The Aftermath of Suffrage

G000155306

Also by Julie V. Gottlieb

FEMININE FASCISM: Women in Britain's Fascist Movement, 1923–1945

THE CULTURE OF FASCISM: Visions of the Far Right in Britain
(*co-edited with Thomas Linehan*)

MAKING REPUTATIONS: Power, Persuasion and the Individual in
Modern British Politics (*co-edited with Richard Toye*)

Also by Richard Toye

CHURCHILL'S EMPIRE: The World That Made Him and the World He Made

THE LABOUR PARTY AND THE PLANNED ECONOMY, 1931–1951

LLOYD GEORGE AND CHURCHILL: Rivals for Greatness

RHETORIC: A Very Short Introduction

THE UN AND GLOBAL POLITICAL ECONOMY: Trade, Finance and Development
(*with John Toye*)

The Aftermath of Suffrage

Women, Gender, and Politics in Britain, 1918–1945

Edited by

Julie V. Gottlieb
Senior Lecturer in Modern History, University of Sheffield

and

Richard Toye
Professor of Modern History, University of Exeter

palgrave
macmillan

First published 2013 by
PALGRAVE MACMILLAN

Palgrave Macmillan in the UK is an imprint of Macmillan Publishers Limited,
registered in England, company number 785998, of Houndmills, Basingstoke,
Hampshire RG21 6XS.

Palgrave Macmillan in the US is a division of St Martin's Press LLC,
175 Fifth Avenue, New York, NY 10010.

Palgrave Macmillan is the global academic imprint of the above companies
and has companies and representatives throughout the world.

Palgrave® and Macmillan® are registered trademarks in the United States,
the United Kingdom, Europe and other countries.

ISBN 978–1–137–01533–4 hardback
ISBN 978–1–137–01534–1 paperback

This book is printed on paper suitable for recycling and made from fully
managed and sustained forest sources. Logging, pulping and manufacturing
processes are expected to conform to the environmental regulations of the
country of origin.

A catalogue record for this book is available from the British Library.

A catalog record for this book is available from the Library of Congress.

Typeset by MPS Limited, Chennai, India.

Contents

List of Illustrations, Tables and Figures

Illustrations

Tables

Figures

Notes on Contributors

Laura Beers is Assistant Professor of History at the American University in Washington, DC. She is the author of *Your Britain: Media and the Making of the Labour Party* (2010), and several articles on British political history.

Adrian Bingham is Senior Lecturer in Modern History at the University of Sheffield. He is the author of *Gender, Modernity, and the Popular Press in Inter-War Britain* (2004), and *Family Newspapers? Sex, Private Life, and the British Popular Press 1918–78* (2009).

Krista Cowman is Professor of History at the University of Lincoln. She has published extensively on the history of suffrage in Britain and on women and politics more generally including *Women of the Right Spirit* (2007) and *Women in British Politics 1689–1979* (2010).

Julie V. Gottlieb is Senior Lecturer in Modern History at the University of Sheffield. She is the author of *Feminine Fascism: Women in Britain's Fascist Movement, 1923–1945* (2000), co-editor of *The Culture of Fascism* (2004) and *Making Reputations* (2005). She has published extensively on women, gender and politics, and she is currently working on a study of gender and appeasement in inter-war Britain.

June Hannam is Professor Emeritus in Modern British History, University of the West of England, Bristol. Her books include *Isabella Ford, 1855–1920* (1989, with Karen Hunt) *Socialist Women, 1880s–1920s* (2002) and *Feminism* (2012). She has published articles on socialism and feminist politics in the late nineteenth and early twentieth centuries, on the Bristol women's movement and on Labour Party women organisers. Her current research interests are women's politics in Bristol after enfranchisement and Labour Party women MPs and candidates in the inter-war years.

Karen Hunt is Professor of Modern British History at Keele University. She has published widely on aspects of local, national and transnational women's politics (1880–1939) as well as on the gendering of politics, including *Equivocal Feminists* (1996) and, with June Hannam, *Socialist Women: Britain, 1880s to 1920s* (2002). She juggles a number of interrelated projects including women and the politics of food on the First World War home-front, the life and politics of Dora Montefiore (1851–1933) as well as a comparative study on the effect of enfranchisement on local women's politics, out of which the chapter in this volume has grown. She continues to delve deeper into the history of Manchester women's politics, particularly how it was experienced in everyday life within local neighbourhoods.

Helen McCarthy is Senior Lecturer in History at Queen Mary, University of London. She studied for her first degree at the University of Cambridge and completed her PhD at the Institute of Historical Research on the topic of interwar internationalism. A revised version was recently published as *The British People and the League of Nations: Citizenship, Democracy and Internationalism, c.1918–1945* (2011). Before joining Queen Mary in 2009, Helen held a Junior Research Fellowship at St John's College, Cambridge. She is a member of the editorial board of *Reviews in History*, Reviews Editor for *Twentieth Century British History* and a Fellow of the Royal Historical Society.

June Purvis is Professor of Women's and Gender History at the University of Portsmouth, UK. She has published widely on women's history in nineteenth and twentieth century Britain and is currently researching the Edwardian suffragette movement. Her many publications include *Emmeline Pankhurst: a biography* (2002) and the co-edited *Women's Activism Global Perspectives from the 1890s to the Present* (2012) in which she has a chapter on suffragette Christabel Pankhurst's text *The Great Scourge*. June is the Editor of *Women's History Review* and also the Editor for a Routledge Book Series on Women's and Gender History. From 2005 to 2010 she was the Secretary and Treasurer of the International Federation for Research in Women's History. She is currently writing a biography of Christabel Pankhurst.

Mari Takayanagi is a full-time professional archivist at the Parliamentary Archives, London, working in public services and outreach. She was awarded a PhD in History by King's College London in August 2012. Her doctoral thesis title is 'Parliament and Women, c.1900–1945' and her research examines the passage of legislation affecting women's lives and gender equality between 1918 and 1928, the role of women on Select Committees and Standing Committees, and the employment of women staff in the House of Commons and House of Lords. She previously read Modern History as an undergraduate at St John's College, Oxford, graduating with first-class honours, and has an MA in Archives and Records Management from University College London.

David Thackeray is a lecturer at the University of Exeter. His book *Conservatism for the Democratic Age: Conservative Cultures and the Challenge of Mass Politics in Early Twentieth Century England* will be published in in 2013.

Pat Thane is Research Professor in Contemporary History, Kings College, London. Her publications include: *The Foundations of the Welfare State* (1982), *Old Age in England: Past Experiences, Present Issues* (2000), *Women and Ageing in British Society since 1500* (co-edited with Lynn Botelho, 2001), *The Long History of Old Age* (editor, 2005), *Britain's Pensions Crisis: History and Policy* (co-edited with Hugh Pemberton and Noel Whiteside, 2006), *Unequal Britain. Equalities in Britain since 1945* (editor, 2010), *Women and Citizenship* *in Britain and Ireland in the Twentieth Century. What Difference Did the Vote Make?* (co-edited with Esther Breitenbach, 2010) and *Happy Families? History and Family Policy* (2010). She is a convenor of History and Policy (www.historyandpolicy.org)

Richard Toye is Professor of Modern History at the University of Exeter. His books include *The Labour Party and the Planned Economy, 1931–1951* (2003), *Lloyd George and Churchill: Rivals for Greatness* (2007), and *Churchill's Empire: The World That Made Him and the World He Made* (2010). Together with Professor Martin Thomas he is currently working on a Leverhulme Trust-funded project, which compares British and French imperial rhetoric from the late nineteenth century to the decolonization period.

Philippe Vervaecke is a Lecturer in British Studies at Lille 3 University. He works on British political culture and parties in the 20th century. He has published books and articles on political history, including *Le Parti libéral, 1906–1924* (with Françoise Orazi, 2010). He recently edited *A droite de la droite. Droites radicales en France et en Grande-Bretagne au XXe siècle* (2012).

Introduction

Julie V. Gottlieb and Richard Toye

There was a momentous sense of achievement when the Representation of the People Act was passed in March 1918 by 385 to 55 in the House of Commons. Amongst other important provisions, the Act granted most women over thirty the right to vote. Of the entirely new elements introduced by the Act – the naval and military voter and the woman voter – the latter excited the most expectation and anxiety. It was reported that while there was never such an outwardly tame general election as that held on 14 December, 1918,

> there was one section of electors to whom, however externally calm, the election must have brought a thrill. The women are said to have voted in crowds, in some London constituencies greatly outnumbering the men, and in their eagerness forming queues at the more populous polling stations, for all the world as though they were out for the impossible butter or meat before the Food Controller took us on hand.[1]

This ravenous anticipation was dampened by frustration on the part of those still excluded from the franchise, and the women's rights campaigner Mary Macarthur pointed to the paradox that although 'the vote was conceded to women on the ground of their services in the war', the Act 'excluded the vast majority of women war-workers'.[2] Another ten years would pass before British women secured the vote on the same terms as men, under the Representation of the People (Equal Franchise) Act (1928).

This, however, was not the end of the story, although it has sometimes been treated as such. In March 2011, during the British referendum campaign on the introduction of the Alternative Vote (AV), a group of leading historians wrote to *The Times*. In explaining their opposition to AV, they referenced the 'long fight for suffrage [which] established the principle of one man or woman, one vote' and claimed that for 'the first time since 1928 and the granting of universal suffrage, we face the possibility that one person's casting ballot will be given greater weight than another'.[3] Leaving

1

aside the merits of their argument about modern day voting reform, what was significant was the way these historians treated 1928 as a great historical end-point. This was misleading. In fact, plural voting for Westminster elections persisted for another twenty years, until the Representation of the People Act (1948) abolished the university constituencies and the right of property owners resident elsewhere to vote in both places. (The Act also did away with the remaining two-member seats, which allowed voters to split their preferences between parties.) Even then, plural voting in Northern Ireland for the Stormont parliament and for local government continued until abolished by legislation in 1968.[4] And even today, plural voting for the City of London Corporation continues: indeed the business franchise there was *increased* in 2002.[5] The 1928 settlement did not even solve permanently what it meant to be politically adult: 18–20 year-olds received the vote only in 1969, and there have been calls since then for enfranchisement at sixteen. Indeed, 16- and 17-year-olds will be able to vote in the referendum on Scottish independence scheduled for 2014.

The messy and partial nature of the post-World War I settlement becomes even clearer if we place the United Kingdom in the context of its Empire. New Zealand women secured the vote in the 1890s, and Australian ones (except for aboriginals!) soon followed. White women secured the vote in Kenya in the 1920s but black ones had to wait until independence in the 1960s. In the interwar years, some British women activists lent their support to calls for women's enfranchisement in India. The Government of India Act (1935) granted votes to women and men on the same terms but because a property qualification was involved only a small number of women actually benefitted.[6] Full enfranchisement had to wait until independence. In other words, even in 1928, the idea of 'one man or woman, one vote' was not held as an immutable principle by the collectivity of Britain's lawmakers. It was a principle that was held to apply in certain important circumstances, but not irrespective of special interests and local conditions.

This book explores the aftermath of suffrage in Britain, keeping in mind the international dimension as well as the connections between gender, electoral law and political culture. We do not see either the 1918 or 1928 Acts as symbols of the termination of a heroic struggle but rather as important landmarks in an ongoing negotiation surrounding citizenship and the public sphere. Nor are we exclusively concerned with women. The 1918 Act was, of course, important for the fact that it granted some women the right to vote in parliamentary elections. But it was equally significant for enfranchising, for the first time, almost – but not quite – all adult men. (Due to residency requirements, only 93 per cent of the adult male population had the vote in 1921. Meanwhile, many who had the parliamentary vote were unable to vote in local elections.)[7] It is hardly possible to account for the impact of these phenomena unless they are considered in parallel. Discussion of appropriate 'feminine' behaviour naturally had to take into account what 'masculine' behaviour was thought to be, and vice versa. Legal equality in terms of voting rights by no means meant that politics lost its gender dimension. And gender discourse remained important even in fields such as imperial and foreign policy where one might not expect gender to have been at issue.[8] Too often, the different literatures on men's and women's politics in this era have failed to engage with one another, but in recent years there have been encouraging signs that this is changing. Although most of the chapters in this book focus on women's politics, they nonetheless reflect an awareness of this need for dialogue. We do not claim that this volume fully achieves the sexual desegregation of modern British political history, but we do believe that it make a contribution towards it.

Equally, the gender politics of the inter-war years cannot be understood apart from the broader context of the period. World War I had left a complex legacy of (contested) state growth and redefinition of national and gender identities. Nicoletta Gullace has argued that the basis for citizenship was recast during the Great War as patriotism, not manhood.[9] From a slightly different perspective, Mary Hilson has suggested that during the 1918 election politicians constructed women's experience of war 'only in terms of their relationships to men, not in terms of their independent experiences: as the heads of households, as consumers struggling with high food prices, or as workers'.[10] After the war an increasingly active proto-welfare state, still committed nonetheless to certain forms of economic orthodoxy such as balanced budgets, was faced with large scale unemployment in traditional industries on the one hand, and the growth of new industries and associated social change on the other. The importance of religion in politics was declining, but there was still a (fragmented) non-conformist vote that was up for grabs as the Liberals struggled.[11] The Empire emerged from the war expanded in territorial extent but militarily overstretched and under challenge from nationalist movements. A relatively benign European outlook in the late 1920s was converted by 1933 to an undeniably threatening scenario: many observers foretold the imminent collapse of civilization.[12]

In party political terms, the Conservatives were dominant but not unchallenged, in an era which saw the first two (minority) Labour governments. The Liberals faced an all-but-unstoppable decline: the genuine multi-party politics of the 1920s was replaced after 1931 by a *de facto* Labour–Conservative two party system. (Ross McKibbin argues that what emerged after 1918 was 'a restored Edwardian politics, together with many of its mental habits and its rhetoric, but without the one thing – the progressive alliance – which gave it life and coherence'.)[13] Changes in political culture and gender roles went hand in hand. Jon Lawrence suggests that politicians became increasingly keen to distance themselves from the rowdy and disruptive behaviour that had become a well established part of electoral ritual.[14] The emergent revised ideas of what constituted political manliness did not just shape arguments between the parties. Rather, ideas about gender were themselves in part the product of the inter-party rhetorical battle.

The relationship between political culture and the legislative framework of electoral politics was also mutually reflexive. The 1918 Act was not only about about a more equalized suffrage (and the extension of vote to servicemen), but also involved important changes to the distribution of parliamentary constituencies, alterations in residence requirements and in the definition of 'household', and changed rules on election expenses.

Given its complexities, it is understandable that the question of its impact on the fate of the parties has been controversial. The 'franchise factor' debate of the 1970s and 1980s centred on the question of how far the rise of the Labour Party could be explained by the expansion of the working-class electorate that the Act brought about. H.C.G. Matthew, Ross McKibbin and J.A. Kay argued that 'Not only was the new electorate divided by class in a way that increasingly excluded the Liberals, but it was less likely to respond to policies that demanded a comparatively high level of political intelligence.'[15] In response, Peter Clarke cast doubt on the assumption that 'the pre-1914 electorate was significantly more open to reasoned argument because it was smaller and richer'. He also argued that 'Labour's electoral support was not socially distinct from that of the Liberal party' and that the Liberals had been successful at playing the new game of class politics prior to the war.[16] Then, on the basis of a more sophisticated understanding of how one qualified to vote under the old electoral system, Duncan Tanner argued persuasively that 'there were no inherent sociological reasons why the newly enfranchised men should have voted solidly for Labour'. Furthermore: 'If they did so after 1918, itself a dubious proposition, then the explanation is to be found not in the simple fact of electoral reform, but in the altered political or social context.'[17] In 1992 Michael Dawson introduced a new factor: the provisions of the Act in relation to election expenses. By restricting what could be spent, in what they thought was their own interests, the established parties succeeded in making it economical for Labour to fight many more seats, including unwinnable ones, with damaging consequences for the Liberals.[18] As these factors affected electoral outcomes and the fates of the parties, so too they shifted the ground on which future elections would be fought.

Indeed, the 1918 Act changed significantly the ways in which parties campaigned and canvassed during elections. Stuart Ball has noted the impact on the Conservative Party of the shift away from an electoral system based on property tenure: 'Local associations during the 1920s [...] evolved from being relatively small groups of men supervising work based on electoral law into much larger popular congregations of both sexes with social, propaganda and campaigning functions.' (This in turn diminished the importance of the Primrose League, a voluntary body allied with the Tory party, which had previously been a key vehicle for such roles.)[19] In the case of Labour, changes in the party's constitution, combined with the effects of war including participation in the coalition government, intersected with the Act to produce a new form of constituency politics.[20] The advent of individual party membership created a new campaigning resource, but the new Constituency Labour Parties (CLPs) also established a potential source of tension with the movement's more powerful trade union wing. Arguably, the Liberal Party's failure in these years was less the product of class-based electoral determinism than of its own inability to come to terms with these new realities as its rivals did (albeit not without difficulties of their own).

An important change over the last forty years, then, is that few historians now think that 'class politics' is a sufficient description of how parties structured their appeals.[21] David Jarvis has shown how the Conservatives, in the new era of mass enfranchisement, did not simply target the working class as a whole, but tailored their message to suit different groups within it, including women.[22] And although, from another perspective, 'high political' approaches remain popular, few historians would now be as confident as Maurice Cowling was in 1971 that there were only fifty or sixty politicians who 'mattered', and that backbench, party and public opinion could be left to one side for the purposes of analysis.[23] Philip Williamson – himself by no means unsympathetic to Cowling – reminds us that 'politicians are not just policy-makers, tacticians, and administrators. They are also public figures for whom speech-making and publication is a principal function, precisely because politics is a *public* activity'.[24] Party politics in the aftermath of suffrage era, moreover, was intrinsically connected to other forms of civil society activity.

Women's historians have tended to approach these issues from different angles. They have been interested in the period after suffrage almost as an afterword to the dramatic narrative of the great struggle and formidable movement, constitutional and militant, for women's suffrage. Historians of British feminism have developed a more nuanced interpretation of what happened to the feminist movement after the vote was won, offering important correctives to the initial impression that the movement lost its cause, its organising zeal, and its personnel and personalities after the First World War.[25] This revision of earlier impressions and prejudices has been facilitated by a newer interest in women's entry into politics in the post-war years.

The majority of the chapters in this volume concern women, both the adjustments they had to make as citizens, either as individuals or in a range of groups, and the way the formal political and party systems integrated their demands and sought to appeal to them. We are thus interpreting the nature of citizenship, both in terms of status and practice, and it will be useful to evoke Rose and Canning's definition: citizenship should be understood as 'a political status assigned to individuals by states, as a relation of belonging to specific communities, or as a set of practices that define the relationships between peoples and states and among peoples within communities.'[26] The gendering of politics, political institutions and political culture, also needs to go beyond high and elite politics, and Thane and Breitenbach have reminded us that 'although representation in formal political institutions is a significant measure of women's exercise of the rights of citizenship, it is not the only means by which women can engage with politics and the state, nor the only means by which they can influence policy'.[27]

In 2000 Pedersen remarked on the paucity of work on women in twentieth century British politics, noting that politics had dropped out of gender history in favour of cultural analyses that offered 'thick description' but sidestepped causal analysis and the study of change.[28] Since Pedersen's provocative thoughts on 'The Future of Feminist History', it is not too much of an exaggeration to say that it is just this approach that has burgeoned. British political history is being gendered, and gender historians are again thinking in terms of political processes. At the same time interest in inter-war politics and the application of new methodologies and theoretical perspectives have advanced the debates and moved us on considerably from empirically driven high politics. The collaboration represented by this collection is the bringing together of these aspects, and by so doing desegregating modern British political history, or at the very least suggesting the ways in which that can and should be done. In this process we can identify a number of leitmotivs in the experience, discourse, and representation of the aftermath of suffrage. What were the popular and personal responses to the achievement of suffrage? Was suffrage revolutionary or did it just feel that way?

Pugh has noted the gradualist and evolutionary nature of suffrage reforms in British history. Aside from annual parliaments, all the objectives of the Chartists were met by 1918, the Chartist movement 'serving as a reminder that an abrupt organisational decline cannot be taken as an adequate indication of failure, but merely represent a stage in the evolution of a movement'.[29] What this suggests then is that women, men, politicians and the Press may have expected revolutionary change with the advent of suffrage, but in keeping with British political traditions, this was to be evolutionary if not long-drawn out. Cowman has more recently also passed an optimistic verdict on women's post-enfranchisement achievements by focusing on their successful integration in party politics, even when this more often than not involved sex-segregated party structures, and on the presentation of party policy. Each party 'clearly believed that there was a collective "woman's vote" to be captured, and that their electoral success could well depend on securing this'.[30]

In the first flush of excitement after the motion passed that women could stand as MPs, 17 did so in the 1918 General Election (on 25 October that year the House of Commons passed the motion that women could stand for Parliament), having only had three weeks to mount their campaigns. This would be a false start for women on the starting line of parliamentary politics. Apart from Constance Markievicz, a Sinn Féin candidate who was elected but who did not take her seat, only Christabel Pankhurst and Mary Macarthur among them had any real prospect of success. It is also significant that, apart from Markievicz, not one of this pioneer group was ever elected as an MP.[31] However, saying this implies that the narrative to come is downbeat, a succession of defeats and disappointments. The promise of suffrage was not only celebrated by the minority of the population who were actively political and joined political parties. Thane has noted women's eagerness to exercise their franchise in the 1922 General Election. *The Times* commented in 1922:

> The greatest surprise which those in charge of polling booths had yesterday was the number of women who appeared to vote immediately after the booths were opened… canvassers found themselves questioned alertly and adroitly on matters not usually considered women's questions. Foreign policy was a strong point moving women in constituencies.[32]

There is evidence then that the novelty of the franchise encouraged political engagement.

So much of the scholarship has adopted the tone of disappointment and grappled with the decline and the schism of feminism in the aftermath of suffrage. In fact, the status and success of inter-war feminism has been hotly debated since the 1920s. The anticlimax of suffrage was expressed with some subtlety by Virginia Woolf in *A Room of One's Own*, published just after the passage of the Flapper's Vote (1928), but referring to the impact, or lack thereof, of the 1918 legislation.

> My aunt, Mary Beton, I must tell you, died by a fall from her horse when she was out riding to take the air in Bombay. The news of my legacy reached me one night about the same time that the act was passed that gave votes to women. A solicitor's letter fell into the post-box and when I opened it I found that she had left me five hundred pounds a year for ever. Of the two—the vote and the money—the money, I own, seemed infinitely the more important.[33]

Ambivalence was widespread. Bringing their thoughts together on a number of different themes, the contributors to *Our Freedom and Its Results* could 'reach no positive conclusion', and all they could agree on was that it was too soon 'to judge what it all amounts to: none of them feel that the freedom of women in society is either really achieved or really stable, or that there is any clear evidence as to what the results of it will be when the time comes'.[34] In past decades we have seen important correctives to the view that feminism failed between the wars, and more nuanced interpretations of the undeniable dispersal of the movement into so many different feminist pressure groups. Thane has argued that

> the proliferation of women's organisations was not a splintering of the women's movement, rather it illustrates how women's organizations came to permeate public life in the decades after the vote was gained, while continuing to co-operate on key issues. These were signs that possession of the vote gave many women a feeling of legitimacy in public life, or their right to promote causes important to them.[35]

Thane's study of the *The Times'* representation of the women voters in the 1920s represented them as thoughtful, independent minded, and 'much like men' in their voting behaviour,[36] a construction of 'the' woman voter that jarred with that disseminated by the populist *Daily Mail*, as Bingham has shown.[37] Cowman has aptly observed that while it has been demonstrated time and again that women do not vote on gendered lines, 'after 70 years of equal voting, the political still tends to be thought of as male and normalised in this way'.[38] Women are regarded as a distinct social group and as a minority akin to an ethnicity, and there is no question that this conceptualization was already well rooted in the immediate post-enfranchisement years.

There was, of course, a backlash against women and feminism after the war due to a combination of economic and cultural factors. A major theme was the new electorate's political ignorance and intellectual inferiority, and the charge that women were politically uneducated.[39] 'As W. Keith pointed out in the *Daily News* in March 1921, in an article titled 'Dislike of Women', 'the attitude of the public towards women is more full of contempt and bitterness than had been the case since the suffragette outbreaks'.[40] The assault on the woman worker was most acute during times of high unemployment, while the 'Missing Generation' was doubly emasculated and ravaged by war injuries and the ascendency of women's power on the home front, with a surplus of women in the population evoking fears of being swamped, and some identifying feminism as 'a far more sinister enemy than any foreign power'.[41] Post-war, post-suffrage Britain was obsessed by a 'Woman Question', or even worse, besieged by a 'Woman Problem'. Virginia Woolf was struck how

> no age could have ever been as stridently sex-conscious as our own. Those innumerable books by men about women in the British Museum are a proof of it. The Suffrage campaign was no doubt to blame. It must have roused in men an extraordinary desire for self-assertion; it must have made them lay an emphasis upon their own sex and its characteristics which they would not have troubled to think about had they not been challenged.[42]

Winifred Holtby observed that 'in the second quarter of the 20th century, the very existence of women appears to challenge controversy'.[43] There was, nonetheless, a spectrum of anti-feminist opinion after the war, with the most misogynist reactions voiced by figures such as Nietzschean eugenicist Anthony Ludovici who was deeply convinced that Britain – and the Anglo-Saxon race – suffered from a 'Woman Problem'. To him 'Feminism means nothing more than the government of odd people, by odd people, for odd people.'[44] He prophesized that the 'regeneration of the Western World which will take ruthless anti-Feminism for granted, is therefore a Masculine Renaissance, a regeneration of Man both as animal and spirit'.[45] It was against this backdrop then that women's citizenship was defined and practised after enfranchisement.

Women MPs were expected to represent all women by dint of their sex, just as women were presumed to be a bloc of voters because they were understood to share the same interests about home, health, and shopping.[46] But many cohorts of women disproved these allegations during the inter-war years. Women MPs themselves recognized the pressure they were under, and as early as 1927 as part of a Deputation to Cabinet, Nancy Astor identified a blame game at work: 'we have always realised that true democracy will have to depend upon men and women, and we realise that when troubles come the women get the hard end of the stick'.[47] Looking into 'this business of women MPs' in 1935, one reporter asked himself 'What would the old suffragettes have thought of it all?' His answer was rife with examples of the trivial questions women MPs raised in Parliament, and he was struck by their interest in foreign rather than domestic affairs, concluding that the 'spirit of 1913 is very hard to trace at Westminster these days'.[48] The press could be more generous too by acknowledging that the nine women MPs in the House in 1936 were good champions of their sex, and during the first six months of the Government 'the feminine point of view has been heard in every important debate'.[49] There was certainly much that rested on the shoulders of women MPs, and sex equality was far from accomplished. But whatever the appraisal, what is most striking is how women MPs were figured as a parliamentary bloc, even though they represented all main parties. Rathbone summarizes the New Feminism and the challenges women faced to get into Parliament:

> That there is only a small number of MPs does not show that women candidates at elections are unpopular, said Miss Rathbone, MP, yesterday. 'What it does show,' she said, 'is that the local party caucuses which select candidates are man-ridden, and, with few exceptions, offer to women only the kind of vacancy which is euphemistically described as offering a 'sporting chance.' [...] Regarding the future of the women's movement, she said: – 'We want to see women peeresses admitted to the House of Lords and to see women eligible for the Diplomatic and

Consular Services. We want women, and a good many of them, in the Indian and Colonial Services, and we want to get rid of the marriage bar wherever it still exists in public services. We want, also, to give a woman married to a foreigner the right to retain her own nationality if she so desires.[50]

Indeed, even if they could transcend party to consider welfare issues and so forth, such non-partisanship was no longer a possibility when it came to foreign policy in the later 1930s, when the Duchess of Atholl, Eleanor Rathbone, Edith Summerskill and Ellen Wilkinson, most prominently, emerged as relentless critics of Chamberlain's foreign policy.

The woman politician and the woman MP was a curiosity but also an easy butt of ridicule and public disdain, conflating in her person the most mistrusted of public figures, the politician, and the misunderstood and reductively homogenized of the two sexes, women. Thelma Cazalet-Keir remarked that

> when I entered the House there was still something slightly freakish about a woman MP, and I frequently saw male colleagues pointing me out to their friends as though I were a sort of giant panda. The House has often been labelled "the best Club in the world," but it was nothing of the sort to women. Not one of the dozen or so women MPs ever entered the Smoking Room where, so rumour had it, as much constructive business is transacted as on the floor of the House.[51]

We find the pillorying of the Woman MP in the political cartoons of W. K. Haselden in the *Daily Mirror*, especially in his series of 1923, 'The Flapper in the House of Commons'. There were warmer parodies as well, such as the 1939 film 'Old Mother Riley MP'.[52] Women MPs did much to excite the imagination about what was possible in post-war politics, but increasingly they were the source of disappointment, their paltry number – only thirty-six during the inter-war period – expected by their champions to remake the world in the period of 'aftershock' (Susan Kingsley Kent),[53] and by their detractors to take the gravity, decorum, and intelligence and responsibility out of politics.

Duff Cooper damned their existence with faint praise:

> I have always had a great respect for the political judgement of women, although I have never thought that the House of Commons was the right arena in which they should display it. The House was fashioned by men in the course of seven hundred years, and men of all parties and classes adapt themselves to its usages with astonishing rapidity. But there is not place in it for women, and women cannot excel there any more than they can on the football field. This does not mean that women's brains are not capable of comprehending and solving political problems.

Politics are not an abstruse science. Common sense, clear vision, knowledge of human nature, courage and patience are the qualities that they demand, and with all these qualities women are endowed at least as richly as men.[54]

Among both their champions and detractors we find, surprisingly, a fair number of women, and it was the mood of these years for Feminists, including those who had fought in the vanguard of the suffrage movement, to feel let down by the patriarchal state but also by their sisters. Among those women who felt the most let down were suffragette leaders Christabel Pankhurst and Norah Elam.[55] While, Elam could only find a solution to this betrayal in British fascism, women of all political hues came to similar conclusions, especially as they looked back on what had been achieved on the eve of yet another war, and when the hope that women might prevent another war by their nurturing and biologically determined abilities to conciliate and reconcile, proved to be bankrupt.

The fault lines were not only drawn between men and women, but also between youth and age. Feminists who had experienced the suffrage struggle were let down by 'modern young women' who knew 'amazingly little of what life was like before the war' and showed 'a strong hostility to the word "feminism"' and all which they imagine it to connote'.[56] Vera Brittain recognized the prevailing stereotype of the feminist as 'spectacled, embittered women, disappointed, childless, dowdy and generally unloved'.[57] Former suffragette Mrs M.H. Harker guffawed: 'Girls to-day? I cannot see much of the old spirit about now, but, of course, there is nothing to fight for.'[58] This generational conflict was, of course, a mirror image of that among men, the young men of the 'Generation of 1914' pitted against the 'old men', 'old gang' and 'old women' who acted as political blocking figures for the young.[59]

In this tense atmosphere, how did Britons celebrate and appreciate those campaigners who had done so much to make the granting of suffrage inevitable? With women going in all political directions after the war, the legacy of the suffragettes was a highly contested one. It was claimed by the Far Left and the Extreme Right, and every other position in between. Sylvia Pankhurst drew on the legacy for the women's peace movement, arguing that if women are to stop war they must 'act nationally and internationally. They must federate all women's peace movements, and take a leaf out of the book of the suffragette, by making themselves felt in a public way'.[60] 'Slasher' Mary, Mary Richardson, claimed the suffragettes for British fascism, while Liberal, Labour and Conservative women all traced their political ancestry to the same mother movement.

Moments of commemoration and real or perceived milestones offer a valuable opportunity to see how contemporaries reflected on the meaning, the achievements, and the disenchantment of momentous historical change.

Cultural historians in particular have made careful studies of these sites of memory. So far there has been more interest in the suffrage movement itself as 'useable history', the dramatic arc of militant acts and the stories of individual heroism and sacrifice making the founding of the WSPU in 1903 a date to be marked – there were a spate of commemorative events in 2003.[61] But milestones of suffrage legislation have also been marked at regular intervals. In terms of suffrage legislation these chronologically determined points of reflection have collided with other major turning points, whether it was the ten year anniversary of the Representation of the People Act coinciding with the Equal Franchise Act, the twenty-first anniversary being marked as Britain was on the brink of another world war, or the fiftieth anniversary actually seen as a spur for Second Wave Feminism: 'Elizabeth Wilson's early account of the growth of WLM situated its origins in part in the 'ferment of political activity' in women's peace groups as they marked their fiftieth anniversary of the vote in 1968.'[62] We can only speculate what may be the backdrop for the centenary of suffrage in a few years time.

As most of the contributors to this volume are interested in the twenty or so years after 1918, the 21st anniversary celebrations of women's suffrage provides an instructive case study. The enfranchised woman turned twenty-one at one of the most portentous moments in Europe's history, and just as Hitler's troops were marching into Prague and making a mockery of Chamberlain's promise of 'peace in our time'. Nonetheless there were many celebrations, the bigger ones in London and Manchester.[63] Lord Cecil, incidentally president of the ailing League of Nations Union, was guest of honour at a party held in the Millicent Fawcett Hall, Westminster at the end of February 1939 to celebrate the NUWSS's contribution to the achievement of women's suffrage, and Nancy Astor came over from the House of Commons to join the celebration.[64] Eleanor Rathbone (former suffragist, post-war president of the National Union of Societies for Equal Citizenship, and crusading anti-appeasement Independent MP) speaking at a luncheon in 1939 to celebrate the anniversary, reflected:

> that on 21st birthdays one usually looked forward, but in their case it was perhaps safer to dwell on the past. They could say that they were now better equipped to face difficult times by their past stern struggles. Everybody now had a share in choosing their rulers, and also a share in the responsibility for the choice...women's organisations had achievements to their credit, in the cause of peace and wider humanity, disregarding national boundaries.[65]

Indeed, it is clear that one of the things that had been achieved was the celebrity status of former suffragette campaigner, whose stories and their own afterlife in the aftermath of suffrage continued to attract media attention. There was a 'where are they now' fascination with the suffragettes, even 30 years after the peak of their activity, and some satisfaction is taken in the fact that even the most radical were pitching in with the war effort, and involved in traditionally women's social and relief work at that.[66] It is interesting to observe that Rathbone, while she certainly noted achievements in social and welfare issues, was most concerned about advances or lack thereof in women's citizenship right, and by extension their ability to take a full part in the pressing issues of the day, namely in the international sphere. Also noteworthy is the cross section of women speaking at this event, absolute pacifists like Royden and Brittain, against the most prominent women anti-appeasers, Rathbone and Summerskill, suggesting that they could still share a platform when it came to feminist politics, while they had become very alien to on another from the perspective of foreign policy and national politics. No matter how deeply divisive the politics of appeasement, feminist solidarity could peek out of the clouds for even a short moment in celebration of women's advances.[67] However, one of the other important things to notice is not what was celebrated but what was absent from these commemorative events – there was no mention of the fact that male citizens too had an important anniversary to mark. Taking our cue from Rathbone, contributors to this volume are asking what had been achieved and what was seen to have remained unattained after suffrage. They are also asking why was it that only women's suffrage was commemorated in this way, and not universal suffrage. Where were the men?

Thinking about commemoration and anniversaries brings to mind the related question of periodization. More often than not the existing historiography on women and politics, and even on post-suffrage politics more generally, takes 1928 as the point of conclusion, as the culmination of a process. The inter-war years are truncated by the 1928 Equal Franchise legislation, and then by the concomitant economic and political crisis. This periodization is adopted, for instance, in important studies by Joanna Alberti, Hannam and Hunt, Cheryl Law, Susan Kingsley Kent, among others.[68] Indeed, Susan Kent sets up some interesting challenges for us as we interrogate our own assumptions about periodization, and in *Aftershocks* she has partly dispensing with a political chronology in favour of the model of the traumatic cycle that was observed in shell shock victims, and projecting this onto the nation as a whole. During the first decade after enfranchisement, interest has centred on how each party adapted itself to mass democracy by rebuilding their respective party structures, and much less attention has been conferred on the, arguably, much more fragmented and schismatic 1930s, messier because the hegemony of a nominally 'National Government' placed these very same party organizations in rather precarious positions.

Arguably, women figure much less in the story of the 1930s, and it is the proverbial problem of the chicken and the egg whether this is due to the relative neglect of the thirties in feminist historiography or the retreat of women's political demands in the face of the Depression and international crises.

Indeed, it is precisely at this juncture that things get even more interesting, and it is in the 1930s when the yet unresolved debates about the scope and nature of women's citizenship collide with international crises and a series of different and varied responses to alternative political extremes. Already in the 1920s there was much unease with mass democracy from various points on the spectrum, the avant-garde pro-fascist Wyndham Lewis frustrated by 'all the humbug of a democratic suffrage' and 'the imbecility that is so wastefully manufactured' which he rejoiced the Italians under Mussolini would be spared.[69] Democracy was itself under great strain and threat during the 1930s, and certainly after the rise of Nazism, and both men and women became more acutely aware of its value but also its fragilities as they contemplated its defeat by extremes of Left and Right.

But if we try to repair the breaks in the periodization and think about our questions over a longer continuum and an expanded time frame, are we still asking the same questions or, inevitably, begging new ones and proposing revised conceptual frameworks as well? Most historians seem to take 1945 as another chronological book end, and in the context of the discussion of gender and citizenship Rose's seminal *Which People's War?*[70] is instructive. Historians working on the 1920s and 1930s will identify many precedents and prefigurations of the pervasive war-time discourse of women's irresponsibility, sexual laxity, and untrustworthiness which makes the whole sex undeserving of the burden of citizenship. However, we can usefully problematize this periodization too, and expand our chronology along different trajectories, for instance, to 1969 when the voting age was lowered to 18, or, looking to the future, to 2018 when centenary celebrations will inevitably prompt new reflections on the significance of the suffrage.

Notes

1. 'A New Experience', *Manchester Guardian*, 16 December. 1918.
2. 'Labour Rights', *Manchester Guardian*, 29 June 1918.
3. David Abulafia, John Adamson, Anthony Beevor *et al.* to *The Times*, published 11 March 2011. Another group of historians, including one of the editors of the present volume, responded with a rebuttal: Stefan Berger, Christine Carpenter, David Cesarani *et al.* to *The Times*, published 18 March 2011.
4. John Whyte, 'How Much Discrimination Was There Under the Unionist Regime, 1921–1968?', in Tom Gallagher and James O'Connell, *Contemporary Irish Studies* (Manchester, 1983), pp. 1–35.
5. Under the City of London (Ward Elections) Act 2002. For discussion, see Nicholas Shaxson, *Treasure Islands: Tax Havens and the Men Who Stole the World* (London, 2011), pp. 265–7.
6. See 'Indian Women Demand Full Political Rights', *Indian Express*, 24 February 1947.
7. Duncan Tanner, *Political Change and the Labour Party 1900–1918* (Cambridge, 1990), pp. 387–9; Chris Cook, *The Age of Alignment: Electoral Politics in Britain 1922–1929* (London and Basingstoke, 1975), p. 49n.

8. For instance, Asquithian Liberal opposition to the Lloyd George Coalition's policy of anti-terrorist reprisals in Ireland was often cast in gender terms. See for example: 'To Every Woman. Do You Like Violence?', in *Pamphlets and Leaflets 1921*, Liberal Publication Department, London, 1922. See also Julie Gottlieb, 'Guilty Women?', *BBC History Magazine*, Vol. 12, No. 13, December 2011, pp. 26–9.

9. Nicoletta Gullace, *The Blood of Our Sons: Men, Women, and the Renegotiation of British Citizenship During the Great War* (Basingstoke, 2002).

10. Mary Hilson, 'Women Voters and the Rhetoric of Patriotism in the British General Election of 1918', *Women's History Review*, 10 (2001), pp. 325–347, at 341.

11. Ross McKibbin, *Classes and Cultures: England 1918–1951* (Oxford, 1998), p. 96.

12. See Richard Overy, *The Morbid Age: Britain Between the Wars* (London, 2009).

13. Ross McKibbin, *Parties and People: England 1914–1951* (Oxford, 2010), p. 33.

14. Jon Lawrence, 'The Transformation of British Public Politics After the First World War', *Past & Present*, 190 (2006), pp. 185–216. See also Kit Good, "Quit Ye Like Men': Platform Manliness and Electioneering, 1895–1939', in Matthew McCormack (ed.), *Public Men: Masculinity Politics in Modern Britain* (Basingstoke, 2007), pp. 143–64.

15. H.C.G. Matthew, R.I. McKibbin and J.A. Kay, 'The Franchise Factor in the Rise of the Labour Party', *English Historical Review*, Vol. 91, No. 361 (October 1976), pp. 723–52, at 749.

16. P. F. Clarke, 'Liberals, Labour and the Franchise', *English Historical Review*, Vol. 92, No. 364 (July 1977), pp. 582–590 at 583–4. Here Clarke was refining claims made initially in his *Lancashire and the New Liberalism* (Cambridge, 1971), to which Matthew, McKibbin and Kay had responded.

17. Duncan Tanner, 'The Parliamentary Electoral System, the 'Fourth' Reform Act and the Rise of Labour in England and Wales', *Historical Research*, 56 (1983), pp. 205–19, at 219.

18. Michael Dawson, 'Money and the Real Impact of the Fourth Reform Act', *Historical Journal*, Vol. 35, No. 2 (June 1992), pp. 369–81. More recently, David Thackeray has drawn attention to the provisions of the Act (further amended in 1922) which prevented election expenditure by persons other than the candidate. The intention of this was to prevent outside organisations (including newspapers) spending money on a candidate's behalf: *Politics for the Democratic Age: Conservative Cultures and the Challenge of Mass Politics in Early Twentieth Century England*, Manchester, forthcoming, 2013.

19. Stuart Ball, 'Local Conservatism and the Evolution of the Party Organization', in Anthony Seldon and Stuart Ball (eds), *Conservative Century: The Conservative Party since 1900* (Oxford, 1994), pp. 261–311, at 264.

20. John E. Turner, *Labour's Doorstep Politics in London* (London and Basingstoke, 1978), p. 4; David Howell, *MacDonald's Party: Labour Identities and Crisis 1923–1931* (Oxford, 2002), p. 18.

21. As Paul Readman notes: 'The debate on the rise of Labour and the concomitant decline of the Liberal party has now reached an advanced level of sophistication, with historians turning away from deterministic class-based "sociological" explanations and toward more fashionable "textual" approaches that place emphasis on the transformative impact of political language' ('The State of Twentieth Century British Political History', *Journal of Policy History* 21 (2009), pp. 219–38, at 220.

22. David Jarvis, 'Mrs. Maggs and Betty: The Conservative Appeal to Women Voters in the 1920s', *Twentieth Century British History*, Vol. 5, No. 2 (1994), pp. 129–52;

idem., 'British Conservatism and Class Politics in the 1920s', *English Historical Review*, Vol. 111, No. 440 (February 1996), pp. 59–84.

23. Maurice Cowling, *The Impact of Labour 1920–1924: The Beginnings of Modern British Politics* (Cambridge, 1971), p. 3.

24. Philip Williamson, *Stanley Baldwin: Conservative Leadership and National Values* (Cambridge, 1999), p. 14. Emphasis in original.

25. See Joanna Alberti, *Beyond Suffrage: Feminists in War and Peace, 1914–1928* (London, 1989); Deidre Beddoe, *Back to Home and Duty: Women Between the Wars, 1918–1939* (London, 1989); Esthere Breitenbach and Pat Thane (eds), *Women and Citizenship in Britain and Ireland in the Twentieth Century: What Difference Did the Vote Make?* (2010); Brian Harrison, *Prudent Revolutionaries: Portraits of British Feminists between the Wars* (1991); Karen Hunt, *Equivocal Feminists: The Social Democratic Federation and the Woman Question, 1884–1911* (London,1996); Cheryl Law, *Suffrage and Power: The Women's Movement, 1918–1928* (London, 1999); Martin Pugh, *Women and the Women's Movement in Britain, 1914–1959* (Basingstoke, 1992); Dale Spender, *There Has Always Been a Women's Movement this Century* (London, 1983); H. Smith (ed.) *British Feminism in the Twentieth Century* (London, 1990).

26. Kathleen Canning and Sonya O. Rose, 'Gender, Citizenship and Subjectivity: Some Historical and Theoretical Considerations', in Kathleen Canning and Sonya O. Rose (eds), *Gender, Citizenships & Subjectivities* (Oxford, 2001), p. 1.

27. E. Breitenbach and P. Thane (eds), *Women and Citizenship in Britain and Ireland in the Twentieth Century: What Difference Did the Vote Make?* (London, 2010), p. 8.

28. Susan Pedersen, 'The Future of Feminist History', *Perspectives*, October, 2000.

29. Martin Pugh, 'The Impact of Women's Enfranchisement in Britain', in C. Daley and M. Nolan (eds), *Suffrage and Beyond: International Feminist Perspectives* (New York, 1994), p. 316.

30. Krista Cowman, *Women in British Politics, c. 1689–1979* (Basingstoke, 2010), p. 149.

31. See Pamela Brooks, *Women at Westminster* (London, 1967), p. 15.

32. *The Times*, 16 November 1922.

33. Virginia Woolf, *A Room of One's Own, and the Three Guineas* (Oxford, 2008; originally published 1929) p. 35.

34. Ray Strachey (ed.), *Our Freedom and Its Results by Five Women* (London, 1936), p. 9.

35. Pat Thane in Thane and Breitenbach, p. 18.

36. See Thane in Thane and Breitenbach, London, 2010, p. 16.

37. Adrian Bingham, '"Stop the Flapper Vote Folly": Lord Rothermere, the Daily Mail and the Equalization of the Franchise 1927–8', *Twentieth Century British History*, 13, 1 (2002), pp. 17–37.

38. K. Cowman, p. 170.

39. A major theme is the political ignorance of the new electorate. 'Elections now represented: "an entirely different proposition to what [they were] before... two thirds of the electorate are politically entirely uneducated... one must not lose sight of the fact that practically half of the electors are women, who are undoubtedly more strongly influenced by an appeal to their senses and are inclined to judge by appearances" (1919 Conservative Agents Journal)' (Cowman, p. 136).

40. Susan Kingsley Kent, *Aftershocks: Politics and Trauma in Britain, 1918–1931* (Basingstoke, 2009), p. 151.

41. *Daily Mail*, 20 December 1927. Quoted in ibid., p. 156.

42. Virginia Woolf, *A Room of One's Own*, p. 92.
43. Winifred Holtby, *Woman and a Changing Civilization* (London, 1934), p. 2.
44. Anthony Ludovici, *The Future of Woman* (London, 1936), p. 149.
45. Ibid., p. 151.
46. What did women do when they did enter Parliament? Brian Harrison has calculated that almost half of their debating contributions in the House of Commons were devoted to housing, health, education, unemployment and labour relations. 'On this basis it can be argued that they had become confined to a limited field of appropriate "women's" topics. But is this a reasonable interpretation? During the 1920s and 1930s these issues were the ones regarded as central by most politicians, regardless of their sex' (M. Pugh, p. 320).
47. 'Equal Franchise: Shorthand Notes of Deputation from the Equal Political Right Campaign Committee', CP 90 (27), 8 March 1927, CAB 24/185, The National Archives, Kew, London
48. 'These Women MPs: The Questions They Ask,' *Daily Mirror*, 4 September 1935.
49. 'Our 9 Women MPs Are Good Champions of Their Sex', *Daily Mirror*, 18 May 1936.
50. 'Why Women MPs Are Few', *Daily Mirror*, 30 November 1935.
51. Thelma Cazalet-Keir, *From the Wings* (London, 1967), pp. 126–7.
52. 'Old Mother Riley MP' (1939), and see also Steven Fielding, 'Cinematic Representations of Politicians and Party Politics c. 1944–1964', *Journal of British Studies*, 47, no. 1, Jan. 2008, pp. 107–28.
53. Susan Kingsley Kent, *Aftershocks: Politics and Trauma in Britain, 1918–1931* (Basingstoke, 2009).
54. Duff Cooper, *Old Men Forget* (London, 1953), pp. 251–2.
55. Julie V. Gottlieb, *Feminine Fascism: Women in Britain's Fascist Movement, 1923–1945* (London, 2000), and Susan and Angela McPherson, *Mosley's Old Suffragette: A Biography of Norah Dacre Fox* (2011).
56. Ray Strachey (ed.), *Our Freedom and its Results by Five Women* (London, 1936), p. 10.
57. Quoted in Cowman, p. 158.
58. 'Suffragettes Fight Their Battles Over Again,' *Daily Dispatch*, 10 May 1939.
59. 'Mr Mauling comes to see me, a young man from Merton who has got his first and wants to know what political party he should join. I say that he had better wait. Every party is crushed by its own old men; out of all this there may emerge a party which young men can join with fervour.' (19th July, 1939, Harold Nicolson diaries, p. 406).
60. E Sylvia Pankhurst, 'Women Can Stop War—and Must!', *Daily Mirror*, 11 October 1935.
61. See Jill Liddington, 'Era of Commemoration: Celebrating the Suffrage Centenary', *History Workshop Journal*, issue 59, (2005), pp. 194–218.
62. Cowman, pp. 164–5.
63. See *Daily Dispatch*, 10 May 1939 for report on a gathering in Manchester 'of the various organisations in the old Women's Suffrage Movement 'to celebrate the 21st anniversary of women's enfranchisement'. The paper noted that 'nearly all these women had been headline news in their day'. Also covered in the *Daily Express*, 10 May 1939, reporting of this reunion of 43 ex-suffragettes.
64. *Manchester Guardian*, 23 February 1939.
65. *Manchester Guardian*, 18 March 1939.
66. 'Women's Defence Work: Former Suffragettes', *Manchester Guardian*, 8 September 1939.

67. Julie V. Gottlieb, '"Broken Friendships and Vanished Loyalties": Gender, Collective (In)Security and Anti-Fascism in Britain in the 1930s', *Politics, Religion & Ideology*, 13 (2012), pp. 197–219.
68. See Joanna Alberti, *Beyond Suffrage: Feminists in War and Peace, 1914–1928* (New York, 1989), June Hannam and Karen Hunt, *Socialist Women: Britain, 1880s to 1920s* (London, 2002), Cheryl Law, *Suffrage and Power: The Women's Movement, 1918–1928* (London, 1997), Susan Kingsley Kent, both her *Making Peace: The Reconstruction of Gender in Inter-war Britain* (Princeton, 1993), and *Aftershocks: Politics and Trauma in Britain, 1918–1931* (Basingstoke, 2009), among others.
69. P. Wyndham Lewis, *The Art of Being Ruled* (London: 1926), p. 370.
70. Sonya Rose, *Which People's War? National Identity and Citizenship in Britain, 1939–1945* (Oxford, 2003).

1
Emmeline Pankhurst in the Aftermath of Suffrage, 1918–1928

June Purvis

Emmeline Pankhurst (1858–1928), the founder of the Women's Social and Political Union (WSPU), which campaigned for the parliamentary vote for women in Edwardian Britain, became the most notorious of the women suffrage leaders.[1] A powerful orator and charismatic yet autocratic leader, she was always in the thick of the action, whether leading her followers in a deputation to Parliament, inciting them to rebellion, supporting their acts of arson and damage to public and private property or undergoing, at great cost to her own health, thirteen imprisonments. Fiery, impetuous, passionate and determined, with a tremendous physical presence, Emmeline Pankhurst was once called the 'enfant terrible' of the British women's suffrage campaign.[2]

She had founded the women-only WSPU in 1903 to campaign for the parliamentary vote for women on the same terms as it is, or shall be, granted to men. For eleven years, from 1903 to the outbreak of the First World War, on 4 August 1914, when she called an end to all forms of militancy undertaken by her followers, Emmeline Pankhurst and her eldest daughter, Christabel, her co-leader of the suffragette campaign, were the scourge of the British Government. With the advent of war, both women became patriotic feminists, supporting their country in its hour of need and urging all suffragettes of the WSPU to do likewise.[3] As Christabel observed, 'As Suffragettes we could not be pacifists at any price. ... To win votes for women national victory was needed for, as Mother said, "what would be the good of a vote without a country to vote in!"'[4] However, Emmeline and Christabel never lost sight of the women's suffrage issue during the war years but encouraged women to engage in war work, believing that the eventual reward for such loyalty would be the parliamentary vote.[5]

Emmeline was in Russia on 19 June 1917, when the House of Commons passed a clause in the Representation of the People Bill conferring the parliamentary vote on women over thirty who were householders, wives of householders, occupiers of property of £5 or more annual value, or university graduates. And when she returned to Britain in the autumn of that year, ill and exhausted, she and Christabel relaunched the women-only WSPU as the women-only Women's Party, an organisation that was to prepare women for their impending citizenship status during wartime and after. But what happened to Emmeline Pankhurst after 6 February 1918, when the Representation of the People Act received the Royal Assent?

It is the aim of this chapter to discuss this issue, placing Emmeline Pankhurst within the social and political context of her time, exploring the various directions that this prominent figure in the suffrage campaign took after partial suffrage for women was won. And as a feminist historian who writes women's rather than gender history, I will discuss both public and private aspects of her life, which, I hope, will help to situate her within debates about what happened to inter-war British feminism. In particular I will discuss four key themes that are pertinent to the last ten years of her life, from 1918 to 1928 – her leadership of the Women's Party, life as a hygiene or social purity lecturer in North America, the raising of her four adopted children, and her candidacy for election to parliament as a Conservative.

By the time the Women's Party was founded in the autumn of 1917, Emmeline who had once been a Liberal and then a member of the Independent Labour Party was profoundly disillusioned with socialism.[6] She believed it was male centred and, in particular, that pacifist socialism, upheld by many in the Labour Party, had not served the national interest during wartime. As she later explained, she felt that pacifist Labour leaders like Ramsay MacDonald and Philip Snowden, 'had tried to betray their country from the very outset'.[7] Nor did the socialism practised by male trade unionists appeal to Emmeline. She had campaigned hard – and successfully – for women's right to war work, meeting stern opposition from British trade unionists who had not only opposed women's entry to the munitions factories but also staged strikes, thus limiting productivity. Such action, she believed, was both sexist and unpatriotic. Nor was Emmeline favourably disposed towards Bolshevism. While in Russia she had witnessed the early stages of the Bolshevik revolution and was despondent about its lack of democracy, rule of terror and oppression of ordinary people, 80 per cent of whom were illiterate. She became scornful of so-called workers' control and rule by committee.[8] Such views, which Christabel also shared, helped to shape the political programme offered by the Women's Party which drew up a manifesto signed by the four key members of the organisation, formerly part of the inner circle of the old WSPU – Emmeline Pankhurst, Honorary Treasurer, Christabel Pankhurst, Editor of its official newspaper *Britannia*, Annie Kenney Honorary Secretary, and Flora Drummond, Chief Organiser.[9]

The Women's Party was in accord with the established political parties that there was a 'woman's vote' that could be secured, irrespective of class or party.[10] Its manifesto outlined many of the ideas that Emmeline had advocated earlier – the importance of the authority of democratic government, the retaining of British control and ownership of industry, and the strengthening of the British Empire. The aims in regard to the war were anti-pacifist and patriotic – 'War till victory' – while in regard to women's issues, a programme of social reform was advocated that incorporated many of the progressive feminist ideas of the time including equal pay for equal work, equal marriage and divorce laws, equal opportunity of employment, a system of maternity and infant care, co-operative housekeeping and co-operative housing schemes that included central heating, a hot water supply, a central laundry, medical services and – if desired – a crèche, nursery, school, gymnasium and reading room.[11]

Thus the Women's Party conflated the winning of the war with the women's cause, a dual aim that was strongly evident in the advertisement for the large 'patriotic' meeting to be held in the Albert Hall on 16 March 1918, in celebration of the women's suffrage victory. Late in the autumn of that year, Emmeline was caught up in another flurry of excitement. On 21 November 1918, just ten days after the First World War ended, a bill was rushed into law making women eligible to stand for election to Parliament, on equal terms with men, ironically allowing those women aged between twenty-one and thirty years to stand for a Parliament they could not elect.[12] Several friends urged the sixty-year-old Emmeline to offer her candidacy, as a leader of the Woman's Party. But feeling her age, and not fully recovered from her Russian trip, Emmeline declined. She wanted this particular honour for Christabel, her eldest and favourite daughter, and sought Lloyd George's help – which he gave. Initially, Christabel was going to stand for the Westbury Division of Wiltshire but switched to the new industrial, working-class constituency of Smethwick in the Midlands. Emmeline campaigned enthusiastically at Smethwick, but Christabel lost the election by just 755 votes to her Labour Party opponent, despite the fact that she had the Coalition Government's 'coupon' or letter of support.[13] Christabel, who had become a Second Adventist, that is a Christian who is expecting the imminent return of Christ, took the news of her defeat better than her mother who was determined that her talented daughter should have a career in politics. But it was not to be. By July the following year, 1919, the Women's Party had faded away.

Emmeline's love and support for her eldest daughter was not the only family matter that impinged on her public political life at this time. She was rarely in touch with her two other biological daughters, Sylvia and Adela, of whom she was deeply ashamed because of their pacifist socialist views.[14] It was not her biological daughters that were on Emmeline's mind at this particular time in her life but the four female 'war babies' she had 'adopted' in the autumn of 1915 and given new names – Kathleen King, Flora Mary Gordon, Joan Pembridge and Elizabeth Tudor.[15] Christabel took responsibility for Elizabeth, or Betty as she was known, but Emmeline worried about how she could provide for the other three children. She had few savings and no professional or vocational training that would fit her for employment.

THE WOMAN'S PARTY.

Patriotic Meeting and Celebration
OF
The Woman's Suffrage Victory.

ROYAL ALBERT HALL,
Saturday Afternoon, March 16th, at 3 o'clock.
DOORS OPEN AT 2 O'CLOCK.

Orchestral Music will be played from 2 till 3 o'clock.

Mrs. PANKHURST will Preside.

Miss CHRISTABEL PANKHURST.
Miss ANNIE KENNY,
and
Mrs. DRUMMOND will Speak.

ADMISSION (including Entertainment Tax):
Stalls, 2/6. Arena, 1/-. Upper Orchestra, 6d. Balcony, 6d.
GALLERY FREE.
Box Seats: Loggia, 2/- each. Full Box, 16/-.
Grand Tier, 3/-. Full Box, £1 10s.
Second Tier, 2/-. Full Box, 10/-.

Tickets should be ordered at once from the Ticket Secretary, 4 William Street, Knightsbridge, S.W., or from the ALBERT HALL, Kensington, S.W.

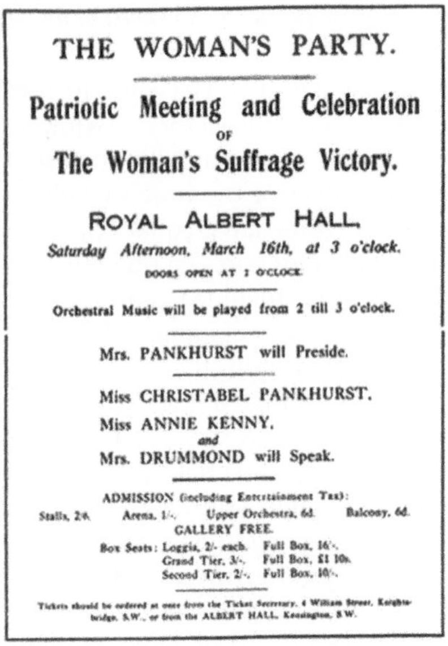

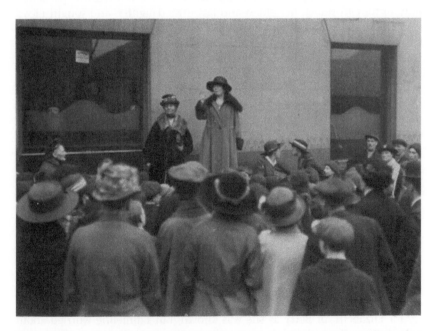

Illustration 1 Advertisement for Woman's Party Meeting, 16 March 1918 (June Purvis Private Suffrage Collection)

Illustration 2 Emmeline and Christabel Pankhurst campaigning in Smethwick December 1918 (June Purvis Private Suffrage Collection)

Illustration 3   Emmeline Pankhurst c. 1919 with her four 'adopted' daughters, from left to right, Elizabeth Tudor, Flora Mary Gordon, Joan Pembridge and Kathleen King (June Purvis Private Suffrage Collection)

Illustration 4   The Unveiling of Emmeline Pankhurst's Statue, Victoria Tower Gardens, Westminster, March 1930 (June Purvis Private Suffrage Collection). It was moved to another site in the Gardens, closer to the Houses of Parliament, in 1956

She had hoped that members of the WSPU would help to financially support the children, but response from suffragettes had been lukewarm and the few contributions that had been made soon dwindled to nothing. Emmeline's salary as a key speaker for the Women's Party had never been enough to cover her personal needs, and now that the Women's Party had faded away she found herself saddled with its liabilities, especially Tower Cressy, a large house that had been bought to convert into a Montessori day school for the little girls and paying pupils. The venture was not a success. To make matters worse, Emmeline also had to pay the expenses for the house she rented, 51 Clarendon Road, Holland Park, the first settled home she had had since giving up her Manchester home in 1907. Never sentimental, she decided that the best way forward was to relinquish her rented house, present Tower Cressy to Princess Alice as a War Memorial Adoption Home, and undertake a lucrative lecturing tour of North America on the evils of Bolshevism.[16] After all, she knew that public speaking was something that she was good at, the North Americans were usually generous with their donations – and there was an emerging hostility towards communism and socialism in that part of the world. Always optimistic, Emmeline told her dear friend Ethel Smyth that now she was free to look solely after her own interests, she would be able 'without difficulty' to earn enough to keep herself and the children for the rest of her days.[17]

In September 1919, now aged 61 years old, a time when most women were considered beyond the age of retirement, Emmeline accompanied by Catherine Pine, an old friend from her suffrage days, sailed to New York leaving her adopted girls behind with a French governess. 'The great work confronting the women now is the suppression of Bolshevism', she told reporters on her arrival. The Bolsheviks were undemocratic and did not represent the working class as whole but only those members who agreed with their doctrines. Through a form of class domination they sought to impose their views on society.[18] The attack on Bolshevism and class conflict were key features of Emmeline's talks in both the USA and Canada where she spoke under the auspices of the Women's Canadian Club. Thus in a talk given in Victoria on 27 November 1919, she spoke to a packed audience of 1,200 on 'Class co-operation versus class war'. Re-asserting her belief in the greatness of the British Empire, she condemned class conflict and expounded on how the cult of Karl Marx had inspired Bolshevism which was 'the absolute negation of everything we have been taught to look upon as right in our civilization – patriotism, religion, family life and the relationship between father and child, husband and wife'. The proletariat, as the lower classes call themselves, she continued, say they cannot rise to the level of the middle class or bourgeoisie and so must drag the bourgeoisie down so that both 'wallow' in a common misery. 'I say it is possible to level up the masses to the place of the middle class', she cried. In conclusion, she appealed for co-operation by the people of the British Empire against the terror of Bolshevism, outlining her plan for an improvement in social conditions in a society based on Christian ideals.[19]

By May 1920, Emmeline had decided to settle in Canada, a country she greatly admired. She stayed in Canada, a Dominion in the British Commonwealth, for five years. During this time, her commitment to the British Empire and imperialism never wavered. An ardent Francophile, perhaps she was particularly attracted to bi-lingual Canada; certainly she wanted to preserve the unity between the British and the French, 'the two greatest races in the world'.[20] Emphasising the cultural heritage that Britain and Canada shared, she represented Britain as the mother of the colonial daughter of Canada, a language that was not unusual for feminist imperialists of the time since it enabled women to participate in the ideological work of empire, shaping what was considered their womanly role and duty.[21] She did not want to break up the British Empire into separate parts, she explained, but to keep all the nations together, in a form of international imperialism where they all worked for the good of the whole. Although it was fashionable to talk of empires as 'oppressive', history had shown that they had accomplished a great deal. 'If, in our modern idea of empire, we eliminate the oppressive, and work for the noble, we will be much better off.'[22] Such statements help to explain Emmeline's transition from the radicalism of her suffrage days to, as we shall later see, Conservatism. Yet we must not forget that many on the Left too saw positive potential in the Empire and acknowledged, as she did, that there was an oppressive element to Empire which could be eliminated. Emmeline's views on Empire may be seen too within the context of ideas expressed by Joseph Chamberlain (1836–1914), a former Liberal who allied himself with the Conservatives and became the leading imperialist of his day. Chamberlain believed that the age of small nations had past and that in the future large agglomerations of countries would be the driving force for change.[23]

Emmeline's popularity in Canada soared. Yet the warm reception she received there was always tempered by worries about her financial situation. 'Now that I have to earn an independence for my old age and also to provide for the infants', she wrote to Ethel Smyth, 'I'm only too thankful I can do it, and in doing it help a little to keep the Empire together and defeat the Bolshevists and *défaitists* who are hard at work here trying to destroy the victory our armies won in the war.' Forced to work 'summer and winter' to support the children she was, nonetheless, determined to fulfil her duties towards them and earn enough to bring them over to Canada.[24] By the summer of 1920, Emmeline felt she had accumulated enough money to do this and so looked for a place to settle. She decided on the small city of Victoria on Vancouver Island, considered the most British of all Canadian cities. Emmeline, who adored small children, was delighted when the little girls arrived in Victoria. 'I am really very reluctant to do anything except potter about, sewing for myself and the children, and reading', she explained wistfully to Ethel Smyth.[25] But such a life could not be embraced. Emmeline, a single parent with few financial resources, had to earn enough to support herself and her dependents. That meant that she was frequently away from home, going away on lecture tours.

A chance meeting with Dr Gordon Bates, a recently demobilised doctor from the Canadian Army Medical Corps and a pioneer in public health, led to Emmeline's appointment as a lecturer for the organisation he had founded, the Canadian National Council for Combating Venereal Diseases. Dr Bates wanted a speaker with the common touch, someone who could relate to ordinary men and women, and Emmeline fitted the bill. For Emmeline, her work with the Canadian National Council seemed 'the logical outcome' of all the other campaigns with which she had been involved.[26] The subject of venereal diseases and their disastrous consequences for unsuspecting wives, their offspring and prostitutes was a subject dear to her heart. She could still remember how long ago, in 1898, when she had taken the job of Registrar of Births and Deaths, after her husband had left her a penniless widow, how venereal diseases were responsible for the death of many babies, a fact often concealed from the grieving mothers who came to register the death, a sealed envelope from a doctor in their hand. And the double sexual stand-ard, venereal diseases and social purity issues had been an integral part of the suffragette agitation which was never a single issue campaign.[27]

Emmeline had strongly endorsed Christabel's *The Great Scourge and How To End It*, first published in 1913, which discussed the degrading effect for women and the British nation of prostitution and venereal diseases, a situ-ation that was a direct consequence of women's subordinate status, as well as men's failure to live up to the moral standards of women. Man-made morality and man-made law upheld a double moral standard, Christabel had argued, whereby sexuality was organised in men's interests and around notions of men's uncontrollable sexual urges. The cure for this unsatisfac-tory situation was twofold – 'Votes for Women', whereby women, exer-cising political power could change the man-made laws that kept them in economic and sexual subjection – and 'chastity for men'.[28] Emmeline was pleased that, once again, she could take up the baton of uplifting the moral outlook of nations. Her wish, as she explained to Ethel Smyth, was to earn enough so that she could purchase 'one of those dear little houses in Victoria with 1 to 3 acres of garden and orchard, where I could live happily and comfortably with the babes, ekeing out my income with a few weeks lecturing and a little writing'.[29]

On 21 April 1921, Emmeline arrived without her second family in Toronto, where the Canadian National Council for Combating Venereal Diseases was located, brimming with her usual energy. As in her suffrage days, she believed that the best way to attract an audience was by working up inter-est amongst the public by giving interviews to the press. Speaking to a keen reporter for the *Toronto Evening Telegram*, she told him that sexual diseases, which come from sexual promiscuity, were closely related to Bolshevism, which was like an infectious mental disease. 'If you get a healthy race ... mental and moral diseases will disappear', she pointed out. The *Toronto Daily Star*, like many other of the Canadian newspapers, were pleased with such comments, praising Emmeline's plea for 'moral sanity' and claiming that she was 'one of the great women or this or any age'.[30]

As expected, crowds flocked to hear Emmeline's address on 'Social hygiene and the world's unrest', given the next day. Keeping a feminist focus, she emphasised that people's health was the cause of women and that women's viewpoint must be adopted when fighting the evil of venereal diseases. While it would be a struggle to eradicate venereal diseases in a crowded country like Britain, in a 'young country like Canada', with its small population, results could be achieved more quickly through educational programmes. 'As a practical woman', she concluded, to much applause, 'and it is the women who are practical; you men are the romancers – I ask you to send cheques as large as the importance of the work to the Council under whose auspices I am speaking to-night.'[31]

Emmeline was so enchanted with Canada that she applied, successfully, for Canadian citizenship. '[T]here seems to be more equality between men and women [here] than in any other country I know ... there are such unlimited opportunities', she enthusiastically told one reporter. The impressed journalist spoke of how 'always beautifully and becomingly gowned' Mrs Pankhurst was and how, during her first six weeks in Toronto she had addressed groups as diverse at the Masonic Lodge, the Canadian Manufacturers' Association, the Imperial Order of the Daughters of the Empire, Women's Institutes, the Women's Law Association, the Women's Press Club, Mothers' Meetings – as well as women in factories, men in factories, the occupants of several men's luncheon clubs, men and women students, church congregations, men's and women's and young people's organisations attached to churches, women in reformatories, printers on strike, and a number of drawing-room gatherings in the homes of influential people in the city.[32] But such an active life, living in hotels away from her second family, was exhausting and lonely. Emmeline decided to bring the children and Catherine Pine from Victoria to Toronto and to rent a house there, at 78 Charles Street West. 'It has been a bit lonely without my babies', she confessed to one reporter, 'and I shall be glad to have them and my own little house and my dear Miss Pyne [sic], with her mending basket, and all the rest of it.'[33]

Yet, despite her love of Canada and Canadians, Emmeline missed her old friends who had served her loyally during her suffrage years – many of whom were anxious about her financial plight. A testimonial fund had been set up in England, in tribute to the work she and Christabel had undertaken for the women's cause, some £3,000 being collected. Half of the money was spent on buying and furnishing a country house at Westward Ho, in Devon, for when she returned to England, and the rest was now sent to the grateful

Emmeline in Canada. Accompanying the gift was a carefully worded letter, written in such a way as to avoid wounding her pride.[34] However, the buying of the house was a 'mistaken kindness' since Emmeline lacked the means to maintain the property, had to let it and, finally, to sell it.[35]

It was probably early in the New Year of 1923 that Emmeline and her family moved house again in Toronto to 76 St Mary's Street, possibly a cheaper residence. But the pace of Emmeline's life did not lessen. She was still a speaker for the Canadian National Council for Combating Venereal Diseases (renamed that year the Canadian Social Hygiene Council), a job that involved extensive travelling on public transport. An engaging and influential lecturer, she would usually tailor her talks to suit her audience. Thus to gatherings of ordinary men and women, she often stressed the responsibilities of parents to raise healthy, moral children, something that was particularly important since every year in Canada, twenty thousand babies died before they were one year old because of the pernicious effects of the venereal diseases of the father which had infected innocent wives, some of whom became infertile. 'There is no crime to compare with that which causes the early death or lifelong suffering of innocent people', Emmeline informed one audience in Saskatoon. 'To bring into the world a child that is blind through venereal disease, is a crime. To cause the lifelong invalidism of a woman, and deny her that greatest joy, the joy of motherhood, is a crime. To cause a child to be born doomed to die, and to suffer very minute during its life, is a crime.'[36] At other times, when speaking to women's groups, she might stress the importance of mothers in racial improvement, especially now that they had won their citizenship. It was the first duty of the woman who had become a citizen, she told her audience at the Women's Canadian Club, 'to defend her own self-respect by fighting the social evil of traffic in human lives that eventually attacks the family'.[37] Ideas about the importance of women's role in the fight against venereal diseases and national degeneracy had already been expressed forcibly by Emmeline during the suffragette campaign. Thus in a major speech in 1913, she highlighted how it was the women's movement that had brought into public debate discussion about the evils of prostitution and venereal diseases, and their destructive effect on the lives of women and children, issues that men had hushed up for too long. She did not then make an explicit link to Empire but had reminded her audience that women had been told that it was their business 'to bring the race into the world; to nurse the babies; to bring them up to be good men and women, the future fathers and mothers', a task that could not be properly done because the authorities were more concerned with notifying diseases such as measles or smallpox than 'the worst disease of all, the most contagious, the most destructive of mind and soul and body'.[38] Emmeline was now reiterating such eugenic beliefs again, in 1923, illustrating how such continuities help us to resolve some of the apparent contradictions between her pre-and post-1914 thinking.

Emmeline's eminence was such that she was elected as a Vice President of the Canadian Public Health Association. But such an honour only added to her workload. The strain of her arduous life now took its toll; her health broke down and the Canadian Government granted its popular speaker six months leave of absence. In the spring of 1924, Emmeline retreated with Catherine Pine and the girls, as well as Christabel and Betty who had come to Toronto two years earlier, to the warm climate of Bermuda. She stayed there for about one year. But without a regular income her savings dwindled rapidly. The sixty-six-year-old Emmeline did not want to return to her lecturing job in Canada; the very thought of travelling on public transport during the severe winters was unbearable. She decide to open a tea shop in the south of France with a close friend of her suffrage days, Mabel Tuke, who offered to put up most of the capital. Christabel, now a success-ful author on Second Adventism, could go with them and continue with her writing. Meanwhile, since her finances were in such a precarious state Emmeline reluctantly decided that Kathleen and Joan should be sent back to England where, through friends, she had arranged for these two girls to be adopted by well-to-do people who could give them the chances in life she could not.[39]

Full of hope, Emmeline travelled to the South of France with Mary, Mabel Tuke and Christabel and Betty. But the 'English Tea-Shop of Good Hope' that she set up in Juan-les-Pins, was not a success. Former suffragettes in England, hearing of her financial plight, rallied to help. Lady Rhondda wrote to Emmeline inviting her to return to England and work for the Six Point Group, a feminist society that campaigned for equality for women, includ-ing an equal franchise for women under thirty. An income of £400 annually, for a minimum of three years, was guaranteed. The proud Emmeline, fearing she was an object of 'charity', declined the offer. She was also of the view that, in a time of world-crisis, when a second world war seemed to be loom-ing, it was undesirable to re-open the franchise question. 'Full and effective use has not been made of the votes we already have', she argued, 'To secure this effective use is the present task.'[40] Perhaps Emmeline was thinking that for women to press their case at this particular moment in time would lead to a charge of 'selfishness' and delay the inevitable electoral reform. She certainly had deep misgivings about working in the women's movement in England with its left-wing, pacifist leanings. Her feminism was now a mater-nal, imperial feminism that gave high priority to women's role in raising the moral tone of the nation and British Empire. She had no sympathy for those so-called 'progressive' left-wing feminists, such as her daughter Sylvia, who advocated an end to imperialism, the overthrow of capitalism, the estab-lishment of a socialist society – and free love.[41] Sylvia had recently joined, but soon left, the British Community Party which Emmeline so hated and, unlike her mother, had turned against the entire concept of parliamentary government.[42]

Just before Christmas 1925, after a six year absence, the nearly penniless Emmeline returned with Mary to England. Initially she stayed with her sister Ada Goulden Bach, in Kensington. Sylvia, who had not seen her mother for a long while, visited only to find that Emmeline refused to speak to her, or even to stay in the same room. Emmeline had heard all the news about her 'wayward' daughter – Sylvia was living, unmarried, with an Italian socialist and anarchist, Silvio Erasmus Corio who had fathered two children in previous liaisons, without a marriage licence. For Emmeline, who had campaigned for the moral uplifting of society, her daughter's behaviour was disgraceful, merely emulating the sexual irresponsibility of men. She did not believe that 'free love' would bring emancipation for women.[43]

The British press was soon buzzing with the news of Emmeline's return to England. Early in 1926 she explained to eager reporters that although a new campaign was beginning to win an equal franchise for women, her next fight would not be for this cause but for industrial peace, improved housing, new electricity schemes for homes and cities – which would take the drudgery out of housework – and the British Empire.[44] Nonetheless, she was soon drawn back into the equal suffrage cause. On 2 March she attended the dinner, organised by the Six Point Group in her honour at which Nancy Astor, the first woman MP, offered to resign her seat in favour of the former militant suffragette leader. Emmeline politely declined but expressed her willingness to contest a seat that might fall vacant.[45]

Emmeline had returned to an England in which class conflict and industrial disputes were endemic, culminating in a General Strike, declared on 1 May, lasting just over a week. Impressed with the way Stanley Baldwin, the Conservative Prime Minister, had dealt with the emergency, she joined the Conservative Party and accepted the offer to stand as a Conservative parliamentary candidate. She needed to earn her living, and the opportunity to become an MP would enable her to indulge her interest in politics – and use effectively her speaking skills. The press in both North America and Britain buzzed with the news of the 'conversion' to the political right of the former notorious suffragette rebel and former member of the Independent Labour Party. When a reporter from the *Morning Post* asked Emmeline why, in view of her previous association with more radical causes, she had decided to stand as a Conservative, she informed him that she no longer believed that the state could do everything. In her younger days, she observed, she had believed in state socialism but now:

I can no longer support the view that State ownership of the means of distribution, production, and exchange would be of any benefit to the community. My war experience and my experience on the other side of the Atlantic, particularly in Canada, where I have spent a considerable time, have changed my views profoundly. Then came the general strike, and I saw that there were only two issues before the country, and that anyone who had the real interests of women at heart would stand firmly behind Mr. Baldwin and the Government. I am now an Imperialist.[46]

Emmeline here accurately reflects how her views had changed over time. Nonetheless, she still kept a feminist agenda firmly in view. If elected to parliament, she asserted, her main concerns would be to work for reforms for women and children, particularly equal suffrage and equal rights for women in all walks of life.[47]

Emmeline Pankhurst had turned to the Conservative Party as the key political force that would uphold the British Constitution and Empire, support democracy, advance the cause of women and resist the communism she so hated. The Labour Party, which had 'consistently' advocated an equal franchise and in its 1923 election manifesto had claimed that it stood for 'equal political and legal rights', had failed to deliver when it was elected to power, for a short time, in 1924.[48] That the first Labour Government, a minority government, should renege on this commitment was no surprise to Emmeline. She had observed that the idea of granting equal suffrage had gradually been gathering support in the Conservative Party, under the leadership of Stanley Baldwin. But there were many feminists campaigning for an equal franchise too, including Lady Rhondda, who sought to invigorate the campaign by asking Emmeline to join the Equal Rights Political Demonstration Committee – which she did, becoming one of the Committee's Vice Presidents. Emmeline was one of the nearly 3,000 women who took part in the procession held on 3 July 1926, which 40 women's groups supported. Her participation in the procession was merely a gesture anyway since she had played her part in securing from Baldwin a promise to implement an equal franchise, a theme of one of his addresses.[49]

Early in 1927, Emmeline was formally adopted as the Conservative parliamentary candidate for the poor, socialist London constituency of Whitechapel and St George's in the East End of London, although the general election was not due until 1929. Since she had no chance of winning the seat, historians have put forward various explanations for her choice. Thus Martin Pugh claims that Emmeline's willingness to accept this nomination was in order 'to spite' her Communist daughter, Sylvia, with her close links to the East End, a verdict with which Shirley Harrison, one of Sylvia's biographers, agrees. Brian Harrison suggests that Emmeline chose Whitechapel and St George's since her support for the British Empire, her distaste for socialism and her support for Baldwin had 'displaced feminism from her list of priorities'.[50] What these historians fail to acknowledge is that Emmeline wanted a working-class constituency since she believed it was the working classes, especially the women, who were most exploited by communism.

Emmeline immersed herself in campaigning, visiting every shop, every tenement, every public house in the area – and holding open-air and women's meetings.[51] 'Our idea is to make friends with everybody and replace class hatred & suspicion by Friendliness and Cooperation', she told one supporter.[52] Emmeline's secretary, Nellie Hall-Humpherson, a pre-war suffragette, recollected that the East Enders 'adored' Mrs. Pankhurst. 'She was a lovely person to them ... she never talked down to them and she was interested in them rather than expecting them to be interested in her. She was a compassionate woman in all her dealings with people, but particularly women.'[53] But Emmeline's election addresses on the importance of a democratic society based on class co-operation where women would work for the moral uplifting of both Britain and the British Empire seemed out of touch with the economic recession of the late 1920s and the rising rate of unemployment. Nor did Emmeline fit in well with Conservative Party Office who found her difficult and not quite 'true blue'.[54]

The sixty-nine year old Emmeline was sitting in the Ladies' Gallery in Parliament when the second reading of the Representation of the People (Equal Franchise) Act was passed on 29 March 1928, giving all women aged twenty-one and over equal voting rights with men. Perhaps she hoped that she would soon be speaking in parliament. But her chances of being elected were slim. In addition to standing for an unpromising seat, her health was failing. 'She looked very frail and old', said one reporter who saw her, 'not even the shadow of an Amazon.'[55]

One month later, the frail Emmeline was struck a cruel blow when, a few hours before she was due to chair a Conservative party meeting, she was warned that she would be asked, at the meeting, whether one of her daughters had had a baby out of wedlock. Unknown to Emmeline, the unmarried Sylvia had given birth to a son, Richard, some five months earlier, on 3 December 1927. At a time when unmarried mothers were stigmatised as wanton, sexually promiscuous women, those close to Emmeline thought it best to carefully keep such news from her, for fear it would have fatal consequences. When the question was asked at the meeting, Emmeline dealt with it by curtly saying that it was not her custom to discuss private matters in public. But the incident, and the resultant publicity, 'cut her to the heart'.[56] On Easter Sunday, 1928, the front page of the *News of the World*, not considered a respectable newspaper, carried an article titled '*Eugenic* Baby Sensation. Sylvia Pankhurst's Amazing Confession'. The article told of how 'Miss' Pankhurst advocated marriage without a legal union and how she considered her son a 'eugenic baby' since she and her 'husband' were both intelligent and healthy people. In particular, Sylvia professed that she could not understand the attitude of her family towards her son. She had written to her mother about the birth of the child, 'but there was no reply'.[57] For Emmeline, such vulgar publicity, repeated around the world, was unbearable. She sunk into a deep depression, weeping all day. Worse, many people thought that the 'Miss Pankhurst' in the headlines referred to Christabel. The scandal also meant an abrupt end to any hopes Emmeline herself had nursed for a political career. 'I shall never be able to speak in public again', she kept saying, between the sobs.[58]

This was not the only worry facing Emmeline. She was living on a pittance and knew she could not afford to give Mary, the 'adopted' daughter she had kept by her side, a good education and good prospects in life. Reluctantly, she asked a wealthy, ex-suffragette friend, Marion Wallace Dunlop, to bring up the twelve-year-old Mary. Alone and burdened with her sorrows, Emmeline took to her bed.[59] She had some comfort from two of her biological daughters. Thus the loyal Christabel visited her mother occasionally and wrote her long, weekly letters. And Adela wrote to her mother too, telling how she and her husband had come around to Emmeline's view about the destructiveness of class conflict and were now promoting the idea of employers and workers acting together, for the common good. The joyful Emmeline immediately replied to her youngest daughter, 'full of regret for the long rift'.[60] But Emmeline refused to forgive or see Sylvia. The 'wayward' daughter and her mother were never reconciled. As Emmeline's health deteriorated, she was moved to a nursing home at 43 Wimpole Street where she died on 14 June 1928, just one month before her seventieth birthday. The royal assent to the Equal Franchise Bill was given on the day of her funeral.

After Emmeline Pankhurst's death, many tributes were paid to her, not for her work post 1918 but for her leadership of the militant suffrage campaign. Some of the former suffragettes set about raising money to commemorate the great leader to which over 700 people from Britain, Canada and the USA contributed. After much wrangling with the Ministry of Works, the British Government finally agreed that a statue could be placed in Victoria Tower Gardens, close to the Houses of Parliament. On 6 March 1930, the ex-Prime Minister Stanley Baldwin, who had once opposed the notorious rebel, unveiled the statue saying, 'I say with no fear of contradiction, that whatever view posterity may take, Mrs. Pankhurst has won for herself a niche in the Temple of Fame which will last for all time.'[61] Since Baldwin, while acknowledging the radical nature of Emmeline's leadership nonetheless placed her within a British tradition of gradual, peaceful reform, one present day historian asserts that Emmeline Pankhurst had been 'domesticated' or tamed.[62] Or had she?

In contrast to the commemoration of Emmeline Pankhurst as a radical suffragette leader before 1918, her life after 1918 has mainly been interpreted as a move to the political right.[63] As we have seen, Emmeline spent five of the last ten years of her life in the more culturally conservative culture of Canada, a British Dominion, mainly because it offered her the chance of employment, an activity that she needed to support herself and the 'war babies' she had adopted. Her time as a lecturer in social hygiene in Canada was formative to her making as an imperial feminist. When she returned to Britain, she found a splintered women's movement and a changed world to which she had difficulty relating. Her views on sexuality and her stress upon the moral uplifting of nations were not embraced by the new generation of feminists. Her attacks on socialism and her ideas about the British Empire were regarded as outdated. Emmeline was out of tune with the times. Yet her commitment to women and broader social reforms remained.

Emmeline Pankhurst joined the Conservative Party since she hoped it would bring in an equal franchise bill – and also because she wanted to lift the standard of living of the working classes, especially of working-class women. But she did not believe that such wide-ranging reforms could be achieved by state socialism alone, but by some mixture of public and private enterprise that emphasised class co-operation rather than class hatred. Class conflict, she believed, undermined the unity of Britain and the bond of womanhood that all women shared, despite their class or wealth. Perhaps, above all, Emmeline Pankhurst's life after 1918 reveals rather than a move to the political right, the difficulties of fitting feminism into any of the main class-based, male dominated political parties of her day. Nonetheless, it is her feminist days as the radical leader of the militant suffrage campaign that are remembered and commemorated. Her figure is very much part of the story of what happened after the achievement of women's suffrage in Britain, even well after her death.

Notes

1. In this chapter I draw upon my *Emmeline Pankhurst: A Biography* (London and New York, Routledge, 2002), esp. pp. 300–63.
2. Comment made by Emmeline Pethick-Lawrence, one of the former leaders of the WSPU, to the journalist Henry Woodd Nevinson. Entry for 23 December 1913, Nevinson Diaries, Bodleian Library, Oxford.
3. Purvis, *Emmeline Pankhurst*, p. 269. For an overview of the vast literature on the suffragette campaign in Britain see June Purvis, Gendering the historiography of the suffragette movement in Edwardian Britain: some reflections, in Lucy Bland and Katarina Rowald (eds) *20 Years of the Women's History Network, Looking Back – Looking Forward*, Special Issue of *Women's History Review*, Vol. 22, No. 4, 2013.
4. Christabel Pankhurst, *Unshackled: The Story of How We Won the Vote* (London, Hutchinson, 1959), p. 288.
5. Purvis, *Emmeline Pankhurst*, p. 269: Angela K. Smith, *Suffrage Discourse in Britain During the First World War* (Aldershot, Ashgate, 2005), p. 32; June Purvis, The Pankhursts and the Great War, in Alison S. Fell and Ingrid Sharp (eds), *The Women's Movement in Wartime, International Perspectives, 1914–19* (Basingstoke, Palgrave Macmillan, 2007), pp. 141–57.
6. She had resigned from the Independent Labour Party in 1907.
7. *Britannia*, 1 March 1918, p. 341.
8. Purvis, *Emmeline Pankhurst*, p. 301.
9. *Britannia*, 2 November 1917, title page.
10. Krista Cowman, *Women in British Politics, c. 1689–1979* (Basingstoke, Palgrave Macmillan, 2010), p. 117.
11. *Britannia*, 2 November 1917, p. 171.
12. Cowman, *Women in British Politics*, p. 116.
13. David Mitchell, *Queen Christabel: A Biography of Christabel Pankhurst* (London, MacDonald and Jane's, 1977), pp. 275–6.

14. See Purvis, The Pankhursts and the Great War, p. 145.
15. Adoption at this time was a very informal process, which had no official status prior to 1926. See Jenny Keating, *A Child for Keeps: The History of Adoption in England, 1918–45* (Basingstoke, Palgrave Macmillan, 2009).
16. Purvis, *Emmeline Pankhurst*, p. 317.
17. Ethel Smyth, *Female Pipings in Eden* (London, Peter Davies Ltd, 1934, second edition, revised), p. 247.
18. *New York Tribune*, 14 September and 2 October 1919; *New York Evening Post*, 14 September 1919.
19. *Victoria Daily Times*, 28 November 1919.
20. Paula Bartley, *Emmeline Pankhurst* (London, Routledge, 2002), p. 211.
21. On this theme see Antoinette Burton, *Burdens of History: British Feminists, Indian Women, and Imperial Culture, 1865–1915* (Chapel Hill and London, University of North Carolina Press, 1994) – and for an informative critique see Susan Pedersen, *Journal of Modern History*, Vol. 69, 1, March 1997, pp. 144–6; Julia Bush, *Edwardian Ladies and Imperial Power* (London, Leicester University Press, 2000), ch. 10.
22. *Toronto Daily Star*, 11 February 1922.
23. I am indebted to the editors of this volume for these insights.
24. Smyth, *Female Pipings*, pp. 250–1.
25. Smyth, *Female Pipings*, p. 252.
26. *Toronto Daily Star*, 11 February 1922.
27. June Purvis, Fighting the double sexual standard in Edwardian Britain: suffragette militancy, sexuality and the nation in the writings of the early twentieth-century British feminist Christabel Pankhurst, in Francisca de Haan, Margaret Allen, June Purvis and Krassimira Dasklova (eds) *Women's Activism: Global Perspectives from the 1890s to the Present*, (London and New York, Routledge, 2013).
28. Christabel Pankhurst, *The Great Scourge and How To End It*, (London, E. Pankhurst, 1913), p. 37 'The real cure of the great plague is ... Votes for Women, which will give to women more self-reliance and a stronger economic position, and chastity for men.'
29. Emmeline Pankhurst to Ethel Smyth, 7 March 1921, Smyth *Female Pipings in Eden*, p. 253.
30. *Toronto Evening Telegram* and *Toronto Daily Star*, 22 April 1921.
31. *Toronto Globe* and *Toronto Mail and Empire*, 23 April 1921.
32. E. Chapman, Mrs. Pankhurst – Canadian, *Maclean's Magazine*, 15 January 1922.
33. *Toronto Globe*, 17 January 1922.
34. Purvis, *Emmeline Pankhurst*, pp. 325–6; C. Pankhurst, *Unshackled*, p. 296.
35. Estelle Sylvia Pankhurst, *The Life of Emmeline Pankhurst: The Suffragette Struggle for Women's Citizenship* (London, T. Werner Laurie Ltd, 1935), p. 169.
36. *Saskatoon Daily Star*, 29 May 1923.
37. *Saskatoon Daily Star*, 29 May 1923.
38. *The Suffragette*, 8 August 1913, p. 738.
39. Purvis, *Emmeline Pankhurst*, p. 337.
40. Smyth, *Female Pipings*, p. 259.
41. Purvis, *Emmeline Pankhurst*, p. 338.
42. Shirley Harrison, *Sylvia Pankhurst: A Crusading Life 1882–1960* (London, Aurum Press, 2003), p. 194, pp. 212–15.
43. Purvis, *Emmeline Pankhurst*, p. 339.
44. *Manchester Guardian*, 28 January 1926.
45. *Toronto Daily Star*, 4 March 1926.

46. *Morning Post*, 3 June 1926.
47. *Toronto Daily Star*, 16 October 1926.
48. Harold L. Smith, *The British Women's Suffrage Campaign 1866–1928* (Harlow, Pearson Education, 2007), p. 95.
49. *Votes for Women at Twenty-one: Extracts from a Speech by the Prime Minister at the Albert Hall, London, May 27* (London, McCorquodale and Co., 1927).
50. Martin Pugh, *Women and the Women's Movement in Britain* (Basingstoke, Macmillan, 2000, 2nd edn), p. 46; Harrison, *Sylvia Pankhurst*, p. 219, Brian Harrison, *Prudent Revolutionaries: Portraits of British Feminists Between the Wars* (Oxford, Oxford University Press, 1987), p. 35.
51. Smyth, *Female Pipings*, p. 263.
52. Emmeline Pankhurst to Margaret Bates, 5 February 1927, June Purvis Private Suffrage Collection.
53. Statement by Nellie Hall-Humpherson, David Mitchell Collection, 73.83/36 (c).
54. Purvis, *Emmeline Pankhurst*, p. 348.
55. Quoted in David Mitchell, *The Fighting Pankhursts,* p. 196.
56. Smyth, *Female Pipings*, p. 266.
57. *News of the World*, 8 April 1928.
58. Smyth, *Female Pipings*, p. 269.
59. Purvis, *Emmeline Pankhurst*, p. 350.
60. Statement by Nellie Hall-Humpherson; Verna Coleman, *Adela Pankhurst: The Wayward Suffragette 1885–1961* (Melbourne, Melbourne University Press, 1996), p. 108.
61. Smyth, *Female Pipings*, p. 278.
62. Laura E. Nym Mayhall, Domesticating Emmeline: representing the suffragette, 1930–1993, *NWSA Journal*, Vol. 11, No. 2, 2000.
63. Julie Gottlieb, *Feminine Fascism: Women in Britain's Fascist Movement 1923–1945* (London, I. B. Tauris, 2000), pp. 157–8; Martin Pugh, *The Pankhursts* (London, Allen Lane, 2001), pp. 351–411.

2

From Prudent Housewife to Empire Shopper: Party Appeals to the Female Voter, 1918–1928

David Thackeray

Over recent years significant attention has been paid to how British political parties responded to the challenge of developing gendered appeals to
new voters in the aftermath of the 1918 Representation of the People Act,
which gave the parliamentary vote to most women aged thirty and over and
all men over the age of twenty-one. Much of this literature has focused on
how parties sought to adapt to female social cultures, most notably David
Jarvis's work on the Conservative party and Pamela Graves's study of the
Labour women's organisation.[1] Few comparable studies have been produced
of how parties developed specific appeals to masculine interests in inter-
war Britain, even though this has been an issue of considerable interest for
historians of the late-Victorian and Edwardian eras.[2] While the following
analysis confines itself to a study of party appeals to the female voter, it is
nonetheless important to emphasise that parties' assumptions about male
and female 'interests' in politics often overlapped.[3] As recent literature on
the Edwardian free trade debate demonstrates, appeals to consumer interests
were by no means confined to women, and the same was true after 1918 as
the politics of the anti-waste movement demonstrates.[4]

Studies of the Conservative and Labour women's organisations have
tended to assess their development in isolation, rather than explicitly seeing
the parties as constantly fighting to construct new ways of appealing to the
female voter and to respond to innovations made by their opponents. This
is not too say that comparative study of the parties' responses to the challenge of female enfranchisement has been neglected. Thanks to recent work
we know much more about the ways in which the political press sought to
appeal to the female voter, of how parties responded to the development
of a vigorous culture of non-party activism, and of the means by which
the culture of British public politics was transformed after 1918, in part,
as a response to the growing prominence of women in political life.[5] All
the same, given the authors' concerns with wider changes in British civic
culture this new literature has tended to pay little attention to how such
developments affected the course of party politics between the wars.

The Liberal women's organisation remains the Cinderella of histories of post-suffrage politics, and its relative neglect, compared to its Conservative and Labour ugly sisters, has stymied the development of comparative studies of women's engagement in party politics. Have no doubt, the problems which the Liberal party faced in sustaining a mass-supported women's organisation after 1918 formed one of the main impediments to its progress in inter-war politics. The Women's Liberal Federation had an impressive paper membership of 115,000 in 1914. Aside from the work of this organisation, Liberal women were also active in the anti-suffragist Women's National Liberal Federation and the Women's Free Trade Union. This record of action compared favourably to the marginal presence which women held within the auxiliary activities of the Labour party at this time. The Women's Labour League, formed in 1906, had a precarious existence and claimed a mere 6000 members.[6] But these positions were reversed during the First World War and its aftermath. The Labour Party's women's sections grew rapidly, with an estimated membership of around 250,000–300,000 by 1928, although this figure was still dwarfed by the one million members claimed by the Conservative women's organisation. The Women's National Liberal Federation (WNLF), formed in 1919 following the amalgamation of the two existing women's Liberal associations, did not fare nearly so well. Membership fell from 95,000 in 1920 to 66,000 in 1923, before making a partial recovery to 88,000 in 1926.[7]

Using popular party magazines, as well as the records of agents and organisers, this chapter explores how British political parties engaged in a competitive dialogue to appeal to the female voter. Through an exploration of these sources it becomes clear that the stagnation of the Liberal women's organisation owed much to its failure to keep up with its rivals' ability to pioneer innovative campaigning techniques, sophisticated media strategies, and popular consumer campaigns, which responded effectively to post-war conditions. For much of the first decade of female parliamentary suffrage the Liberal women's organisation struggled to present itself as a modern alternative to its rivals, and seemed stuck in pre-war modes of politics.

Perhaps the main innovation in party appeals to women after 1918 was the proliferation of popular political magazines aimed at the female voter. The monthly *Labour Woman* had been in production since 1911, and was joined by a Conservative magazine, *Home and Politics*, in 1921, which started life as a special edition of an existing party publication, the *Popular View*. Liberal party magazines aimed at the female voter went through various incarnations. Although sometimes stocked by sympathetic newsagents, such literature was usually distributed at cheap rates to constituency party associations, and sold door-to-door by women workers.

The Conservative women's periodical, *Home and Politics*, seems to have been a particular success and by 1929 it claimed a monthly circulation of 200,000 copies.[8] Notes on party organisation sat together with features typical of a contemporary women's lifestyle magazine, including advice on household chores, cookery, and dress. Incorporating these ostensibly non-political features into party literature was seen as vital in appealing to women, especially those of the lower middle and working classes. When the Conservatives ran a one-off magazine aimed at women under thirty who had gained the vote in 1928, a central office memorandum noted that 'it was agreed that generally speaking pamphlets and leaflets, obviously political in character...were liable to be disregarded by the millions of women of these classes'.[9]

Part of the appeal of *Home and Politics* was that it could easily be localised, enabling women to keep up-to-date with the political and social activities of their constituency association. Local editions often contained a page relating to the work being undertaken by the prospective Conservative candidate, and enabled the party to mould its appeals to suit a variety of localised social cultures. By 1926 there were thirty-nine local editions of *Home and Politics*, usually paid for by advertising, with inserts varying from four to sixteen pages, and localisation was increasingly becoming the norm for other party magazines such as *Man in the Street* at this time.[10] Conservative Central Office assisted this proliferation of literature through the activities of its Lobby Press Service, which provided a steady stream of articles and notes that papers were free to localise.[11]

Labour attempts to develop a syndicated press service met with less success. By 1924 only thirteen local parties were using articles provided from head office in London and the news service closed down two years later.[12] Nonetheless, special local election newspapers appear to have become common by the mid-1920s, with commercial companies like Reynolds providing assistance to local Labour parties with their provision of standardised templates and occasional news copy.[13]

Although Labour arguably lagged behind the Conservatives in terms of developing a local media appeal, its party magazines still managed to provide women with an array of advice on organisation and campaigning. Marion Phillips, Labour's Chief Woman Officer, was a regular contributor to the *Labour Organiser*, and regional agents such as Elizabeth Andrews and Annie Somers wrote women's pages for local party publications.[14] By encouraging targeted electioneering techniques they were able to develop a variety of discourses aimed at different groups of women. Labour canvassers were encouraged to fit their discussions around the concerns of the particular woman they were addressing:

> If she is suffering from unemployment, tell her about the Labour Party and the right to work or maintenance. If she is a housewife, tell her how much money she pays for tea or sugar is a tax which the Labour Party wants to do away with. If she has a little baby, tell her about the Labour Party's fight for free or cheap milk.[15]

Much like the Conservative activists who promoted localised magazines, Labour effectively broke the female electorate into a variety of interest groups and sought to target each individually. Phillips encouraged women organisers to arrange special meetings for supporters of the co-operative movement, and the wives of trade unionists. Furthermore, activists were also encouraged to distribute suitable literature outside of mothers' meetings at churches and chapels.[16]

After 1918 the Liberals struggled to match their opponents' experiments with targeted appeals to the woman voter. Given that the parliamentary Liberal party remained under the leadership of Asquith, who had been a convinced opponent of women's suffrage, it was poorly placed to develop an effective programme of appeals to the new female voter. But it was also hampered by the lack of an effective party women's magazine to compete with *Home and Politics* and *Labour Woman* until 1925. The *Women's Liberal Magazine* restricted itself to a weekly digest of branch news and the activities of the national organisation, harking back to the format of Edwardian party magazines. By late 1920 the publication was making a substantial loss with only 104 out of 815 Women's Liberal Associations bothering to subscribe, subsequently it was cut back to a four-page monthly and relaunched as the *Federation News*.[17] Yet this name change had little effect on the magazine's content. Whereas rival party magazines for women gave regular advice on innovative ways to run constituency branches, it was only after the 1923 election that the *Federation News* began to pay serious attention to offering advice on organisation.[18]

Finally, in January 1925 the Liberal party launched two popular magazines, the *Liberal Women's News* and *Liberal Pioneer*. The former heavily imitated the style of the Conservative *Home and Politics*, addressing party policies in a simple fashion, and including household hints and competition pages. This change in approach brought some belated success, whereas *Federation News* had 3000 subscribers at the time of its demise, the relaunched *Liberal Women's News* reached a circulation of 10,000 by May 1925. But even so, less than ten percent of Women's Liberal Association members were subscribing to the magazine two years later.[19] With such low circulation figures localisation of Liberal party magazines was effectively a dead letter.[20]

Prior to the party reunification in 1923 the Asquith and Lloyd George Liberals appear to have taken somewhat different approaches to the question of appealing to women, with the latter being the more progressive. This appears to have been thanks in part to the influence of Constance Williams, an occasional contributor to the *Lloyd George Liberal Magazine*.[21] By comparison with the Labour party, the Asquithian Liberals appear to have been hesitant in embracing the need to develop targeted appeals directed towards different sections of voters. Remarkably, a record of the discussion of election methods at the Liberal agents' annual meeting in 1920 stated that 'special appeals for the votes of ex-service men is pure waste. There is no solid Women's Vote as such. As evidence secured by special tests proves that 90 per cent of the women vote the same way as their husbands do'.[22] Some Asquithian Liberal agents appear to have supported the production of specialist literature for interest groups, but overall the evidence suggests that they struggled to match their rivals' targeted electioneering techniques.[23]

The issue of ex-servicemen's welfare provides a good example of Asquithian Liberals' failure to keep up with their rivals in developing new appeals to the woman voter. Given that ex-servicemen made up much of the long-term unemployed in post-war Britain, politicians who claimed to represent their interest were effectively making a wider claim to represent deprived working families whose breadwinners had lost their jobs with the onset of economic recession. Conservative and Labour appeals to female voters often highlighted the issue of party efforts to provide assistance to ex-soldiers in finding work, gaining benefits, and securing affordable housing.[24] Asquithian Liberals made few effective interventions in the debates on the welfare of ex-servicemen's families, which were dominated by arguments between the Lloyd George Coalition, in which the Conservatives formed a majority, and the Labour Party.

All parties recognised that they needed to pay significant attention to creating mass supported organisations after 1918. Whereas pre-war party associations had devoted much of their energies to training women who were keen to be of practical service at elections as canvassers, helpers, and speakers, it was now understood that simpler meetings were necessary to appeal to the female voter who may previously have had little interest in party politics. Women's meetings were often organised in mid-afternoon to suit the working day of housewives and all parties experimented with 'cottage meetings', where women would be invited to a meeting held in a neighbour's house. The informal setting had the advantage that women did not need to change out of their work dress; moreover, they could take their children along to the meeting or leave them under the supervision of a neighbour. Activists were encouraged to provide tea and newspaper articles to discuss, but 'taking the chair' or making speeches was frowned upon in such settings.[25]

Annie Townley, the Labour women's organiser for south-west England, encouraged her colleagues to take note of the methods that rival parties were using in establishing successful women's branches. She observed that the Conservatives and Liberals were taking an informal approach to meetings and thereby appealing to housewives keen for company and a break from monotonous routine:

> Obviously, the method is not to try and teach these women the particular Party programme, but first to attract the women to cheerful meetings, as bright as possible – with always a cup of tea. So dull and dreary becomes

the life of the average working-class mother, so over-worked is she, that only by providing some relaxation and real change can we gain her interest.[26]

In much the same spirit as the cottage meeting, Labour introduced the technique of 'mass canvassing' during the early 1920s. This involved holding open-air meetings in residential streets and distributing literature to house-bound women. In taking the meeting to the terraced streets of industrial Britain Labour sought to demonstrate that only it could represent the interests of working-class communities. A party of canvassers would go around each house and inform the women that a twenty-minute meeting would be held shortly in the street, and those unable to attend due to house-work or childcare duties received some literature, while canvassers engaged in informal chats following the meeting.

Jessie Stephen, a Labour woman organiser, thought that mass canvassing touched many women who would not attend a conventional party meeting. She singled out 'women who are so poverty stricken that they have not the necessary clothes to go out in. Their pride is such that if they cannot go respectably dressed, they will not go out at all. This group is larger than many suppose'.[27] Labour organisers sought to give such women a sense of dignity. Elizabeth Andrews, the woman organiser for Wales, claimed that workers who engaged in mass canvassing with her in mining districts even lent their clothes and shoes for some of the poorest women to go out and vote in.[28] Mass canvassing was recognised as one of the most effective weapons that Labour possessed.[29] Subsequently, the Liberal women's organisation imitated it, engaging in occasional 'mass attacks', which involved a concentrated campaign of meetings scattered over a few adjoining constituencies.[30]

Mass canvassing and its imitators may have been eye-catching, however, we should be careful not to exaggerate their importance to the culture of women's party activism in the 1920s. It should be noted that this was an extremely resource-intensive form of campaigning. When Jessie Stephen was brought into Wakefield to work at the 1922 election, she spent two days recruiting workers and undertook 280 mass canvassing meetings over the following eight days. As such, the campaigning technique was effectively confined to a small number of constituencies during by-election and general election campaigns.

Conservatives developed a more effective means to engage working-class women with their party's activities through the creation of political clubs in industrial districts. One of the earliest and most successful of such organisations was the Unionist Women's Institutes created in 1919 by Annie Chamberlain, wife of the future Conservative Prime Minister Neville Chamberlain. Based on the model of the Women's Institutes – they aimed to provide women with a social centre along with talks on citizenship, although, unlike the WIs, they had an explicit party bias. Meetings were staged on an informal basis. Indeed, when Neville Chamberlain gave a talk to a Ladywood institute he felt the scene 'seemed more like an infant welfare centre than a political gathering'.[31]

As well as providing their babies with a hearty dose of Tory politics, Birmingham women could participate in sewing clubs and see demonstrations on topics such as economical hay-box cookery. In Ladywood, simple political talks were given on subjects like 'The A.B.C. of Unionism', the Conservative-led council's attempts to improve housing, and 'What the city is doing for the children'.[32] The Unionist Women's Institutes spread rapidly throughout the industrial centre of the city and were also promoted in the surrounding region by Annie Chamberlain in her capacity as head of the West Midlands Women's Unionist Organisation.[33] Similar movements emerged across the country such as the Fuschia Clubs, which claimed to be open to all women of 'constitutional' views, and these organisations also organised ancillary activities such as Empire bazaars and thrift clubs.[34]

Part of the appeal of these Conservative women's clubs was that they imitated the culture of non-party organisations such as the Women's Institutes and Townswomen's Guilds, which thrived in inter-war Britain and had a more democratic and less hierarchical structure than traditional constituency party associations. Conservative women's branches made great use of speakers and literature from such non-party organisations as their services were often available at a nominal cost. A Conservative handbook produced in 1925 noted that propaganda literature 'is offered free by non-party organisations to such an extent that the [Conservative] Central Office is frequently expected to forego its charges' for pamphlets, leaflets and other publications'.[35]

Each of the main political parties, not least the Conservatives, expressed some wariness regarding the activities of the non-party movement.[36] Even into the 1930s Conservatives voiced fears that rival parties would come to dominate decision-making in the local bodies of organisations like the Women's Institutes unless their supporters made an effort to attend meetings.[37] Moreover, as Pat Thane discusses elsewhere in this volume, for some people participation in a non-party organisation was seen as an alternative to involvement in a political party.[38] But for many others activism in both types of organisation was common, and all parties sought to imitate aspects of the culture of non-party leagues. As we have seen, party activists understood that their meetings needed a strong social and ostensibly apolitical element if they were to attract large numbers of women. The Conservatives may ultimately have been most successful in developing a 'non-political' appeal but they were certainly not acting in isolation. Nor was there anything particularly novel about the appeal of such cultures in inter-war Britain. The rapid growth of the Primrose League and Women's Liberal Federation in the late-Victorian period owed much to their function as social centres, and this was especially true of rural areas where these organisation's annual dance or summer fete was often the main social event of the year.[39]

What seems puzzling is that the Liberal party also sought to develop a similar culture of popular women's clubs but with nothing like the success of their Conservative rivals. Admittedly, some of the Liberal clubs appear to have achieved impressive growth. In Penzance, isolated in western Cornwall, membership grew from 50 to 540 in four years. Weekly meetings usually began with a thirty minute concert, there would be a sing-song or a dance, with a ten to fifteen minute talk on politics and obligatory cup of tea sandwiched inbetween. The High Wycombe Liberal Women's Club hit upon a similar winning formula combining an informal discussion on current affairs with a sewing club and yet more afternoon tea.[40] But these were scattered achievements.

It may have been the case that whereas Conservatives saw party and non-party associations as filling separate, albeit complementary, spheres in Britain's associational life, non-party activism provided a more attractive route for Liberal women than participation in its beleaguered party organisation. Certainly, the *Liberal Agent* suggested that recruiting new blood was a problem. One correspondent voiced his frustrations in early 1921: 'Do not our women's organizations in the main, still comprise a few enthusiastic women – not exactly young – but loyal and true workers, remnants of the pre-war era'[41] This state of affairs should not come as much of a surprise given that the Liberal party was a divided force, and its women's magazine was effectively a cipher at this time. The League of Nations Union was one non-party organisation which drew support from large numbers of Liberal activists, and erstwhile Liberals. This body tapped into the party's traditional Nonconformist support base, particularly in Wales, where strong links were forged with the Free Churches. League of Nations Union meetings in some regions began with prayer or took place on church premises.[42] It could be surmised that working within such an organisation, which had 300,000 members at its peak, may have offered a more appealing prospect for many women than devoting ones service to the Liberal party organisation.

As the chapters in this volume by Bingham, and Hunt and Hannam demonstrate, newspapers and party literature commonly addressed women as consumers between the wars.[43] Consumer politics had played a vital role in women's integration into party politics before 1918. The housewife became a totemic figure in the free trade/tariff reform debate of the Edwardian period, which acted as a training ground for an army of female speakers, canvassers and organisers. In fact, the Women's Unionist and Tariff Reform Association formed the organisational backbone, and much of the leadership, of the Conservative party's women's organisation, which was established in the final months of the First World War. In addition, the labour movement widened its appeal to women in wartime Britain by advancing a new consumer politics. Faced with food shortages, labour organisations attacked profiteering and successfully called for rationing and food controls. Several women who subsequently became Labour party organisers had participated in these campaigns during the war through their work with the co-operative movement. After the war, Conservative literature rarely addressed women as wage workers, focusing instead on their household duties and role as consumers. This outlook was reflected in the party's 1922 campaign guide, which noted that 'the problems of a changeful time need the co-operation of the woman, who sees them from the kitchen and nursery window, with the man, who looks through the office or workshop'.[44] This focus on woman as a consumer may have been influenced by the limited female franchise. And yet the same outlook was apparent in Conservative publications directed at the young 'flapper' voter after 1928. Chief amongst these was *Women of Today and Tomorrow*, a one-off magazine, of which 8.5 million copies were printed.[45] Aside from images of glamorous film stars and the better-looking male Conservative MPs, this publication focused on the home with sections on housewifery, better buying and the cost of living. One feature sought to warn readers of the perils of Socialism by noting that Russia had only one artificial silk factory whereas the production of artificial silk stockings had thrived in Britain under a Conservative government![46] Conservative Central Office justified this strategy of focusing on the female consumer by claiming that less than 20 per cent of the new 'flapper' voters were industrial workers.[47]

Labour Woman paid significantly more attention to wage workers, producing a regular feature on working conditions in common careers for women, and highlighting the plight of the unemployed woman.[48] But during the 1920s Labour pamphlets ultimately spent more time addressing women as consumers. This approach was a particular feature of the 1924 election, where attention was focused on the Labour government's promotion of 'the free breakfast table'. Philip Snowden, the chancellor of the exchequer, claimed to have introduced a 'housewife's budget' reducing food duties by £30 million.[49] Labour presented Conservative plans for economy as being opposed to the interests of the working mother. Voters were instructed to remember that 'a well spent rate is the truest economy', and that a Labour government would create a more efficient and healthier society through housing reform, improved schooling, and better infant welfare services.[50] This focus on appealing to the voter through providing value-for-money public services was also a feature of Labour's municipal politics, particularly in London where the party was under the stewardship of Herbert Morrison.[51]

In municipal politics both Labour and the Conservatives often sought to appeal to the prudent consumer who wanted low rates and efficient municipal services. At times it could be hard to differentiate the language of these parties. This was the case in Salford, Lancashire, during the 1921 municipal elections where it was observed that 'most of the candidates lay claim to the "anti-waste" label in some form or other, either by adopting it as a title or propounding some form of it in their addresses'.[52] Perhaps more than has previously been realised, many Conservative leaders were uncomfortable with the calls for drastic retrenchment which were a staple feature of articles in the *Daily Mail* and *Daily Express* at this time.[53]

Conservatives sought to develop a progressive appeal in local politics to counter the consumer politics developed by Labour politicians like Herbert Morrison. In towns like Birmingham and Barnsley Conservatives championed major house building programmes.[54] With Labour and the Conservatives seeking to occupy the centre ground in municipal politics Liberal influence waned, further undermining the vitality of the party's women's organisation. Conservative-Liberal pacts became a common feature in inter-war politics, usually with the Tories eventually emerging as the dominant partner, much to the frustration of a correspondent in the *Liberal Women's News* who feared that the growth of municipal alliances was demoralising the party.[55]

The Liberals were further handicapped by their inability to develop a distinctive consumer politics which could revitalise their women's organisation. When Liberal publications aimed at women addressed consumer issues, it was usually to attack the approaches of rival parties. As Chancellor of the Exchequer, Winston Churchill was presented as robbing the working-class housewife by introducing new taxes.[56] These Tory taxes, supposedly directed at imported goods, were, it was claimed, an attempt to introduce protectionism by stealth.[57] Furthermore, the *Liberal Pioneer* claimed that Labour's advance threatened the private trader and would lead to less choice for the female consumer: 'The Socialists are to get control on the municipal councils and then the council is to finance the co-operative stores and encourage them to branch out in all directions...this will gradually ruin the other retail traders.'[58] The party developed few new consumer campaigns of its own. True, Lloyd George's land campaign, with its plans to tax land values, was presented as a means to reduce indirect taxes on food and drink.[59] But when Lloyd George adopted radical public works schemes to deal with unemployment at the 1929 election, activists in Liberal strongholds like Devon and Cornwall still tended to focus on the need for free trade and retrenchment, a creed little changed since the First World War.[60]

Whilst Labour was also a free trade party, it developed a much more wide-ranging appeal to the consumer after 1918. As Frank Trentmann has demonstrated, the labour movement created a new consumer politics which shifted attention away from free trade's focus on cheapness to a new emphasis on developing state food controls to make nutritious products like milk accessible to all. *Labour Woman* attacked the private companies who acted as a 'profit vampire', keeping milk consumption rates in Britain low. Labour claimed the milk production could be made more efficient and economical by running it as a national service.[61] The second Labour government expanded on this politics, and sought to use the state to protect the interests of the working-class consumer against high food prices through the creation of a Consumers' Council, although this measure fell by the wayside due to the growing crisis in the state's finances. The Hire Purchase Bill, introduced by Ellen Wilkinson in 1931 to provide protection for the consumer's payments if they fell into financial difficulties, initially met the same fate, before being successfully implemented in 1937.[62]

Conservatives developed their own consumer politics through a campaign to encourage housewives to buy goods from Britain and the Empire in preference to foreign goods. *Home and Politics* presented buying imperially as a duty to help kith and kin: 'What would be said of a woman who went down the street, marketing-bag on arm and who passed by her son's grocery shop to make her purchases in the establishment of a stranger.'[63] Empire shopping clearly owed much to the Edwardian tariff reform campaign. Creating 'imperial preference' through high import duties on goods from outside the Empire had been at the heart of Joseph Chamberlain's politics. But Empire shopping was also promoted as a way to aid the interests of the consumer both at home and in the Dominions at a time of economic hardship, without resorting to the expensive, and potentially counter-productive forms of state intervention proposed by the Labour party. It was claimed that Labour's Consumers' Council Bill would create more bureaucracy and waste and ultimately lead to a rise in prices.[64] The Empire buying campaign was publicised widely by *Home and Politics* after 1925 and supporters were encouraged to promote the cause through Empire fetes and pageants. Furthermore, an 'Empire Cookery Book' was also promoted by the women's Conservative organisation, with the endorsement of Mrs. Baldwin.[65]

The cause of imperial shopping was not only championed by the Conservative party organisation, a government-sponsored Empire Marketing Board (EMB) was set up in 1926, which appointed a woman officer to liaise with civic organisations such as the Women's Institutes and Women's Co-operative Guild, who sought to champion the cause of buying Empire goods.[66] This development appears to have alarmed the *Liberal Pioneer*, which ran a fictional article, the following year, about the discussion of Empire buying at a Women's Institute meeting.[67] The EMB's attempts to market the idea of imperial consumption followed much the same lines as the Conservative women's campaign. EMB posters used the argument long employed by tariff reformers that the Empire was a family whose bonds needed to be strengthened. Typical slogans included: 'You are partners in an Empire make it prosperous' and 'The Empire is one large family'.[68] The Board's campaign also relied heavily on the consumer, Empire shops were set up in major cities, which were given over to products from the various Dominions for a fortnight.[69]

In 1922 an election manual produced by the independent agent, Henry Houston, claimed that bread-and-butter issues were the key to the woman's vote:

> Never mind about the Treaty of Sevres. It is very important, no doubt, but seventy five percent of electors have never heard of it. What they do understand – especially the women – is the purchasing power of the pound and the problem of unemployment. Tell them how your policy will affect those.[70]

This was a lesson that the Conservative and Labour parties took to heart. Realising that they now needed to widen the appeal of their politics beyond the activist minority to the many women who had hitherto taken little interest in party politics, both sought to adapt their appeals to suit working women's social cultures. In practice this meant holding afternoon meetings in neighbourhood settings which combined straightforward political education with social activities. Women were also kept up-to-date with the respective parties' activities through popular magazines, which could be adapted for localising.

The claim that only working women could speak for working women was regularly voiced by Labour women organisers, and they sought to demonstrate this through perhaps the most dramatic campaigning innovation of the early 1920s, 'mass canvassing'. Yet this was a claim that the Conservatives countered through the development of organisations like the Women's Institutes and Fuschia Clubs, which penetrated into the back-to-back terraces of working towns, which mass canvassing sought to claim for the Labour party. For sure, the Unionist Women's Institutes' claims to be a democratic form of organisation should be treated with some caution given that they relied on the patronage of traditional social leaders and educated social workers to get them off the ground. But they were clearly successful in widening the appeal of the women's Conservative organisation. If anything, elite patronage may well have been an advantage in what was still a highly paternalistic and deferential society. Henry Houston, who had overseen several successful campaigns by 'anti-waste' candidates during the early 1920s in southern England, observed that 'happy is the agent who has on his staff a woman who holds the keys to the humble homes of the division. She must be of good breeding, for the working woman still loves "a lady"'.[71]

That the Liberal women's organisation should have proved so ill adept at responding to these innovations was by no means inevitable, indeed it seems remarkable given the embryonic nature of Labour's women's section before 1914, and the party's continued dominance by male trade unionists after the war, which often hampered the interests of women activists.[72] Undoubtedly, the Lloyd George-Asquith split put Liberal women at a unique disadvantage, dissipating activists' energies and finances into two rival organisations made it doubly hard to win over the new woman voter. The Liberal party's media strategy also exacerbated their problems, they did not develop a popular magazine for women until 1925, by which time rival publications were already well established.

But perhaps the most important reason why the Liberal women's organisation stagnated was its inability to develop a mass-supported consumer campaign. The Liberals' continued emphasis on free trade as the key means to nurse Britain's economy back to health increasingly seemed like an outdated and hollow message by comparison with its rivals' consumer policies. Labour women built on their wartime campaigns for food control, acknowledging that free trade alone was no longer enough to secure the interests of the consumer, which could only be guaranteed by state measures to curb food profiteering and secure the cheap provision of key staples such as milk. Conservatives countered by arguing that Britain's economic problems could be dealt with most effectively by consumers mobilising to buy only goods from home and Empire where possible. Fired by this campaign the Conservative women's organisation claimed to have recruited 150,000 members in the year after April 1925 alone, comfortably more than the total paper membership of the Women's Liberal Federation.[73] Whilst the Conservatives responded to the challenge of the 'flapper voter' by producing a 1928 publication with the optimistic sounding title of *Women of Today and Tommorow*, Liberal women increasingly seemed to be the women of yesterday.

Notes

I would like to thank Laura Beers and the editors for their helpful comments on earlier versions of this chapter.

1. D. Jarvis, 'Mrs. Maggs and Betty: the Conservative appeal to women voters in the 1920s', *Twentieth Century British History*, 5 (1994), pp. 129–52; P. Graves, *Labour Women: Women in British Working-class Politics, 1918–1939* (Cambridge, 1994); See also J. Hannam and K. Hunt, *Socialist Women: Britain, 1880s to 1920s* (2001), there have been a range of other studies which discuss specific localities and political organisations.
2. For the pre-1918 period see in particular J. Lawrence, 'Class and gender in the making of urban Toryism, 1880–1914', *English Historical Review*, 108 (1993), 629–52; M. Roberts, 'W.L. Jackson, exemplary manliness and late Victorian popular Conservatism', in M. McCormack (ed.), *Public Men: Masculinity and Politics in Modern Britain* (Basingstoke, 2007), pp. 123–42; For the inter-war period see D. Jarvis, 'The Conservative party and the politics of gender, 1900–1939', in M. Francis and I. Zweiniger-Bargielowska (eds), *The Conservatives and British Society 1880–1990* (Cardiff, 1996), pp. 172–93; D. Thackeray, 'Building a peaceable party: Masculine identities in British Conservative politics, c.1903–24', *Historical Research*, Vol. 85, 230 (2012), 651–73 (online early, http://onlinelibrary.wiley.com/doi/10.1111/j.1468-2281.2012.00600.x/pdf).
3. For a detailed discussion of the role of gendered appeals in politics which focuses on the Conservative party see D. Thackeray, *Conservatism for the*

Democratic Age: Conservative Cultures and the Challenge of Mass Politics in Early Twentieth Century England (Manchester, 2013).

4. F. Trentmann, *Free Trade Nation: Commerce, Consumption, and Civil Society in Modern Britain* (Oxford, 2008), pp. 69–80; D. Thackeray, 'Rethinking the Edwardian crisis of conservatism', *Historical Journal*, 54 (2011), pp. 191–213 at pp. 197–8.

5. A. Bingham, *Gender, Modernity, and the Popular Press in Inter-War Britain* (Oxford, 2004), pp. 127–35; H. McCarthy, 'Parties, voluntary associations and democratic politics in Interwar Britain', *Historical Journal*, 50 (2007), pp. 891–912; J. Lawrence, *Electing Our Masters: the Hustings in British Politics from Hogarth to Blair* (Oxford, 2009), ch. 4.

6. Membership figures from L. Walker, 'Party political women: a comparative study of Liberal women and the Primrose League, 1890–1914', in Jane Rendall (ed.), *Equal or Different: Women's Politics 1800–1914* (Oxford, 1987), pp. 165–91 at p. 169 (Liberal); M. Pugh, *Women and the Women's Movement in Britain, 1914–1999* (Basingstoke, 2000), p. 130 (Labour); G.E. Maguire, *Conservative Women: a History of Women and the Conservative Party, 1874–1997* (Basingstoke, 1998), p. 80 (Conservative).

7. Figures from Pugh, *Women and the Women's Movement*, pp. 131, 140.

8. Figure cited in Jarvis, 'Mrs. Maggs and Betty', p. 132.

9. Memorandum by J. Ball, 20 March 1929, Conservative Party Archive (CPA), Bodleian Library, Oxford, CCO170/5/47.

10. John Ramsden has claimed that there were 144 local editions of Conservative party publications by 1928, see his *The Age of Balfour and Baldwin 1902–1940* (1978), p. 233.

11. In June 1927 Conservative Central Office estimated that newspapers printed 353 leading articles, 535 notes and 35 special articles based on materials provided by the press service, R. Cockett, 'The party, publicity, and the media', in A. Seldon and S. Ball (eds), *Conservative Century: the Conservative Party since 1900* (Oxford, 1994), pp. 547–77 at pp. 551–2.

12. C. Howard, 'Expectations born to death: local Labour party expansion in the 1920s', in J. Winter (ed.), *The Working Class in Modern British History: Essays in Honour of Henry Pelling* (Cambridge, 1983), pp. 65–81 at pp. 75–6.

13. 'Reverberations', *Labour Organiser*, January 1924, p. 1; L. Beers, 'Selling socialism": Labour, democracy and the mass media, 1900–1939' (Unpublished PhD thesis, Harvard, 2007), pp. 217–18.

14. Elizabeth Andrews wrote for the *Colliery Worker's Magazine*, the paper of the South Wales Miners' Federation. For examples of Andrews' journalism see her *A Woman's Work Is Never Done*, ed. U. Masson, (Dinas Powys, 2006, originally published 1957); Annie Somers was a regular contributor to the *London Labour Chronicle*.

15. M. Phillips and G. Tavener, *Women's Work in the Labour Party: Notes for Speakers' and Workers' Classes* (1923), p. 11.

16. M. Phillips, 'Organising the women electors', *Labour Organiser*, February 1922, p. 6.

17. For the publications financial problems see *Women's Liberal Magazine*, December 1920, p. 153.

18. For rare examples of advice on organisation in *Federation News* before 1924 see H. Storey, 'What is a study circle?', March 1923, p.19; 'Practical hints on election work', December 1923, p. 81.

19. *Liberal Women's News*, June 1925, p. 2; October 1927, p. 120.

20. The *Lloyd George Liberal Magazine* had separate English, Welsh and Scottish editions, but they were identical except for a page largely given over to branch news.

21. Constance Williams appears to have produced the first election manual aimed specifically at women, *How Women Can Help in Political Work: Practical Hints on Local Organisation and Electioneering* (1905). She began her political work as Assistant Secretary to the Women's Liberal Federation and acted as a speaker and organiser for the Free Trade Union.
22. 'Discussion of election methods', *Liberal Agent*, October 1920, p. 7.
23. For the use of specialist literature by Liberal organisers see R. Jones, 'What I should like to do before October 15th 1921', *Liberal Agent*, July 1921, p. 19.
24. for examples of Conservative and Labour literature on this theme see 'Activities of the Banbury Conservative Association', *The Popular View in North Oxfordshire*, July 1924, p. 4; 'Why I shall vote Labour. A working woman's letter from "Blighty"', Labour party MSS, microfiche, 1919/36; D. Rider, 'Wanted – a Rents Reduction Act', *Labour Woman*, September 1922, p. 135.
25. 'The organisation of Liberal women', *Liberal Agent*, April 1920, p. 36; C. Williams, 'Women's work and outlook: how women can help in politics', *Lloyd George Liberal Magazine*, November 1920, p. 81; E. Davis, 'Cottage meetings', *Home and Politics*, July 1923, p. 5.
26. A. Townley, 'A woman's page', *Labour Organiser*, January 1922, p. 14.
27. J. Stephen, 'Some lessons of the election', *Labour Woman*, January 1923, p. 7.
28. E. Andrews, 'Wales – then and now: 1919–1947', *Labour Woman*, February 1948, reprinted in her *A Woman's Work*, ed. Masson, p. 114.
29. M. Phillips, 'Women's work in the election. What are you prepared to do?', *Labour Woman*, November 1922, p. 174.
30. 'The Sussex mass attack', *Liberal Women's News*, March 1928, p. 40.
31. N. Chamberlain to H. Chamberlain, 26 September 1920, in R. Self (ed.), *The Neville Chamberlain Diary Letters, vol. 1: The Making of a Politician, 1915–1920* (Aldershot, 2000), p. 388.
32. Mrs N. Chamberlain, 'Clubs for Unionist women', *Home and Politics*, March 1921, p. 2; 'Unionist Women's Institute: Interesting development in the Ladywood division', *Straight Forward*, January 1921, p. 4.
33. See the following articles in the Birmingham Conservative magazine *Straight Forward*, 'Doings in the divisions', February 1921, p. 2; 'Women and politics: success of the institute movement', April 1921, p. 6; 'Women's activities', December 1921, p. 3.
34. National Union of Conservative Associations [NUCA], *Handbook on Constituency Organisation* (1928), pp. 115–17.
35. NUCA, *Handbook on Constituency Organisation* (1925), p. 26.
36. For examples of wariness towards non-party organisations expressed by activists from across the political spectrum see McCarthy, 'Democratic politics in inter-war Britain', pp. 901–7.
37. National Society of Women's Organisers' minutes, 30 September 1936, Conservative Party Archive, CCO170/2/1/1.
38. P. Thane, 'The impact of mass democracy, 1918–1939'.
39. P. Lynch, *The Liberal Party in Rural England 1885–1910: Radicalism and Community*, (Oxford, 2003), pp. 51, 85; J. Robb, *The Primrose League 1883–1906* (New York, 1942).
40. M. Christophers, 'How Penzance won the recruiting cup', *Liberal Women's News*, June 1927, p. 95; G. Humphrey, 'The Women's Liberal Club at High Wycombe', *Liberal Women's News*, May 1927, p. 75.
41. H. Dowsett, 'Women's work in political organizations', *Liberal Agent*, January 1921, p. 13.

42. H. McCarthy, 'Democratizing British foreign policy: rethinking the Peace Ballot, 1934–1935', *Journal of British Studies*, 49 (2010), pp. 358–87 at pp. 374, 378, 381.

43. A. Bingham, 'Enfranchisement, feminism and the modern woman: Debates in the British popular press, 1918–1939'; K. Hunt and J. Hannam, 'Towards an archaeology of interwar women's politics: the local and the everyday'.

44. NUCA, *The Campaign Guide* (1922), p. 981.

45. A.R. Linforth to J. Ball, 20 March 1929, CPA, CCO170/5/47.

46. NUCA, *Women of Today and Tommorow* (1928).

47. NUCA, 'The new women voters', n.d. [1928], CPA, CCO170/5/47.

48. See for example the following articles from *Labour Woman*, 'The domestic worker and the unemployed woman', March 1919, p.26; E.H. Howse, '"Sorry you've been troubled": the work of the telephonist', February 1922, p. 25; M.J. Symons, 'The girl who serves the meals', January 1922, p. 9.

49. P. Snowden, 'The housewife's budget', 1924/84; see also 'I am voting Labour', 1924/31; 'Food prices down', 1924/2; 'Why all workers by hand or brain should join the Labour Party', 1924/49, all Labour Party MSS, microfiche, pamphlets card 92.

50. 'To working women: Remember! A well spent rate is the truest economy', 1924/92; see also 'Why all workers by hand or brain should join the Labour Party' 1924/49, card 92; 'Do you know how important the County Council Election will be for your children' 1922/8, card 72, 'Mrs. Job's talks. Why women should vote Labour' 1922/44, card 79, all Labour Party MSS, microfiche.

51. A. Somers, 'M.R's and women. Observations on a silly leaflet', *London Labour Chronicle*, November 1922, p. 2; for Labour's focus on moderate social reforms in municipal government see also D. Tanner, 'The pattern of Labour politics, 1918–1939', in D. Tanner, C. Williams and D. Hopkin (eds), *The Labour Party in Wales 1900–2000* (Cardiff, 2000), pp. 113–39 at pp. 117–24; M. Savage, *The Remaking of the British Working Class 1840–1940* (1994), pp. 84–5.

52. *Salford Reporter*, 29 October 1921, p. 5.

53. For a longer discussion of this point see Thackeray, *Conservatism for the Democratic Age*, ch. 9.

54. S. Davies and B. Morley, *County Borough Elections in England and Wales 1919–1938: A Comparative Analysis, vol. 1* (1999), pp. 14, 226.

55. S. Davies and B. Morley, 'Electoral turnout in county borough elections, 1919–1938', *Labour History Review*, 71 (2006), pp. 167–86 at p. 169; 'Conservative and Liberal pacts by a young Liberal', *Liberal Women's News*, February 1927, p. 26.

56. F.C. Thornborough, 'The new budget taxes', *Liberal Women's News*, September 1928, p. 117; see also the following articles from *Liberal Pioneer*, 'The Tory tax on women's clothes', July 1925, p. 4; 'Women and Winston', June 1927, p. 6.

57. See for example the following Liberal Publication Department leaflets, 'Creeping paralysis' (1926), leaflet 2698; 'Women of England. Your household bills are heavy because of protective taxes' (1928), leaflet 2549.

58. 'When a woman goes shopping', *Liberal Pioneer*, March 1928, p. 6.

59. 'Taxation of land values', *Liberal Pioneer*, October 1925, p. 4.

60. M. Dawson, 'Liberalism in Devon and Cornwall, 1910–1931: 'The old time religion'', *Historical Journal*, 38 (1995), pp. 425–37 at p. 430.

61. 'A call to housewives!', *Labour Woman*, October 1924, p.158; in the same issue see also 'No dirty milk', p. 161; the labour movement's campaigns for improved access to milk are described in more detail in F. Trentmann, 'Bread, milk and democracy: consumption and citizenship in twentieth century Britain', in M. Daunton and M. Hilton (eds), *The Politics of Consumption: Material Culture and Citizenship in Europe and America* (Oxford, 2001), pp. 129–63 at pp. 143–5.

62. For these measures see N. Robertson, 'The Labour government and the consumer', in J. Davis, J. Shepherd and C. Wrigley (eds), *The Second Labour Government, 1929–1931* (Manchester, 2011).

63. M. Fedden, 'Empire catering', *Home and Politics*, May 1928, p. 9; see also 'The shoppers' slogan', *Home and Empire*, April 1930, p. 20.

64. 'Shopkeepers as criminals', *Home and Empire*, June 1930, p. 1; in the same publication see also 'No help for the consumer', July 1930, p. 1.

65. 'Food for Thought: The Dinner Table and the Empire', *Home and Politics*, May 1926, p. 9.

66. Empire Marketing Board, *The Work of the Empire Marketing Board*, report no.2, October 1926, p. 7.

67. 'Beggar my neighbour', *Liberal Pioneer*, April 1927, p. 4.

68. S. Constantine, *Buy and Build: The Advertising Posters of the Empire Marketing Board* (1986), p. 12.

69. W. Elliot, 'Empire Marketing Board', *Journal of the Royal Society of Arts*, June 1931, pp. 735–47.

70. H.J. Houston and L. Valdar, *Modern Electioneering Technique* (1922), p. 20.

71. Houston and Valdar, *Modern Electioneering Practice*, p. 148.

72. For male trade unionists' hostility to family allowances, a policy promoted by the Labour women's section see S. Pedersen, *Eleanor Rathbone and the Politics of Conscience* (New Haven, CT, 2004), p. 216.

73. 'Unionist Women's Conference', *The Times*, 30 April 1926, p. 16.

3

The Impact of Mass Democracy on British Political Culture, 1918–1939

Pat Thane

We have perhaps not reflected enough on the peculiarities of British political history between the two world wars. It was the first period of mass democracy – almost so in 1918 when all men got the vote at age 21 and women at 30, if they were local government electors (i.e. tenants or owners of property and paying local rates) or wives of electors. Full democracy came in 1928 when all women were enfranchised at age 21. The electorate tripled in 1918 from 7.6 million to 21.7 million and rose to 28.8 million in 1928 – a major transformation unprecedented in Britain. It was also the one period of the twentieth century when the party political system was peculiarly weak. Later in the century it was assumed as the norm that Westminster politics consisted of two big parties fighting it out, taking turns to govern, with a third party and some very minor parties trailing behind. There were one-party, majority governments for only seven years between the wars, 1922–late 1923 and 1924–29, both Conservative governments. There were minority Labour governments in 1924 (for a little over nine months) and 1929–31. The Coalition government of 1918–22 was Conservative dominated, though with a Liberal prime Minister, Lloyd George, as was the National Government from 1931, especially from 1935, this time with a 'National Labour' leader, Ramsay MacDonald, from 1931 to 1935, and Conservatives, Stanley Baldwin, then Neville Chamberlain, from 1935 to 1940. For the remainder of the Second World War there was another coalition, led by Winston Churchill. The fact that governments felt that they had at least to appear to be coalitions, or 'national' – representative of and speaking for the nation – must tell us something about the prevailing political culture or, at least, about how politicians perceived that culture and felt that they should present themselves to the expanded electorate.

At the same time, despite what can be seen as the instability of the political system and the prolonged economic depression, this was a period of remarkable social and political stability in Britain, especially compared with many other European countries, or even with the strikes, suffragette demonstrations and trouble in Ireland of pre-1914 Britain. The only General

Strike ever to occur in Britain came in ten days in 1926, but it was tame by European standards of the time. It did not threaten the political order and was not so intended by the trade union leaders involved. There were demonstrations by unemployed people, by women campaigning for the equal franchise before 1928, by fascists and anti-fascists in the 1930s, but none of these threatened the political order or the political elite. Extreme political groups, whether communist or fascist, were weak. The most votes gained by the Communists in any inter-war election was 74,824 in 1931. The New Party, precursor to the British Union of Fascists gained only 36,377 votes in the same election. It did not contest the election of 1935 and was proscribed by the government in 1940.[1]

Why did British political culture take this form between the wars and to what extent, if at all, was this connected with the extension of the franchise? Some stimulating reflections on the relative stability of British politics at this time can be found in Keith Middlemas' *Politics in Industrial Society: The Experience of the British System since 1911* (1979).[2] He argued that established politicians were well aware of the potential danger to the familiar political order from the national and international movements of the time and learned how to manage British public opinion in order to avert disorder. As Middlemas put it, they learned how to:

> extend the state's powers to assess, educate, bargain with, appease or constrain the demands of the electorate, raising to a sort of parity with the state the various competing interests and institutions to which voters owed allegiance... they sought to avoid by compromise, crises in sensitive areas like wages and conditions, public order, immigration and the position of women... not by invoking authority, but by the alternate gratification and cancelling out of the desires of large well-organized, collective groups to the detriment of individuals, minorities and deviants.[3]

Middlemas saw certain 'large, collective groups' independent of party, as gaining increasing power, increasingly integrated into the political system, becoming what he called 'governing institutions'. He gave particular salience in this process to associations representing employers and workers, employers' associations and trade unions, the two sides in the class war that it was vital to avoid in the aftermath of the Russian Revolution. Middlemas argued that the importance of these institutions and their assimilation into the political system had been overlooked because historians had focussed on political parties and the 'high politics' of Westminster, overlooking and underestimating the roles of other political actors in influencing government action.

Helen McCarthy and I have agreed, broadly, with Middlemas' argument in a recent publication[4] but have discerned a larger number and range of non-party associations active and influential in inter-war British politics, whose roles need to be assessed. We argue that this is another of the unusual characteristics of the political culture of the period. Of course there have long been pressure groups active in British politics, before the inter-war years and since. Precise quantification is difficult and probably impossible given how numerous they were, many of them ephemeral and poorly recorded. But it is likely that there were more of them, engaged in more sustained campaigns and with discernible influence upon government actions at this time than before or at some other times in the later twentieth century. For some people, engagement with such groups was an alternative to support for a political party. Others were also active in party politics and/or in more than one group. The roles of these organizations, as we discuss below, have perhaps been underestimated because much of their activity consisted of lobbying government quietly behind the scenes rather than the dramatic public demonstrations which demand attention in the pre-World War 1 period, but they were not necessarily less, and may have been more, effective.

Our article arose from Helen McCarthy's work on the League of Nations Union and other inter-war associations[5] (discussed elsewhere in this volume) and mine on women's campaigns of the period by the National Union of Societies for Equal Citizenship, among others (discussed later in this chapter),[6] and on the role of the voluntary sector in the formation and implementation of state welfare policies in twentieth century Britain.[7] I have argued that women's political participation after they partially gained the vote in 1918 often took this collective form because they found it hard to make an impact on politics as individuals in party politics, especially as parliamentary candidates. It was very difficult for women to gain selection for winnable parliamentary seats, as all too many of them quickly discovered, and few were elected to parliament between the wars or for or long after. In 1918 women were 1 per cent of parliamentary candidates and just one woman was elected (the Sinn Fein candidate for Dublin, St Patrick's, Countess Markiewicz, who like the other 72 MPS elected for her party, did not take her seat). The largest percentage of female candidates between the wars (five) and MPs (2.4 per cent, 15 MPs) came in 1931.[8] Many women discovered that they could best make an impact on parliamentary politics through collective action, forming or joining associations to campaign on a wide range of issues of particular concern to them.

This form of activism by women, and its effectiveness, has been underestimated because it was long assumed that few women were elected because few put themselves forward, that, indeed most women lost interest in political campaigning once they gained the vote, believing that they had achieved the equality they sought.[9] This was never very convincing and was denied by suffrage campaigners at the time. They realized that the opposition had not gone away and that the struggle to make a reality of gender equality must continue. The militant suffragist, Viscountess Rhondda, commented in 1921 that, in gaining the vote, women 'had passed the first great toll-bar on the road which leads to equality' but 'it is a far cry yet to the end of the road'.[10] Her biographer suggests that 'while welcoming the 1918 Representation of the People [Act] she was neither naive enough nor complacent enough to expect that such a limited measure would break down the still significant barriers to full emancipation'.[11] This view was shared by leading suffrage campaigners with otherwise differing perspectives, including the militant Sylvia Pankhurst and the moderate Eleanor Rathbone. They recognized that the battle must continue, if by different means, as Rathbone put it, if women were to take advantage of their new political rights, new methods were needed, for women were no longer seeking 'a big, elemental... simple reform', such as enfranchisement, but the 'difficult re-adjustments of a complicated... antiquated structure of case law and statute law' which required sober and tricky negotiation.[12] The extent of female involvement in interwar campaigning suggests how widely this view was shared.

If newly enfranchised women felt the need to form or join campaigning associations in order to have a political voice because they were excluded from conventional parliamentary politics, this does not explain the spread of associational activity among middle and upper class men in the interwar years. They had long had the vote and could not claim to be under-represented in parliament.

Yet many men as well as women clearly wanted to campaign for government action in a variety of areas and opted to do so though organizations other than political parties. Their presence in non-party organizations suggests that they did not always believe that their objectives could be achieved through party affiliation alone. For example, the League of Nations Union was formed in 1919 to promote a new world order based on international co-operation. Many of its leaders and members, including its initiator Lord Robert Cecil, were active members of political parties but they, rightly, believed that their objectives cut across parties and that, by detaching the campaign from party, they would attract a wider range of support.

Many men and women, sometimes the same men and women, were also motivated by the belief that the new political landscape, with a mass electorate, required new approaches and structures to draw in new voters and educate them to use the vote, to be good citizens, contributing to a stable democracy. The term 'citizenship' – previously regarded as rather un-British, even French – and the concept of education for citizenship of a new, inclusive democracy took on an unprecedented salience in British political discourse at this time especially among the liberal elite. It largely disappeared again after World War II. It had a particular resonance in the political culture of the inter-war years.[13]

One example of the concept in action between the wars was the Council for Education for Citizenship, founded in 1934 by the former Liberal MP and former Lord Mayor of Manchester, Ernest Simon, his wife Shena, a suffragist, feminist and also a former leading Liberal councillor in Manchester, and Eva Hubback, also a suffragist and a leading member of the National Union of Women's Suffrage Societies, which in 1919 became the National Union of Societies for Equal Citizenship (NUSEC, see below). Hubback had studied at Newnham College, Cambridge, with Shena Simon and had introduced her to Ernest. The Simons and Hubback embodied many of the characteristics and ideas of inter-war democratic idealism. All three were progressive reformers active in a variety of causes. Hubback was an active campaigner for divorce reform, birth control, better care and nutrition for children, among other things. She had no party affiliation between the wars but became a Labour member of the London Country Council in 1946. Shena Simon led on educational reform and council house building on Manchester City Council. Both Simons became disillusioned with the Liberal Party, he after losing his parliamentary seat in 1931. He had come to feel that the partisan atmosphere of parliament militated against achieving real progressive change. He strongly believed in local government and non-party organizations as upholders of democracy against excessive central power.

The Council for Education for Citizenship initiated and financed a campaign to promote the teaching of civic and social philosophy in secondary schools. Ernest Simon and Hubback co-wrote *Training for Citizenship* in 1935, which expressed their views that the survival of democracy depended as much on the education of the citizen, beginning early in life, as on the machinery of government. Simon contested a by-election as an Independent in 1946, unsuccessfully, and then joined the Labour Party, to whose intellectual wing he had long been close. Shena Simon had joined Labour in 1935. He supported Labour in the House of Lords which he entered in 1947.[14]

The prominence of the concept of democratic citizenship between the wars suggests a desire among the pre 1918 voting classes, that went wider than the government, to maintain social stability, at a time when instability was extensive and growing elsewhere in Europe, including in other newly democratized countries such as Germany. The aim was to integrate the new voters into the political system by fostering 'active citizenship', participation in campaigning groups that were independent of political parties, which would help to make a reality of democracy without political upheaval.

The language of citizenship and the desire to help and encourage new voters to use their new political rights, preferably for progressive causes, was very evident among former suffragists. Even before the passing of the Representation of the People Act, suffrage societies began to organize to raise political awareness among women, to inform them about important political issues and train them in procedures of campaigning, public speaking, committee work, and other essential skills of public life. As early as 1917, the National Union of Women Workers (from 1918 renamed the National Council of Women) formed a network of Women's Citizens Associations (WCAs) throughout the country to provide this training. The first of these was formed by Eleanor Rathbone in Liverpool in 1913.[15] Membership was open to all women at age 16, so that political education could begin early in life. The role of WCAs was to 'foster a sense of citizenship in women. Encourage the study of political, social and economic questions; secure the adequate representation of the interests and experience of women in the affairs of the community'.[16] Shena Simon was an active member of the NCW and a founder of the Manchester and Salford WCA.[17]

The National Union of Women's Suffrage Societies (NUWSS) moved smoothly from its major role in helping to bring about the Representation of the People Act[18] to enabling women to make use of their new political legitimacy. It published pamphlets guiding women through the complexity of getting onto the voting register and using the vote, including: *And Shall I have the Parliamentary Vote?; Six Million Women Can Vote; The New Privilege of Citizenship* and *How Women Can Use the Vote*. In 1919 it changed its name to National Union of Societies for Equal Citizenship to signal its new role. It devoted itself to encouraging and supporting women's organizations to campaign and lobby government on issues which concerned them, assisting them to draft legislation, organize delegations to Ministers, to make contact with sympathetic MPs and guide legislation through parliament. Eva Hubback played a leading role in these activities. Supportive MPs were, unavoidably, mainly male, a small group of whom consistently supported issues promoted by women's organizations, though their biographers have, equally consistently, overlooked these activities.[19] They included Neville Chamberlain who guided through parliament a Bill drafted by the National Council for the Unmarried Mother and her Child, (founded 1918, of which he was a strong supporter and future President) which, in 1923, became the Bastardy Act and enabled children to be legitimated on the subsequent marriage of their parents, increased the amount of maintenance payable by fathers of illegitimate children, and improved the procedures by which unmarried mothers claimed this.[20] Women campaigners, often assisted by NUSEC, supported by sympathetic MPs, had a number of other legislative achievements in the 1920s including improving the custody rights of mothers, equalizing divorce rights between men and women and the introduction of widows and orphans pensions.[21] Women used their votes and the campaigning associations effectively.

In 1924 NUSEC merged with the WCAs. Both organizations were determinedly non-party. This did not mean that all their supporters were hostile to political parties, but a substantial section of the pre-First World War women's movement – as of other sections of British society – was critical of the adversarial party system, believing that party organization and discipline undermined the democratic process, serving the ends of its leaders and not of the wider population. When pre-war suffragists were asked what difference the vote would make, some of them replied: 'the automatic disappearance of party government' and 'the subordination of party considerations to principle'.[22] In consequence many women ran for election as Independents. Eleanor Rathbone was an Independent member of Liverpool city council from 1910 until the mid-1930s and an Independent Member of Parliament from 1929 until her death in 1946.

Rathbone held one of the long-established, anomalous, university seats[23] which regularly returned Independents to parliament. Until 1950, when they were abolished by the Labour government as an affront to democracy, all university graduates, including women after 1918, held a second vote which returned members of parliament for a number of university seats. Oxford, Cambridge and Trinity College Dublin (until 1922) had two each, London University one, the Combined English Universities (for whom Rathbone sat) two, the Scottish Universities three, the University of Wales one, Queens University, Belfast, one. Unusually in the British electoral system at this time, from 1918 they were elected by the Single Transferable Vote, not by the normal 'first-part-the-post' system. There was a substantial, though unsuccessful, campaign for the adoption of some form of proportional representation between the wars, another symptom of discontent with the prevailing party system.[24] It was almost impossible for an Independent to be returned for a non-university constituency at any other point in the twentieth century, in peacetime.[25]

The relationship of women's non-party organizations with the political parties was a source of debate and tension in the parties and the organizations. There were conflicts between the Labour Party and NUSEC over such issues as birth control and protective legislation for women workers (which NUSEC opposed as promoting gender inequality, but Labour women supported as necessary protection for non-unionized working women).[26] But there was also overlapping membership between the parties and the feminist organizations and the WCAs and NUSEC were prepared to work in elections and give support to party candidates, mainly female, but also male, who were active in causes favoured by the women's movement. They were anxious in principle to promote and support women as candidates in national and local elections including the many women who were party members and activists. By 1927 the Labour Party had about 300,000 female members, about half the total individual membership of the party. At this time the Liberal Party had about 100,000 and the Conservatives over one million women members.[27]

Also the feminist organizations recognized that the political culture in some parts of the country was more receptive to independent candidates than in others. Of the 13 women elected to Cambridge City Council between 1918 and 1930, 10 were independents. All of the 39 women elected to Manchester City Council between 1908 and 1939 were party representatives.[28] Of the 52 women elected to Liverpool City Council between the wars, 17 were not representatives of the three major parties, four were Independents, the remainder were scattered among a variety of organizations including the

Co-operative Party (4), the Communist Party (1), the Protestant Party (2) and the 'Anti-Waste' campaign (opposed to what they regarded as excessive government spending).[29] There was frequent collaboration between party and non-party women at local level despite the disapproval of national party leaders.

A formal attempt to co-ordinate the activities of party and non-party women was made by the Consultative Committee of Women's Organizations (CCWO). This was initially formed by the NUWSS in 1916 to co-ordinate the demand for the vote. It became more active in 1921 when Lady Astor reorganized it to provide a link between members of parliament (at the time she was the only sitting female MP) and women's organizations. Forty-nine women's societies affiliated, including the NUSEC, the National Council of Women (NCW), the Six Point Group and the Liberal and Conservative, but not Labour, Party women's organizations. It promoted networking, often at parties thrown by the wealthy Lady Astor, among women activists and politicians, seeking to draw women into the normal processes of political lobbying. It had some success in the 1920s but declined somewhat in the 1930s, as Lady Astor's concern to appease Nazism diverted her attention and lost her much support in women's Associations.[30]

Alongside the women's organizations, such as NUSEC, that were primarily dedicated to encouraging women to use the vote, associations with other objectives were also committed to the political education of female voters. The Women's Institutes (WIs)[31] were founded in 1915 by suffragists, some of them former militants, to give the large numbers of British country-women opportunities for personal and political development, partly by providing them with a social space which was under their own control and independent of the traditional rural social hierarchy, with the squire's wife at the apex, and the wife of the parish clergyman a little below. The demo-cratically elected committees of the WIs aimed at initiating a shift in rural power relationships among women, while giving them experience of politi-cal organizing. Equally important, they encouraged women to value their work and their skills in the home and to campaign to improve conditions of work in the home – their workplace. These aims they held in common with the women of the Labour Party.[32] The two organizations co-operated on campaigns to improve the quality of housing, pressing local authorities to take advantage of inter-war housing legislation to build more and better homes. WIs in particular campaigned for improvement in the appalling state of much rural housing, and access to piped water and electricity sup-plies, which were lacking in much of the countryside in the 1930s. The gradual spread of improvements in such essential facilities owed much to pressure from the WIs.

But they did not campaign only on domestic and gender issues. The National Federation of Women's Institutes strongly supported the League of Nations and the LNU, sending representatives to meetings of the League in Geneva and to international peace conferences in the 1930s.[33] Both WIs and Labour women encouraged women, as men were doing at the time, to seek reduced hours of work and a wider range of leisure activities, while encouraging sociability and activities such as drama and craft work and day trips.[34] Sociability, building informal links between people, often of different backgrounds, was an important objective of many inter-war associations, male and female, as contributing to building a sense of national solidarity.

In 1932 the NUSEC established Townswomen's Guilds (TGs) as small town analogues of the WIs, in acknowledgement of the success of the WIs in providing a space for women previously excluded from the political culture. The TGs had an impressive 54,000 members by 1939.[35] A similar role of encouraging political awareness and political education among women, alongside other goals, was performed by women's trade unions, professional, confessional, and single-issue groups such as the National Union of Women Teachers, the Council of Women Civil Servants, the (Roman Catholic) St Joan's Social and Political Union, the Union of Jewish Women, the Women's Sanitary Improvement and Health Visitors' Union, the working class Women's Co-operative Guild, and many others. At least 130 such organizations were active in the 1920s, almost certainly drawing into public life a larger number and wider social range of women than ever before.[36]

Women challenged with a new vigour the established gender order in one of the key institutions of the English cultural hierarchy: the Church of England. The Church League for Women's Suffrage (CLWS) was founded in 1909 as a democratic organization, including both men and women, initiated mostly by individuals with backgrounds in Christian Socialism. In 1919 it renamed itself the League of the Church Militant, protesting, convincingly, that the Church was 'not half militant enough'.[37] It campaigned thereafter for greater representation of women within the Church and, particularly, for the ordination of women, which was finally achieved in 1994. Women were admitted more readily to the Ministry of Non-Conformist religious institutions: by the Congregationalists in 1917 and the Baptists in 1926.[38]

The League was one of many organizations which both campaigned on single issues and worked with others in support of causes in which the variety of women's associations felt a common interest, especially the campaign between 1918 and 1928 to equalize the franchise and the longer struggle against the marriage bar.[39] In the 1930s women showed a distinct preference for membership of more specialized women's organizations over those whose central commitment was more broadly to gender equality. The membership of professional, confessional, and other organizations grew as that of the NUSEC (from 1932 the National Council for Equal Citizenship) declined. The number of societies affiliated to the NUSEC fell from 2,220 in 1920 to 48 in the later 1930s.[40] This proliferation of women's organizations was not a splintering of the women's movement, rather it illustrates how women's organizations came to permeate public life in the decades after the vote was gained while continuing to co-operate on key issues and making considerable impact, not least in achieving legislative change. The women's organizations provide just an example of wider movements in inter-war British political culture.

In all three major political parties as well as in non-aligned organizations, women worked hard to help women acquire the skills of political campaigning. Many women argued that in a political system so dominated by political parties as the British, there was no alternative but to seek to influence the parties and to use the potential power of the vote to pressurize them, fully aware of how difficult this would be. Arguably these and other organizations contributed to political stability by enabling more voters to feel included in the political system and that they had the possibility of achieving change within it.

Another important but under-researched and underestimated component of the political culture of the inter-war years was local government. Local authorities at this time had considerably more power and independence than in the later twentieth century. Inter-war local councils could, and many, such as Manchester, did deliver improved housing, education, healthcare and other services. The local franchise was also extended in 1918 and 1928. The 1918 Representation of the People Act granted the local government franchise to all men at age 21 and to married women at age 30. Unmarried women (including widows) continued to qualify for the local vote on the terms conceded to them in 1869: they qualified at age 21 if they were (i) occupiers, owners or tenants of land or premises; (ii) joint occupiers of land or premises; (iii) occupiers of unfurnished lodgings; or (iv) inhabitants of a dwelling by virtue of office or employment.[41] The number of female local government electors increased from 1 million to 8.5 million. From 1928, married women – who could not normally be legal owners or tenants of any property, which was the automatic right of their husbands – could vote in local elections from age 21.

Election to local government office was more accessible to women than selection as candidates for Westminster, though still not very accessible. Local government, dealing as it did with social issues such as health and education, had long been regarded as lying particularly within woman's sphere, including by many women. It was also more compatible with domestic duties since it did not require long absences from home. Women's representation in local government had grown steadily since unmarried and widowed women with suitable property qualifications were granted the local vote in 1869.[42] It grew further between the wars until by the late 1930s they were represented (if often in small numbers) on almost two-thirds of local authorities and were 16 per cent of elected members for London Boroughs (compared with only 5 per cent of members of City and Borough Councils throughout England and Wales)[43]. Twenty-four of the 144 members of the London County Council were female.[44] As we have seen, many women stood as Independents, their affiliation influenced by the local political culture. The greater possibility of standing as Independents, though it may have weakened in the 1930s as the parties tightened their grip of local government in more localities,[45] also assisted women to stand successfully.

Local government provided another channel whereby people who felt excluded from influencing central government could participate. The Labour Party was never a majority governing party nationally between the wars but it had growing success at local level, gradually taking majority control of big city councils, starting with Sheffield in 1926, until by the mid-1930s it controlled most cities and the important London County Council. The real improvements in health, education and social services achieved by many local authorities between the wars are likely to have contributed to social stability, especially in areas of high unemployment and poverty, including parts of London. Non-party organizations, including women's organizations, campaigned with real success, for policy change at local as well as central government level: for better housing, more maternal and child welfare clinics, wash-houses and other services.[46]

To maintain social stability, successive governments recognized that it was important not only to foster harmonious industrial relations but also to ensure that social conditions did not worsen, and, if possible, improved, even in a period of economic depression. This was not easy at a time when poverty, bad housing, unemployment, high infant mortality and malnutrition were all too common. Nevertheless there was a steady increase in public expenditure on social welfare between the wars, improvements in working-class housing, health and education, the expansion of unemployment benefits (which for all their deficiencies were better than ever before), the introduction of pensions for widows, orphans and blind people and much else.[47]

In these and other activities governments worked closely with voluntary organizations both in the formulation of new policies and their administration. Voluntary organizations, some new, some founded in the previous century, campaigned vigorously for more state welfare. They provided where they could for the needs of the groups on whose behalf they campaigned, but were well aware that only the state had the resources to meet national needs adequately and comprehensively. They included voluntary adoption societies, institutions caring for disabled people or the unemployed, maternal and child welfare clinics, charities providing country holidays for poor children, free legal advice, the National Council for the Unmarried Mother and her Child and many more. Such organizations engaged in regular discussions with central and local government about the need for more state provision and the forms it should take. The National Council of Social Service, set up in 1919, was designed to continue and extend the considerable wartime cooperation between voluntary and statutory bodies and to coordinate the work of voluntary agencies. One of its stated aims was 'to co-operate with Government Departments and Local Authorities making use of voluntary effort', as it did. It acted as a channel through which statutory funding was dispersed to voluntary bodies, as it increasingly was, produced policy documents to inform social legislation and held regular conferences on a broad range of subjects.[48] Voluntary organizations identified social problems, devised solutions, urged the state to adopt them, then often worked with the state to administer the newly implemented policies. Then as now, voluntary associations and the state collaborated in the development of a 'mixed economy of welfare' rather than competing. The 'Big State' did not squeeze out the 'Big Society' as some would argue; they worked together.[49]

Organizations of this kind were different from the campaigning associations described above. Essentially they were service providers, providing *for* those in need rather than necessarily seeking to empower them or to extend citizen rights, though some combined both roles. The important point is the range and number of influential voluntary associations playing complementary roles alongside, in dialogue with and influencing party politics in inter-war Britain, assisting in maintaining a stable democracy.[50]

Non-party associations in Britain also actively sought to achieve peace and stability internationally, pre-eminently the mixed-sex League of Nations Union, as Helen McCarthy has described. The women's associations were part of an international expansion of women's organizations world-wide, while newly founded male organizations such as Rotary Clubs, founded in Britain in 1905, then rapidly spreading internationally, becoming Rotary International in 1925. Among younger people, the youth movements founded in pre-1914 Britain spread equally fast around the world: the Boy Scouts (founded 1907) and Girl Guides (founded 1910, when girls showed an unseemly desire to join the Scouts), both dedicated to nurturing good citizenship and international fellowship in the young. Like the women's organizations, these non-party bodies came together (and with the women's organizations) in support of common causes, such as the local peace campaigns held in some districts in the later 1930s.[51]

Some British organizations were affiliated to international organizations, as the National Council of Women was to the International Council of Women and a number of organizations to the Women's International League for Peace and Freedom. Regional federations grew up world-wide, such as the Pan-Asian and Pan-Pacific women's organizations, as did federations with other international connections, such as the British Commonwealth League.[52] The growth of many of these organizations was stimulated by the foundation of the League of Nations and the hopes it engendered for world peace, social progress and international co-operation. Many of them, including women's organizations, actively lobbied the League on a range of issues including aboriginal rights in Australia and women's issues such as maternity leave.[53] They found the League often more receptive than their own governments and hoped through the League to put pressure on these governments. Early in its history the League agreed to the appointment of women to its senior posts and a number were appointed, at a time when it was rare for women to be formally involved in international diplomacy.

Another important dimension to international politics concerned the movements for colonial freedom, which came to fruition after the next war. British associations supported the Indian independence movement among others. Many British feminists supported in particular the demands of the Indian women's movement for equal rights during the long debates over the reform of the Indian constitution between the wars, though Eleanor Rathbone MP, a member of the all-party parliamentary committee which reviewed Indian constitutional arrangements in 1927–30, angered the three main Indian women's associations – the Women's Indian Association, the National Council of Women in India and, the most importantly, the All-India Women's Conference – by supporting only a limited franchise for women in India which she believed was more immediately attainable than the universal adult suffrage which they demanded.[54] These movements and connections merit more attention than they have received from historians of Britain.

This chapter explores the proliferation of highly political, but non-party, associations and their roles in politics in inter-war Britain. It asks why the biggest ever extension of the franchise in Britain and the achievement, at last, of formal democracy was followed by apparent widespread scepticism about the established party political system and a preference for voluntary campaigning and service organizations of various kinds. It examines the evident political influence and success of many of them in achieving change in legislation, in the provision of welfare services and influencing political debate on key issues. It also asks whether this changed political culture helped keep British society and politics relatively stable in a period of international instability.

Certainly this was the explicit aim of many of the organizations in question, which sought to educate the new (and old) electorate in 'good citizenship', in a collective determination to contribute to building a good, cohesive society, seeking to involve them actively in political discourse and action. And it was certainly the desire of the main political parties and a likely reason for their willingness to co-operate with so many non-governmental organizations. These organizations drew large numbers of voters into the local and national political arenas, giving them voices and channels for expressing their views, enabling them to feel included, not excluded, from political processes which affected their lives and those of others they cared about. Like all political campaigns, not all of these were successful, for example, in achieving world peace, but there were enough real, if more modest, achievements to give hope and encouragement, such as the changes in family law and the expansion of social welfare provision even in a time of economic depression.

The growth and vibrancy of non-party action in inter-war Britain was part of wider international movements in a period when international communication – by telephone, radio, air – was taking new forms and expanding, and international co-operation and understanding were urgently needed. These international changes were important in themselves and influenced British political culture. After World War II, the party system reasserted itself in Britain, but there have been times, including the present, when scepticism about it, a feeling among many voters of exclusion from the political system, and the search for alternatives has revived. Perhaps the study of the inter-war years can help us to understand why.

Notes

1. David Butler and Gareth Butler *Twentieth Century British Political Facts, 1900–2000*. (London, 2000), pp. 179, 235.
2. Keith Middlemas *Politics in Industrial Society: The Experience of the British System since 1911*. (London, 1979).
3. Ibid., pp. 18–19.
4. Helen McCarthy and Pat Thane 'The Politics of Association in Industrial Society' *Twentieth Century British History*, Vol. 22, No. 2, 2011, pp. 217–229.
5. Helen McCarthy *The British People and the League of Nations. Democracy, Citizenship and Internationalism, c 1918–45* (Manchester, 2011).
6. Pat Thane 'What Difference Did the Vote Make? in Amanda Vickery ed. *Women, Privilege and Power. British Politics 1750 to the Present* (Stanford, 2001) pp. 253–88.
7. Pat Thane 'The "Big Society" and the "Big State": Creative Tension Not Crowding Out' *Twentieth Century British History* (forthcoming).
8. Butler and Butler *Political Facts*, p. 261.
9. Barbara Caine *English Feminism, 1780–1980* (Oxford, 1997), pp. 173–255.
10. Ibid. p.183.
11. Shirley M. Eoff *Viscountess Rhondda. Equalitarian Feminist* (Colunbus, 1991), p. 64.
12. Eoff *Rhondda* p. 174.
13. Abigail Beach and Richard Weight eds *The Right to Belong: Citizenship and National Identity in Britain, 1930–1960* (London, 1998).
14. Brendon Jones 'Simon [*née* Potter] Shena Dorothy, Lady Simon of Wythenshawe (1883–1972)'; Brendon Jones 'Ernest Emil Darwin Simon (1879–1960)'; Gillian Sutherland 'Eva Marian Hubback (1886–1949'. All *Oxford Dictionary of National Biography* (Oxford, 2004–11).
15. Susan Pedersen *Eleanor Rathbone and the Politics of Conscience* (New Haven and London, 2004) pp. 128–9.
16. Cheryl Law *Suffrage and Power. The Women's Movement 1918–1928* (London, 1997) p. 113.
17. Jones 'Shena Simon'.
18. Sandra Stanley Holton *Feminism and Democracy: Women's Suffrage and Reform Politics in Britain* (Cambridge, 1986).
19. Particularly active in women's causes in parliament were Lord Robert Cecil, a Conservative MP, though increasingly at odds with his party between the wars, Martin Ceadel 'Cecil (Edgar Algernon) Robert Gascoyne [known as Lord Robert Cecil] Viscount Cecil of Chelwood' *ODNB*; and Major Jack Hills MP,

also a Conservative and a brother-in-law of Virginia Woolf, EWW Green 'Hills, John Waller (1867–1938)' *ODNB*. Neither biography, nor those of Chamberlain, mentions their interest in women's issues, though Hills' biographer comments that he wrote 'one of the finest books on dry fly-fishing ever written'.

20. Pat Thane and Tanya Evans *Sinners? Scroungers? Saints? Unmarried Motherhood in Twentieth Century Britain* (Oxford, 2012).
21. Thane 'What Difference' pp. 273–82.
22. Brian Harrison *Separate Spheres. The Opposition to Women's Suffrage in Britain* (London, 1978) p. 229.
23. Graduates, male and female, could vote both in their constituencies and for a separate list of university candidates.
24. Jenifer Hart *Proportional Representation: Critics of the British Electoral System* (Oxford, 1994).
25. David Butler and Gareth Butler *British Political Facts* (London, 2000) pp. 167–8.
26. Pat Thane 'Women of the British Labour Party and Feminism, 1906–1945' in HL Smith ed. *British Feminism in the Twentieth Century* (Aldershot, 1990) pp. 124–43.
27. Pat Thane 'Women and Political Participation in England, 1918–1970' in Esther Breitenbach and Pat Thane eds *Women and Citizenship in Britain and Ireland in the Twentieth Century. What Difference Did the Vote Make?* (London, 2010), pp. 11–28.
28. Janet Howes, '"No Party, No Sect, No Politics" The National Council of Women and the National Women's Citizen's Association, with particular reference to Cambridge and Manchester in the inter-war years' (PhD thesis, Anglia Ruskin University, 2003).
29. Sam Davies *Liverpool Labour. Social and Political Influences on the Development of the Labour Party in Liverpool, 1900–1939.* (Liverpool,1996) pp. 247–361.
30. Pugh, *Women's Movement* pp. 70–1.
31. Maggie Andrews *The Acceptable Face of Feminism. The Women's Institute as a Social Movement* (London, 1997).
32. Thane 'Women of the Labour Party'.
33. Andrews *Women's Institute*.
34. Ibid. Thane 'Women of the Labour Party'.
35. Pugh *Women's Movement* pp. 240–1.
36. Law *Suffrage.* pp. 232–7. Andrews *Women's Institutes;* Caitriona Beaumont 'Women and Citizenship: a Study of Non-feminist Women's Societies and the Women's Movement in England, 1928–1950' (PhD thesis, University of Warwick, 1997).
37. Jacqueline R. deVries 'Challenging Traditions: Denominational Feminism in Britain, 1910–1920' in Billie Melman ed. *Borderlines. Genders and Identities in War and Peace, 1870–1930.* (London and New York, 1998), pp. 265–84. Sheila Fletcher A. *Maude Royden. A Life.* (Oxford, 1989).
38. I am grateful to the late Sue Innes for this information.
39. Law *Suffrage.*
40. Pugh *Women's Movement.* pp. 241–2.
41. Patricia Hollis *Ladies Elect.: Women in English Local Government,1865–1914* (Oxford, 1987).
42. Ibid.
43. Pugh *Women's Movement* pp. 57–8.
44. Ibid. p. 59.
45. Ibid.
46. Michael Savage *The Dynamics of Working Class Politics: The Labour Movement in Preston, 1880–1940* (Cambridge, 1987). E.Peretz 'Local Authority Maternity Care

in the Interwar Period in Oxfordshire and Tottenham' in J.Garcia *et al. The Politics of Maternity Care* (Oxford, 1990).

47. David Vincent, *Poor Citizens: The State and the Poor in Twentieth-Century Britain* (London, 1991); Jose Harris, 'Society and State in Twentieth-century Britain' in F.M.L. Thompson ed. *The Cambridge Social History of Britain, 1750–1950: Volume 3: Social Agencies and Institutions* (Cambridge, 1990), pp. 63–117.

48. Katherine Bradley *Poverty, Philanthropy and the state: Charities and the Working Classes in London, 1918–79* (Manchester, 2009); Margaret Brasnett, *Voluntary Social Action: A History of the National Council of Social Service, 1919–1969* (London: NCSS, 1969).

49. 'Thane 'Big Society' Matthew Hilton and James McKay eds *The Ages of Voluntarism. How We Got to the Big Society* (Oxford, 2011).

50. Ibid. Nick Crowson, Matthew Hilton and James McKay eds *NGOs Contemporary Britain. Non-State Actors in Society and Politics since 1945* (London, 2009). Nicolas Deakin and Melanie Oppenheimer eds *Beveridge and Voluntary Action in Britain and the Wider World* (Manchester, 2011).

51. McCarthy *League of Nations* p. 230.

52. Marie Therese Sandall '"International Sisterhood"? International Women's Organizations and Co-operation in the Interwar period' (PhD thesis, Royal Holloway, University of London, 2007); Angela Woollacott 'Inventing Commonwealth and Pan-Pacific Feminisms: Australian Women's Internationalist Action in the 1920s–30s' *Gender and History,* 1998, Vol. 10. pp. 425–48.

53. Carol Miller 'Lobbying the League: Women's International Organizations and the League of Nations'(D.Phil. thesis, University of Oxford, 1992).

54. Pederson *Rathbone*, pp. 250ff. Mrinalini Sinha 'Suffragism and Internationalism: the Enfranchisement of British and Indian Women under an Imperial State' in Ian Fletcher *et al.* eds. *Women's Suffrage in the British Empire: Citizenship, Nation and Race* (London, 2000) pp. 224–39; Geraldine Forbes *Women in Modern India* (Cambridge, 1996) pp. 92–120.

4
The House of Commons in the Aftermath of Suffrage[1]

Richard Toye

What role did the House of Commons play in the political life of the nation in the aftermath of suffrage?[2] There is surprisingly little historiography to help answer the question. We have accounts by Brian Harrison of the role of women MPs and by P.J. Waller of the role of political humour.[3] S.A. Walkland's edited volume on the Commons in the twentieth century contains useful information, although it focuses on procedure and organization, not on the part that that the House played in public life as a whole.[4] Of course, we have plenty of knowledge of events that took place *in* the Commons. No biography of an MP would be complete without an account of his or her maiden speech and any celebrated parliamentary episodes they may have been involved in; and, in addition to *Hansard*, numerous published diaries and autobiographies provide the raw materials from which such accounts can be fashioned. Yet we have little understanding of how to interpret such events, not merely as building blocks in accounts of the success or failure of policies and individuals, but as part of what Alan Finlayson and James Martin have called the 'symbolic ritual dimension of politics'.[5] Thus we have excellent accounts by H.C.G. Matthew and Jon Lawrence respectively of the culture of public speech outside parliament, and these include the aftermath of suffrage period, but no one has attempted anything similar for the Commons.[6] Nor, indeed, do we have systematic analyses of how interwar MPs saw their role (which lay at the nexus between high and grassroots politics) or of how parliament was reported in the press.[7] Stuart Ball wrote over twenty years ago that 'Parliament has been viewed as the place where events occur, rather than as a factor shaping the events themselves.' In spite of Ball's own valuable article on the Commons in the 1900–51 period, and of Paul Seward and Paul Silk's equally useful survey of the twentieth century as a whole, we still need to know more about what the institution was *for* at the advent of universal suffrage, and what the impact of full democracy upon it was.[8]

As we will see, parliament in the aftermath of suffrage era was in some respects a highly contested institution. At the same time, paradoxically, it was regarded by many with considerable complacency. There were not many academic treatises on Parliament at this time; one of the most substantial, by the then LSE academic W. Ivor Jennings, was published in 1939, and was shot through with Whiggish assumptions. Jennings wrote: 'Members of Parliament [...] know the People of England to be a free people, and themselves the representatives of that freedom. [...] British constitutional history is a story of resistance to oppression, often temporarily unsuccessful, but ultimately resulting in its abolition.'[9] The same assumptions informed Josiah Wedgwood's History of Parliament project, launched in the 1920s.[10] In the political sphere, while there were many proposals (especially in the 1930s) for reform of Commons procedure, there was little deep thinking about the nature and purpose of the institution. The Weimar theoretician Carl Schmitt argued in the 1920s that no new principled (as opposed to pragmatic) arguments for parliamentarism had been advanced 'since about 1848'.[11] It is certainly difficult to think of anything in British interwar thought that would contradict him.

There were a small number of 'Diehard' Conservatives who, from the Edwardian period onwards, became alienated from parliamentary politics.[12] Overwhelmingly, however, the main political parties saw parliament as a useful and important body that was worth defending from the threats posed to it not only by communism and fascism but also (supposedly) by each other. Notwithstanding their failure to provide it with new intellectual underpinnings, then, it cannot be said exactly that they took parliament for granted. But with few exceptions (notably Ball, and Seaward and Silk), that is what historians have tended to do; or at the very least they have often allowed themselves to make sweeping assertions about it without detailed justification. This is true across the spectrum. Ralph Miliband made the influential argument, from a Marxist perspective, that Labour throughout its history had been defined by its 'parliamentarism', but had little or nothing to say about the party's actual behaviour in the Commons.[13] From a social democratic viewpoint Ben Pimlott in effect accepted Miliband's premise about the party's electoralism but presented this as commendable pragmatism rather than dogma.[14] Philip Williamson's admiring book on Stanley Baldwin rightly discusses parliamentarism as a key part of Baldwin's public doctrine; but we learn relatively little about how this affected his actual behaviour in the Commons.[15] Keith Middlemas, for his part, has argued that 'Long before 1945, Parliament had ceased to be the supreme governing body [...] parties and Parliament subordinated themselves to the administrative and managerial powers of the state apparatus.'[16] But again we are not told about what this alleged decline meant in terms of what MPs actually did, this apparently being taken as irrelevant in the face of more powerful exogenous factors. Nor have those scholars interested in why extremist challenges to parliamentary government failed said much about parliament itself, or what its appeal may have been.[17] And surely, any account of 'the transformation of British public politics after the First World War' needs to consider Parliament if it is to be complete.[18]

This chapter does not aspire to provide a complete review of all aspects of the Commons during the period. It does, however, aim to raise some pertinent questions and offer some hypotheses. It explores how the extensions of the franchise in 1918 and 1928 (and the election of the first women MPs and the new influx of Labour MPs after the Great War) affected the culture of the House of Commons. It considers the extent to which post-war Commons practices marked a break with the past, by reflecting, for example, on the legacy of the now-defunct Irish Parliamentary Party. It asks how MPs' practices within the Commons chamber (including symbolic disruption tactics) were understood and contested. It reflects on the role of the Prime Minister within the Commons and what this tells us about how the power of that office was exercised. Finally, it considers the degree to which the impact of the suffrage extensions on the Commons can be disentangled from other factors which affected parliamentary politics. All this must be seen in the longer-term perspective of twentieth century developments. Executive control of parliament increased, and there was a growing volume of legislation. At the same time, the importance of the Commons to the political process as a whole decreased, although we must always be wary of accepting too readily the declinist views of contemporaries.[19]

We may begin by asking, what was the socio-economic background of MPs in the aftermath of suffrage? Naturally this varied between parties. Using figures provided by Michael Rush, we may see that 47.9 per cent of Conservative MPs elected at general elections between 1918 and 1935 were drawn from the professions, representing little change from the previous era. However, the 38.1 per cent of this cohort drawn from business represented a significant increase, on the back of a trend that had been rising since the late nineteenth century. This growth was largely accounted for by the decline of Conservatives relying on private means, down to 4.6 per cent of those elected from 1918 to 1935 from 31.4 per cent of those elected from 1868 to 1895 and 15.3 per cent of those elected from 1900 to 1910. The introduction of payment of members in the Edwardian period may have been a factor in this. The percentage of Conservatives and Liberals drawn from business were now roughly in line, and with 43% of Liberals elected from 1918 to 1935 coming from a professional background the party was not far behind the Tories in that respect. The Liberals did do slightly better in that period than the Tories in terms of the percentage of working-class MPs, but this was still trivial in both cases – 3.4 per cent as opposed to 1.1 per cent. By contrast, of course, the new influx of Labour MPs (the big breakthrough coming in 1922) substantially increased the working-class element in the Commons. At the same time, even as their numbers increased, the *percentage* of Labour MPs from working backgrounds declined. Although Rush uses slightly different periodisation for Labour than he does for the other parties, he shows that the share of working-class Labour MPs declined from 89.5 per cent of those elected at general elections between 1900 and 1918 to 56.2 per cent of those elected between 1922 and 1935, 1935 being the last year in which they formed a majority of the Parliamentary Labour Party.[20] These figures help explain both why class became an important element in 1920s arguments over parliamentary methods and behaviour, and also why the tensions it produced were relatively short-lived. We may also note the strong ex-service element in the post-war Commons. According to Richard Carr's work on Conservative ex-servicemen MPs, there were 200 of them by 1924, which meant that nearly half the parliamentary party had served in the Great War; after the 1935 election, there were still 171.[21]

MPs were increasingly busy. Although the volume of business had been increasing before the war, there had still been some years when there was no autumn session of parliament. In 1907, for example, Winston Churchill had used the autumn for the expedition that resulted in the publication of his book *My African Journey* (1908). After the war, autumn sessions were an inescapable fact of life, although some still put up resistance. Churchill himself argued that the near-continuous sittings had diminished public interest in Parliament.[22] The Conservative cabinet minister Arthur Steel-Maitland protested, to no avail, that 'An Autumn Session is a handicap to every sitting Member. It is the best time for work in the constituency and for holding meetings.' It was also, he argued, 'a peculiar handicap to the Unionist Party', as Tory MPs tended to live further away from their constituencies than others did.[23] As this shows, partisan interests were involved here; there was also an ideological dimension. The Conservative MP Earl Winterton distinguished between the views which, he said, obtained on different sides of the political spectrum:

> Those on the Left consider that [...] the happiness and well-being of the community can best be secured by the widest measure of House of Commons control of the financial and economic activities of the Nation. [...] For that reason they desire that Parliament should sit for most of the year, and membership of the House of Commons be a "whole-time" job. Those on the Right wish Parliament to restrain itself within the limits, so far as modern conditions allow, of what have been its historic duties to the Nation; they do not believe that a vast output of legislation and administrative control of the individual at every point makes for content or security; they consider that members of the House of Commons will perform their task best if they are not prevented, by too constant sittings of the House, from carrying out their ordinary avocations.[24]

In fact, the interwar Conservative Party did pass much legislation, including social reform measures about which it boasted proudly. To a considerable extent this may have reflected the party attempting to anticipate the desires of the new mass electorate rather than responding to them directly, although some of the 1920s rash of 'women's legislation' can be attributed to women's campaigning networks.[25] Some politicians felt, in fact, that there was less popular interest in legislation than there had been before the war, partly because more business was being conducted in committee, away from the floor of the House. Churchill was of this view, observing in 1931 that in pre-war days 'There were two or three great Bills each year, but they were great Bills – much larger than the Bills that are going through now and much more controversial.' There were now many more Bills 'of the second order, of the second rank of importance', and the public lost sight of them.[26] MPs were now working harder, judged by their participation in debates, on committees, at question time, and by their voting records. This was a continuation of a long-term upward trend; Rush also finds that 'from some time between 1913 and 1928, the opposition became more organized and systematic', in view of the increase in the number of speeches made in debate by opposition frontbenchers.[27] Still, it was possible for MPs to get away with only a minimal contribution if they wanted to. Frank Gray, briefly a Liberal MP and a Junior Whip, noted in 1925: 'How some Members – and they are many – go there day after day content to sit in the House or the smoke-room without either participating, or appearing to desire to participate personally, is a little difficult to understand.'[28] Inactivity was taken to an extreme by Sir John Leigh, who served as a Conservative MP from 1922 to 1945 and who appears never to have spoken in the Chamber at all (although he did table some questions).[29]

MPs were also increasingly expected to attend to the personal problems of their constituents. The Labour MP Harry Snell recalled that 'One of the chief torments of a member's life is the answering of letters, most of which should not have been written, and some of which reflect considerable discredit on those who write them. No inconsiderable number of the British public appear to think that the chief duty of a member of parliament is to attend to their personal claims, and that he should always place these before the needs of the nation.'[30] (Women MPs faced additional pressures, receiving letters from women outside their constituencies who regarded them as MPs for women in general.)[31] Some members were more conscientious than others. The ILP MP Jennie Lee recalled that her colleague James Maxton found her dealing with constituency work on a side-table in one of the division lobbies (members did not have offices). 'Looking quizzically down at me, he tapped with his long brown fingers the enormous bundle of letters I was ploughing my way through and said in his slow disarming drawl, "You had better make up your mind, you know, whether you mean to be a socialist Member of Parliament or another b----- welfare worker like Geordie" – chuckling and nodding in the direction of his bosom pal George Buchanan M.P.'[32] Neglect of constituents was, of course, potentially perilous. The Liberal MP Percy Harris complained in his memoirs that 'A member who rarely speaks in the House but is always visiting his constituency, opening bazaars, or attending to their [i.e. constituents'] personal grievances, receives far more appreciation than another who may be assiduous in discharging his parliamentary duties and fighting the people's battle on the floor of the House.'[33]

It was not the case, however, that there was no overlap between Commons and constituency. One pseudonymous writer in the *Conservative Agent's Journal* described how, in the 'new conditions of electioneering' that had come about with the growth of the electorate, MPs needed to recruit American style 'boosters' to sing their praises to fellow voters. The article explained:

> In better class districts "boosters" are developed from those well meaning individuals who pose as authorities on the affairs of the day and like to express freely their views in their particular circle of friends. As soon as an individual of this kind is noticed, he is sent a ticket for the strangers' gallery of the House of Commons, together with a note requesting that if he cannot use it himself to return it at once. He has not been very long in the Gallery before the Member makes his appearance, and greeting him by name invites him to dinner, which they take tete-a-tete, and another "booster" is born. Women "boosters" are developed in the same way, only they are usually invited to take tea on the terrace.

The writer added: 'One is not very proud of this type of supporter, and it feels like undressing in public to speak of them.'[34] This speaks marvellously both of Conservatives' discomfort with mass politics and their ability to swallow their distaste in order to take advantage of it. It also demonstrates that the Commons itself could be a site of engagement between high and low politics, with the MP acting as interlocutor between the two worlds.

At the same time, there was an element of popular suspicion of Parliament – or at least some MPs so perceived. It is doubtful of course that this was a new phenomenon, although the pre-war introduction of payment of MPs may have exacerbated it. Harry Snell, in his pamphlet *Daily Life in Parliament* (1930) was at pains to emphasise that MPs were hardworking and that the then salary of £400 a year (approximately £22,000 at 2012 values) did not stretch as far as many people seemed to suppose. He also went to lengths to repudiate the well-known description of the Commons as 'the best club in London'. He argued: 'This stupid phrase has done untold harm, and it has popularised an entirely false conception of what social life in Parliament is like.' He pointed out that the facilities for MPs were lousy, and that the Commons at any rate did not choose its own members. There was deeper point, too, aimed at those critics who had suggested 'that the social life of Parliament is so destructive to political independence that the party hostility which is displayed on the floor of the House is a mere masquerade meant to deceive the public'. This comment was probably aimed in part at Labour left-wingers who felt that the seductive atmosphere of the Commons had dulled the parliamentary party's edge. Snell claimed never to have seen evidence of personal friendships between MPs leading to a loss of fighting spirit: 'and personally I experience no difficulty in harbouring a genuine regard for men whose political opinions I most cordially detest'.[35] By contrast, Hugh Dalton was later proud to boast that 'I did not take any particular trouble to get to know Tories or Liberals. Socially, at Westminster, I was a strong Party man.'[36]

Whether or not fraternisation between MPs of different hues did in fact modify the asperity of party warfare – or indeed render it fraudulent – is a moot point. Undoubtedly, though, exposure to the culture of the Commons did alter the behaviour of new members in significant ways. Recent work in political science/discourse analysis has considered the modern Commons as a 'community of practice' in which newcomers adopt the socio-cultural habits of the institution (including its rhetorical norms) through 'situated learning'.[37] This approach is also applicable to the aftermath of suffrage era. Many MPs' memoirs emphasise this learning process. Herbert Morrison (Labour) recalled how his failed maiden speech taught him his 'first lesson on the unique character of debate in the Mother of Parliaments'.[38] Herbert Williams (Conservative) recalled being reproved for heckling on the first day of debate he attended, 'which was thought very bad manners on the part of an entirely new Member'.[39] According to Harold Macmillan (also Conservative), 'For a young member, coming for he first time to the House of Commons is very like going to the House of Commons is very like going to school, and the atmosphere of the place is very similar [...] front-bench figures constitute a society of prefects who rule the school under the general guidance of the head-master or Speaker.'[40] (Macmillan clearly had in mind here his own public school background, which he shared with over 60 per cent of his fellow Tory MPs and with just under 40 per cent of Liberal ones.)[41] Memoirists frequently emphasised both the power of the institution and its timeless qualities, transcending the proclivities of individual members. As John Buchan (Conservative) wrote:

> The customary platitudes about the House of Commons happen to be true. Individual members may be ill-bred; the House itself has a fine taste and breeding, and a sure instinct in matters of conduct. [...] The flashy platform demagogue has to change his methods if he is to win its favour. It demands specific qualities – a certain decency in debate and a certain respect for itself and its ancient ritual. The sansculotte who refuses its demands is speedily silenced, for the House has immense powers of neglect and disapproval. The man who has won fame in some other walk of life, like the public service, business, science or literature, is given a respectful hearing, but he has to show the specific House of Commons gifts before he is accepted.[42]

This superficially appealing picture cannot be taken wholly at face value.[43] There was quite a strong correlation between the 'customary platitudes' and the highly partisan claims advanced by Conservatives about Labour's attitude to Parliament. These became particularly pronounced after the major influx of Labour MPs, including the 'Clydesiders', at the 1922 election. On the one hand, there were the denunciations of 'the Socialists, who think that the House of Commons is a fine place to repeat their street-corner harangues',[44] and whose speeches were supposedly 'intended to bring Parliamentary institutions into hatred and contempt'.[45] On the other there was the claim that, in due course, the Commons itself would take the socialist rowdies in hand and tame them by teaching them good manners.[46] In 1923 a cartoon in the Conservative Party publication *The Popular View* showed the Mother of Parliaments giving a bawling 'Red' a bath in Parliamentary Manners. Belittling Labour members by suggesting that they would be tamed, the legend ran: 'The Mother of Parliaments has to take the Socialist MPs in hand, as their leader cannot manage them.'[47] (See Illustration 5.)

The prediction that the atmosphere of the Commons would exert a moderating influence on Labour members was not a bad one. Arguably the process took rather longer than some Conservatives envisaged, but it had mainly been accomplished by the 1930s. By the time of World War II, those Clydesiders who were still in the Commons had ceased to be symbols of 'Bolshevist frightfulness' and become much-loved parliamentary figures.[48] Thus when James Maxton and other MPs took part in a 1943 radio discussion broadcast to America, the parliamentary 'scenes' that had caused so

The Mother of Parliaments has to take the Socialist M.P.s in hand, as their leader cannot manage them.

Illustration 5 Cartoon from *The Popular View*, March 1923 (reproduced courtesy of the Conservative Party)

much controversy at the time had become a matter of laughter and mutual congratulation.[49] However, the process was not achieved by the impersonal forces of 'the mother of parliaments' but by the agency of individuals within it, in combination with the broader political strategies of the main parties and their leaders. Here, J.H. Whitley, who served as Speaker from 1921 to 1929, stands out as an important figure.[50] Some Conservatives felt that he showed 'excessive patience which erred on the side of weakness' when dealing with Labour, but this was a misjudgement, as Bonar Law for one appreciated.[51] According to Ralph Verney, who served as Speaker's Secretary during these years, Whitley's 'treatment of the Labour Party was deliberate, and he was not diverted by any hostile criticism: he was out to help them to take their position as His Majesty's Opposition, though never allowing them to transgress the Rules of Order or to act contrary to recognized Procedure, which, when necessary, he used to take great trouble in explaining personally to individual Members in the privacy of his Library'.[52] Ramsay MacDonald referred to this obliquely in his tribute to Whitley on his retirement: 'You have shown us in a most remarkable way how to be patient and courteous without being lax; how to be strict and severe without being mechanical and formal; and you have also demonstrated to us, in a way that few of your predecessors have done, how gentleness can rule and how persuasiveness can subdue.'[53]

MacDonald, of course, did not feel that he himself was in any great need of such lessons – but he may have found Whitley a useful ally in the process of educating those Labour members 'who have no sense of Parliamentary methods & who expect Front Bench leaders to live in a perpetual state of fighting exaltation & be noisy'.[54] His efforts to inculcate what he saw as the correct methods fitted in with his broader efforts to make Labour respectable. Laura Beers has suggested that 'the hysterical representation of socialist politics by Labour's opponents helped to reinforce pre-existing tendencies towards gradualism, parliamentarism and financial orthodoxy within the movement, as party and trade union leaders shied away from policies and actions which could be presented as reckless or unconstitutional'.[55] Indeed, Labour was quite prepared to counter-attack by disputing the Conservatives' constitutional credentials. For example, MacDonald claimed in 1923 that 'But for the stand which the Labour party had made for honest politics and proper Parliamentary action there would be no means for constitutionalism in this country at the present time.'[56] The Liberals also contested this ground: during the Coalition period, the Asquithians claimed that they were 'the only party' that was truly committed to parliamentary government.[57]

The idea of the timeless traditions of the mother of parliaments was thus to a great extent a fiction under which all parties sought to advance their own claims to be the true defenders of the constitution. It should not blind us to the real changes that the Commons did experience in these years. The most obvious of those was the presence of the first women MPs. Their impact on the atmosphere of the Commons may not have been very dramatic, given their small numbers (an interwar peak of fifteen in 1931).[58] For many decades after they first arrived – arguably even to the present day – the House retained a distinctly masculine character. The women themselves were frequently the victims of bawdy jokes which provoked loud laughter in the chamber but went unreported in the press.[59] Nevertheless, as Harrison has shown, the early female members did carve out a 'distinct rhetorical space' for themselves, albeit at the cost of accepting that there were particular 'women's issues' on which they should concentrate their efforts.[60] Moreover, their impact on the way that the Commons was perceived by the public may have been more dramatic, as is suggested by the flood of letters to Nancy Astor by women from across Britain who considered her to be 'their' MP. Beers has shown how the media treated some women MPs as celebrities and demonstrated a fascination with their clothing.[61] Female MPs may therefore have had an impact on British political culture that was disproportionate to their numbers.

It would be easy for the very visible arrival of women MPs to blind us to an equally significant departure: that of the majority of Irish MPs, the refusal of the Sinn Féin members elected in 1918 to take their seats being followed by the creation of the Irish Free State in 1921–22. (There remained in the Commons some vestiges of the Irish Parliamentary Party: seven Redmondites survived the cull of 1918, and T.P. O'Connor, who sat for a Liverpool seat, was Father of the House at the time of his death in 1929.) This has, of course, often been seen quite rightly as a bonus to the Conservative Party, through the removal from Westminster of a bloc opposed to it.[62] What has not been considered is the impact on the atmosphere of the Commons itself. By 1914, the IPP was no longer the extreme disruptive presence it had been during the high years of Parnellism, and its members had gained something of a reputation for distinctive humour. Earl Winterton commented in 1930 on how the present-day Commons contrasted with the pre-war era:

> There are fewer "scenes" in the course of debate, and I consider that there is a better feeling between Parties and individuals. This, no doubt, is partly due to the disappearance of the Irish Nationalist Party, whose presence in the House seldom made for harmony. On the other hand, Parliament, by this disappearance, has lost a fund of genuine eloquence, wit, and debating power which has never been replaced from other sources.[63]

Churchill, for his part, saw the rigidity of the parliamentary timetable in the modern era, and its domination by government business, as the legacy of Nationalist obstruction in the late Nineteenth Century:

> I think that the old flexibility of the English procedure was destroyed by the attacks made on it by the Nationalist party – completely destroyed

and greatly altered, and since the Nationalist Party, with all their Parliamentary qualities, which were very great, have left us and are entirely replaced by British Parties, I notice a very much greater possibility of returning to the old procedure.[64]

That, of course, did not happen. Nor did the Labour Party seek to imitate the IPP. 'I am sometimes told to study the Irish party and follow it', wrote MacDonald in 1922. 'I shall do nothing of the kind, because my task is quite different from that of any Irish Party.' This, he argued, was because Parnell had had a single, limited objective – Home Rule – and at the same time stood no chance of gaining a majority and forming a government. Labour by contrast did have this latter object in view and, in order to help win over public opinion, needed to 'work Parliament in Parliamentary ways'.[65] Predictably, though, Labour's opponents continued to offer harsh criticisms on the party's actual parliamentary conduct. In his 1920s prime ministerial letters to the King, outlining daily developments in the Commons, Baldwin was scathing of the 'violent and abusive tactics' adopted by labour backbenchers and contrasted them with the 'quite remarkable patience and conciliation' with which Conservatives had met them.[66]

These letters, it should be noted, were likely the work of secretaries or junior whips rather than the Prime Minister himself. Nonetheless, they are a fascinating source for the study of parliamentary activity. The institution of the daily prime ministerial letter had been revived by Bonar Law (in the Edwardian period the task of writing them had devolved on the Home Secretary) and was continued by MacDonald during his 1924 government but appears to have been discontinued by him in 1929 and was not thereafter revived.[67] We may deduce that Bonar Law's intention, in part, was to distinguish his style of government from his predecessor, Lloyd George, who as Prime Minister had not had much time for Parliament (and perhaps not much for the King either). A further flavour of the correspondence – which was always written in the third person – can be gleaned from a Baldwin letter of April 1927, the theme of which has considerable relevance for the present volume:

The Prime Minister's quiet, simple and brief announcement during Question time that the Government had decided to introduce a Bill during the next Session of Parliament to give women the franchise at the age of twenty-one would not have led a stranger to the House of Commons to think that the House was hearing for the first time of a constitutional change of first class importance and of a decision which had provided himself and the Government with the most harassing problem which they have had to tackle since coming into office. The decision is one which is bound to be unpopular in many Conservative quarters and its quiet reception yesterday is no indication of the opposition which may have to be faced. Naturally, the Socialists greeted the announcement with cheers.[68]

These letters reinforce the importance of the Commons to Baldwin's style of government, which has been rightly emphasised by Philip Williamson. Although he was by no means the perfect parliamentary performer, his presence in the Commons for up to nine hours a day (not all of that time in the Chamber) cemented his authority over his MPs.[69] His powers of control depended less on the authority of the Whips than on the mild put-down in the Chamber or on the disapproving verdict passed on to a rebel via a fellow MP.[70]

Baldwin's habits need to be seen in long-term perspective. Dunleavy *et al.* have carried out a pioneering analysis demonstrating a decline in prime ministerial activity in the Commons since the 1880s; they concluded that this led to a decline in accountability. Implicitly, they argue that Prime Ministers have increased their own powers (through the avoidance of scrutiny) by speaking less; they do not consider any positive benefits that may accrue to prime ministers from parliamentary speech.[71] The example of Baldwin – and indeed other inter-war Prime Ministers – suggests a more complex picture. The hours he spent taking the temperature of the Commons and influencing its mood were not wasted time; it is not obvious that he would have made himself stronger by withdrawing himself elsewhere. On the other hand, such behaviour no longer seemed quite as natural as it would have done in Gladstone's day. The Labour MP George Strauss recalled that, as National Government Prime Minister after 1931, MacDonald spent much time sitting next to Baldwin on the front bench: 'His critics said this was to avoid the tedium of ministerial work in Downing Street. Others said it was because he so loved watching the proceedings and moods of the House.'[72] These, then, were years of transition. While Prime Ministers still gained something from workaday engagement with the House, too much of it might help gain them a reputation for indolence. One might suggest that, in the longer run, Prime Ministers did not suck power away from the Commons by progressively extracting themselves from it; rather they increasingly kept away because they shared the growing general sense that its power had already gone elsewhere.[73]

This leads, in conclusion, to some fundamental questions about the Commons in these years. Did it, as Middlemas's claims imply, become progressively hollowed out, preserving its outward form whilst surrendering its power to the state bureaucracy? Alternatively, did the power move to party machines organised around socio-economic interest groups, as Schmitt suggested in relation to Weimar in an arresting passage in *The Crisis of Parliamentary Democracy*:

The situation of parliamentarism is critical today because the development of modern mass democracy has made argumentative public discussion an empty formality. Many norms of contemporary parliamentary law, above all provisions concerning the independence of representatives and the openness of sessions, function as a result like a superfluous decoration, useless and even embarrassing, as though someone had painted the radiator of a modern central heating system with red flames in order to give the appearance of a blazing fire.[74]

Neither model seems perfectly applicable. On the one hand, parties remained more important than Middlemas suggests; on the other, those parties were not merely the slaves of interest groups, important as the latter were. Nevertheless, there is a change to be seen over the course of the period. The 1920s were a time of flux and of genuine multi-party politics, and it often seemed as though the Commons itself could be a decisive arena.[75] 'Nothing is so important as constant attendance at the House', wrote the then Asquithian Liberal William Wedgwood Benn in 1922.[76] Although the Commons occasionally did do surprising things, as in the Anglican prayer book controversy of 1927–28 (which saw the rejection of reforms proposed by the Church of England), one should not exaggerate its unpredictability. Nevertheless, the contrast with the 1930s is palpable. After 1931, *de facto* two-party politics, combined with the crushing National Government, meant that the chances of a debate in the Commons actually changing anything were very slight indeed. 'We do not have any longer the clash of debate and the confrontation by effective champions of great bodies of organized opinion', complained Churchill early in 1939. 'In the main, it is the Government of the day contending, none too well, with overwhelming preponderant difficulties, and the rest of the House either backing them up or making a formal effort at criticism.'[77] Nevertheless, the Norway debate of 1940 showed that the Commons – in conditions of crisis – was still capable of triggering the fall of a government.[78]

Moreover, the Commons ended World War II with its reputation enhanced.[79] This suggests that any narrative of 'decline' cannot be a straightforward one. Moreover, as we have seen, the changes that took place during the aftermath of suffrage can by no means be attributed exclusively to the extension of the franchise itself, especially since the connection between enfranchisement and the rise of the Labour Party was by no means as simple as was once thought.[80] Some trends, such as the growing volume of business, had been in place prior to 1918; others, such as the withdrawal of the Irish, were not obviously connected to the rise of mass politics. The growing pressures on MPs – the increased postbag, the greater demands of the constituency, the more extensive committee work – were doubtless accelerated by the franchise extension but the changes were evolutionary not revolutionary. The Woman MP, was, however, a wholly new and significant feature of national public life, notwithstanding the small numbers of female members and their relatively small impact on the life of the House itself.

On the whole, the House of Commons changed not in response to overt popular pressure but rather in the face of a fair measure of popular indifference.

The press may have turned some MPs into celebrities but many others felt that their activities did not receive enough coverage in the face of 'competition from film stars and cricketers'.[81] In the aftermath of suffrage, the House of Commons remained an important focus of national political life, and a contested one at that. MPs did, however, suffer from a growing anxiety about their role, and as to whether the public was really listening to them. Ironically, in the developing era of committee work and of the 'hard-working MP', they also had significantly less time to listen to each other.[82]

Notes

1. I am grateful to John Whitley for access to the papers of J.H. Whitley and for helpful comments on an earlier draft of this chapter. I am also grateful to the participants at the Aftermath of Suffrage conference for comments and suggestions. Any errors that remain are, of course, my own responsibility.
2. Although 'Parliament' and 'House of Commons' are used more or less interchangeably here, it is the Commons that is the focus, as in this period it was unequivocally the dominant chamber.
3. Brian Harrison, 'Women in a Men's House: the Women MPs, 1919–1945', *Historical Journal* 29 (1986): 623–654; P.J. Waller, 'Laughter in the House: A Late Nineteenth and Early Twentieth Century Parliamentary Survey', *Twentieth Century British History* 5 (1994): 4–37.
4. S.A. Walkland (ed.), *The House of Commons in the Twentieth Century*, Clarendon Press, Oxford, 1979.
5. Alan Finlayson and James Martin, '"It Ain't What You Say ...": British Political Studies and the Analysis of Speech and Rhetoric', *British Politics* 3 (2008): 445–64, at 448.
6. H.C.G. Matthew, 'Rhetoric and politics in Britain, 1860–1950' in P. J. Waller (ed.), *Politics and Social Change in Modern Britain* (1987): 34–58; Jon Lawrence, *Electing Our Masters*, Oxford University Press, Oxford, 2009.
7. However, much useful information on MPs' backgrounds and parliamentary participation can be extracted from Michael Rush, *The Role of the Member of Parliament Since 1868: From Gentlemen to Players*, Oxford University Press, Oxford, 2001.
8. Stuart Ball, 'Parliament and Politics in Britain, 1900–1951', *Parliamentary History* 10 (2008): 243–276, at 243; Paul Seaward and Paul Silk, 'The House of Commons', in Vernon Bogdanor (ed.), *The British Constitution in the Twentieth Century* (2003): 139–188. Another work deserving of mention is Philip Norton (ed.), *Eminent Parliamentarians: The Speaker's Lectures*, Biteback, London, 2012, which contains some very helpful insights on the parliamentary contributions of key figures such as Lloyd George.
9. W. Ivor Jennings, *Parliament*, Cambridge University Press, Cambridge, 1939. p. 506.
10. Paul Mulvey, *The Political Life of Josiah C. Wedgwood: Land, Liberty and Empire, 1872–1943*, Royal Historical Society, London, 2010, pp. 164–77.
11. Carl Schmitt, *The Crisis of Parliamentary Democracy*, MIT Press, Cambridge MA, 1988, p. 4. This work was first published in 1923, with a new edition appearing in 1926.
12. Martin Pugh, *'Hurrah for the Blackshirts!' Fascists and Fascism in Britain between the Wars*, Pimlico, London, 2006, p. 16.
13. Ralph Miliband, *Parliamentary Socialism*, George Allen & Unwin, London, 1961.
14. Ben Pimlott, *Labour and the Left in the 1930s*, Cambridge University Press, Cambridge, 1997.

15. Philip Williamson, *Stanley Baldwin,* Cambridge University Press, Cambridge, 1999, pp. 75–6, 117–18, 136, 210, 241–2.
16. Keith Middlemas, *Politics in Industrial Society* (1979): 22.
17. See, for example, Andrew Thorpe (ed.), *The Failure of Political Extremism in Inter-War Britain,* Exeter University Press, Exeter, 1989.
18. Jon Lawrence, 'The Transformation of British Public Politics After the First World War', *Past & Present* 190 (2006): 185–216. By 'public politics' Lawrence meant 'extra-parliamentary politics', which is sufficient for the purposes of his article but is in general too narrow a definition.
19. Seaward and Silk, 'The House of Commons'. As they show (pp. 161–2), the increase in the volume of legislation was not in terms of the number of bills, but in terms of the number of pages that each bill took.
20. Rush, *The Role of the Member of Parliament,* pp. 98–105.
21. Richard Carr, 'Veterans of the First World War and Conservative Anti-appeasement', *Twentieth Century British History,* Vol. 22, No. 1, 2011, pp. 28–51, at 31, 34.
22. 'Special report from the Select Committee on Procedure on Public Business', HMSO, London, 1931, p. 142.
23. Arthur Steel-Maitland, 'Autumn Session, 1928', 17 Oct. 1928, Baldwin Papers 59, Cambridge University Library.
24. 'Special report from the Select Committee on Procedure on Public Business', HMSO, London, 1931, p. 329.
25. Daniel J.R. Grey, 'Women's Policy Networks and the Infanticide Act 1922', *Twentieth Century British History,* Vol. 21, No. 4, 2010, pp. 441–63.
26. 'Special report from the Select Committee on Procedure on Public Business', p. 148.
27. Rush, *The Role of the Member of Parliament,* pp. 146–56. Quotation at 146.
28. Frank Gray, *Confessions of a Candidate,* Martin Hopkinson & Co., London, 1925, p. 157.
29. Rush, *The Role of the Member of Parliament,* pp. 140–1.
30. Lord Snell, *Men, Movements and Myself,* J.M. Dent and Sons Ltd., London, 1936, p. 213.
31. There is no evidence that male MPs felt particular new anxieties about dealing with demands from female constituents – perhaps because the women MPs were taking the heat.
32. Jennie Lee, *To-Morrow Is a New Day,* The Cresset Press, London, 1939, p. 128.
33. Percy Harris, *Forty Years In and Out of Parliament,* Andrew Melrose Ltd., London, n.d. (c. 1947), p. 114.
34. 'Thirty-Three Division' [pseudonym], 'Some Thoughts on Electioneering', *The Conservative Agent's Journal,* March 1923.
35. H. Snell, *Daily Life in Parliament,* George Routledge & Sons, Ltd, London, 1930, pp. 65, 67.
36. Hugh Dalton, *Call Back Yesterday: Memoirs 1887–1931,* Frederick Muller Ltd., London, 1953, p. 256.
37. Sandra Harris, 'Being Politically Impolite: Extending Politeness Theory to Adversarial Political Discourse', *Discourse & Society.,* 12.4 (2001): 451–72.
38. Herbert Morrison, *An Autobiography,* Odhams Press Limited, London, 1960, p. 95.
39. Herbert Williams, *Politics – Grave and Gay,* Hutchinson & Co. Ltd., London, 1949, p. 93.
40. Harold Macmillan, *Winds of Change 1914–1939,* Macmillan, London, 1966, p. 156.
41. By contrast, only about 10 % of Labour MPs elected between 1922 and 1935 had gone to public schools, although this in itself marked a sharp increase over the previous era. *Rush, The Role of The Member of Parliament,* pp. 99, 102, 105.

42. John Buchan, *Memory Hold – the Door*, Hodder and Stoughton Ltd, London, 1940, pp. 226–7.
43. Ball accepts, too easily, that Labour MPs' use of 'the devices of platform speaking' in the Commons was a sign of 'ineffectiveness': 'Parliament and Politics': 274.
44. 'Lobby Notes by the new "M.P."', *The Popular View*, December 1922.
45. 'Frightfulness in Parliament', *The Morning Post*, 25 Nov. 1922.
46. John Ramsden notes a similar dichotomy with respect to the first Labour government: 'In 1924 the Unionists were able to have it both ways to quite a remarkable extent: they had only allowed labour into office because they recognized that labour was moderate and would be powerless, but they then set about denouncing the same men as irresponsible and dangerous.' *The Age of Balfour and Baldwin 1902–1940*, Longman, London, 1978, p. 199.
47. *The Popular View*, March 1923.
48. 'Frightfulness in Parliament', *The Morning Post*, 25 Nov. 1922.
49. Transcript of 'Answering You – No. 101', broadcast 28 June 1943, Parliamentary Archives, HC/50/2/4.
50. The other Speakers during the inter-war period were J.W. Lowther (who served from 1905 to 1921) and E.A. Fitzroy (1928–43).
51. Bonar Law to George V, 14 Dec. 1922, Baldwin Papers, 60.
52. Ralph Verney to Lord Hemingford (formerly Dennis Herbert), 5 Jan. 1945, J.H. Whitley Papers, courtesy of the Whitley family.
53. Parliamentary Debates, House of Commons, 5th Series, Vol. 218, 19 June 1928, col. 1597.
54. Ramsay MacDonald diary, May 1923, PRO 30/69/1753, The National Archives, Kew, London (henceforward TNA). All publications quoting these diaries are obliged to explain that MacDonald meant them simply 'as notes to guide and revive memory' and did not intend them to be published.
55. Laura Beers, 'Counter-Toryism: Labour's Response to Anti-Socialist Propaganda', in Matthew Worley (ed.), *The Foundations of the British Labour Party: Identities, Cultures and Perspectives, 1900–39*, Ashgate, Farnham, 2009, pp. 231–54. Quotation at 233.
56. 'Labour Leader's Vision', *The Times*, 3 Dec. 1923.
57. 'How To Get Real Progress', in *Pamphlets and Leaflets for 1919*, Liberal Publication Department, London, 1920.
58. Harrison, 'Women in a Men's House', p. 623.
59. Earl Winterton, *Orders of the Day*, Cassell and Company Ltd., London, 1953, p. 94.
60. Harrison, 'Women in a Men's House', p. 635.
61. Laura Beers, 'A Model MP? Ellen Wilkinson, 'star culture' and the changing boundaries of the political in interwar Britain', forthcoming.
62. For example, John Ramsden, *An Appetite for Power: A History of the Conservative Party Since 1830*, HarperCollins, London, 1998, p. 236.
63. 'Special report from the Select Committee on Procedure on Public Business', p. 328.
64. Churchill, apparently forgetting about Northern Ireland, further remarked that Parliament now consisted 'entirely of British people from this single island'. Ibid., p. 149.
65. J. Ramsay MacDonald, 'The Session', *Forward*, 23 Dec. 1922.
66. Stanley Baldwin to George V, 17 Feb. 1927, Baldwin Papers 62.
67. Bonar Law's letters to the King can be found in the Baldwin Papers, 60; MacDonald's are in TNA PRO 30/69/228.
68. Baldwin to George V, 14 Apr. 1927, Baldwin Papers, 62.

69. Williamson, *Baldwin*, pp. 74–8.
70. Williams, *Politics – Grave and Gay*, p. 107.
71. Patrick Dunleavy and G.W. Jones with Jane Burnham, Robert Elgie and Peter Fysh, 'Leaders, Politics and Insititutional Change: The Decline of Prime Ministerial Accountability to the House of Commons, 1868–1990', in R.A.W. Rhodes and Patrick Dunleavy (eds), *Prime Minister, Cabinet and Core Executive*, St. Martin's Press, Basingstoke, 1995), pp. 275–97.
72. George Strauss, unpublished memoirs, p. 56, George Strauss Papers, Churchill Archives Centre, Cambridge, STRS 1/1.
73. On changing patterns of prime ministerial speech in the later period, see Richard Toye, 'The Rhetorical Premiership: A New Perspective on Prime Ministerial Power Since 1945', *Parliamentary History*, 30 (2011), pp. 175–92.
74. Schmitt, *Crisis of Parliamentary Democracy*, p. 6. Cf. Austen Chamberlain's comment: 'that which in the olden days would have been decided on the floor of the House, and perhaps affected by the trend of the discussion in the House, is now sometimes decided upstairs in a Party meeting or a committee meeting of the Party, which really takes all the life out of the debate, and you merely come down to the House of Commons to register a decision which has been taken upstairs': 'Special report from the Select Committee on Procedure on Public Business', p. 224.
75. Maurice Cowling presents 1920–24 as the decisive period: *The Impact of Labour 1920–1924: The Beginnings of Modern British Politics*, Cambridge University Press, Cambridge, 1971.
76. William Wedgwood Benn diary, 16 May 1922, Stansgate Papers ST 66, Parliamentary Archives.
77. Winston Churchill, 'Parliament is the Stage of Empire Drama', *News of the World*, 1 Jan. 1939, in Michael Wolff (ed.), *The Collected Essays of Sir Winston Churchill*, Vol. II, Library of Imperial History, London, 1976, p. 429.
78. Of course the vote itself – which the government actually won – did not lead directly to the fall of Neville Chamberlain. He could have survived had the Labour leaders decided they were willing to serve under him: Nick Smart, 'Four Days in May: The Norway Debate and the Downfall of Neville Chamberlain', *Parliamentary History*, Vol. 17, no. 2 (1998), pp. 215–43.
79. Philip Norton, 'Winning the War but Losing the Peace: The British House of Commons During the Second World War', *Journal of Legislative Studies*, 4 (1998), pp. 33–51.
80. See Duncan Tanner, 'The Parliamentary Electoral System, the 'Fourth' Reform Act and the Rise of Labour in England and Wales', *Bulletin of the Institute of Historical Research*, 56 (1983), pp. 205–19.
81. Comments of Earl Winterton: 'Special report from the Select Committee on Procedure on Public Business', p. 336. See also the comments of Austen Chamberlain and J.M. Kenworthy: pp. 223, 308.
82. See, for example, the comments of Austen Chamberlain, ibid., p. 224.

5
Enfranchisement, Feminism and the Modern Woman: Debates in the British Popular Press, 1918–1939

Adrian Bingham

'If a future chronicler were to study the files of our newspapers,' speculated the novelist Rose Macaulay in a lecture to the feminist Six Point Group in November 1925, 'he would get the impression that there had appeared at this time a strange new creature called woman who was receiving great attention from the public.'[1] Because 'men insisted on generalising about women', Macaulay noted, newspaper readers were faced with the 'great and increasing nuisance' of articles about women's lives and interests; 'I am,' she lamented, 'always being rung up or written to by some newspaper and asked what my opinion is.' The questions posed by the press ranged from dilemmas in personal lives – 'should clever women marry?' – to the impact of female enfranchisement. '"How will the women vote!" they ask before elections', she observed, identifying too the implication that 'sex formed some kind of bond in the women's political world, and that neither temperament, nor education, nor economic conditions counted for anything.' If too much was written about Woman 'with a capital W', joked Macaulay, 'she may come to life like Frankenstein's monster.'[2]

Examining the newspaper files from the 1920s, the 'future chroniclers' of Macaulay's imagination may not find 'strange new creatures' or 'Frankenstein's monster', but they certainly will not miss the insistent journalistic fascination with modern women and changes in femininity. This endless stream of newspaper articles both reflected and shaped the intense national debates about gender relations in the years after the First World War. Daily newspapers were one of the most successful products of the inter-war period, and moved right to the heart of popular culture in this period: circulation doubled in the twenty years after 1918, and by 1939 some two-thirds of the population regularly saw a daily paper.[3] Newspapers played a significant role in setting the agenda for public and private discussion, and in providing interpretative frameworks through which readers made sense of the world.[4] Newspapers are valuable sources for the gender historian not just because of their cultural significance, but also because the diversity of their contents – covering everything, as Macaulay recognised, from marriage proposals to voting intentions – allows us to trace the interaction of different forms of gendered discourse. This chapter will argue that it is important not to isolate debates about enfranchisement and feminism from broader social and cultural discussions about gender relations; ideas about 'modern women' and the nature of post-war British society significantly influenced perceptions of the political impact of women. As Karen Hunt and June Hannam argue in this volume, we need to be wary of writing parallel histories that over-compartmentalise the different elements of women and men's lives. By placing popular notions of 'modernity' at centre stage, this chapter also challenges the resilient interpretation that the mass media were responsible for fostering an 'ideology of domesticity' in this period as part of a 'backlash' against the apparent advances of the First World War.[5] It will propose a more nuanced argument that the popular press generally came to terms with, and sometimes even enthused about, the developments of modernity, while seeking to blunt the appeal of the more radical and threatening aspects of changes in gender relations, and underplaying the need for further feminist effort.

The chapter is in three sections. It begins by examining how the popular press integrated new female voters into their political discourse. After the heated debates of the Edwardian period, it is striking how quickly and decisively women were brought into the political nation. Newspapers addressed considerable amounts of material – some of it, indeed, featuring explicitly feminist voices – to female readers, and emphasised not only the duties of citizenship but also the power that women now wielded in the political system. The right-wing press, in particular, placed the housewife at the heart of its influential political crusade against inflation, high prices and government 'waste'. Considerable attention was also paid to female candidates, and there were high expectations of the transformative potential of women politicians. The second section argues that the perception that politics had been dramatically changed by female enfranchisement was sustained and reinforced by a wider belief that the Great War had fundamentally reshaped British society, and that an essential feature of this post-war modernity was an inexorable momentum towards equality and the emergence of a more confident and accomplished generation of women. The equalisation of the franchise in 1928 gave a powerful boost to this interpretation. The final section will suggest that this rhetoric of transformation and change disguised the persistence of gendered stereotypes that continued to restrict and limit women's contribution. As Macaulay emphasised, journalists and commentators continued to generalise about women in a way that was unimaginable when writing about men. The notion that female voters and politicians were preoccupied with a set of 'women's issues' was very tenacious. The assumption, moreover, that fundamental change had already occurred in relations between the sexes had a tendency to leave feminism appearing shrill and outdated. The press may have encouraged women to seize new freedoms and exercise their political rights, but it also encouraged the belief that the women's movement was no longer necessary.

Popular newspapers had powerful commercial and political incentives to take female readers and voters seriously. Women made up around 45 per cent of the popular newspaper audience in this period, and they were far more valuable than men as a target for branded advertising.[6] At the same time, papers such as the *Mail* and *Express*, driven on by interventionist proprietors such as Northcliffe, Rothermere and Beaverbrook, actively sought to mobilise readers behind their political campaigns; the new female electorate provided a new, and potentially receptive, audience to convert. Once the suffrage issue was resolved in the early months of 1918, there was a conspicuous desire in Fleet Street to rally behind the decision and to draw a line under previous controversies. A consensus formed around the belief that women 'deserved' the right to vote after their contribution to the 'Home Front', and it was widely accepted that women had a vital role in post-war reconstruction. 'Women demonstrated their right to the privileges of citizenship by the enthusiasm for service that they have shown since the beginning of the war', declared the *Daily Express* on the passage of the Representation of the People Bill through the House of Commons in January 1918.[7] Ten months later, with the war concluded and an election campaign under way, the *Daily Mail* voiced similar sentiments, decisively turning its back on the paper's pre-war opposition to 'votes for women':

> The need for the association of women in the deliberations and governance of national affairs was never greater than now. ... Now that we have admitted and realized the rights of women it seems almost incredible that we should have attempted to touch even the fringe of such problems [of social reform] while more than half of the population were excluded from any share in the management of the nation's affairs.[8]

Nor was there any appetite to reheat the pre-war controversies about female members of Parliament. 'The woman politician will humanise politics,' argued the *Express* in January 1918, 'and her help will be invaluable in the rebuilding that must follow the war.'[9] Another editorial in November suggested that 'No Parliament would be truly representative of the country which did not contain women members.'[10] The *Daily Mirror* also dismissed anxieties about the introduction of female MPs: 'we cannot foresee the end of everything in the admission of women to debates they will already be influencing by their voting capacity'. The paper argued that 'women speakers seem to be remarkable for their lucidity and swiftness', observing that Beatrice Webb, as one example, 'can be quite alarming in the steely beauty of the practical style'.[11] The *Mail* similarly praised Ray Strachey (standing as an independent candidate in the 1918 election) 'as a woman of quick decision' who spoke 'rapidly and eloquently with a telling gift of repartee'.[12] The belief that female politicians would bring a new sensitivity and expertise to welfare questions was such that on polling day, the *Mail* advised undecided voters in constituencies where women were standing that they should vote for them if there was 'any doubt' about the male candidates, 'if only because the new houses for the people have got to be provided and women naturally know more about houses than men'.[13] In the early 1920s, indeed, the *Mail* went one step further by supporting Lady Rhondda's unsuccessful campaign to enable women to enter the House of Lords.[14] 'Since women are now admitted to the House of Commons,' the paper claimed, 'there is obviously no reason – apart from petty litigious obscurities – why they should be excluded from the House of Lords. The one is but a natural consequence of the other.'[15]

During the election campaign of 1918, the press emphasised time and again the importance of women involving themselves in the political process, understanding the issues under discussion, and casting their vote. Popular newspapers saw themselves as having an important role in educating women for citizenship. My content analysis of the final week of the campaign indicates that between one-quarter and one-third of total election coverage in the *Mail*, *Express* and *Mirror* was dedicated to 'women's issues' and female candidates, while in the liberal *Daily News* the proportion was about one-seventh.[16] 'Mind You Vote', insisted an *Express* editorial a week before polling day: 'the *Daily Express* appeals especially to women to vote in force. They now have the privilege; it is for them to show that they realise the responsibility'.[17] 'Vote! Vote!! Vote!!!' implored the women's page of the *Mail*: 'Women Must Do Their Duty Today as Parliamentary Voters'.[18] Several leading members of the women's movement, including Millicent Fawcett, Ray Strachey, Eva Gore-Booth and Marion Phillips, were given a platform to address readers and explain why voting was important; Violet Markham, a noted anti-suffragist who had recanted in time to stand as an Independent Liberal candidate in 1918, was also given space by the *Mail* to encourage women to go to the polling booths: 'We do not want a man-made world or a woman-made world,' she argued, 'but a world to which thoughtful and patriotic citizens of both sexes are making the best possible contribution.'[19] The unity of former opponents behind the wider goal of encouraging women's citizenship powerfully symbolised the emergence of a new age.

There was a similar consensus around the need to persuade women that politics was not abstract and distant, but significantly shaped the realities of everyday life. The *Mail*'s women's page published a message from the National Union of Women's Suffrage Societies (NUWSS) that sought to address women's uncertainties over their new role:

> You feel, perhaps, that politics are something remote, something not women's concern at all. And yet there is no one more concerned than the British woman with the politics of today. For this is what the politics of

today mean - the terms on which women shall be allowed to work, the trades in which they shall work, the wages they shall earn, the education that shall be given to their children...[20]

Ray Strachey, also writing in the *Mail*, insisted that 'Politics are not really dull', explaining that they affected 'what kind of a house you live in, what kind of food you can buy and at what price, what kind of work and pay you or your menfolk get, what kind of schools your children can go to'.[21] The authors of the *Mail's* Labour column[22] similarly sought to counter the perception among some women 'that the things done in Parliament do not concern them, and so they are not going to bother about the election'. On polling day itself, the *Express* invited veteran suffrage campaigner Millicent Fawcett to address female readers: 'Remember you are voting for your work, your wages, the education of your children, the guardianship laws that concern them, for your homes, for your citizenship. And then do not hesitate, but Go To The Poll!'[23] Politics was consistently translated into the language of the domestic and the familial in a bid to reach women perceived to be immune to appeals to party or national interest.

Newspapers even began to compete on the quality of their election coverage for female readers and their editorial attentiveness to issues facing women. The liberal *Daily News* capitalised on its long history of support for the suffrage movement by including a daily advert that proclaimed it was 'The Paper that said women must have the vote, and the Paper that the woman voter must have.'[24] Having been a 'consistent advocate of the elimination of sex discriminations from the sphere of political life', an editorial declared 'profound satisfaction' at the 'achievement of this great reform on the eve of the new era which lies before this country and the world'.[25] The *Mirror's* history, by contrast, was one of opposition to enfranchisement, but it now turned a fresh page and gave a high profile to election appeals to women; it prominently advertised the editor's 'special article' on 'Why Women Should Support Mr Lloyd George' in rival paper the *Express*.[26] The *Mirror* promised that henceforth its political writing for women would be expansive and inclusive, because 'the great human, personal and national interests, the things that matter, the deeper issues of life, touch the two sexes equally, and concern them both'.[27] Such promises were rarely honoured, of course, because the notion of separate gendered interests was much too firmly entrenched; they did, however, testify to the editorial desire to find ways of appealing to the female audience. The *Daily Express* meanwhile, publicised telegrams of support the paper had received from female parliamentary candidates for its scheme offering its advertising columns free of charge to women war workers seeking alternative employment.[28] The *Mail*, for its part, gave strong backing to Lloyd George's call for 'complete sex equality', and in particular supported the women's movement campaign for equal pay. This demand, an editorial noted, was made with 'complete justification. ... Really equal pay for really equal work is unanswerable'.[29] Fleet Street's battle to appeal to this significant body of new and potentially uncommitted female voters had the effect of pushing women's issues up the political agenda.

Once polling had been completed in 1918, the popular press was, moreover, keen to celebrate the diligence and maturity of the new voters. The overall turnout, at 58.9 per cent, may have been disappointing but women were conspicuously excluded from any blame. 'Not even the most ardent women suffragists... anticipated such a remarkable demonstration of women's interest in their new prerogative,' declared the *Express*: 'While the men were apathetic, the women turned out everywhere.'[30] The *Mirror* agreed: 'This election has been marked by a great number of abstentions: not amongst the women. The women voted.'[31] 'Two facts stand out from the polling' observed the *Mail*. 'First the public apathy; second the great strength of the women's vote...nearly as many women voted as men.'[32] The inclusion of women into the political system appeared to have been a resounding success – and as a *Mail* editorial shortly before the election noted, the gloomy predictions of the anti-suffragists had proved to be wide of the mark: 'Those good if slightly out-of-date politicians who used to paint lurid pictures of a world which included women voters may be relieved to know that the worst results they anticipated seem quite unlikely to be realised.'[33] The salient phrase here was 'out-of-date': in this post-war modernity the denial of citizenship to women seemed entirely anachronistic.

The journalistic preoccupation with female voter in 1918 was unusually intense, underpinned as it was by the obvious news value of women visiting the polling booths for the first time; unsurprisingly, the coverage of 'women's issues' was not as extensive in subsequent elections in the inter-war period.[34] Yet the efforts to integrate women into the political realm were by no means restricted to the noise and drama of election campaigns. Women's pages periodically lifted their horizons from the usual diet of fashion, housewifery and childcare advice to extol the virtues of public engagement. 'Learning To Be Citizens – A Matter of Importance' declared a headline on the *Mail* women's page in September 1919, above an article insisting that 'no woman should forget that whether her sphere be compassed by the office or the home, she has wider interests because she is also a citizen'.[35] Three months later, the *Mail* invited Ray Strachey – 'whose knowledge of politics' was described by the paper as being 'probably greater than that of any woman in Great Britain' – to write a series of weekly articles on 'Womanly Politics'. 'Everyone who has a vote ought to think and know about politics,' she wrote, 'but for a woman it is doubly necessary to do this because we have to train up the next generation of voters as well. That is why current politics is woman's job, and why it is possible to call politics "womanly".'[36] Strachey's column touched on a wide range of issues ranging from the everyday (such as housing, and the price of milk and coal) to questions of imperial reform in India and Ireland.[37] Such features became less common after the early

1920s as female voters increasingly became an accepted part of the political landscape, but they did further encourage women to embrace citizenship.

Perhaps more significant in emphasising the changed nature of politics were the attempts to mobilise women behind high-profile campaigns. Karen Hunt has discussed how some socialist publications before and during the First World War attempted – with limited success – to create a space for a gendered politics of consumption.[38] In many respects it proved easier for conservative newspapers such as the *Mail*, the *Mirror* and the *Express*, already characterised by an ethos of consumerism and an emphasis on the domestic, to pose as the champion of the housewife in the political sphere.[39] The *Mail* and the *Mirror*, in particular, idealised the housewife as a citizen-consumer whose preoccupation with living-standards and domestic efficiency made her a 'natural' opponent of government 'squandermania'. In February 1920, for example, the *Mail* printed letters describing the 'widespread anxiety and alarm felt by women at the continued rise in prices'. 'Many women ask us what they are to do', the paper noted. 'They have enormous power; of the 21, 392,000 voters in this country no fewer than 8,479,000 are women. Let them use this power.' The 'best and most practical way' of exercising this power was declared to be writing to MPs: 'Government extravagance is the first cause of high prices. ... Women should, then, make Government economy the first plank in their campaign.'[40] The *Mail* suggested a form of words that women could use on postcards or letters.[41]

The following year the *Mirror* and its sister paper, the *Sunday Pictorial*, took the campaign a step further by forming an Anti-Waste League and supporting candidates at by-elections. The dramatic successes of Anti-Waste candidates at Dover in January 1921 and at Westminster in June were widely assumed to be a demonstration of the power of the female voter.[42] The *Mirror* missed few opportunities to develop its gendered political rhetoric. 'The old political parties never took the smallest heed of the women's point of view', wrote Rothermere, the paper's proprietor, in a signed article in August 1921. By contrast, he proclaimed, 'from the very start women and the votes of women have been the mainstay of the Anti-Waste League!' Women

> wanted to know why prices were so high, why rates and taxes were so crushing, why the husbands of so many could not get work, why they were feeling the pinch so much after a glorious victory. In the propaganda of the Anti-Waste League the women electors found the answer to their inquiries.[43]

The anti-waste crusade fizzled out when Lloyd-George's Coalition Government reacted by forming the Geddes committee to identify severe cost-cutting measures, but by then it has already made a significant political impact, reinforcing the perception that women could have a decisive electoral impact even before the equalisation of the franchise.[44]

In the early 1930s, the housewife also became a central figure in the *Mail* and the *Express*'s joint 'Empire Free Trade' campaign to create an imperial trading zone protected by tariffs.[45] The papers suggested that the shopping choices of ordinary housewives had a direct and immediate impact on the domestic and international economy. By buying British or imperial goods, and spending what they could afford rather than saving, women could lubricate the wheels of the nation's faltering economy:

> There is no actual tariff yet. But at all costs she must, wherever possible, buy British, thus setting up an imaginary tariff wall for herself. ... Every woman should spend as much as she can afford, always remembering, however, that every pound expended on foreign scents, cosmetics and clothes is contributing to a trade balance that is already weighted against her country.[46]

'Buying British', moreover, entailed no real sacrifice: 'there are opportunities in every shop for each purchase to be a British article at a price no greater, when quality is compared, than the price of a similar article made abroad'.[47] The needs of the family and the nation were not, of course, contradictory for the patriotic *Mail* and *Express*. Just as the press translated political debates into the language of everyday life, so too did they try to render meaningful the economic problems of the depression. If women were to be encouraged to spend their money in particular ways, the underlying reasons needed to be made clear. Articles therefore explained 'What the Stable Pound Means to the Housewife' in 'commonsensical' terms, underlining that it was far more than 'a mysterious happening connected with high finance'.[48] The popular press, in short, both shaped and reinforced the consumer politics that, as David Thackeray demonstrates in this volume, was becoming increasingly central to party campaigning during the inter-war period.

Both during and between elections, then, the popular press encouraged female voters to take politics and citizenship seriously. This involved persuasion as much as education, and this kind of popular political journalism could be viewed as nothing more than the cynical output of papers seeking to secure the support of female readers for particular political agendas. Journalists often spoke for readers without listening to their voices, or listening only to those voices they wanted to hear. But there were few disinterested parties in the political sphere, and popular newspapers did not try to disguise their political affiliations. For many people in the inter-war period, moreover, the daily newspaper reading habit was a new one, and the press was exposing some of its audience to regular political debate for the first time. Indeed, given its attempts to demonstrate how politics affected the lives and well-being of ordinary women, it would not be unreasonable to place the popular press alongside a range of mainstream women's organisations, including the Women's Institutes and the Mothers' Union, who shied away from 'feminism' but played a significant role in encouraging women to embrace their citizenship.[49]

As Macaulay noted in her speech to the Six Point Group, assessments of the impact of female voters made up only a one strand of much broader public debate about modern women and gender relations in the 1920s. We cannot fully understand these political assessments without placing them in this wider context and examining contemporary beliefs about the nature of this post-war modernity. In the years after 1918, and particularly after the Sex Disqualification (Removal) Act of 1919, newspapers were filled with stories about women's 'firsts', as women moved into new public and professional roles. These reports were usually accompanied by grand proclamations about the significance of women's first steps. 'The empanelment of women jurors... is another long stride towards civic equality with men', declared the *Daily Mail* in January 1921; 'the last traces of women's long dependence are quickly wearing off with increasing practice in public life'.[50] When, the following year, Ivy Williams was called to the Inner Temple as the first female barrister, the *Mail* observed that 'the changed status of women in regard to public affairs grows more marked every day...women are finding more and more useful public work they can perform in their changed status'.[51] Voting was only one aspect of women's new role in British public life, and evidence of these fresh opportunities was presented in newspapers on an almost daily basis.

This process affected far more than the serious business of public affairs: women appeared to be demonstrating their abilities in a wide range of fields. Pioneering sportswomen, channel swimmers, and aviators, such as Suzanne Lenglen, Gertrude Ederle and Amy Johnson, received considerable publicity from popular newspapers and were held up as models of a new athleticism and bravery. The press also displayed an intense interest in the new fashions, hairstyles and body shapes of the 1920s, which all seemed to express a rejection of the fussiness and restrictiveness of Victorian clothing. Countless photographs and cartoons of the flapper's short hair and slim silhouette gave repeated visual reminders of this apparent break with the past.[52] All of this material reinforced the widely held perception that gender relations had been transformed by the war and a new generation of more assertive women was emerging. Ellen Wilkinson, the Labour MP, noted in 1931 that 'women doing startling new things fill the papers until one begins to wonder if men are doing anything at all... [women are]apparently beating men at their own games all along the line...the impression gets about that all England's women are barristers, or aeronauts or crack channel swimmers'.[53]

If the recent war marked a fundamental rupture with Victorianism, the future seemed to offer the prospect of an inexorable movement towards greater equality. In 1926, the *Daily Mail* asked the engineer and inventor 'Professor' A. M. Low to predict 'Our Lives in 1950'; he forecast that

> The next twenty years will undoubtedly see a great advance in the position of women. With the gradual erosion of physical disabilities I do not believe that women will trouble to stay at home. ...Women will cease to expect the suggestion of protection.[54]

Similar predictions were made when a newspaper dated 1 January 2000 was produced for the *Mail*'s Ideal Home Exhibition in 1928. The sports pages of this millennium edition reported that a woman had knocked out the male champion boxer, and described the tremendous shock when a British man overcame the top female French tennis player.[55] Two years later the *Manchester Evening News* quipped that 'Before long we shall probably see a girl bowler dealing with Bradman.'[56] 'There is little doubt that fifty years will see women almost completely supreme in most things', claimed a contributor to the *Daily Herald*'s women's page in 1933. 'One only has to keep one's eyes and ears open to see evidence of this wherever one goes.'[57] This narrative of progress was influential across the spectrum of the press.

These assumptions about the momentum towards greater equality helped to shape political discourse throughout the 1920s, and into the 1930s. Newspaper commentaries frequently focused on the potential power of female voters and MPs, and raised expectations that women would transform the political system. Even in 1918, when male voters still constituted a clear majority of the electorate, commentators suggested that women might be 'a decisive factor' and that 'the election will turn largely upon the women's votes'.[58] There were also predictions that women would dominate men in the Commons. The *Mirror* published a cartoon in which the Houses of Parliament were reduced to a cradle and screaming politician-children were admonished by a giant mother figure. 'There appears to be some fear amongst male politicians,' observed the caption wryly, 'that their feminine rivals will completely control them.'[59] When Nancy Astor was elected to the House of Commons in November 1919, there were predictions of a flurry of further female entrants. Having won the 'confidence of the public' during the war by proving their 'gifts of intellect, energy and courage', the *Mail* anticipated 'a large increase in the number of women members, where there is so much legislative work for which they are peculiarly qualified waiting for them to do'.[60] It is perhaps unsurprising that the 1928 Ideal Home Exhibition's paper for 2000 predicted that Britain would have a female prime minister.[61]

The equalisation of the franchise lent further credibility to this progress narrative. When the Prime Minister, Stanley Baldwin, pledged in June 1924 to lower the female voting age to 21, the *Mail* predicted a dramatic increase in the political influence of women:

> If the women use their power (and they may gradually come to do so) they can dominate the state and control all its departments. They will almost certainly claim in the immediate future a much larger proportion of appointments, so that men will be steadily dislodged.[62]

The equalisation was eventually accepted as inevitable by most newspapers, but, as is widely known, it was vehemently opposed by the *Daily Mail* and the *Daily Mirror*. This 'Flapper Vote' campaign was not representative of press political discourse in this period, and, as I have argued at length elsewhere, the dominant motivation for the campaign was not anti-feminism, but the rabid anti-socialism of the papers' idiosyncratic proprietor, Lord Rothermere.[63] Examining the rhetoric of the 'flapper vote crusade', it is clear that the prospective voters were regarded with suspicion not so much because they were women, but because they were young, likely to be employed, and therefore susceptible to propaganda from unions and the labour movement: 'The case against Votes for Flappers,' argued that *Mail*, 'is really to be compressed into this: that Socialists are convinced such a measure will place them in power for many years.'[64] For present purposes, though, more significant than the *Mail* and *Mirror*'s opposition was the way in which the equalisation of the franchise reinforced assumptions about the momentum towards gender equality and encouraged a renewed emphasis on women's political power. The fact that female voters outnumbered male voters was a constant theme of the coverage of the next general election in 1929; headlines and cartoons repeatedly speculated about the political impact of young women. It was easy for commentators to portray equalisation as a culmination of women's progress since the war. During the war, observed an editorial in the *Express*, it was clear that 'there was nothing in the way of sacrifice, hardship, endurance that the young women of Great Britain would not gladly meet for their country's sake':

> The type has not altered since then. The younger generation is just as splendid. ...Our conviction is firm that they value the privilege which has been extended to them, and that they will use it intelligently, with more independence and with a greater sense of responsibility than accompanies most men when they enter a polling booth.[65]

The 1929 election was perhaps the high point of this emphasis on the power of the female voter, but similar observations continued to be made throughout the 1930s. On the day of the general election in November 1935, for example, the *Daily Mirror*'s main feature article, by regular contributor Ursula Bloom, was headlined 'Women! Today It's Up To You!': 'This is a woman's election. Its trend will be decided by women and its canvassing has been very largely accomplished by women. Women's influence is enormous...the future lies in her hands.'[66] In the *Daily Mail*, meanwhile, a political correspondent was adamant that women were more active citizens than men: 'women are taking more interest in this election than men. ...Women are asking more intelligent questions than men....There are more volunteer women workers at the committee rooms than men.'[67] As Julie Gottlieb observes in Chapter 9 in this volume, moreover, peace-seeking female voters were often perceived to be a decisive force in the by-elections held in the wake of the Munich crisis in 1938. Two decades after enfranchisement, commentators continued to portray women as a coherent electoral force, poised on the verge of transforming the political system.

Popular papers did, then, make genuine efforts to include women in their political discourse, and repeatedly emphasised the rights and responsibility of citizenship to their female. The *Mail* and *Mirror*'s hostility to women's political participation demonstrated in the 'Flapper Vote' campaign was by no means typical. Yet at a deeper level there were still a variety of assumptions and silences that worked to limit and restrict the female voter. Most obvious was the resilience of the idea of 'women's issues'; popular journalists across the period, as Macaulay noted in 1925, found it difficult to escape the notion that women's voting priorities were determined by their shared sex. Favoured stereotypes did vary slightly according to political disposition. The right-wing papers, the *Mail*, the *Express*, and (until the mid-1930s) the *Mirror*, placed the image of the cautious 'domestic chancellor' at the heart of their political discourse. The housewife, responsible for family expenditure, was portrayed as seeking above all low prices, low taxes, and economic stability: these were the essential preconditions for maintaining a decent standard of living. On the left, the rhetorical strategy was usually based around the 'compassionate mother', whose overriding concern was for the health of her family and the prospects of her children. From this perspective, 'women' wanted constructive reforms such as better housing, welfare benefits, and improved education. Female politicians found it difficult to escape similar stereotypes about the issues on which they would speak or show particular expertise. As Laura Beers has noted, moreover, the press scrutinised the appearance and personal lives of female MPs far more intensely than their male counterparts.[68] Mary Agnes Hamilton, Labour MP for Blackburn between 1929 and 1931, lamented in 1932 that 'Women MPs get an immense publicity, not for their work, but for their clothes, their hobbies, their husbands, any and every extraneous thing they do.'[69] Such coverage inevitably made it more difficult for women to appear as serious political figures, although some, such as Ellen Wilkinson, sought to use this press interest positively by diverting it towards their own campaigns.[70]

Repeatedly associating women with a particular set of issues inevitably suggested that other topics were not so relevant to women or so amenable to 'women's understanding'. 'She may not particularly care whether we sign a treaty with Albania or not because the whole thing is too distant,' argued Morton Wallace in the *Mirror*, 'but every housewife cares very considerably whether the price of sugar is to be 2d. per pound cheaper or not.'[71] Important questions of fiscal strategy, industrial policy, and union legislation, for example, were frequently regarded as of little interest to women, and even when they were presented to female readers it was often in such a way as to reinforce this political 'separation of spheres'. Such topics were reduced to practicalities as quickly as possible, and there was little encouragement for women seeking a more sustained analysis.

This reflected a deeper scepticism about women's interest in politics. Journalists seeking to appeal to the new female voters constantly struggled against powerful Fleet Street voices doubtful of the value of such material. Discussing the make-up of the *Express* in a letter to Beaverbrook in 1932, Beverley Baxter, the editor, accepted that 'the most important thing about the *Daily Express* is its political policy and especially its Empire policy'. Nevertheless, he continued 'it is essential that we maintain our hold upon the general public, and we would be foolish if we failed to realise that not one woman in a hundred reads political, financial or industrial news'.[72] For that reason, he argued, every effort had to be made to ensure that 'heavy' material was not too prominent, and that women's other interests were adequately catered for. Looking at the inter-war popular press as a whole, Robert Ensor, an experienced leader-writer himself (and later historian) believed that similar calculations had been made across Fleet Street. Editors analysing circulation results, he claimed in 1947, had concluded that

> women (in the mass that is) have no day-by-day interest in politics. They will not patronise a paper that obtrudes much serious politics upon them. They have very little interest in doctrines, arguments or serious specula-tions of any kind. ...Women's concern is not with ideas or principles, but with persons and things.[73]

Readership surveys from the 1930s onwards supported these anecdotal impressions. Research carried out by the London Press Exchange for the *News Chronicle* in 1934 found that while parliamentary and domestic news reports had a strong appeal for a significant proportion of male readers, they were less popular with women.[74] Political and Economic Planning's *Report* in 1938 presented evidence that women newspaper readers displayed a 'lack of interest in public affairs', while Mass Observation noted more than once the different levels of interest in political reports displayed by men and women.[75] It was perhaps not surprising that as this commercial evidence accumulated in the 1930s, and as the journalistic interest in the new female voters faded, the amount of political material directed specifically at women declined, and politics disappeared almost entirely from the women's pages themselves. From the mid-1930s, indeed, the most serious and challeng-ing women's page of all, that in the *Manchester Guardian* under Madeline Linford, reduced its political coverage.[76] Few journalists were prepared to think critically about the reasons for women's apparent lack of interest in the political reporting they were providing.

At the same time, the press narrative of modernity and female progress distorted the realities of inter-war society. Women's 'firsts' were news and were treated as such, yet thereafter women's experiences rarely hit the head-lines. Popular newspapers tended, then as now, to concentrate on concrete happenings and the particular achievements of individuals: this fulfilled the requirements of 'human interest'. More general, structural issues of progress and prejudice were much less easy to fit into the popular format. The exceptional difficulties that faced women entering these new spheres, or the frustrations of those who failed to break into their chosen field, were not usually pursued. As a result, the number of women who overcame the obstacles in front of them was repeatedly overestimated.

These tendencies did not help a feminist movement seeking to mobilise support for the continuation of the campaign to improve the position of women. The popular press was by no means consistently hostile to feminism, especially as espoused by relatively moderate figures such as Eleanor Rathbone.[77] Ray Strachey, Lady Rhondda, Vera Brittain, and Winifred Holtby were all fairly regular contributors to popular newspapers. Leading figures from the pre-war suffrage campaign were treated much more positively than they had been at the time. A serialisation of Christabel Pankhurst's memoirs ran for over three months in the *Weekly Dispatch* in 1921, and Emmeline Pankhurst was generously commemorated on her death in 1928.[78] But the women's movement struggled against being stereotyped as 'old news' and found it more difficult to capture headlines now that it was attempting to remedy broad and complex problems of social and economic inequality rather than the obvious injustice of exclusion from the franchise. While conservative papers could be sympathetic to moderate 'new feminist' proposals focusing on marriage and motherhood, they were far less amenable to the more challenging egalitarian agenda. The language of 'rights' was an uncomfortable one: the *Mirror* wrote of its frustration at continuing feminist references to the battle for 'those silly old rights we've heard so much about'.[79] The *Express* praised the Federation of Women's Institutes because 'it speaks with a woman's voice and works in a woman's way'; it 'has no bone to pick, and has no "cause" to make its voice strident'.[80] In the 1930s feminist attempts to resuscitate the question of equal pay, for example, received only very occasional coverage. Significant challenges to the status quo were typically presented as sectional and divisive, especially in times of economic dislocation.

The discourse of modernity encouraged the perception that changes were happening quickly enough as a result of the 'emancipation' brought by war, and journalists suggested that women now had the political power to remedy grievances themselves without the aid of 'crusading' organizations. The massive social and cultural obstacles that remained in the path of women all too often lay obscured. Reviewing advances up to the beginning of 1927, for example, the *Daily Mail*'s women's page could declare that 'a casual person asked about women's achievements in the past year might think the position analogous to Alexander – "no new fields left to conquer"'. It noted that men 'are beginning to talk of the necessity for real sex equality, or, at least, a Men's Rights Defence League'.[81] When the feminist and musician Dame Ethel Smyth claimed the following year that women were still not competing on equal terms with men, James Douglas of the *Express* accused her of suffering from 'conspiracy mania': men would, he argued, 'in the new era of equal opportunity for both sexes hold their own against women only by being better at their job'.[82] Similarly, a contributor to the *Mirror* claimed in 1929 that 'Women are already equal with men. They have the right to work, the right to own property, and the right of political action. We can be fairly sure that what they want, they will get.'[83]

Such attitudes made it difficult for the feminist movement to continue to justify its existence and draw attention to issues of inequality. Vera Brittain commented that some elements of press opinion could be 'gently patronising, lightly chaffing those women who share in feminist activities, and jocosely suggesting that their enthusiasm is just a bit behind the times'. Some journalists believed, she thought, that 'feminism is merely hysterical, since it is now quite unnecessary'.[84] By presenting modern young women almost as if they were, as Macaulay suggested, a new species, newspapers raised the prospect that they were free from the accumulated prejudices and inequalities of the past. Wiser voices knew that there were still many battles yet to be fought.

It is difficult to disagree with Laura Beers's recent assertion that '[w]hile women were now technically included as members of the political nation, the media represented and appealed to them as unequal citizens'.[85] Stereotypes about 'women's interests' remained firmly entrenched, and female politicians and feminists often struggled to get their opinions, rather than their fashions, noticed by the press. If, as Lady Rhondda claimed, the 'real task of feminism' after the war was to 'wipe out the overemphasis on sex that is the fruit if the age-long subjection of women', there was still much work to do.[86] Yet, as Pat Thane has observed, 'there is a danger of measuring the impact of vote by impossible standards'.[87] It is hardly surprising that such long-standing patterns of gendered thought were not eroded quickly. The persistence of these stereotypes should not obscure the real shifts in political discourse brought about by enfranchisement and the desire to appeal to the new female voters. The popular press played an important role in the relatively smooth integration of women into the political system, and contributed to a wider political effort to emphasise the value of female citizenship. Against an international backdrop in which democracy was under severe threat, the value of such support for political participation should not be underestimated. 'Women as News' may have been, as Macaulay complained, a 'nuisance' in the 1920s, but it was still probably better than being ignored altogether.

Notes

1. *Manchester Guardian*, 13 Nov. 1925, cited in *The Guardian Century: The Twenties* (London: The Guardian, 1999), p. 5.
2. Ibid.

3. G. Harrison with F. C. Mitchell and M. A. Abrams, *The Home Market* (London: G. Allen & Unwin, 1939), ch. 21; A.P. Wadsworth, 'Newspaper Circulations 1800–1954', *Manchester Statistical Society Transactions*, 4, Session 1954–55; C. Seymour-Ure, 'The Press and the Party System between the Wars', in G. Peele and C. Cook (eds), *The Politics Of Reappraisal* (London: Macmillan, 1975), pp. 233–9; T. Jeffery and K. McClelland, 'A World Fit to Live In: The *Daily Mail* and the Middle Classes 1918–39' in J. Curran, A. Smith and P. Wingate (eds), *Impacts and Influences: Essays on Media Power in the Twentieth Century* (London: Methuen, 1987), pp. 28–39.

4. On the significance of the press in British culture, see A. Bingham, *Family Newspapers? Sex, Private Life, and the British Popular Press, 1918–78* (Oxford: Oxford University Press, 2009), pp. 15–28. For a useful summary of agenda-setting and interpretative frameworks, see C. McCullagh, *Media Power: A Sociological Introduction*, (Basingstoke: Palgrave, 2002).

5. See, for example, B. Melman, *Women and the Popular Imagination in the Twenties: Flappers and Nymphs* (Basingstoke: Macmillan, 1988); D. Beddoe, *Back to Home and Duty: Women Between the Wars 1918–39* (London: Pandora, 1989), p. 8; M. Pugh, *Women and the Women's Movement 1914–59* (Basingstoke: Macmillan, 1992), chs 4, 7; C. Law, *Suffrage and Power: The Women's Movement 1918–28* (London: I.B. Tauris, 1997), p. 205; S. Bruley, *Women in Britain since 1900* (Basingstoke: Macmillan, 1999), p. 62.

6. See A. Bingham, *Gender, Modernity and the Popular Press in Inter-War Britain* (Oxford: Oxford University Press, 2004), ch. 1.

7. *Daily Express*, 11 Jan. 1918, p. 2.

8. *Daily Mail*, 26 Nov. 1918, p. 2.

9. *Daily Express*, 11 Jan. 1918, p. 2.

10. *Daily Express*, 28 Nov. 1918, p. 4.

11. *Daily Mirror*, 23 Oct. 1918, p. 6.

12. *Daily Mail*, 13 Dec. 1918, p. 6.

13. *Daily Mail*, 14 Dec. 1918, p. 4.

14. Women were finally admitted to the House of Lords in 1958, the year that Lady Rhondda died.

15. *Daily Mail*, 3 Mar. 1922, p. 8.

16. For the figures, see Bingham, *Gender*, p. 125.

17. *Daily Express*, 7 Dec. 1918, p. 4.

18. *Daily Mail*, 14 Dec. 1918, p. 7.

19. *Daily Mail*, 12 Dec. 1919, p. 7.

20. *Daily Mail*, 7 Dec. 1918, p. 7.

21. *Daily Mail*, 13 Dec. 1918, p. 7.

22. Northcliffe donated a daily column in the *Mail* to the Labour party to compensate for its lack of press representation: the *Herald* could only afford to publish weekly during the war until March 1919.

23. *Daily Express*, 14 Dec. 1918, p. 1.

24. *Daily News*, 30 Nov. 1918, p. 4.

25. *Daily News*, 10 Dec. 1918, p. 4.

26. *Daily Express*, 9 Dec. 1918, p. 2.

27. *Daily Mirror*, 10 Dec. 1918, p. 7.

28. *Daily Express*, 9 Dec. 1918, p. 5; 10 Dec. 1918, p. 1.

29. *Daily Mail*, 10 Dec. 1918, p. 4.

30. *Daily Express*, 16 Dec. 1918, p. 7.

31. *Daily Mirror*, 31 Dec. 1918, p. 5.
32. *Daily Mail*, 16 Dec. 1918, p. 5.
33. *Daily Mail*, 4 Dec. 1918, p. 4.
34. For figures on the press coverage of later elections see Bingham, *Gender*, p. 125. There was a noticeable spike in coverage in 1929, when women for the first time voted on the same terms as men.
35. *Daily Mail*, 11 Sept. 1919, p. 9.
36. *Daily Mail*, 1 Dec. 1919, p. 15.
37. *Daily Mail*, 8 Dec. 1919, p. 15; 15 Dec. 1919, p. 15; 22 Dec. 1918, p. 9; 29 Dec. 1918, p. 9.
38. Karen Hunt, 'Negotiating the boundaries of the domestic: British socialist women and the politics of consumption', *Women's History Review*, 9/2 (2000), pp. 389–410.
39. Bingham, *Gender*, ch. 3.
40. *Daily Mail*, 23 Feb. 1920, p. 6.
41. Ibid., p. 7.
42. K. Morgan, *Consensus and Disunity: The Lloyd George Coalition Government 1918–1922* (Oxford: Oxford University Press, 1986), p. 154.
43. *Daily Mirror*, 24 August 1921, p. 5.
44. Morgan, *Consensus and Disunity*, pp. 244–6.
45. On the Empire Free Trade campaign see A. Chisholm and M. Davie, *Beaverbrook: A Life* (London: Hutchinson, 1992), chs 14–15.
46. *Daily Mail*, 18 Sept. 1931, p. 10.
47. *Daily Mail*, 25 Sept. 1931, p. 5.
48. *Daily Mail*, 9 Sept. 1931, p. 7.
49. On these mainstream organizations, see C. Beaumont, 'Citizens not Feminists: The Boundary Negotiated between Citizenship and Feminism by Mainstream Women's Organisations in England, 1928–39', *Women's History Review*, 9/2, 2000, pp. 411–29.
50. *Daily Mail*, 12 Jan. 1921, p. 6.
51. *Daily Mail*, 9 May 1922, p. 8.
52. See Bingham, *Gender*, chs 2, 5.
53. *Daily Mail*, 19 May 1931, p. 10.
54. *Daily Mail*, 1 March 1927, p. 10.
55. *Daily Mail*, 2 Apr. 1928, p. 10.
56. *Manchester Evening News*, 21 July 1930, p. 4, cited in C. Langhamer, *Women's Leisure in England, 1920–1960* (Manchester: Manchester University Press, 2000), p. 55.
57. *Daily Herald*, 21 Oct. 1933, p. 5.
58. *Daily News*, 29 Nov. 1918, p. 6; 30 Nov. 1918, p. 4.
59. *Daily Mirror*, 30 Nov. 1918, p. 5.
60. *Daily Mail*, 2 Dec. 1919, p. 6.
61. *Daily Mail*, 2 Apr. 1928, p. 10.
62. *Daily Mail*, 4 June 1924, p. 6.
63. A. Bingham, '"Stop the Flapper Vote Folly": Rothermere, the *Daily Mail* and the Equalisation of the Franchise 1927–28', *Twentieth Century British History*, 13/1, (2002), pp. 17–37.
64. *Daily Mail*, 27 Apr. 1927, p. 10.
65. *Daily Express*, 23 May 1929, p. 10.
66. *Daily Mirror*, 14 Nov. 1935, p. 10.
67. *Daily Mail*, 14 Nov. 1935, p. 9.

68. L. Beers, '"A timid disbelief in the equality to which lip-service is constantly paid': gender, politics and the press between the wars', in L. Beers and G. Thomas (eds), *Brave New World: Imperial and Democratic Nation-building in Britain between the Wars* (London: Institute of Historical Research, 2012), pp. 129–48.
69. Cited in ibid., p. 145.
70. Ibid. pp. 143–7.
71. *Daily Mirror*, 29 Oct. 1924, p. 5.
72. House of Lords Record Office, Beaverbrook Papers, H/91, Beverley Baxter to Beaverbrook, 5 Jan. 1932.
73. R.C.K. Ensor, 'The Press', in Sir Ernest Barker, (ed.), *The Character of England* (Oxford: Clarendon Press, 1947), pp. 418–19.
74. J. Curran, A. Douglas, and G. Whannel, 'The Political Economy of the Human-Interest Story', in A. Smith, (ed.), *Newspapers and Democracy: International Essays on a Changing Medium* (Cambridge, Mass.: MIT Press, 1980), pp. 294, 318–19.
75. Political and Economic Planning, *Report on the Press* (London, 1938), p. 250; Bodleian Library, Oxford, X. Films 200, Mass Observation, File Report A11, 'Motives and Methods of Newspaper Reading'; Dec. 1938, p. 15; File Report 126, 'Report on the Press', May 1940, p. 4; File Report 1339, 'Report on *Daily Express* Readership', June 1942, p. 18.
76. M. Stott (ed.), *Women Talking: An Anthology from the Guardian Women's Page* (London: Pandora, 1987), p. xv.
77. In 1931, for example, the *Daily Mail* supported two measures put forward by the women's movement, namely Eleanor Rathbone's bill to improve the situation of widows by preventing disinheritance, and international proposals to amend the nationality legislation for the benefit of married women: *Daily Mail*, 24 Mar. 1931, p. 10; 25 Mar. 1931, pp. 11; 25 May 1931, pp. 8–9. The *Daily News* and the *Daily Herald*, meanwhile, frequently carried reports of the activities of organizations such as the National Union of Societies for Equal Citizenship and the Women's Cooperative Guild.
78. *Weekly Dispatch*, 6 March 1921, p. 1, and subsequent editions into June; *Daily Mirror*, 19 June 1928, p. 20; *Daily Mail*, 29 May 1929, p. 8.
79. *Daily Mirror*, 19 June 1935, p. 11.
80. *Daily Express*, 15 May 1929, p. 3.
81. *Daily Mail*, 1 Jan. 1927, p. 15.
82. *Daily Express*, 17 Mar. 1928, p. 8.
83. *Daily Mirror*, 23 May 1929, p. 11.
84. V. Brittain, *Why Feminism Lives* (London, 1927), cited in P. Berry and A. Bishop, (eds), *Testament of a Generation: The Journalism of Vera Brittain and Winifred Holtby* (London: Virago, 1985), p. 97.
85. Beers, 'A timid disbelief', p. 130.
86. Cited in P. Thane, 'What Difference did the Vote Make?' in A. Vickery (ed.), *Women, Privilege and Politics* (Stanford, Calif: Stanford University Press, 2001), p. 255.
87. Ibid., p. 254.

6
'Doing Great Public Work Privately': Female Antis in the Interwar Years[1]

Philippe Vervaecke

'The last lap of the Suffrage struggle was rather too much for me. (...) Now the question is what the women will do with their vote', Mary Ward wrote to her formerly anti-suffragist, by then staunch suffragist, friend Mrs Creighton a few months after the enfranchisement of women. In January 1918, Lord Curzon, both leader of the National League for Opposing Women's Suffrage (NLOWS) and of the House of Lords, had indeed failed to sway the votes of his fellow Peers in January 1918, much to Ward's dismay. The weariness one notices in Mary Ward's remarks must have been shared by many of her female associates in the anti-suffragist cause. In spite of their last-ditch attempts to call for a referendum on the question, female anti-suffragists had not only lost, but they could also feel betrayed by their leader and many of their male associates both in the Commons and the Lords. Ward's words also suggest a readiness to look forward and to view enfranchisement with an attitude of 'benevolent neutrality on the merits of the question', as Ward's daughter contends in the biography she dedicated to her mother.[2]

Ten years or so later, for all the railings against the Equalization Bill which appeared in the *Daily Mail*, the last anti-suffragist campaign in 1927–28 was a low-key, almost an exclusively male affair, with only a smattering of Tory backbenchers ready to obstruct the principle of franchise equalization.[3] David Low nicely captured this sense of masculine, rearguard isolation in 1927 and 1928 when he depicted Colonel Gretton, one of the most vociferous opponents to the flapper vote in Parliament, chained to the railings in front of 10 Downing Street in a desperate attempt to deny young women the vote, while a sprightly Joan Bull, personifying the new electorate, knocks on the door of the Prime Minister's residence and casts a puzzled glance at the protest staged by Gretton.[4]

What this chapter addresses is not so much what female Antis 'did with their vote' after 1918, to use Ward's phrase, than the part played by former anti-suffragists in public life in the interwar years. Women's involvement in anti-suffragism from 1908 and 1918 is now a thoroughly researched subject, thanks to the work of Brian Harrison and Julia Bush.[5] Anti-suffragist discourse and networks, which for many years were the poor relative in studies of suffragism and of the women's movement, have been by now systematically charted, but apart from a few pages dedicated by Bush to the women leaders of the NLOWS in the interwar years, little has been written on the plight of anti-suffrage élites after 1918.[6] History, as the axiom goes, is written by the victors, so this neglect for the plight of anti-suffragists after 1918 is yet another confirmation of the validity of the phrase.

Building upon Bush's account of the post-enfranchisement trajectory of leading suffragists, this chapter analyses the public roles undertaken by over a hundred activists in the interwar years. The objective of such a prosopographic endeavour is to determine how far there was distinctive 'Anti' behaviour after 1918 and to retrieve the type of public activities, philanthropic, party political or otherwise, to which female 'veterans' from the anti-suffrage campaign participated.

Considering the historiographical discussion over the alleged decline of interwar British feminism and over the extent to which a "conservative" political culture prevailed at the time, studying female Antis in the post-enfranchisement context offers a useful insight into a group which was so much indebted to traditional assumptions about gender, Empire and democracy – and which, in a somewhat self-contradictory way, had disseminated this viewpoint in such a vocal, articulate and well-organised manner. A good many female Antis ended up among the busybodies within women's organisations in the interwar years, albeit in those organizations which allowed them to remain consistent with their own, gendered vision of how women should intervene in public life.

* * *

The chapter starts with a presentation of a sample of 111 former members of the Women's National Anti-Suffrage League (WNASL) or NLOWS used in the survey. The profile of this group of anti-suffragist ladies is outlined in generational, political and social terms, among other characteristics.

This discussion tackles the scale and range of interwar public activities, from charitable work to civic responsibilities, undertaken by the group. Bush's study underlines the passing of the older generation of Antis after 1918, but also the remarkable careers of well-known figures like Katherine Atholl, Gertrude Bell and Violet Markham. Obviously, all three of them have been included in the sample, but the focus in this chapter is placed upon more obscure anti-suffragist figures. The picture which emerges from the study suggests that interwar paths like that of Atholl or Markham are exceptional, while the rule for many anti-suffragist ladies, even the most articulate of them, was that they chose to remain aloof from involvement in party politics, and even more so from the 'rough-and-tumble' of elections. For some among them it even appears that commitment to anti-suffragism is among the few overtly political stances they chose to adopt, and that their public duties remained carefully confined to non-political, 'womanly' work. One is indeed struck how much these ladies' post-1918 paths through life reveal continuities in their approach to public work. Pre-war religious, philanthropic and educational bodies remained the privileged medium through which many former Antis took part in public life, even if some of them did join such conservative-minded bodies within the interwar women's movement as the Townswomen's Guild or the Mothers' Union. Cooperation, as Bush insists in her study, did exist before and during the war between suffragists and anti-suffragists.[7]

The bulk of former anti-suffragists abstained altogether from taking part in the new, often women-only, party structures which appeared after 1918. Given the prevalence of Conservative and imperialist opinion among female Antis, it is little surprise that right-wing female Antis maintained their commitment to Conservative and imperialist organisations after the war, as the continued importance of the Primrose League and of the Victorian League to some of the anti-suffragist stalwarts tends to show. At the height of the suffrage controversy, both organisations did welcome suffragist and anti-suffragist members alike, but Antis were a majority then and even more after the war. One may even contend that the Victoria League, with its emphasis on womanly duty and imperial service, was an ideal recruiting ground for Antis. After 1918, both leagues appeared as safe-havens for female Antis and acted as a congenial, mostly female and at the same time mixed-sex context for the defeated anti-suffragists. This continued involvement helped both leagues, for all their seeming Victorian out-datedness, to survive into the interwar years.

* * *

The sample analysed in this chapter includes individuals who took part in the anti-suffragist campaign in a number of ways.[8] What has been attempted is a systematic study of women who either signed anti-suffrage petitions between 1908 and 1916, or who appeared on the platform at anti-suffragist meetings in Scotland, in London or in the local branches of the WNASL or the NLOWS.[9] At times, it has been impossible to definitely identify participants to such events. In cases where it proved impossible to clearly identify some of those protagonists of the anti-suffrage campaign, the individuals in question were left out. But I was confronted with few instances of that type, and it has been possible to find data on most anti-suffrage activists. The anti-suffragists on whom further information would be needed were usually NLOWS or WNASL permanent staff like Helena Norris, Agnes Stewart and Cordelia Moir, or local activists like Jeannie Ross (assistant secretary of the Kensington branch of the WNASL) and Agnes Hills (West Sussex branch). But given the high social profile of the sample, a significant amount of data was accessible.

Obviously, this somewhat skews the complexion of the whole sample in favour of the most notorious figures in the movement. One needs to insist on the fact that the findings are thus partial at best and that a more thorough study is required, especially on anti-suffragist circles outside London which would include senior provincial figures whose presence is not noted in metropolitan gatherings.[10] Indeed, little is known about the profile of the anti-suffragist rank-and-file.[11] The degree of commitment to the cause may vary from one case to another, but all held strong enough feelings about the issue to lend their name to it on petitions or to be reported as participants at anti-suffragist events at least once, and in most cases on multiple occasions.

Considering the ten years which elapsed between the initial stages in the Edwardian anti-suffragist mobilisation and the passing of the Representation of the People Act in 1918, another precaution which needs to be taken is to ascertain the generational profile of anti-suffragists. One reason why the plight of Antis after 1918 has been neglected is the passing of many high-profile workers for the anti-suffragist cause after 1918 and even before. As a form of mobilisation, anti-suffragism was delivered a death-blow in 1918, with the NLOWS folding in the wake of the passing of the Representation of the People Act. After that date, some of the most prominent female Antis were simply too old to take any share in public life. Even before the Great War, surviving signatories of the 1889 Anti-Suffrage Appeal, who had formed the backbone of the WNASL and later that of the NLOWS, were a disappearing cohort. Octavia Hill had died in 1912; anti-suffragist leader Mary Ward died in 1920. Lesser anti-suffragist figures like the headmistress Lilla Strong died in 1914; and others like the educationalist Lucy Soulsby or Lady Wantage retired from public and/or professional life during the war or just after. Even among the younger generation of pre-war Antis, there had been premature deaths. Beatrice Chamberlain did witness the final stage in the anti-suffragist battle, but she died in late November 1918, before having the opportunity to vote at the 1918 election.

Still, one should not overlook the fact that a younger generation of anti-suffragists had appeared on the scene between 1908 and 1914. Year of death has been retrieved for 106 of the 121 ladies included in the sample. While only 9 of these ladies died before 1918, the bulk of the sample survived well into the 1920s and beyond: 27 died between 1918 and 1928; 69 lived to witness franchise equalization; and 45 died in 1939 and after. Data on year of birth confirms this pattern, with 35 out of the 79 individuals for whom precise date of birth has been retrieved who were in their fifties or younger in 1918, and 35 in their sixties or older at the end of the Great War.[12] So there was the possibility for a significant number of former WNASL or NLOWS members one could expect to be in a position to be active in public life after 1918. And even among the older generation of Antis, the range of interwar activities undertaken by someone like Lady Jersey, though already in her

69th year in 1918, is there to remind us that advancing years, in some cases, need not necessarily be equated with withdrawal from public life. Among those in their early or mid-50s or younger in 1918 one may mention, among others, actresses Rosina Filippi (born in 1866), Phyllis Broughton (born in 1862) and Mabel Terry Lewis (born in 1872); writer and teacher Enid Moberley Bell (born in 1881), daughter of C. F. Moberley Bell, the anti-suffragist managing director of *The Times*; civil servant Janet Hogarth (born in 1865); orientalist and diplomat Gertrude Bell (born in 1868); former Free Trade Union Secretary Ivy Pretious (born in 1880), and Lady Charnwood (born in 1876).

In terms of social standing and networks, anti-suffragists were also a close-knit, well-connected group. As one of their suffragist opponents noted, anti-suffragist élites were indeed 'women in Society with a big "S"... women with their feet in the fender, who do not realise how the possession of the suffrage would strengthen the position of women who possibly have no fender to put them in'.[13] Among the lot, one spots the presence of the Bischoffsheim family (Lady Ellen Desart; her mother and her aunts Mathilde Langenbach and Miss Mundella), which was among the wealthiest in the country. Among other groups of relatives who rallied to the anti-suffragist cause, one may note Lady Wantage and her niece Lady Jane Lindsay, and of course the Ward family, with Mary and her daughter Dorothy.

Antis recruited in circles which were very close to the Court, among whom were the elderly Lady Victoria Buxton (1839–1916), goddaughter of Queen Victoria; Lady Bradford (1848–1936), Extra Lady of the Bedchamber for Queen Mary in 1905 and 1910 and Lady Calthorpe, friend of the Queen and a guest on the Isle of Wight. In the group, well-known hostesses included Lady Edith Allendale (1850–1927), a friend of M. Paul Cambon, French ambassador in London between 1898 and 1920 and Miss Mary Mundella; and Lady Ilchester. As a number of Antis were foreign-born or of foreign origins (for example, Mary Harcourt, Lady Hadfield and Mrs Wilton Phipps, all three American-born; Miss Mary Mundella, of Italian origins; Rosina Filippi, born in Venice), many within the group were active in the social life gravitating around embassies and in the charitable organisations for the welfare of foreigners. Both Mary Harcourt and Lady Hadfield belonged to the Society of American Women in London, while Mary Mundella was active in the British Italian League and Miss Lawrence Alma-Tadema was involved in Polish relief committees in the 1930s.

This, combined with the fact that many among the group were active in the Royal Amateur Art Society, for example, Mathilde Langenbach and Ethel Pease, gives an undeniably High Society flavour to a group of noted socialites whose privileged life was more often than anything reported in the 'Court Circular' section of *The Times*.[14] And yet, Antis recruited beyond such social strata and welcomed women with less glowing pedigrees. Many came from more ordinary family backgrounds and owed their prominence in Anti circles to their own individual achievements and expertise in their fields, whether as educationalists, writers, journalists, actresses or political activists, among others Janet Hogarth, Elizabeth Burgwin, Frances Low, Ivy Pretious, Gladys Pott, Lucy Soulsby, Ermine Taylor and Jessie Phipps.

Family connections were thus not the only ties that had facilitated the early stages of recruitment, and shared professional background and associational networks also had provided opportunities for the mobilisation of anti-suffragist sentiment. Jessie Phipps, Margaret Macmillan, Ellen Pinsent and Elizabeth Burgwin all shared a similar commitment to the welfare and education of 'feeble-minded' and 'crippled' children.

Authors and writers formed another sub-group. Ethel Colquhoun had peevishly replied to suffragist insinuations that 'the great majority of educated and thinking women [were] found in the suffrage ranks' that this was 'a ridiculous assertion'.[15] Apart from notorious cases like Mary Ward and Ethel Harrison, who regularly contributed to *The Nineteenth Century*, a number of other anti-suffragists like Nina Kay-Shuttleworth, Lady Elizabeth Biddulph of Ledbury or Lady Theodora Guest were published writers in their own right, though on a more modest scale.[16]

Two organizations constituted ideal recruiting grounds for Antis: the Primrose League and the Victoria League. Though both bodies insisted on their non-alignment over women's suffrage, one is struck by how many anti-suffragists belonged to one of those organisations, and at times to both of them, like Lady Jersey.[17] The theatrical profession was also well-represented, with Phyllis Broughton, Mabel Terry Lewis and Lady Tree, wife of Herbert Beerbohm Tree, who had joined the Primrose League and with whom Rosina Filippi, another NLOWS supporter, had worked.[18]

In terms of religious affiliation, anti-suffragists constituted a diverse group, for whom religious faith was often not just a private issue, but a matter of public commitment. A dedicated Catholic, Josephine Ward had taken part in the Eucharist Congress in 1908. The Duchess of Newcastle, another Catholic, was vice-president for the Association of Perpetual adoration which provided help to poor Catholic churches and missions, and a member of a host of other Catholic organisations like the Catholic Truth Society, the Catholic Seamen's Home and Institute and the Catholic Discharged Prisoners' Aid Society. Lady Desart, who came from a Jewish family, became a patron of the Society for the Protection of Jewish Girls and Women. Among the Anglicans of note, Lady Victoria Buxton, an invalid for most of her life, was nonetheless active in the cause of the Christian Social Union and the Young Women's Christian Association.

Politically speaking, the sample under study also shows that one cannot conceive anti-suffragism solely as a Conservative affair. Among ladies with Liberal connections, one notices the presence of Ethel Pease, wife of Jack Pease, Liberal Whip; Lady Haversham, wife of Arthur Hayter, Liberal MP and Lord of the Treasury; Edith Massie, a member of Women's National Liberal

Association in the 1890s and wife of the Liberal Whip John Massie; Mrs Clarendon Hyde, wife of the Liberal candidate for Cardiff for 1910; Lady Catherine Robson, member of the Liberal Social Council and wife of Lord Robson, Attorney-General in Asquith's Government and Lady Charnwood, wife of Godfrey Benson, Liberal MP between 1892 and 1895. Many within Anti élites were indeed political wives, married to peers and MPs from both sides of the House. Of course, women from a Conservative background represented the bulk of the group. Beatrice Chamberlain, daughter of Joseph and sister of Austen, is a case in point. Her dedication to the Conservative cause earned her recognition within the Conservative party hierarchy. *The Times* obituary announcing Beatrice Chamberlain's death reminded readers that she had been 'opposed to the vote being given to women, but the minute it was given she used all her energy in trying to educate them to use it rightly'.[19] Chamberlain had indeed been very active both in the Women's Unionist Tariff Reform Association (WUTRA) and the body that had later replaced this Chamberlainite organisation, the Women's Unionist Organisation (WUO), which was to be the chief channel of integration of women within the party in the 1920s.

To judge from Beatrice Chamberlain's case, one should not equate commitment to anti-suffragism with political apathy. Indeed, one finds numerous instances of active Antis who had undertaken political work before, during and after their commitment to organised anti-suffragism, as shown by the previously mentioned cases of such Liberals as Edith Massie and Lady Robson, and by that of Mary Mundella, another Anti member of the Women's National Liberal Association. Tariff reform had attracted the active support of Beatrice Chamberlain, Lady Talbot, Lady Ilchester and Lady Ancaster. Conversely, Ivy Pretious had been Secretary of the Free Trade Union. For Lady Eustace Cecil, who had canvassed for Evelyn Cecil in the Eastern Division of Hertfordshire in 1898, and Lady Talbot, who took part in her husband's election campaign in Chichester in 1906, there was no incompatibility between their commitment to anti-suffragism and active involvement in electioneering to support their relatives.[20] Similarly, after the war, the Catholic writer and anti-suffragist Josephine Ward is reported as 'sharing the labours' of her son Herbert in the Southern Division of East Ham 'even to the extent of speaking at meetings'.[21] Mary Mundella is presented in her *Times* obituary as a 'keen politician' who took part in her father's contests in his constituency.[22] In some cases, active political work may well have caused women to join the anti-suffragist ranks. One startling example of this is the case of Ivy Pretious, whose task as Secretary of the Free Trade Union seems to have been made extremely difficult owing to suffragist heckling. On one occasion, Pretious went as far as barring women – even journalists – from attending an FTU meeting, probably so as to protect the prestigious speakers of the day, Asquith, Lord Avebury and Lord Balfour, from disruption by female hecklers.[23]

Quite consistently with the so-called 'Forward' policy supported by Mary Ward, who called for anti-suffragist support for greater involvement in local authorities on the part of women as this meant intervening in allegedly womanly spheres such as education and poverty relief, a handful of anti-suffragists were active in local government before the war. Ward, with similar-minded Antis like Elizabeth Burgwin, had set up the Local Government Advancement Committee within the NLOWS, the objective of which was to spread knowledge of the opportunities of local government among women and to promote the candidatures of women at municipal elections. Burgwin's support for the 'Forward' policy was in line with her career as a member of the London School Board in the 1890s to promote the welfare of 'feeble-minded children' and later occupied the job of Superintendent of Special Schools for the London County Council. There she found another anti-suffragist co-worker and fellow member of the National Association for Promoting the Welfare of the Feeble-Minded, Jessie Phipps, who sat on the Education Committee of the London County Council. Phipps's work received recognition from the Conservative Municipal Reform Party, which proposed her name as alderman in 1913. One type of political activity anti-suffragists were becoming involved in before the war was parliamentary committee work, in particular the Joint Parliamentary Advisory Council, to which both Mary Ward and Lady Talbot participated in their capacity as recognised experts on question of welfare and social work. This advisory council had been set up to get the 'women's point of view into the House of Commons'.[24] Lady Talbot became one of the most ubiquitous women members of the various official committees which enlisted the help of women before, during and after the war. Talbot took part in the Home Office Committee on Industrial and Reformatory Schools in 1913, the Committee on Unmarried Mothers chaired in 1915 by the Archbishop of York to investigate the increase of illegitimate births, and the Departmental Committee set up in 1916 by the President of the Board of Education to make provision for the education of children and young persons after the war. Talbot's distinguished public career did not end with the war, as shall be seen later on. This trend continued during the war, when various parliamentary committees, like the Food Economy and War Savings, or the Luxury Duty Committee, benefitted from the help of anti-suffragists like Beatrice Chamberlain.[25] Increased wartime intervention on the part of Government provided opportunities for some Antis. Gladys Pott became inspector of the Women's Branch at the Board of Agriculture in 1916 and organised the Women's Land Army.

After the time the anti-suffrage movement got off the ground, several types of public campaigning seem to have been popular with Antis. The first one is the mobilisation against Lloyd George's Insurance Act, with such Antis as Lady Tweedy, Lady Ellen Desart, Lady Eustace Cecil and Lady George Hamilton all attending an Albert Hall meeting held in June 1912 to protest against a policy likely to affect them as employers of servants.[26] The second one is the war effort, with anti-suffragists like Ethel Colquhoun taking part in the recruitment drive to enlist volunteers at the beginning of the Great War, while others directed their energies towards relief work. During the War, the Red Cross seems to have been among the favourite charitable institutions patronised by Antis, as one notes the involvement of Lady Wynne, Lady Beachcroft and Lady Lubbock, for example. But to some Antis, wartime charitable work should not be indiscriminately pursued by upper-class ladies. Ethel Colquhoun thus warned wealthy ladies against the potential consequences of inordinate voluntary work: 'It is not advisable for well-to-do women to increase or even create unemployment among those who must work for a living. In many cases, it is better for a well-to-do lady to deny herself the luxury of voluntary work and to pay a poorer sister to make shirts, address envelopes, or tie up parcels', as there were already 'numberless secretaries, typists, shop girls, needle-women and others thrown out of work because of the war'.[27] Notwithstanding those recommendations, Colquhoun's anti-suffragist associates were undeniably not lagging behind their suffragist rivals in such wartime work. Mrs Clarendon Hyde was for instance the busy-body behind the creation of a club for the wives and women dependants of sailors and soldiers on active service, while Lady Charnwood started to work from 1915 onwards on a hospital located in a *péniche* on a Belgian canal.

The picture which emerges from this survey of the associational networks to which anti-suffragists belonged before 1918 is that of a set of public-spirited ladies whose patriotism was spurred by the outbreak of war. For many of these women, anti-suffragism was only one aspect of the manifold public and political duties which their social position or professional status allowed them to shoulder. What shall now be outlined is how, given the features outlined in the sample under study, these women adjusted to the post-war, post-enfranchisement context.

The first feature allowing us to appreciate the anti-suffragists' interwar trajectories is the generational factor. The first decade after the Great War coincided with the disappearance of the older generation of anti-suffragists. When Lady Theodora Guest, 'a *grande dame* of the old school', died in 1923, the *Times* noted that 'her death sever[ed] a remarkable link with the society of the Victorian age'.[28] A similarly elegiac note was struck in 1927 on Lady Edith Allendale's death, when in a tribute to her, her friend Professor J. H. Morgan lamented that with her disappeared a figure defined by 'a certain stateliness of manner and personal dignity which, one sometimes think, were the secret of the Victorian Age'.[29] But as shown earlier, a significant portion of anti-suffragists were young, educated and articulate enough to make their mark on interwar public life. How far did they?

The first feature of anti-suffragist trajectories in the post-war era is the complete disappearance of organised anti-suffragism after 1918. Even a convinced Anti like Violet Markham recognised that anti-suffragist women had to move on and to admit that the war had brought about a sea-change, which had provided ample justification for enfranchisement. Markham, who was a candidate as an independent, unofficial Liberal in December 1918 made it clear that she was thus breaking away from her past as an anti-suffragist and that 'her old views were mistaken', women having 'splendidly justified the new rights they [had] obtained'.[30]

Once the Conservatives floated the idea of franchise equalization at the 1924 election, few veterans from the WNASL challenged that policy. Frances Low was one of those lone voices who attacked the idea of introducing the so-called flapper vote, an initiative she lambasted in a letter to the Editor of the *Times* in which she expressed her fear that this would mean 'the weakening and final surrender of masculine force':

> A small Committee is deciding what is most revolutionary, momentous, irrevocable, and that has elements of disintegration, one of which will be the deterioration of the home, to which Bolshevism is a mere child's play. The argument, most shallow and specious, is that the granting of this vote is merely "logical", as if the practical affairs of this world were settled, not on grounds of wisdom, prudence, experience, but on grounds of pure logic. One understands, and who can blame it, the Labour Party pushing forward this measure. But do mature men and women realize it means a permanent majority of women in every constituency, the governance of this country by women, and the best women have something better to do with their unique gifts and functions than politics?[31]

Given the prevalence of Conservative, imperially minded, anti-socialist ladies among Antis, it may seem surprising that Lord Rothermere's anti-flapper-vote campaign, which was largely predicated upon anti-Socialist sentiment, did not elicit support from former NLOWS activists. But even Rothermere's *Daily Mail* was after all very isolated in its hostility towards franchise equalization, as the rest of the Conservative press viewed the whole issue with equanimity.[32]

Beyond this disappearance of organised feminine anti-suffragism, one notices a range of continuities in the Antis' commitment to interwar public life, especially concerning the type of philanthropic or party political activities anti-suffragists took part in.

For some anti-suffragists, commitment to that cause had been an exception within a public life confined to charitable causes. That brand of anti-suffragists simply retired from public life after that or returned to low-key, low-profile public duties once the fight was lost. But old age is not the only factor explaining the relatively low profile adopted by many former Antis in public life after 1918. Marriage, as in the case of Ivy Pretious, explains the gap between her pre-war work for the FTU and for the WNASL and the paucity of evidence concerning the public responsibilities she undertook after the war. After her marriage to Sir Charles Tennyson, the poet's grandson, she retired from public life, restricting her work to help for the Central Council for the Care of Cripples, for which she was awarded an OBE. For the anti-suffragist thespians, for example, active support for anti-suffragism seems to have constituted an exception, rather than the norm in their approach towards public life. Mabel Terry Lewis did support the Actors' Benevolent Fund and the Hospital for Sick Children, and after the war Phyllis Broughton remained after the war a member of the Theatrical Ladies' Guild and the Rehearsal Club, a charitable institution established in 1892 to provide 'a quiet retreat for the girls who take smaller parts in theatrical productions during rehearsals and between afternoon and evening performances'.[33] This pattern of retreat into philanthropy is replicated among many of the titled ladies who joined anti-suffragist bodies. Lady Weardale's commitment to anti-suffragism must have been reinforced when she witnessed an attack at Euston Station against her husband, who had been mistaken for Asquith, by a suffragette wielding a dog whip.[34] Widowed from 1923, she retired from public life, remaining committed to the Save the Children Fund, of which she became vice-president when her husband, the first president of that body, died.[35]

One type of charitable institution which seems to have been an interwar favourite among former Antis, who counted numerous wives and daughters of Army and Navy officers, are the various societies promoting the welfare of veterans and their families. Lady Fremantle, wife of Admiral Sir E. R. Fremantle, was active in the Soldiers' and Sailors' Families Association, for example. But the most dedicated of those workers for the welfare of veterans was Lady Annie Plumer, wife of Field-Marshal Plumer. In 1926, she contributed to the foundation of the King's Roll Clerks' Association, whose aim was to place disabled men in permanent posts. She was also active in the Toc H League of Women Helpers and in the Ypres League, taking part in Ypres Day celebrations through the interwar years. Her activities for the benefit of ex-servicemen earned her an OBE too.

Among the many charitable undertakings patronised by former Antis, the Personal Service League, established in 1909, provides a convincing illustration of the patrician dimension of the philanthropic work shouldered by Antis. That organisation was set up as, in the words of Lord Salisbury at the society's inauguration meeting, 'money by itself could achieve very little in helping those in distress. It was easy for the rich man to write a cheque, but what was wanted was personal service'.[36] Lady Talbot and Violet Markham both took part in the creation of that body, which went into abeyance after the war but was resurrected in 1932 to help the unemployed, with prominent former Antis in its ranks, including Lady Hadfield, Jessie Phipps and the Duchess of Montrose. The League, which insisted on its non-party, non-denominational nature and which received the patronage of Queen

Mary, organised work parties and counted 400 depots in 1936.[37] This complemented in a secular way the work of the Charity Organisation Society, an important Anglican philanthropic organisation with a focus on promoting self-sufficiency among the poor, to which Sophia Lonsdale and Edith Corry belonged. It also resembled such High Society charitable agencies as the Friends of the Poor, to which Margaret Macmillan contributed. Child welfare had been one of the pet causes defended by anti-suffragists. Lady Talbot, Lady George Hamilton and Lady Jersey had been active in the Happy Evenings' Association before the war, an organisation which was disbanded in 1919 much to Mary Ward's dismay, who protested that recreational initiatives for children remained a voluntary affair, with only two of the London play centres managed by the Evening Play Centres Committee receiving subsidies from the London County Council.[38] The range of charitable duties taken up by former anti-suffragists shows how much their approach to public work remained as gendered as ever.

By contrast, former Antis remained aloof from many of the organisations which appeared after the war. The League of Nations Union was noticeably absent from the bodies they joined, which is foreseeable considering the appeal of imperial patriotism among anti-suffragists. Lady Jersey remained a member of the board of the Victoria League until 1925, and in that organisation she worked alongside such former associates as Mrs Max Müller. Mrs Yorke Bevan and Lady Talbot belonged to the Ladies' Imperial Club, while Lady Lubbock remained a patroness of the League of Empire and Lady Hadfield a member of the British Empire League in the 1930s. Many female imperialists – though not all – had indeed joined anti-suffragist organisations as they believed that women's enfranchisement would weaken the 'Imperial Parliament' and jeopardise Britain's imperial mission, which to them was best left in the hands of men. For imperially-minded anti-suffragist women, women had to be active in the promotion of Empire, but mostly in a role subservient to that of men, as may be seen in the case of the Victoria League, a very popular organisation among female Antis. The Victoria League thus promoted 'practical' imperialism and mobilised women across the Empire in a range of philanthropic tasks, such as school twinnings or the sending of parcels to isolated colonials, so as to foster a sense of unity among the 'Britannic' race spread across the world.[39] The involvement of numerous female Antis in such imperialist bodies as the Victoria League among others shows that for all the supposed lack of interest of women for foreign affairs, which, as Adrian Bingham notes, was circulated in the Conservative popular press, female Antis remained keenly interested in the fate of the Empire and actively tried to forge a sense of imperial unity through such bodies.

One spots few cases of involvement in women's civic groups. Ethel Pease was active in the Townswomen's Guild, but this stands as an exception, and no evidence of support for the Mothers' Union or the Young Women's Christian Association (apart from Ethel Pease again, who came from a Liberal background) has been observed among the sample. For all its alleged conservatism, the women's movement held little appeal for anti-suffragists, probably owing to emphasis on active citizenship in many of those organisations.[40]

Although Markham's candidacy in 1918 was a one-off only, her subsequent activities offer one clear example that active anti-suffragism was no impediment to the enjoyment of a successful public career after 1918. Here, the major change was not so much enfranchisement but the removal of disabilities for women concerning the magistracy in particular. Soon after the war, Mary Ward, Lady Jersey and Janet Hogarth became JPs for the County of London, and other anti-suffragists followed suit in the interwar years, for example, Margaretta Lemon, Reigate Borough JP.[41] Jessie Phipps became vice-chairman of the London County Council in 1920, and became the first woman to occupy that position, while Violet Markham became Mayor of Chesterfield in 1927. Anti-suffragist participation in parliamentary committees and official bodies also continued after the war. Lady Talbot was appointed a member of the Consultative Council on General Health in 1920; Janet Hogarth worked as Adviser on Staff Welfare at the Ministry of Munitions in 1920. Gladys Pott became chairman of the Society for the Oversea Settlement of British Women, which operated under the supervision of the Dominions Office. She, like many other anti-suffragists who received such distinctions, was made a CBE in 1937 for her achievements. Violet Markham reached recognition when she was appointed Deputy Chairman of the Assistance Board in 1937. In 1924 Atholl became the first woman to become a member of a Conservative government, in which she served at the Board of Education.

Among those evincing keen interest in political organisation both before and after 1918 is Flora Fardell. Before the war, Fardell had been a Primrose League stalwart and sat on the League's Literature Committee, where she worked with a fellow Anti, Lady Ancaster. She was among the League's nominees for the Council of the National Union of Conservative Associations, together with Lady Jersey and Lady Talbot, and she continued to work on the League's Grand Council all through the interwar years.[42] Fardell was one of those Conservatives who saw the danger that anti-Socialism could slide into apparent hostility to the working classes as a whole. In February 1920, on her suggestion, the League's Grand Council passed a resolution stating that 'given the Primrose League always found it possible to work in harmony with all classes, the statements made by certain politicians and newspapers that it is necessary to unite against Labour, should be publicly controverted in the press and on the platform'.[43] True to that cross-class perspective, Fardell created the Young Conservatives' Union in 1924 so as to promote cooperation between the classes in the London area.[44] Mrs Yorke Bevan was another committed activist, with a very similar profile. She belonged to the Ladies' Imperial Association and to the Ladies' Grand

Council of the Primrose League, and took part in the High Church mobilisation against the revision of the Prayer Book in 1927 and 1928 as she joined
the Committee for the Maintenance of Truth and Faith which opposed the
alternative communion service.[45]

The post-war career of Lady Jersey, former president of the NLOWS,
stands as the clearest illustration of both change and continuity in the anti-
suffragists' approach to public life. Margaret Jersey took advantage of the
new opportunities offered to women when she was appointed a magistrate
in the Juvenile Courts. Jersey also continued to support both the Victoria
League and the Primrose League after the war. She retired from the Grand
Council of the Primrose League in 1935, once deafness and failing sight
became too much of a handicap.[46] Until that resignation, she had been
among the most assiduous members of the Primrose League's Ladies' Grand
Council, which she presided over from 1921 onwards.[47] She also worked
on the League's mixed-sex Grand Council, in which she repeatedly made
stridently anti-socialist recommendations. Just after the issue of women's
enfranchisement had been settled, Jersey warned her Primrose League colleagues that they had to be wary of 'certain Socialist, "pacifist" and other
bodies' who were' rying to get hold of the new women voters'. 'It would be',
she thought, 'no violation of the party truce to be on their guard against
this'.[48] In 1920, she advised her Primrose League colleagues to be vigilant
about the National Young Labour League, which, she feared, would 'teach
children a camouflaged communism'. Three years later, she urged the
League to counter 'the ceaseless and untiring propaganda of the Socialist
Party', against which, she believed, one could not count on the 'merely passive belief in the good sense of the electorate'.[49] One cannot help wondering
how Jersey appreciated the speech made by William Joynson Hicks, then
Home Secretary, at the League's Grand Habitation in 1928 to defend his
policy of franchise equalization:

> He hoped to see the extension of the franchise triumphantly carried. He
> could understand those people of his own age saying: 'Why should we,
> who have borne the burden and heat of the day, call into our councils
> these five million additional women voters?' But they could not set back
> the tide. They had to see that the tide was with them and not against
> them. They had to realize that the future of the country lay these young
> men and women (Cheers).[50]

Jersey's loyalty towards the Primrose League was not an isolated instance,
as Laura Fardell, as seen earlier, but also Edith Milner among others,
remained faithful to the Primrose League after 1918. The League continued to appeal to former anti-suffragists after the war, much more than the
women-only WUO, in which only Beatrice Chamberlain, Lady Talbot and
Lady Theresa Londonderry were involved just after enfranchisement. For

Conservative Antis, the sex-segregated WUOs were probably too daunting a proposal, while the cooperation between the sexes which was the hallmark of the League offered a more reassuring framework of action, which did much to ensure the survival of the League in the interwar years.[51]

This survey of anti-suffragist public work before and after 1918 is by no means the final word on the subject. More research is required on this group, especially at local, grass-roots level. Still, several conclusions may be drawn from the study of the sample.

The first one is that anti-suffragism was, for many of the women involved in that campaign, only one among many other public or political responsibilities. The second one is that hostility towards women's suffrage before 1918 was no obstacle for subsequent involvement in public affairs, especially for those Antis who subscribed to Ward's Forward policy and who found opportunities to enjoy fulfilling public careers after 1918. The most important variable here is not so much enfranchisement, but the removal of the restrictions imposed upon women in other fields, especially in terms of access to the magistracy. Within the group under study, Katherine Atholl stands out as an exception : she was the only former Anti to become an MP. The other Antis who took on public responsibilities were either appointed (as Lady Desart, who became an Irish Senator in 1922) or co-opted into governmental agencies. That few Antis actually went into the 'rough-and-tumble' of elections should not be considered as confirmation of their dislike for women's participation to politics. After all, many suffragists quickly realised that obtaining the right to vote was only one step towards political influence, and that exerting direct influence on Parliament – or on local authorities – would be an uphill struggle in what remained all through the interwar years a male-dominated field. The third conclusion is that for many anti-suffragists, involvement in the WNASL or the NLOWS was a parenthesis in public careers that eschewed active involvement in politics. Once anti-suffragism was definitely defeated, many retreated into the type of gendered public activities which they deemed suitable to their condition. For many within anti-suffragist élites, philanthropic work was the most proper, not to say the only, type of public work that women could undertake. If one leaves out the handful of female anti-suffragists who had high-profile political careers after 1918, the Aftermath of Suffrage era chiefly meant, for many among anti-suffragist veterans, continuing to perform 'great public work privately', very much as they had done before getting involved in anti-suffragism. Most female Antis thus returned to obscurity after 1918, working whether as 'Lady Bountifuls' for various charitable undertakings or as mere decorative adjuncts for party-political organisations.

All in all, the idea that 1918 constituted a neat dividing line is at best misguided. If the cause espoused by female anti-suffragists was lost, the reasons why they had chosen to mobilise against enfranchisement and the underlying 'feminist' assumptions with which many of them equated suffragism with remained relevant afterwards. The gendered, imperialist world-view most Antis held before 1918 remained the hallmark of their public actions in the aftermath of suffrage. For pre-war Antis, women should safely remain with the gendered precinct of philanthropic action, and womanliness required great caution towards, not to say downright abstemiousness from party politics and electoral competition. This outlook perfectly suited female Antis for the interwar political culture, which, even if it coincided with unprecedented numbers of women joining political parties, also put a premium on cross-party women's organisations. In these, some Antis did play a prominent role – very much as the most public-spirited among them had done before the war. Within such organisations, female Antis were able, as some of them had done even at the height of the suffrage controversy, to find common ground with more "feminist" activists. But for the bulk of the Antis who have come under study in this chapter, in the interwar years, 'public' work did not mean involvement in 'public' life but all too often in charitable work only, as philanthropic action remained the type of gendered task that the elites of the Anti movement, which had so heavily recruited in the highest circles of society, were expected to perform.

Notes

1. The title of the paper is a quotation from *The Times* obituary of a prominent Anti, Lady Wantage (*The Times*, 10 August 1920, p. 20).
2. Mary Ward to Louise Creighton, 14 March 1918, quoted in Janet Penrose Trevelyan, *The Life of Mrs Humphry Ward*, London: Constable, 1923, pp. 244–5.
3. Adrian Bingham shows that the anti-flapper-vote stance of the *Daily Mail* was unrepresentative of wider Conservative opinion. To judge from the attitude of other Conservative newspapers like the *Daily Express*, the enfranchisement of women over 21 was viewed with equanimity, while anti-feminist discourse became in fact more muted, including in the *Mail*, the hostility of which towards equalization had more to do with anti-socialism, as Bingham convincingly contends. Adrian Bingham, '"Stop the Flapper Vote Folly": Lord Rothermere, the *Daily Mail*, and the Equalization of the Franchise 1927–28', *Twentieth Century British History*, 13, 1 (2002), pp. 17–37.
4. David Low, 'History repeats itself – with a difference', *Evening Standard*, 29 March 1928, British Cartoon Archive reference number LSE 0376. The cartoon is accessible on the British Cartoon Archive website, http://www.cartoons.ac.uk/.
5. Julia Bush, *Women Against the Vote: Female Anti-Suffragism in Britain*, Oxford: Oxford University Press, 2007; Brian Harrison, *Separate Spheres: The Opposition to Women's Suffrage in Britain*, London: Croom Helm, 1978.
6. Bush, *Women Against the Vote*, pp. 290–6.
7. Bush, *Women Against the Vote*, pp. 12–14.
8. The whole sample is accessible in .pdf format at the following address : http://cecille.recherche.univ-lille3.fr/auteur/philippe-vervaecke.
9. *The Times*, 'Women's National Anti-Suffrage League. Enthusiastic Meeting', 22 July 1908, p. 14; 'Women's Anti-Suffrage League. Meeting at Queen's Hall', 27 March

1909, p. 10; 'Anti Woman-Suffrage Appeal', 21 July 1910; p. 9; 'Anti-Suffrage Meeting. Speeches by Lord Curzon and Mr. Hobhouse', 21 January 1913, p. 6.

10. Only five local activists (Bertha May Broadwood, Edith and Margaret Corry, Georgina King Lewis, Beatrice Jefferis, all active in the Croydon branch of the NLOWS) not present in London-based gatherings have been included in the sample. More research on anti-suffragist grass-roots would be welcome. I am indebted to Ruth Davison for having helped me identify these local activists of the NLOWS. See her doctoral thesis, 'Citizens at Last: Women's Political Culture and Civil Society, Croydon and East Surrey, 1914–39', Royal Holloway, University of London, 2010.

11. The NLOWS claimed 50,000 members in 1914, but there are no extant membership files. For an analysis of membership and local branches, see Bush, pp. 212–18.

12. Only 9 individuals in the whole sample had died before the December 1918 elections.

13. Lady Louisa Knightley, *The Queen*; 29 August 1908, p. 383, quoted in Mitzi Auchterlonie, *Conservative Suffragists: The Women's Vote and the Tory Party*, London/New York: Tauris Academic Studies, 2007, p. 95.

14. Bush's findings on NLOWS local élites confirm this. Out of a total of 119 Branch presidents, 54 were titled ladies. Bush, p. 213.

15. *The Times*, 'Letters to the Editor', 1 November 1913, p. 10.

16. Kay Shuttleworth wrote articles in the *National Review*; Biddulph of Ledbury had published a biographical portrayal of her father; Lady Guest was author of *A Round Trip in North America*, published in 1895.

17. On the Primrose League and the suffrage controversy, see my chapter, 'The Primrose League and Women's Suffrage, 1883–1918', in Myriam Boussahba-Bravard (ed.), *Suffrage Outside Suffragism. Women's Vote in Britain, 1890–1914*, Basingstoke: Palgrave/Macmillan, 2007, pp. 180–201.

18. Primrose League Papers, Minutes of the Grand Council, folio 532, 19 March 1908.

19. *The Times*, 'Beatrice Mary Chamberlain', 22 November 1918, p. 11.

20. *The Times*, 16 June 1898, p. 7; 11 January 1906, p. 10.

21. *The Times*, 30 November 1923, p. 14.

22. *The Times*, 11 November 1922, p. 13.

23. *The Times*, 5 March 1909, p. 10.

24. In 1920, the president of that council, the Conservative MP Sir Arthur Steel-Maitland, paid tribute to that body in a manner leaving no doubt as to the diminutive role MPs were ready to give to those female experts, when he praised the 'experience' of those 'women of authority' which 'was brought to bear in a businesslike way for the amendment, where necessary, of non-contentious Bills'. 'Women's Aid to Parliament. Council of Social Experts', *The Times*, 18 February 1920, p. 11.

25. For women MPs' participation in select committees, see Mari Takayanagi's Chapter 10 in this volume.

26. *The Times*, 28 June 1912, p. 9.

27. *The Times*, 14 August 1914, p. 9.

28. *The Times*, 26 March 1924, p. 16.

29. *The Times*, 23 May 1927, p. 19.

30. *The Times*, 'Miss Markham's Contest', 4 December 1918, p. 10. Markham had presented herself to her constituents as a bit of a maverick not ready to 'take kindly

to the crack of the party whip', an attitude she shared with another anti-suffragist, the Duchess of Atholl, and more widely, with another women politician from the other side of the suffrage divide, Nancy Astor. Katherine Atholl was among the few veterans from anti-suffragist organizations who expressed her opposition to franchise equalization in 1928. See Bush, p. 296.

31. *The Times*, 'Votes for Girls', 21 June 1924, p. 8.

32. W. K. Haselden, the Daily Mirror cartoonist, had been relentless in his denunciation of suffragist violence before 1914. By the early 1920s, his attitude had very much mellowed regarding women's participation to politics. On Haselden's series of cartoons on the flapper as a candidate for Parliament, see my article '"The Rough-and-Tumble of Politics": Interwar Cartoon Representation of Women's Involvement in British Elections, 1918–1935', in Kornelia Slavova and Isabelle Boof-Vermesse (eds), *Gender/Genre*, Sofia: Saint Kliment Ohridski University Press, 2010, pp. 203–16. On how the popular press appeared sceptical about women's interest in politics, see Chapter 5 by Adrian Bingham.

33. *The Times*, 'The Rehearsal Club', 12 April 1916, p. 10.

34. *The Times*, 'Suffragist Assault on a Peer', 19 February 1914, p. 6.

35. *The Times*, 'Lady Weardale', 18 October 1934, p. 17.

36. *The Times*, 'Personal Service Association', 13 May 1909, p. 9.

37. *The Times*, 'Personal Service League', 15 October 1936, p. 16.

38. The association, which provided entertainment to children, was dissolved in 1919 after thirty years' work, allegedly because educational authorities had started subsidising recreational activities for children. *The Times*, 'Happy Evenings Association', 1 March 1919, p. 8; 'Evening Play Centres', 5 March 1919, p. 11.

39. As David Thackeray observes in his Chapter 2 in this volume, Conservative women's organisations developed a range of imperially-minded activities and often attempted to imitate non-party organisations, so as to allow as many women as possible to take part. At constituency level, this Conservative cocktail of imperial zeal, of womanly activities such as bazaars, together with the refusal of being overtly party-related, must have proved appealing to former anti-suffragists.

40. On the emphasis placed upon citizenship in the women's movement in the interwar years, see Caitriona Beaumont, 'Citizens not Feminists: The Boundary Negotiated Between Citizenship and Feminism by Mainstream Women's Organisations in England, 1928–1939', *Women's History Review*, 9, 2 (2000), pp. 411–29; Helen McCarthy, 'Parties, Voluntary Associations, and Democratic Politics in Interwar Britain', *Historical Journal*, 50, 4 (2007), pp. 891–912.

41. Davison, p. 276.

42. Primrose League Papers, Minutes of the Grand Council, folio 112, List of Committees 1909-1910; folio 271, 6 June 1918; f. 402, f. 407, 4 March 1920.

43. Primrose League Papers, Minutes of the Grand Council, f. 402, 5 February 1920.

44. *The Times*, 'Political Ideals', 17 March 1924, p. 13.

45. *The Times*, 18 April 1927, p. 13.

46. Violet Powell, *Margaret Countess of Jersey. A Biography*, London: Heinemann, 1978, p. 184.

47. Lady Jersey had been among the original members of the Ladies' Grand Council of the Primrose League, which had been created two years after the foundation of the League in 1883. Her resignation from the League in 1935 coincided with the fiftieth anniversary of her presence in the Ladies' Grand Council.

48. *The Times*, 18 May 1918, p. 3.

49. Primrose League Papers, Minutes of the Grand Council, f. 435, 4 March 1920; f. 603, 1 February 1923.
50. *The Times*, 'Home Secretary and the Franchise. Speech at Primrose League Demonstration', 5 May 1928, p. 14. *The Times* reports that the audience was mostly composed of women, Grand Habitation, the League's yearly assembly, having attracted 10,000 people that day, which is evidence that that organisation, for all its out-datedness and Victorian flavour, continued to enjoy massive support at that stage, especially among women.
51. On tensions between WUOs and male-dominated Conservative associations, see John Brennan, 'The Conservative Party in the Constituencies, 1918–1939', PhD, Oxford, 1994, pp. 85–95.

7

Towards an Archaeology of Interwar Women's Politics: The Local and the Everyday

Karen Hunt and June Hannam

In 1924 the suffragist Helena Swanwick observed:

> It is obvious to anyone who has lived an active political life for the past twenty years that politics are being profoundly modified in precisely the way the Suffragists foresaw. Not that there would be a woman's party; not that there would be any marked opposition between men and women politicians, but that, insensibly, the actual and potential presence of women in politics affects the thoughts of men. ... They are becoming sensitive to women and women's side of life work.[1]

This chapter considers Swanwick's optimistic assessment of the aftermath of suffrage not in the more familiar national arena but in the place where the new woman citizen went about her everyday life: her local neighbourhood. As Swanwick suggests, once women had achieved enfranchisement in 1918 contemporaries expected that politics would be different.[2] Winning the principle that sex no longer disqualified women from formal political citizenship was bound to change the nature and practice of politics, but it was not entirely clear what the shape of that politics would be.

From the beginning there was a lively debate, especially within women's and feminist organisations, about what citizenship meant to women and on what basis they should participate in political life.[3] These issues have also been explored by historians, in particular for the interwar years. They have examined the extent to which newly enfranchised women continued to seek to improve their position as women, whether they chose mixed-sex political parties, women's organisations or feminist groups as the best means to achieve their goals, and whether they were able to exert an influence on policy-making. This essay shifts the focus of attention to the local level. Although it grows out of extensive research into two cities which had strong pre-war suffrage movements, Bristol and Manchester, our intention here is not to provide a detailed case-study, or simply to add another layer to a well-known historical narrative. Instead, we argue for a new archaeology of 'women's politics' which poses a challenge not only for how we explain what happened after the vote was won but also how we conceive of politics more generally. The aim is to map the effect of enfranchisement on how women understood and 'did' politics at a local level. By turning to the locality – the space in which everyday politics was experienced – it becomes possible to raise new questions that can lead to the reframing of interwar women's politics. It is argued here that we should expand our understanding of what constitutes 'women's politics' and then explore the interrelationship between the changing possibilities it presented. Women's politics must be situated not only within the swift moving politics of its times but also within local political cultures and histories of women's neighbourhood activism. Such a broadening and deepening of our understanding of interwar women's politics will provide a much more nuanced picture of the aftermath of suffrage. To the rich mix of what we already know about separate elements of interwar women's politics, we want to add the local and the everyday.

Key issues explored by historians interested in women's political activism after enfranchisement have been the extent to which there was a greater participation of women in public life, whether there were continuities or discontinuities before and after suffrage and whether women continued to have collective goals. Did they seek to improve their own position as women or was their emphasis on campaigning for broader social changes to benefit humanity as a whole?[4] Research into these questions has either tended to use a biographical approach, in which individual lives are used as a way to map change, or has concentrated on particular organisations, thereby compartmentalising women's political activism.[5] When women did campaign to improve their position as women, historians have debated the extent to which they were able to exert influence on policy-making at either a national or at a local level.[6] Women's organisations, including women-only groups within political parties, provided another focus for political action, but here too their aims were complex.[7] Some women's groups defined themselves explicitly as feminist, whereas others, such as the Townswomen's Guild and the Mothers' Union rejected this label. Nevertheless they all sought to educate women into being active citizens and recognised 'the rights of women to the benefits of political and social citizenship'.[8]

Other studies have focused on political culture, using the national press to discuss representations of the new woman voter.[9] Across the political spectrum, parties needed to communicate with the new, mass electorate and began to recognise that the housewife could be a key source of support. It has been argued, therefore, that the representation of women voters within political parties and the popular press, in particular through the image of the housewife, in itself played an important part in defining the nature of women's political engagement.[10] However, this literature is less concerned with the agency of the woman voter or housewife herself. Nor are local political cultures and their representation in the still-thriving interwar local press central to their concerns. Although the figure of the housewife is frequently invoked, she is rarely interrogated. Did she have a coherent identity? How was her voice articulated and to what extent was it inflected with class identities? These are issues that comparative local studies of interwar women's politics can address.

It is argued here that a new approach is needed. It is important to break free from parallel histories and to look at the interrelationship between different forms of women's formal and informal political activity. We should ask whether political women of whatever affiliation had more in common with each other than those who were unaligned or indifferent. To do this we need to consider all the spaces in which 'women's politics' could be made – pressure groups and voluntary organisations as well as parties.[11] This will enable us to acknowledge that women's political activity is dynamic, can involve multiple affiliations and can change over time. We would suggest that the most effective way to do this is to refocus on the local.

It is at the level of the local that the relationship between different groups, and between the activist and her newly enfranchised, unorganised sister, can best be pursued through a meticulous search of the spaces in which women carried out and developed their politics. After all, it is locally that the majority of women (and men) engaged in or encountered politics. It was here that they attended meetings, organised political and social events and carried out the patient electoral work of canvassing door-to-door. In the 1920s and 1930s, this was recognised by all the political parties who made a greater effort to build up a grassroots membership and to engage with the new electorate. Today, when the political process appears more and more remote from people's lives, it is instructive to examine a period in which emphasis was placed on encouraging active citizenship with a focus on immediate concerns that could then link to broader political perspectives.

Studies of the suffrage and labour movements have shown the importance of looking at the local as a space to understand the meaning of politics and have drawn attention to the ways in which local, national and international political activities were intertwined. Thus, the locality was not only the place in which women were drawn into suffrage activities, but could also shape the characteristics of the movement as a whole. Local suffrage histories have shed new light on the national movement, including who was involved, the nature of militancy and the relationship with other political movements.[12] Similarly, studies of organising the grassroots of the Labour Party have looked at the complex relationship between the national and the local. They explore political cultures as well as organisational structures and examine how far political organisation touched everyday life.[13]

Work has already begun in mapping interwar women's politics within localities. Women's organisations have been examined, for example, by Valerie Wright and Esther Breitenbach in Scotland and Ruth Davidson in

East Surrey.[14] They show the variety of groups in which women were active and that feminist issues had not disappeared. There is also a wealth of research on women and local Labour politics in the interwar years.[15] This includes explorations of the extent to which interwar Labour and socialist parties informed, and were informed by, everyday life. For example, Ann Marie Hughes argues that it was working-class women's experiences of everyday life that politicised them.[16]

Nonetheless these studies still tend to compartmentalise women into specific organisations, or groups of organisations, and while sometimes raising questions about everyday life do not take this further to explore whether a different kind of politics was being developed across, between and even beyond parties and women's organisations. That is what our proposed archaeology of women's politics intends to do. First, we have to map the site: tracing the effect of enfranchisement on how women understood and 'did' politics. But we also need to excavate what lies below the surface to uncover how individual women made their political choices over a long period of time. Context tells us much – politics was and is about the interaction between parties, pressure groups and civil society as well as between the politically engaged and the ordinary citizen. Admitting women in some cases for the first time, or in far greater numbers than before, made a difference to the context of political life as well as to women's experience of it. Comparative local studies are crucial in order to develop a new understanding of the nature and meaning of British women's politics. They make it possible to assess patterns of similarity and difference and to trace continuities and discontinuities across time and between organisations. However, comparison should not be limited to other British examples. For example, recent studies of housewife activism in Australia and Canada in the first half of the twentieth century can help us to look beyond formal women's politics and connect the everyday with 'the political'.[17]

We suggest that four key issues need to be explored in any comparative local study in order to develop a deeper understanding of interwar women's politics. These are the issues arising from separatism, the nature and effect of 'women's issues', the connections between politics and everyday life as well as the emotional architecture of women's politics. All of these will be discussed in greater depth below. Since women's politics occurred in many different spaces it is essential to always ask the same questions whatever is being investigated in order to identify patterns beyond specific organisations, places and times. Wherever appropriate, examples will be drawn from our own research on Manchester and Bristol, two cities that were centres of the pre-war suffrage movement but had their own distinctive economic and social structures as well as political cultures which affected the political choices that women activists made.

One issue that concerned women both before and after enfranchisement was the question of separate women's organisation.[18] We need to know in what circumstances political women viewed separate women's organisations or sections as appropriate, useful or even essential. Their views could be a function of their party affiliation, generation, experience of suffrage politics or the character of local women's organisations/sections. They could also change over time, as when Independent Labour Party (ILP) women in the 1920s reversed their longstanding opposition to women's auxiliaries.[19] It is also important to recognise the ways in which earlier local political cultures created the possibilities in the interwar period for women to make their own political journeys, as well as shaping the networks between political women and the choices made on whether to pursue a particular issue through mixed-sex, feminist or women's organisations.

In some local contexts, for instance, it could be difficult for women who sought election as local councillors to remain outside party politics. In Bristol, Emily Smith and Lilian Meade King stood as independent candidates before the war. Smith, the president of the National Union of Women Workers and of the local branch of the Women's Local Government Association, believed that women would be able to improve their own and other women's lives through work on municipal bodies but denounced the role of party politics in local government. After 1918, when antagonism between the Conservative and Liberal parties on the one hand and the Labour party on the other was far more pronounced in Bristol, Smith, along with Lilian Meade King, stood successfully as Conservative candidates.[20] In contrast, of the thirteen women elected to Cambridge City Council between 1918 and 1930, ten were Independents.[21] Over the same period eighteen women sat on Manchester City Council. Two were elected pre-war as Independents and a further two were part of the local Municipal Progressive Union, but the rest were Liberal, Labour or Conservative. Both cities had local Women Citizens' Associations encouraging women to be active citizens but they responded to the local political cultures in different ways.

These examples suggest that there are significant interrelationships between organisations at a local level that need to be contextualised, for instance, between the Women Citizens' Associations (WCA), which declared themselves to be non-party, and party women. The character of local WCAs varied, as Innes has shown for Edinburgh and Savage for Preston, but they all worked in a context in which party was increasingly dominant in local politics.[22] In Manchester, the WCA had unsuccessfully tried to get its own candidate elected to the City Council in 1919, but then adopted a more pragmatic position: as an association the WCA does not 'support candidates who are put forward by their political parties, but it does urge very strongly those of its members who are party women to support and work for those women candidates, irrespective of party, to do all in their power to help to return the women who are now standing for election'.[23] A number of the first generation of Manchester women councillors were active in the WCA, such as Mary Kingsmill Jones (Conservative) and Shena Simon (Liberal), but all stood on party tickets.

Relationships between parties and women's non-party organisations were not easy in the interwar period. The issue was seen as one of loyalty. The tensions were most profound for Labour women. At the 1920 Labour Women's Conference, Marion Phillips moved the resolution which instructed members 'to avoid dissipating their energies in non-party political organisations', by which she meant any part of the women's movement. In the debate, a number of Labour women spoke up in favour of the WCAs as an *additional* space in which to make their politics. Annot Robinson drew on her own experience of socialist, suffrage and peace activism in Manchester to argue 'women had for years been associated with other organisations, and had obtained special knowledge therefrom, which had been of immense value'.[24] So how did these relationships work on the ground? Despite the non-party position of WCAs, we know that Labour women were involved in local branches. Hannah Mitchell, whose principal loyalty in the 1920s was to the ILP, wrote for the local WCA's paper *Manchester and Salford Woman Citizen* and her fellow Labour councillor, Dora Taylor, was a member of Crumpsall WCA. These relationships need to be plotted carefully through the interwar period as Labour women's sections become more insular and it became more difficult to maintain feminist and Labour affiliations. However, this can be overstated. When in 1928, a Manchester branch of the explicitly feminist Open Door Council was formed, its chairman was the Labour councillor Hannah Mitchell.[25] Nonetheless, crossing boundaries between organisations and sustaining multiple memberships did become more difficult in the 1920s. Any mapping of interwar women's politics has to explore how this affected women in local communities, particularly their everyday experience of citizenship and attitude to politics.

The many women who chose party membership after 1918 had to decide where, how and to what extent they wanted to give their individual energies.[26] Political parties saw their women's auxiliaries as the way to recruit the new voters and to cement women's loyalty to party. Yet many activist women were ambivalent about separate women's sections in their own parties. In Bristol, women councillors addressed meetings on political issues but only a minority took part in the work of these groups: councillor Mrs Robinson was the 'energetic and hard-working secretary' of the women's branch of the Conservative Association of the Stapleton and Easton wards, while Emily Webb was crucial to the success of her local Labour Party women's section.[27] It was more usual, however, for activist women to seek office in the local mixed-sex party structures as a way to ensure greater influence and to further their careers, although they might first need to build a profile in the women's organisations. Kate Gleeson, for example, a Labour Party councillor in Bristol after 1936, first represented the women's central committee on the Executive of Bristol East Labour Party and then in the post war years was chairman of the St George West Ward Labour Party.[28] Women's choices were shaped by local responses to women's activism and often to fears of feminism but as important was the priority given within local party branches to what were deemed 'women's issues'.

When women did get involved in local politics – whether through attending meetings, joining campaigns or standing for election to municipal bodies – what were the issues that galvanised them? Research at a local level adds to our understanding of what made a demand a 'woman's issue' and the success women had in determining their own agendas, as well as those of their parties and organisations. It also allows us to trace what they learnt from the strategies adopted by other political women and the extent to which women were willing to work together across political boundaries.

There were plenty of women municipal candidates in the interwar period who emphasised their concern for what they saw as women's issues, especially social reforms, and their track record in the field. Emily Webb, who had been a Poor Law Guardian in Bristol since before the war, presented herself as particularly suited and experienced as a woman to work to improve conditions for the poor and unemployed when she sought election to the Council in 1929.[29] The Conservative councillor Emily Smith expressed similar views. In her 1913 election campaign as an Independent, she suggested that women had skills that were different from men and claimed that her main interest was in municipal lodging houses for women, an issue that was also supported by Bristol ILP.[30] In the early 1920s she joined with women from the Labour party to lobby the Health Committee on this question and in 1922 the Council purchased a property to use as a women's lodging house.[31] Patricia Hollis's work on women and local government before the First World War has made Webb's and Smith's experience seem familiar.[32] Nonetheless, studies of women councillors in other localities show a greater range of earlier experiences and forms of self-representation. In Coventry, for example, the Labour councillor Alice Arnold identified herself principally as a worker, indeed a militant unionised worker, rather than as a de-classed representative of her sex.[33] Although her biographer Cathy Hunt suggests that Arnold was exceptional, there is evidence from Manchester that other Labour women were uncomfortable with the assumption that their sphere of interest was mothers, welfare and washhouses. Certainly there was a strong sense that an issue did not have to be domestic to be seen as a woman's issue, as one woman commented in 1928, 'One of the most hopeful signs of recent years is the way that women of all parties have resolutely set their faces against a militaristic outlook. The World War made war a "women's topic".'[34] Many suffragists had been peace campaigners and they continued in the interwar years to emphasise that this remained a woman's issue. So too did the Women's Co-operative Guilds. The various Guilds who were part of the Failsworth (Manchester) Co-operative Society not only had speakers in the 1920s on the No More War demonstration and the Peace Crusade but a Guildswoman gave a report on her experience as a delegate to Russia.[35] Connections were being drawn between the local and the international, just as when Katherine Bruce Glasier spoke from the women's platform of a Gorton ILP meeting and 'dealt with the position in China and its relation to the cotton workers of Lancashire'.[36]

Just as party political women had to decide whether to be part of separate women's auxiliaries, so political women more generally found they had to take an attitude to the notion of 'women's issues' and the implicit gendering of politics which it represented. When Mary Kingsmill Jones was interviewed in 1924 she was both a WCA activist and a Conservative city councillor. Her views on what constituted 'women's issues' were typical:

> there are certain aspects of ...[the City Council's work] which from their very nature are bound to make a close and direct appeal to women – such as any aspect of the housing question, whether it be the necessary provision of houses or the saving of all unnecessary labour in these houses when provided; questions of public health, more especially those directly concerned with maternity and child welfare; and of course all matters pertaining to education.

However, she was not convinced by the need to municipalise the milk supply (a common demand of women's organisations) and although she thought there should be special relief for unemployed women, she did not see unemployment as a gendered problem.[37] Others saw the continuing battle for the provision of women police as the key women's issue for the municipality.[38]

The existence of women's issues politicised matters previously seen as beyond politics but then it was often presumed that these issues were all that a woman would be interested in. When Shena Simon remembered Manchester's first woman councillor, Margaret Ashton, she captured the dilemma of the political woman: 'The methods of the "womanly woman" may lull the opposition to sleep for the time being, but they never can meet and defeat it. Those of us who followed Miss Ashton on the City Council found that thanks to her, all the barriers had been stormed, and that we were accepted as naturally as if we were men.'[39] Other women councillors in interwar Manchester admired the pioneering work of Ashton but were less sanguine about the council itself. Describing a local victory when the proposal that women teachers should be forced to retire on marriage was defeated, Councillor Hannah Mitchell commented: 'But the anti-feminist undercurrent still flowed.'[40]

A key issue for the interwar period is how the new electorate affected both the definition of 'women's issues' and also their ranking on the political agenda, and whether this led to a reconfiguring of the gender division of politics. Women did try to alter council priorities. For example, Lillian Pheysey, a Labour member of Bristol City Council, challenged her own party when she opposed the proposal for new City Council buildings in 1929 on the grounds that if an 'Aladdin's cave' were erected they would be told that there was no money left for other services such as health and new council housing.[41] Frustration continued for women who struggled to get women's issues taken seriously within their political parties. In 1935 Manchester Labour Women's Advisory Council resolved 'That on matters of party policy dealing with such questions as Education, Housing and Maternity services there shall be an immediate cessation of free voting on the part of the Labour Group in the City Council.'[42] For party women, translating a private matter into a political one had no effect unless it was recognised as a priority for their party, one which its representatives were obliged to support.

Women's minority position in local government and the opposition that they often faced, even from members of their own parties, led activists to pursue their goals in other, less party political, spaces. In some areas new organisations were formed to bring different women's groups together. In Bristol, for example, the Soroptimist Club was involved in a number of projects in the 1930s, including the question of lodging houses and residential flats for young women. When a meeting was organised with a speaker from London invitations to attend were sent to the National Council of Women (NCW), the Federation of University Women and the Electrical Association for Women.[43] The Club was also active in raising funds to help the Walker Dunbar hospital to establish a medical annexe for elderly women who needed care and nursing. It was to be named after Dr Elizabeth Blackwell, the first woman to qualify as a doctor.[44] Others continued to use the umbrella organisations that had developed before the war as a means to network on a largely agreed list of 'women's issues'. It has been assumed that these fora were eschewed by party women, yet the NCW (formerly the National Union of Women Workers) could bring together women across what elsewhere would be seen as insuperable barriers. The 1925 Report of the Manchester and Salford NCW reveals representatives of a wide range of philanthropic and welfare organisations from the Crippled Children's Help Society to the Council for the Unmarried Mother and her Child, but it also includes non-party political organisations such as the WCA as well as a Labour Party women's section. Labour councillor Dora Taylor attended as a representative of the Home Help Society and the Liberal councillor Janet Zimmern was the branch treasurer. However, to underline the ambivalence of many party women to such non-party women's groups, a local Women's Cooperative Guild had disaffiliated the same year. An important issue for the Manchester NCW was the campaign for women police, an undoubted 'women's issue', and the branch was predictably represented at conferences on temperance and on moral welfare but also at a No More War conference. In January 1926, the branch organised a two-day conference on one of the key women's issues of the interwar period, maternal mortality.[45] This is women's politics as much as the pioneering and often embattled women councillors.

The effect of the few successful political women on local women's politics could vary. Their energy could galvanise other women, although this depended on whether they identified as political *women*. They could break through cultural constraints and outright prejudice, as shown by Hannah Mitchell's attempts in the early 1920s to get selected as a Labour municipal candidate in Manchester.[46] However, the dominance of these women could also shut down other opportunities. Some, like Bessie Braddock in Liverpool, did not foster other women's participation in existing local political structures.[47] Others slotted in to what had already become accepted as a constricted space. For example local initiatives in World War One such as Food Control Committees had already established the idea that one woman was sufficient to represent undefined women's interests.[48]

Women's issues were not just those that related to the welfare of women as mothers, and to their children, although many were, or were figured in this way, such as peace. For instance, Annie Townley urged Bristol Labour women to follow the lead of those in Sheffield in trying to establish a peace day in schools in order to 'instil a love of peace in all children'.[49]

The interwar era saw new 'women's issues' cohere and seek space on the wider political agenda, notably housing.[50] Women claimed that they were experts in housing since their homes were their workplaces and therefore they argued that women should be central to the drafting of housing policy and the design of public housing. Celebrating ten years of work, the Manchester & Salford WCA included in its list of achievements the adoption of labour-saving suggestions for Corporation houses and a successful fight to secure a subsidy for the parlour house.[51] The full spectrum of women's political spaces were used to make the case for housing as a women's issue, for example arguing that new Corporation flats should have lifts: 'Of what use the outcry about maternal mortality if expectant mothers are forced to add the climbing of three flights of stairs many times a day to all their other inevitable fatigues?'[52] Here was an issue which directly linked to the experience of the 'unorganised housewife', whose daily life was affected by inadequate housing. Everyday life could be linked to women's politics: but could women activists connect with the housewife in her home?

Comparative local studies allow us to consider the effect of the experience of everyday life, not just on the particular practice of political women but also on their understandings of politics themselves. What did politics mean in everyday life and could a politics be made which bore a closer relationship to the everyday experience of unpoliticised women?

One space in which such issues were being explored in the interwar period centred on the figure of 'the housewife'. The issue was whether the ordinary housewife was only to be a passive audience for political propaganda or whether she could have a voice of her own and a means to articulate that voice. We know more about this in relation to the Second World War and beyond when housewives leagues finally become a British phenomenon.[53]

However, to understand the relationship between the housewife and interwar women's politics, it is crucial to explore continuities with earlier attempts to galvanise the housewife such as the pre-First World War efforts of socialist women to construct a gendered politics of consumption as well as the opportunities presented by the wartime politics of food.[54] It is significant that the longest lasting column in *Labour Woman* during the interwar period was titled 'The Housewife'. This was often a space where the politics of food was addressed as a 'woman's issue'. In 1920 readers of the column were told, 'It is no use grumbling; it is necessary to take action' and examples were given of local campaigns by Labour women to achieve the municipalisation of the milk supply.[55] Across the 1920s the purpose of this column varied. Pieces reporting on activism around food and exhortations to vote Labour in order to improve the conditions of the daily struggle of the housewife jostled for space with recipes and domestic hints. In contrast in the regular column headed 'Domestic' in North Bristol's Labour paper, *Bristol Forward*, women wrote articles on aspects of women's politics, such as local government, education or peace, rather than on domestic subjects. Their aim was to ensure that women voters should realise that 'politics touches the home life at all points. ... As soon as she rises in the morning and strikes a match to light the fire she is taxed. When she makes her tea for breakfast again she is taxed. ...Taxes are imposed by the government and she has to pay whether she likes it or not, and that's politics'.[56]

In a period traditionally characterised by a return to domesticity, the figure of the housewife was often invoked by politicians but her experience as a potential political force in the 1920s and 1930s has rarely been considered. Hannah Mitchell, in her journalism and political practice in Manchester in the 1920s, often addressed 'the housewife' but hers was not a conservative (with a small c) message. Her argument that 'no section of the community is more closely affected by the methods adopted by our local governing bodies than the woman in the home' was not that unusual or radical. The same could be said of her observation that the work of the City Council 'bears some analogy to the work of the women in the home: a sort of larger housekeeping'.[57] Yet her emphasis in discussions of 'the unemployed' on how women are never seen as unemployed and how there is no drive to limit the housewife's working week, was more challenging. She consistently emphasised how women's daily lives were affected by politics, for example by exploring the links between election day and washing day. She called for women to 'down washing tools and vote for more public washhouses'.[58] Here the home was a space which was not only affected by politics but out of which a new form of politics might emerge. Domesticity did not need to be conservative or confining, but according to Mitchell, it *had* to be addressed. There are certainly connections here with arguments made before the war by socialist women who tried to create a gendered politics of consumption as a way to reach and then to galvanise the ordinary working-class woman in her daily life.[59]

Exploring the links it made with the everyday is one way in which local women's politics can be seen as distinctive. Another approach is to reinstate emotion into our understanding of the meaning and experience of politics and the spaces in which the activist and the unorganised woman encountered one another. As political scientists have noted, too often academics portray human beings as rational and instrumental in their political views and actions and 'ignore the swirl of passions all around them in political life'.[60] This has gender implications since women's political claims are often belittled as 'emotional' with women voters portrayed as being particularly susceptible to emotional appeals. However, in certain historical circumstances the emotions that might be associated with, for example, women and family life, can become powerful political tools when women campaign for social welfare reforms or for other political causes.[61] Emotions can motivate individuals to become involved in social movements, create solidarities with others and sustain activities over a lengthy period. How does this apply to women's politics specifically? Often subject to criticisms – for neglecting husbands and children if they were married or for failing to follow the usual path towards a fulfilled life if they were not – women activists frequently used selfless dedication to a higher cause to validate their activities. Lilian Fenn, a Labour Party women's organiser, emphasised the emotional satisfaction she gained from her job since 'it was a great joy to have work furthering the principles and causes in which I believed' and to work with others to end the 'twin evils of poverty and war'.[62] Women such as this, who were confronted daily with the poverty of working-class women, did not just construct a narrative of their work in terms of an available discourse, unconnected to the suffering that they described, but expressed a specific 'structure of feeling that was rooted in a particular historical context'.[63]

Activist women made use of emotion to connect with the unorganised newly-enfranchised woman. One example is the effect of the Miners' Strike of 1926 on local non-mining communities. The chief woman officer of the Labour Party coordinated national efforts to provide relief for miners' families through a central women's committee but the practical work was conducted locally. The emphasis placed on relief for mothers and babies not only helped to motivate members of local Labour women's sections who raised money, collected clothing and organised its distribution, but it also enabled them to appeal to women in neighbourhoods who were not political activists. At the same time and separately, ILP and Communist women undertook solidarity work with miners' families, mobilising emotional engagement between, on the one hand, working-class women struggling to make ends meet outside mining communities, and on the other, with those suffering the additional deprivations of the miners' lockout.[64] These activities drew on, and in some cases helped to politicise, existing everyday networks of support between women in local neighbourhoods, resonating with earlier international examples of industrial solidarity which had successfully mobilised women within their local communities.[65]

The experience of the strike and subsequent lockout also led some women to think about a different kind of politics. Elizabeth Andrews, Labour Party women's organiser for Wales, described the dispute as an 'industrial war' which 'maimed mothers and babies' and therefore argued for a 'newer conception of politics' based on the model of the women's committees which put the needs of children at the centre of their efforts.[66] She wrote 'if we could only approach all our Economic, Social, National and International problems from this point of view, making the welfare of the child the basis of human relationships in Human Society, we would soon solve these problems'.[67] This was in tune with views that had already been expressed in *Labour Woman* that women's participation in politics 'would tend much to humanise what is now too mechanical in the machinery of politics'.[68] However, this was not just the province of Labour women. Conservative Nellie Beer said when elected to Manchester City Council in 1937: 'There are many domestic questions in which women can interest themselves, and I should like to have the opportunity of serving on such committees as housing, public health, or public assistance, which have the closest bearing on the homes of working families.'[69] However, how these aspirations materialised could result in different priorities and practices. It cannot be assumed that interwar women's politics was homogenous.

Comparative local studies enable us to explore the complexities of the everyday experience of women's politics, but they also challenge the assumption that the interwar period itself was homogenous. Our studies of socialist women and of communist women, have made us wary of generalising about the 1920s.[70] The character of the immediate post-war period, of the early twenties, the period around the General Strike and the later 1920s all differed and as the context changed so did the possibilities and practicalities of women's politics. Nor should it be assumed that women's politics in the 1930s was characterised by an ungendered focus on the effects of mass unemployment and the rise of fascism. Indeed, the biggest issue for women's politics in Manchester in the 1930s was maternal mortality, prompted by the Molly Taylor case, which led to a cross-party women's campaign for reform.[71] Similarly in Liverpool Bessie Braddock worked with a variety of non-party women's groups to organise a national conference on maternity and child welfare.[72] In the later 1930s, campaigning around the cost-of-living once again became a galvanising issue for political women as they reached out to the experience of 'the ordinary housewife'.

Focusing on the local gives a new perspective on the interrelationship between the local, the national and the international and how these were experienced in daily life. Mapping how the twists and turns of 'mainstream politics' affected women's politics in particular is important in itself and also because it is another part of the continuing story of the gendering of politics.

For women in their neighbourhoods in the interwar period a number of these sets of interrelationships can be illuminating: not only the changing relationship between the international and the local over the issue of peace (a significant element within women's politics of the period); but also the interplay between the national and the local, as politics became increasingly dominated by party, parliament, 'the national' and the metropolitan. The latter is apparent in examples where women's politics was affected by tension between the culture and politics of a local ward and a party's central office. Bristol East, for instance, dominated by the ILP for many years, had supported the pre-war suffrage campaign and had a record of encouraging women to stand as candidates for local government. However, in 1929 when the local party selected Leah Manning, a teacher, as their parliamentary candidate the national party intervened and imposed the 'unknown lawyer', Stafford Cripps.[73] Nonetheless, the local political culture remained intact so that during the Second World War Bristol East members were prepared to defy the official policy of the Labour party by supporting Jennie Lee who stood as an independent socialist for Bristol Central.[74] A full archaeology of interwar politics will allow us to not only to map the continuities, changes, fractures and reformations that characterised women's politics in the immediate decades after enfranchisement, but to explain them too.

In conclusion, therefore, we are suggesting that interwar women's politics should be reframed. The key is to follow the example of some revisionist suffrage historians in reconfiguring the national story by focusing on the local to explore the nature of women's networks; how women negotiated multiple and changing affiliations; and the interrelationship between women's organisations and other political organisations and pressure groups. Instead of compartmentalising women's experience in the parallel histories of particular parties, movements and organisations, women's politics should be seen as something which happens in a range of spaces. The connections between women's experiences of formal and informal politics in the interwar period allow us to foreground the extent to which the creation of a new female electorate made a difference to the practice and experience of politics in women's daily lives.

We therefore propose an archaeology of women's politics. It will place the interrelationship between the possible spaces for everyday politics – that individual women identified with, combined, moved through or rejected – within the context of the changing politics of the time. Equally important will be to recognise the role of preceding political cultures and experiences in shaping the possibilities for a women's politics in the aftermath of suffrage. The creation of this archaeology of women's politics will pose challenges for existing explanations of what happened after the vote was won but also how we understand politics more generally. We are not claiming that stories of women's politics can only be told when anchored within local political cultures but without this we only have a partial, patchy and even a distorted national picture. The national story of women's politics will change when it is rebuilt out from the neighbourhood – from the local and the everyday.

Notes

1. *New Leader*, 16 May 1924.
2. P. Thane, 'What difference did the vote make?', in A. Vickery, ed., *Women, Privilege and Power. British Politics, 1750 to the Present*, Stanford, CA, Stanford University Press, 2001, pp. 257–8. Although some suffragists, after experiencing the War, saw enfranchisement as an anti-climax. See M. Hilson, 'Women voters and the rhetoric of patriotism in the British General Election of 1918', *Women's History Review*, 10, 2, 2001, pp. 325–48.
3. C. Law, *Suffrage and Power. The Women's Movement, 1918–28*, London, IB Tauris, 1997, ch. 4.
4. K. Offen, *European Feminisms, 1700–1950: A Political History*, Stanford, CA, Stanford University Press, pp. 369–75.
5. For example, see J. Alberti, *Beyond Suffrage: Feminists in War and Peace, 1914–28*, Basingstoke, Macmillan, 1989; S. Pedersen, *Eleanor Rathbone and the Politics of Conscience*, New Haven, CT, Yale University Press, 2004.
6. P. Thane, 'Women in the British Labour Party and the construction of state welfare, 1906–39', in S. Koven and S. Michel, eds, *Mothers of a New World: Maternalist Politics and the Origins of Welfare States*, London, Routledge, 1993; P. Graves, 'An experiment in women-centered socialism: Labour women in Britain', in H. Gruber and P. Graves, eds, *Women and Socialism: Socialism and Women: Europe between the Two Wars*, Oxford, Berghahn, 1998; D. Tanner, 'Gender, civic culture and politics in South Wales: explaining Labour municipal policy, 1918–39', in M. Worley, ed., *Labour's Grass Roots: Essays on the Activities and Experiences of Local Labour Parties and Members, 1918–45*, Aldershot, Ashgate, 2005.
7. For example, see P. Thane, 'The women of the British Labour Party and feminism, 1906–1945', in H.L. Smith, ed., *British Feminism in the Twentieth Century*, Aldershot, Edward Elgar, 1990; P. Graves, *Labour Women: Women in British Working-Class Politics, 1918–39*, Cambridge, Cambridge University Press, 1994; D. Jarvis, '"Behind every great party": women and conservatism in twentieth century Britain', in Vickery, ed., *Women, Privilege and Power*; C. Beaumont, 'Citizens not feminists: the boundary negotiated between citizenship and feminism by mainstream women's organisations in England, 1928–39', *Women's History Review*, 9, 2, 2000, pp. 411–29; M. Andrews, *The Acceptable Face of Feminism: The Women's Institute as a Social Movement*, London, Lawrence and Wishart, 1997; G. Scott, *Feminism and the Politics of Working Women: the Women's Co-operative Guild, 1880s to the Second World War*, London, UCL Press, 1998. For an overview of the women's movement between the wars, see B. Caine, *English Feminism, 1780–1980*, Oxford, Oxford University Press, 1997.
8. Beaumont, 'Citizens not feminists', p. 425.
9. See, for example, Adrian Bingham, *Gender, Modernity and the Popular Press in Inter-War Britain*, Oxford, Oxford University Press, 2004; H. McCarthy, 'Parties, voluntary associations and democratic politics in interwar Britain', *Historical Journal*, 50, 4, 2007, pp. 891–912; J. Lawrence, 'The transformation of party politics after the First World War', *Past and Present*, 190, 2006, pp. 185–216; L. Beers, *Your Britain. Media and the Making of the Labour Party*, Harvard University Press, 2010.

10. D. Jarvis, 'Mrs Maggs and Betty. The Conservative appeal to women voters in the 1920s', *Twentieth Century British History*, 5, 2, 1994, pp. 129–52; M. Hilton, 'The female consumer and the politics of consumption in twentieth century Britain', *Historical Journal*, 45, 1, 2002, pp. 103–28. See also Chapter 2 in this book by David Thackeray.

11. For a discussion of the meaning of 'women's politics', see K. Hunt, 'Rethinking activism: lessons from the history of women's politics', *Parliamentary Affairs*, 62, 2009, pp. 211–26.

12. For an overview of local suffrage activities, see J. Hannam, '"I had not been to London". Women's suffrage – a view from the regions', in J. Purvis & S.S. Holton, eds, *Votes for Women*, London, Routledge, 2000; L. Leneman, 'A truly national movement: the view from outside London', in M. Joannou and J. Purvis, eds, *The Women's Suffrage Movement: New Feminist Perspectives*, Manchester, Manchester University Press, 1998.

13. Examples include Worley, ed., *Labour's Grass Roots*; S. Davies, *Liverpool Labour: Social and Political Influences on the Development of the Labour Party in Liverpool, 1900–39*, Keele, Keele University Press, 1996; N. Evans and D. Jones, '"Help forward the great work of humanity": women in the Labour Party in Wales', in D. Tanner *et al.*, eds, *The Labour Party in Wales, 1900–2000*, Cardiff, University of Wales Press, 2000.

14. V. Wright, 'Education for active citizenship: women's organisations in inter-war Scotland', *History of Education*, 38, 3, 2009, pp. 419–36; E. Breitenbach, 'Scottish women organising and the exercise of active citizenship c.1900–c.1970', in E. Breitenbach and P. Thane, eds, *Women and Citizenship in Britain and Ireland in the Twentieth Century*, London, Continuum, 2010; R. Davidson, 'Citizens at last: women's political culture and civil society, Croydon and East Surrey, 1914–39', PhD, Royal Holloway, 2010.

15. For example, see J. Hannam, 'Making areas strong for socialism and peace: Labour women and radical politics in Bristol, 1906–1939', in K. Cowman and I. Parker, eds, *Radical Cultures and Local Identities*, Newcastle upon Tyne, Cambridge Scholars Publishing, 2010; C. Hunt, '"Success and the ladies": an examination of women's experiences as labour councillors in interwar Coventry', *Midland History*, 32, 2007, pp. 141–59; L. Newman, '"Providing an opportunity to exercise their energies": the role of the Labour women's sections in shaping political identities, South Wales, 1918–39', in Breitenbach and Thane, eds, *Women and Citizenship*; D. Tanner, 'Gender, civic culture and politics'.

16. K. Hunt, 'Making politics in local communities: Labour women in interwar Manchester', in Worley, ed., *Labour's Grass Roots*; A.M. Hughes, *Gender and Political Identities in Scotland, 1919–1939*, Edinburgh, Edinburgh University Press, 2010.

17. J. Guard, 'A mighty power against the cost of living: Canadian housewives organize in the 1930s' and J. Smart, 'The politics of the small purse: the mobilization of housewives in nterwar Australia', *International Labor and Working-Class History*, 77, 2010, pp. 27–47, 48–68.

18. See, for example, K. Hunt, *Equivocal Feminists. The Social Democratic Federation and the Woman Question*, Cambridge, Cambridge University Press, 1996, ch. 9.

19. See J. Hannam and K. Hunt, *Socialist Women. Britain, 1880s–1920s*, London, Routledge, 2002, pp. 94–6.

20. *The Bristolian and Clifton Social World*, October 1913. See also C. Haskins, 'Elected women in local government in Bristol during the interwar years', MA, University

of the West of England, 2001. Useful comparisons can be drawn with Devon: J. Neville, 'Challenge, conformity and casework: the first women councillors in interwar Devon', paper presented at Aftermath of Suffrage Conference, Sheffield, June 2011.

21. P. Thane, 'Women and political participation in England, 1918–1970', in Breitenbach and Thane, eds, *Women and Citizenship*, p. 17.

22. S. Innes, 'Constructing women's citizenship in the interwar period: the Edinburgh Women Citizens' Association', *Women's History Review*, 13, 4, 2004, pp. 621–47; M. Savage, *The Dynamics of Working-Class Politics: The Labour Movement in Preston 1880–1940*, Cambridge, Cambridge University Press, 1987.

23. *Manchester & Salford Woman Citizen* (hereafter *Woman Citizen*), 28 October 1929.

24. *Labour Woman*, May 1920.

25. *Manchester Guardian*, 31 October 1928.

26. M. Pugh, *Women and the Women's Movement in Britain, 1914–59*, Basingstoke, Macmillan, 1992, pp. 61–6.

27. *Bristol Evening News*, 25 June 1924; St George West Ward Women's Section Minutes, 1920s, BRO, 40488/M/9.

28. Bristol East Labour Party, Minutes of General Council, 1946–1948, BRO, 4088/M/9/3.

29. T. Sinnett, 'The Labour Party in Bristol, 1918–1929', PhD, University of the West of England, 2006, pp. 176–7; ch. 4.

30. *The Bristolian and Clifton Social World*, October 1913.

31. This was discussed in an article written two years later: *Bristol Evening News*, 13 June 1925.

32. P. Hollis, *Ladies Elect. Women in Local Government, 1865–1914*, Oxford, Clarendon Press, 1987.

33. C. Hunt, '"Everyone's poor relation": the poverty and isolation of a working-class woman local politician in interwar Britain', *Women's History Review*, 16, 3, 2007, pp. 417–30.

34. *Leeds Weekly Citizen*, 6 April 1928.

35. *The Failsworth Industrial Society's Monthly Messenger*, August 1923; May 1929; December 1928.

36. *Labour's Northern Voice*, 19 June 1925.

37. *Woman Citizen*, 16 October 1924.

38. Councillor Annie Lee in *Manchester Evening News*, 12 July 1934.

39. *Woman Citizen*, December 1937.

40. H. Mitchell, *The Hard Way Up*, London, Virago, 1977, p. 218.

41. Sinnett, 'The Labour Party in Bristol', ch. 6.

42. Manchester Labour Women's Advisory Council Minute Book, 1 April 1935, Manchester Central Library (MCL), M449/1.

43. Soroptomist Club of Bristol, projects, 1934–1939, BRO, 31642(21)d.

44. Ibid. correspondence, 18 February and 25 March, 1938.

45. 29th Annual Report of National Council of Women (Manchester, Salford and District Branch), 1925, MCL, 396 N15.

46. Mitchell, *The Hard Way Up*, pp. 194–5.

47. Davies, *Liverpool Labour*, pp. 179–81.

48. K. Hunt, 'The politics of food and women's neighbourhood activism in First World War Britain', *International Labor and Working-Class History*, 77, 2010, pp. 12–15.

49. Bristol Labour Party Central Women's Committee minutes, BRO 40488/M/4/3, 14 September 1934.

50. Manchester Women's History Group, 'Ideology in bricks and mortar. Women and housing in Manchester between the wars, *North West Labour History*, 12, 1987, pp. 24–48; K. Hunt, 'Gendering the Politics of the Working Woman's Home' in E. Darling & L. Whitworth, eds, *Women and the Making of Built Space in England, 1870–1950*, Aldershot, Ashgate, 2007.
51. *Woman Citizen*, 15 October 1923.
52. Letter, *Manchester Evening News*, 13 September 1934.
53. See, for example, J. Hinton, 'Militant housewives: the British Housewives League and the Attlee government', *History Workshop Journal*, 38, 1994, pp. 129–56.
54. K. Hunt, 'Negotiating the boundaries of the domestic: British socialist women and the politics of consumption, *Women's History Review*, 9, 2, 2000, pp. 389–410; Hunt, 'The politics of food'.
55. *Labour Woman*, March 1920. For a discussion of the politics of milk, see F.Trentmann, *Free Trade Nation*, Oxford, Oxford University Press, 2008.
56. *Bristol North Forward*, February 1922
57. *Labour's Northern Voice*, 22 October 1926.
58. *Labour's Northern Voice*, 21 October 1927.
59. See Hannam & Hunt, *Socialist Women*, ch. 6.
60. J. Goodwin *et al.*, 'Introduction: Why emotions matter', in J. Goodwin *et al.*, eds, *Passionate Politics: Emotions and Social Movements*, Chicago, University of Chicago Press, 2001, p. 1.
61. C. Florin, 'Heightened feelings. Emotions as 'capital' in the Swedish suffrage movement', *Women's History Review*, 18, 2, 2009, pp. 181–201.
62. L. Fenn, 'I liked my job', *Labour Woman*, January 1954.
63. J. Sangster, *Transforming Labour: Women and Work in Post War Canada*, Toronto, University of Toronto Press, 2010, p. 258.
64. S. Bruley, *The Men and Women of 1926*, Cardiff, University of Wales Press, 2010.
65. E. Ross, 'Survival networks: women's neighbourhood sharing in London before World War I', *History Workshop*, 15, 1983, pp. 4–27; A. Cameron, *Radicals of the Worst Sort. Laboring Women in Lawrence, Massachusetts, 1860–1912*, Urbana, University of Illinois Press, 1993, ch. 4.
66. U. Masson and L. Newman, 'Andrews, Elizabeth (1882–1960): Labour Party women's organiser for Wales', in K. Gildart *et al.*, eds, *Dictionary of Labour Biography, Volume X1*, Basingstoke, Palgrave Macmillan, 2003.
67. *Colliery Workers' Magazine*, January 1927, quoted in ibid., p. 8.
68. *Labour Woman*, February 1920.
69. *Daily Dispatch*, 3 November 1937.
70. Hannam & Hunt, *Socialist Women*; Hunt and Worley, 'Rethinking British Communist Party women'.
71. For a contemporary account of the Molly Taylor case, see *Labour Woman*, January 1935. For the context, see J. Emanuel, 'The Politics of Maternity in Manchester, 1919–39', MSc, Manchester University, 1982.
72. Davies, *Liverpool Labour*, p. 180.
73. L. Manning, *A Life for Education: An Autobiography*, London, Victor Gollancz, 1970, p. 81.
74. R. Whitfield, *A Brief history of Bristol South East Constituency Labour Party, 1918–1950*, 1979, Pamphlet 1115, BRO.

8
'Shut Against the Woman and Workman Alike': Democratising Foreign Policy Between the Wars

Helen McCarthy

In her 1936 novel, *Honourable Estate,* Vera Brittain tells the story of Ruth Allendeyne, an intelligent, soulful young woman born into a wealthy, Midlands manufacturing family, and her search for a purpose in life. After the war claims her beloved brother, best friend, and the dashing American officer with whom she enters into a passionate love affair, Ruth eventually finds this purpose with the intellectual Denis Rutherford, a young man schooled in the values of mutually respectful, companionate marriage by the unhappiness of his own mother, the victim of a possessive and patriarchal husband. The story ends with Ruth's victory as a Labour candidate at the election of 1929 and her early career as a pioneering woman MP, work she combines with motherhood, a status happily and voluntarily entered into, thanks to her knowledge of birth control and to Denis's spousal cooperation.

Honourable Estate is a rich, multi-layered novel which gives imaginative life to the questions preoccupying its author in the mid-1930s, questions about the new possibilities created by women's enfranchisement; about the social and political implications of an increasingly organised and assertive working class; and about what might be done to halt the drift towards another catastrophic war. For Vera Brittain, these questions were intimately inter-connected. As Denis tells Ruth shortly after their first meeting in 1922:

> I don't believe there'll ever be a lasting peace until politically-minded women give their minds to it in the same way as they gave them to the suffrage movement. For one thing, they're more biologically interested than men in eliminating war – and then, like the suffragettes, they've often got a capacity for dramatising things that men can't equal.[1]

With her sharp intellect and flair for public speaking, Ruth, Denis urges, must become one of the 'men and women who'll make these issues dynamic and urgent from public platforms the world over. It's the man in the street we want to get at', he continues:

> in spite of all the politicians who suffer from stupidity or vanity or megalomania, war doesn't happen nowadays through the mysterious influence of omnipotent "authorities". No authority on earth could force war on a democratic people unless their inextinguishable aptitude for cherishing wrong-headed notions made them ready and even anxious to accept it.[2]

With Denis as her mouthpiece, Brittain seeks to persuade her readers that war *can* be prevented if only the good sense of the mass electorate, and especially its newly enfranchised female members, would mobilise against the destructive forces of militarism and nationalism.

In making the connection between universal suffrage and international peace, Brittain was far from a lone voice between the wars. The confident claim that mass democracy would moralise foreign policy was made repeatedly in this period by progressives, who enthused about the demise of aristocratic monopoly and secret diplomacy and trumpeted the potential of public opinion to bring war-mongering governing elites to heel. This chapter aims to show how the introduction of universal suffrage generated in Britain a renewed idealism concerning the possibilities of a 'democratised' foreign policy, but one which was distinctively gendered. As the editors of this volume point out, the impact of mass democracy and the passage of female enfranchisement cannot be studied or understood separately, yet these phenomena have usually occupied distinct and disconnected literatures. Historians have studied at great length the resurgence of popular pacifism and the evolution of new ideas about international relations in the decades following the war.[3] They have also explored in depth the impact of enfranchisement upon the scale and scope of women's participation in British political life, including non-party pressure groups dedicated to the pursuit of peace and international understanding.[4] Despite this gendering of interwar political history, however, what the existing literature largely fails to spell out is the intimate connection between the democratic idealism of the immediate post-war era and women's political agency in the sphere of foreign affairs. As Julie Gottlieb notes in Chapter 9 in this volume, there was much speculation between the wars as to how the new female electorate would engage with questions of foreign, imperial and defence policy, all areas of government which anti-suffragists had earlier placed beyond women's 'natural' sphere of knowledge and interests. As this chapter argues, it was the mothers of the world who were expected to form the front line in the war on war, emboldened, in Britain at least, by their new-found electoral power. For some feminists this aspiration extended to include women's direct access to the foreign policy-making process through their admission to the diplomatic profession, which remained a male preserve between the wars.

Nonetheless, as the chapter goes on to reveal, by the mid-to-late 1930s, when *Honourable Estate* had barely left the printing press, these ideals were fading fast, overshadowed by international events and overpowered by the resilient defences of the old diplomatic ways. Ultimately, and despite the best efforts of the real-life Ruths and Denises of Britain, democracy could not force entry into this still secretive branch of government and drag foreign policy decision-making into the glare of publicity. Priya Satia has pushed this argument further, claiming that the advent of mass democracy forced the state to go to ever greater lengths to keep foreign policy in the hands of officials and elite 'experts' by cultivating public ignorance of its shadowy activities in Britain's new empire in the Middle East.[5] Whilst the development of 'official secrecy' was undoubtedly a notable feature of the interwar imperial state, this chapter places greater emphasis on debates concerning the possibilities and limitations of public opinion in relation to international affairs more broadly. By the late-1930s, those stressing the limitations appeared to be winning the argument. The door to foreign policy influence remained, as one commentator observed in 1938, 'shut against the Woman and Workman alike'.[6]

* * *

That popular government could somehow 'moralise' the conduct of diplomacy was an idea dating back at least to the radical politics of the late eighteenth century, and one which remained a significant strand within political discourse through most of the Victorian period.[7] It was from the late-nineteenth century onwards, however, and against the backdrop of an increasingly democratic franchise, the growth of a mass-circulation press, and intensifying imperial rivalries abroad, that this radical critique moved towards the centre of political debate. Secrecy in government, according to such critics as E.D. Morel, J.A. Hobson and H.N. Brailsford, served the interests of financiers and armaments firms by concealing from the public their shadowy role in fomenting capitalist–imperialist war, aided by a complicit 'yellow' press. In his lacerating critique of the government's handling of the Moroccan Crisis of 1911, later republished as *Ten Years of Secret Diplomacy*, Morel argued that Britain had been brought to the very brink of war as a result of 'the intrigues, the lack of straightforward dealing, and the absence of foresight on the part of diplomacy working in the dark and concealing its manoeuvres from the national gaze'.[8]

These radical perspectives were further amplified by fears of an all-powerful Foreign Office and dismay at the secrecy surrounding Britain's entry into the War in August 1914, a point taken up with great energy after that date by the

Union of Democratic Control (UDC).[9] On platforms and in pamphlets, UDC leaders accused the government of conniving to minimise Parliamentary scrutiny of foreign policy and to keep the British public entirely ignorant of decisions taken in their name. 'The present Government's tenure of office has been marked by an almost complete abstention from public reference to foreign affairs', read one early tract. 'The public has been treated as though foreign affairs were outside – and properly outside – its ken.'[10] Radical MP and former diplomat Arthur Ponsonby devoted the greatest attention to this theme, authoring multiple works in which he pressed for urgent and systemic reform.[11] His programme included increased public oversight of all Foreign Office business, Parliamentary consent as a requirement for making declarations of war or signing treaties and, finally and most importantly, the education of the electorate so as to dampen the 'bellicose and combative passions' inflamed by press, music hall and warmongering demagogues and to nurture instead the 'rational and pacific instincts'. He continued:

> The peoples must tear the bandage from their eyes, cast the gag from their mouths, and prepare themselves; so that, seeing and understanding, they may help in the councils of the world with a better chance than their Governments, their statesmen, and their diplomatists, whom they have allowed too long to exercise, behind closed doors, the sole management of affairs which concern their national existence.[12]

The feminist Helena Swanwick, one of the few prominent female members of the UDC, added an important gender analysis to this radical critique, explicitly connecting the cause of democratic control to the cause of women's suffrage. Women, she argued in 1915, 'whose physical force is specialised for the giving and nurture of life', suffered worst from rampart militarism and stood to gain most from the establishment of a moral law amongst nations.[13] Women's enfranchisement, she reasoned, would speed the latter and eliminate the former, a proposition echoed in the writings of other anti-militarist feminists such as Catherine Marshall, Isabella Ford, Kathleen Courtney and Mary Sheepshanks. In a speech of 1915, Marshall argued that 'the experience and habits of mind which women acquire as mothers of families and as heads of households' equipped them perfectly for the larger task of building 'a better system of international relations which would make impossible the repetition of such a tragedy as that in which we are now involved'.[14] Although feminist pacifism remained a controversial stance during the war, this linking of women's maternal and pacific qualities to their political rights and civic duties would become a commonplace within interwar internationalism. As Hunt and Hannam note in Chapter 7 in this volume, anti-militarism in the 1920s provided a means of extending the scope of maternalist politics beyond 'mothers, welfare and washhouses'.[15]

More generally, the proposition that foreign policy should, in future, become more 'democratic' had moved into mainstream political debate by the end of the war, when many in Britain turned their thoughts towards the possibilities of international government for preserving peace amongst nations. The Foreign Office convened a committee of experts in 1918 to consider these possibilities in depth; in their report, they identified a growing conviction amongst the peoples of Europe that the experience of total war, together with the toppling of autocratic regimes in its wake, would necessitate a wholesale transformation in the conduct of foreign policy:

> At a moment when the forms and spirit of popular government are acquiring a noticeable accretion of strength in every direction, and when the vast majority of those who have to fight are not only voters but civilians by profession and inclination, it is becoming an article of faith widely and sincerely professed in most countries that there is no quarrel between nations for which an equitable settlement could not be found without recourse to war, provided the voice of the people could make itself heard, and the necessary machinery were called into existence.[16]

For many, the League of Nations – the intergovernmental body created at the Paris Peace Conference – appeared to embody this new democratic idealism which placed the 'voice of the people' at its heart. In Britain, its cause was taken up by the League of Nations Union (LNU), a new internationalist pressure group which was notably more centrist and broad-based in character than the UDC.[17] Robert Cecil, LNU Chairman and later President, believed that the League had the potential to eradicate secrecy and intrigue from international relations for good by substituting in their place transparent structures which allowed for rigorous public scrutiny. As he explained to the Prime Minister, Stanley Baldwin, in 1926: 'One of the chief principles on which the success of the League depends is that the general public opinion of the world is in favour of peace, and that in international difficulties an appeal shall be made to this opinion.'[18] The LNU, for its part, attempted to mobilise and vocalise British public opinion through a flurry of activities – from public meetings and pamphleteering to theatrical pageants and study circles – building, in the process, a mass movement comprised of thousands of local branches and organisational affiliates. The latter included such organisations as the National Council of Women, the British Legion, the Scout Association and Rotary International, alongside the Anglican and nonconformist churches.[19]

Public opinion thus acquired a new significance in the discussion of international relations, and the League of Nations became an important arena for its expression. Yet if public opinion were to act as the new arbiter between nations, it needed to be educated as well as mobilised. As the LNU's monthly journal, *Headway,* told its readers in 1929: 'What is wanted is not merely abstract sympathy with the League's endeavours, but a reasonably accurate general knowledge of what the League has done in the past and an intelligent understanding of what it is endeavouring to do in the present.'[20] The LNU was not alone in wishing to educate the British people on the subject of international affairs, nor in believing that there existed a new appetite amongst the public for greater understanding of the forces making for conflict between nations. As one academic surveying the growth of interest in international studies in the late 1930s remarked: 'The deep emotional and intellectual impression left by the War and its aftermath has created an unwonted desire to take stock of the conditions of the modern world, and to grapple with the new problems of social conduct and organisation to which the changes of the last one hundred and fifty years have given rise.'[21]

It is difficult to quantify this upsurge of interest with any precision, but the fact of its existence can be inferred from the founding of bodies such as the Council for the Study of International Relations, Chatham House and the Geneva School of International Studies; the introduction of 'international relations' to undergraduate degree courses, extra-mural syllabi and adult school classes; the extensive educational activities of the LNU itself; and the lectures, study circles and educational overseas tours arranged by a wide range of organisations, from Women's Institutes, YMCA clubs and Free Church Councils to Women's Co-operative Guilds, Labour Colleges and trade union branches.[22] Not all of these groups explicitly linked the study of international affairs to the radical democratic control agenda, and some were more obviously aimed at policy elites or dedicated political activists rather than the general masses. But most did acknowledge the duty of citizens in a democratic society to be better informed about such matters and better prepared to hold their governments to account.

Women, with their newly won political rights, were identified as an especially crucial target group for political education of this kind. One leaflet produced by the LNU in 1921 and addressed to the 'Women of England', reminded its readers of their potential political influence but also their responsibility as citizens of the world. 'You have achieved political power,' it began:

> Your voices form a majority in this State. You can have your will. Would it not be a great thing to open the era of your full citizenship by exercising that power, not to benefit a class, not to gain some selfish end, but to confer upon the whole world the gift for which it is praying – Peace.[23]

Many women's organisations made the same link between responsible citizenship and knowledge about international affairs, setting up dedicated 'Peace' or 'League of Nations' committees and pledging support to LNU campaigns. Over fifty organisations had affiliated to the LNU's Women's Advisory Committee by 1922 in order to keep abreast of League affairs and to co-ordinate activities on themes ranging from disarmament and arbitration to humanitarian relief and the welfare of women in the new mandated territories.[24] Some went further by encouraging local branches to affiliate to the LNU as 'corporate members' or 'associates'. 572 individual Women's Institutes had done so by 1934, encouraged by national headquarters 'to keep themselves informed of the work of the League and to do all they can to further its efforts to create a well-informed public opinion on the many questions that arise in the greatest effort ever made to promote real friendship among the peoples of the world'.[25]

Women's active participation in foreign policy debates was demonstrated with particularly dramatic effect in the LNU's famous Peace Ballot of 1934–5, a voluntary referendum designed to gauge opinion on Britain's membership of the League, international control of armaments and the use of collective sanctions against aggressor nations.[26] Half-a-million volunteers were recruited to carry out the onerous task of delivering paper forms to households throughout the country, many of them mobilised through the LNU's organisational affiliates, including a strikingly large number of women's organisations. No fewer than 21 of the 38 participating national organisations in England and Scotland were women's associations, and the separately-organised Welsh effort received similar levels of assistance from women.[27] The loyal service of this 'door-knocker parade' (as they became known) was routinely trumpeted in *The Ballot Worker,* a monthly newssheet for volunteers; it listed details of women's imaginative fund-raising efforts, of whole districts worked almost exclusively by women's organisations, and of the valuable effects upon female volunteers and voters alike. 'It was very educative,' a canvasser from the Baptist Women's League observed, 'for we had to know the facts, and how best to deal with all types of questions.'[28] Meanwhile an organiser in Birmingham was delighted to find that the women in her district wanted 'to discuss matters they never bothered about before'.[29]

Although the Ballot created some controversy and drew criticism from supporters of the National Government, the sheer number of Britons prepared to complete the Ballot papers – which totalled nearly 12 million, or about a third of the adult population – was widely acknowledged to be an astonishing feat.[30] Ballot supporters frequently alluded to the ordinariness of the 'quiet citizens' who had seized this opportunity to make their views known.[31] For some feminists, the Ballot was proof of the seriousness with which women took their duties as newly enfranchised citizens. Veteran suffragist Kathleen Courtney was convinced that the Ballot's democratic character had factored heavily in winning women's support, as she told Prime Minister Stanley Baldwin during a deputation to the Foreign Office in July 1935. 'The recognition of the value of the judgment and intelligence of the ordinary woman for whom I speak was of the essence of the National Ballot and the ordinary woman responded to it.'[32]

As well as arguing for women's inclusion in public debate concerning international affairs, interwar feminists also called for direct access to the foreign policy-making process through the admission of women to Britain's Diplomatic Service. The Sex Disqualification (Removal) Act (SDA) of 1919, which swiftly followed female suffrage, paved the way for women's admission to the prestigious administrative grade of the Home Civil Service but left overseas posts reserved to men. These included the Diplomatic and Consular Services, the Colonial Service, the Indian Civil Service and the Trade Commissioner Service, all of which remained off limits to women. These restrictions attracted little comment at the time; Parliament debated the question only briefly during the passage of the SDA, and even those who defended women's right to jobs in the Home Civil Service drew the line at sending them abroad.[33] Women's societies deplored these restrictions, but there was little opportunity to revisit the issue before 1929, when a Royal Commission on the Civil Service (the Tomlin Commission) was appointed to look into – amongst other issues – the employment of women in public service.

The women's societies who appeared before the Commissioners treated the question of women's admission to the Diplomatic Service not merely as a matter of employment rights, but one connected to wider questions concerning women's substantive contribution to international understanding and accord. The representatives of the National Union of Societies for Equal Citizenship (NUSEC) argued for the opening of diplomatic careers to women in recognition of the much broader range of issues, including those of a social and economic nature, with which modern diplomacy was now forced to deal: 'The presence of responsible women attached to Embassies and Legations,' they argued, 'would bring the world of international diplomacy into wholesome relation with the standards and social practices of the world of politics and economics, from which in the past it has been disastrously remote.' They added: 'It is in fact one aspect of the democratisation of international diplomacy which is a condition of constructive internationalism'.[34]

This identification of women with the 'social' dimensions of international diplomacy was equally evident in the arguments placed before the Interdepartmental Committee appointed by the Foreign Office in 1934 to consider the question of women's admission to the Diplomatic Service at greater length. A female diplomat, as the London and National Society for Women's Service argued, would be much better equipped to report on the changing social conditions of women in the country to which she was posted, and to get in touch with women's movements, whose part 'in the development of civilisation was speedily increasing all over the world', particularly in those states which had granted female suffrage.[35] A number of witnesses endorsed, on these grounds, the appointment of specialist women attachés in selected posts as an interim measure should the Committee fail to accept the case for full equality with immediate effect. Akin to the naval or military attachés routinely posted to embassies, they would exist, as Dame Edith Lyttelton explained, 'for the sole purpose of gathering and understanding what it is the women in enfranchised countries especially are thinking and doing'.[36]

Lyttelton had herself demonstrated just how much a suitably qualified woman could contribute through her service as substitute-delegate for Britain at the annual Assembly of the League of Nations on no fewer than five occasions. Tellingly, she chose for her debut speech to the Assembly in 1923 the subject of educating children for peace. 'If all the women combined all over the world to teach the children to hate war,' she declared to the assembled delegates, 'and if they fostered the ideals of brotherhood, there would not be any war. If women chose to combine they could disarm the world.'[37] Lyttelton sat, like women from other member-state delegations, on the Assembly's Fifth Committee, whose remit covered assorted questions of a social or humanitarian nature, including the opium trade, the relief of refugees, child welfare and trafficking in women. Lyttelton took a special interest in the first and last of these issues, convinced that international cooperation could combat such evils far more effectively than disparate national endeavours. This was a view shared by Rachel Crowdy, chief of the Social Questions Section and the highest-ranking woman in the League secretariat. After her appointment in 1919, Crowdy became an instant magnet for the international women's societies swarming into Geneva to lobby delegates and officials on their favoured causes; she used what influence she possessed to divert League resources towards these problems, and won an impressive victory in 1923 when the League appointed a special Commission to investigate the scale and nature of the global trade in women and children.[38]

Some voices questioned this tendency to identify women's international interests with 'social' questions. Helena Swanwick, who took Lyttelton's place in the delegation the following year, described the Fifth Committee's remit as 'a sort of rag-bag of miseries and forlorn hopes' and remarked ruefully of its typical agenda: 'A woman, it appeared, was assumed to be well-informed about Opium, Refugees, Protection of Children, Relief after Earthquakes, Prison Reform, Municipal Co-operation, Alcoholism and Traffic in Women.'[39] Swanwick did, as it so happened, know a little about the last of these subjects, but as for the rest was as ignorant as her fellow male delegates. Swanwick recalled in her memoirs that she would have far preferred to sit on a Committee dealing with issues on which she possessed proper expertise, such as Disarmament, and was mildly irritated when the other women delegates asked her to address the Assembly on their behalf on the subject of the Geneva Protocol. This desire to avoid being restricted to dealing with questions deemed of a 'feminine' nature was also evident amongst some advocates of women's admission to the Diplomatic Service.

The Council for Women Civil Servants, for instance, played down the 'special contribution point', insisting that diplomacy required qualities and attributes which could be found in equal measure in both sexes. They therefore rejected the idea of women attachés on the grounds that it boxed women into a separate, specialist career track and delayed their employment on mainstream diplomatic work.[40]

These critical perspectives underlined a broader ideological tension present within interwar feminism concerning the place of maternalist understandings of sexual difference within the wider struggle for equality.[41] Yet they never threatened to displace the widely-held belief that women had a 'special' contribution to make in the international sphere. Women's 'natural' affinity with matters of a social or humanitarian nature was frequently linked in public discourse to their maternal status (actual or potential), and to their special interest in peace. This very obviously echoed aspects of wartime feminist anti-militarism, which conceptualised war as an affront to the 'mother-heart of womanhood', in Marshall's words.[42] Vera Brittain rehearsed the very similar sentiments she was shortly to put in the mouth of Denis Rutherford in a piece for a woman's magazine in early 1934:

Because women produce children, life and the means of living matter to them in a way that these things can never matter to men. Yet too many wives and mothers make a virtue of taking no interest in 'politics', although it is only by political methods that a new and yet vaster annihilation of human life can be prevented.'[43]

She went on:

It is useless to have a nursery if you do nothing to prevent that nursery from being blown to bits within the next few years. I believe that women of the world could stop war if they ceased to be completely absorbed in themselves and their homes and their children, and began to realise that their duty to mankind extends beyond their own little doorstep.[44]

This framing of women's international responsibilities in maternalist terms, which inflected so much interwar feminist discourse, had a wider cultural purchase. This same maternalist–pacifist trope was present, for example, in such ideologically disparate organs as the journal of the Women's Institutes and that of the Labour Party women's organisation, *Labour Woman*. Writing in the former in 1934, a Mrs G. Marriage of Kelsale and Carlton remarked that the question of peace was 'a matter on which all women should make their voices heard, urging all those in authority to do their utmost for Peace. Those of us with sons growing up especially realise the need for urgent action'.[45] Similarly, readers of *Labour Woman* were asked against the backdrop of the Disarmament Conference in 1932 to ponder the question:

> Are we training our children to have a Peace mentality?...Has each of us, as a wife and mother, done her utmost to protect the children of the future? Do not let us mince words or have muddled ideas about the matter. DISARMAMENT IS THE RESPONSIBILITY OF THE MOTHERS OF THE WORLD.[46]

Finally, this trope could also be found in much LNU literature, which urged women to mobilise around the ideal of international government, not merely as new voters, but as mothers. 'War is the negation of all women's primary instincts', a leaflet of 1934 told its readers: 'War means *destruction*. Women are concerned with *construction;* with bearing and rearing children, with home-making, with caring for the weak, the sick, the aged, with preserving the lives that War must destroy.'[47] Strikingly, internationalist appeals targeted at *men* adopted gendered language of a very different kind, typically invoking the ex-serviceman's harrowing experience of combat in the Great War and playing up the supposedly dire consequences of any future war for the pay-packet of the family breadwinner.[48]

The 'democratisation' of foreign policy was, thus, a powerful proposition within interwar public debate, and of particular resonance within discourses concerning women's special responsibilities as both newly-enfranchised citizens and mothers. But it was also, in many respects, a highly problematic proposition, and one which, in the final analysis, failed to gain any real traction over the conduct of British diplomacy or foreign policy decision-making. The major explanation for this failure is the gulf of understanding which existed between advocates of democratisation and Britain's governing elites – a gulf which even the LNU, with its well-connected leaders, failed to bridge. These elites were far from convinced of the case for democratic control, or even for greater measures of openness and transparency in their dealings with other nation-states. The Conservative or Conservative-led governments, which dominated the period, were generally sceptical of the League's efforts to foster cooperation between the nations, whilst Whitehall officials remained attached to more traditional and closed forms of diplomacy. In a letter to Cecil in 1933, the powerful Cabinet Secretary Maurice Hankey defended these methods, arguing that secrecy was often crucial for the successful outcome of negotiations, whilst publicity had to be handled with care. 'At the right stage public meetings are essential,' he wrote, 'at the wrong stage they are disastrous.'[49] Even when Ramsay MacDonald and Arthur Ponsonby, former UDC radicals, entered government in 1924, they found themselves unable to transform the prevailing culture in the Foreign Office; Ponsonby registered a minor success with the introduction of the 'Ponsonby Rule', which required all treaties to be placed before the Commons for 21 days before receiving ratification, thus facilitating scrutiny and discussion.[50] Yet this reform, on its own, could not effect a recalibration in the balance of power over foreign policy towards Parliament.

The persistence of traditionalism also put paid to feminist designs on the Foreign Office. Given the dim view which Foreign Office chiefs took of general arguments in favour of democratisation, it was hardly surprising that they failed to see the force of the feminist case for women's admission to the Diplomatic Service, rooted as it was in assumptions about the broadening remit of diplomacy in the contemporary world. The claim that women's movements overseas were now worthy of the Foreign Office's attention did not persuade the Ambassador in Buenos Aires, Sir Henry Chilton, who told the Interdepartmental Committee in 1934 that the women's suffrage movement in Argentina was 'not taken very seriously' in political circles.[51] Sir Ronald Graham, a former ambassador to Rome and a Foreign Office representative on the Committee, interrupted Edith Lyttelton as she gave her evidence to remark that the task of keeping in touch with local female opinion was already performed perfectly adequately by (unpaid) diplomatic wives: 'I have had the most important information given me by ladies of the Embassy and by my own wife', he insisted. 'The female channel is not entirely closed.'[52] Another official, RCS Stevenson, agreed that the special expertise which might be supplied by a woman diplomat was unnecessary, but for a different reason: 'Just as soon as a women's movement becomes of political importance,' he told the Committee, 'then men can keep an equally effective watch on it as a woman can.'[53]

There were further objections to the proposed admission of women to diplomatic careers. Foreign officials, it was said, would not take a female diplomat seriously and British interests would therefore be compromised; female diplomats, it was further assumed, would be limited in their geographical mobility – and hence their value to the state – as a result of marriage and motherhood; and finally, women, it was alleged, were physically and temperamentally too delicate for overseas service, and especially for consular work, which often involved dealing with unsavoury characters in ports. These arguments won the day, and women were denied the opportunity of entering the Diplomatic Service until after the Second World War.[54] This victory for the masculine status quo was yet further indication of the barren ground upon which arguments for democratisation fell at the Foreign Office. Quite apart from the question of women, the case for broadening the social spectrum from which *male* diplomats were recruited had secured only the mildest expressions of support in the 1920s. The old property qualification was abolished in 1919, accompanied by minor changes to the form of the competitive entrance exam, but there was little sense that Britain's diplomatic corps had – or, indeed, in the future *should* – become a mirror of the wider society. A pamphlet published by the Fabian Society in 1930 revealed the continuing dominance of public-school educated males at the Foreign Office and Britain's embassies abroad.[55]

The gulf of understanding separating Britain's governing elites and advocates of democratisation was deepened further by the often uncritical assumptions held by the latter concerning the capacities of 'public opinion'. The case for democratisation rested on an assumption about the willingness of mass electorates to engage in serious, well-informed discussion of foreign policy matters, and the further assumption that public opinion, once educated, would always swing behind the cause of peace and reconciliation. Both assumptions were doubtful in interwar Britain. British people, as a whole, were undoubtedly better informed on international affairs between the wars than at any point previously, and they could, as the Peace Ballot demonstrates, be mobilised *en masse* on occasion. There is certainly little basis for suggesting that interwar Britons were apathetic towards foreign policy; the tone and content of much party-political debate suggests that politicians certainly *believed* that voters cared about international affairs.[56] Yet it was, undeniably, only ever a minority who were involved in sustained activism through the LNU or other political bodies.

Furthermore, whilst it is reasonable to say that the core tenets of liberal internationalism won support across a wide political spectrum, they were never hegemonic; more belligerent and nationalistic sentiments were evident on the diehard right of the Conservative party and in certain sections of the right-wing popular press. Coverage of the League was consistently hostile in the *Daily Express* in the 1930s, for instance, with the Peace Ballot repeatedly coming under fire throughout 1934 and 1935.[57] The elision of public opinion with the cause of international peace was rendered more problematic in the 1930s by the emergence of an assertive, physically demonstrative anti-fascist movement on the left, and by the growing conviction amongst some LNU loyalists that Hitler's designs on Europe needed now to be actively resisted. Naturally, there had been divisions and differences within internationalist circles before, but, as the international crisis deepened in the later 1930s, any notion of a unified 'public opinion' in support of some generalised and under-theorised conception of 'peace' became impossible to sustain.

The desire to educate citizens so as to understand better the twists and turns of international affairs was not lost. The LNU's work amongst schoolchildren was continued into the 1940s and beyond by a new body, the Council for Education in World Citizenship, whilst the LNU itself, having been renamed the United Nations Association (UNA) in 1945, extended its activities amongst university students; these included the popular 'Model United Nations' programme in which thousands of young people in Britain participated – and continue to do so, even today.[58] Yet the democratic idealism which captivated so many at the end of the First World War, when it seemed possible to remake the world through international cooperation and friendship, was not renewed in 1945. At the UNA's first post-war meeting in the Albert Hall in autumn 1945, veteran internationalist Gilbert Murray noted that amongst the crowds there was 'not the same buoyant hope, not the same expectation of a millennium'.[59] The United Nations failed to inspire the extraordinary levels of enthusiasm and devotion lavished upon the League thirty years earlier. As Kathleen Courtney noted in 1949, the post-war public was altogether more sceptical of grand schemes for international peace, particularly in light of the unfolding ideological struggles of the Cold War: 'The United Nations Association', she wrote:

> faces public opinion in a very different mood. The League of Nations had been tried and did not prevent a second world war. A new world organisation naturally met with a somewhat cool and critical reception and the events of its first years have brought further doubt and disillusion.[60]

It would seem, in fact, that even Vera Brittain recognised the failure of the democratic ideal, or at least the fragility of its aspirations, when she wrote *Honourable Estate* over a decade earlier. Ruth asks Denis if he thinks that the League of Nations will do any good, and his answer is prophetic:

> It might. I think it would, if we could only obliterate the diplomats and politicians who were in charge of everything before the War. Their minds are hard set in the old ways...I wouldn't mind betting you that ten or fifteen years hence, the pre-war statesmen will still be running our foreign affairs. By that time, if the League exists at all, they'll have turned it into a convenient instrument of the old diplomacy, doing their work for them all the more effectively under a safe camouflage of altruistic benevolence.[61]

Notes

1. Vera Brittain, *Honourable Estate* (London: Virago, 2000, first published 1936), p. 442.
2. Ibid.
3. See, for example, Martin Ceadel, *Semi-Detached Idealists: the British Peace Movement and International Relations, 1854–1945* (Oxford, 2000); Cecilia Lynch, *Beyond Appeasement: Interpreting Interwar Peace Movements in World Politics* (London, 1999); Donald Birn, *The League of Nations Union 1918–1945* (Oxford, 1981); David Long and Peter Wilson, eds, *Thinkers of the Twenty Years' Crisis: Inter-war Idealism Reassessed* (Oxford, 1995); Jeanne Morefield, *Covenants Without Swords: Idealist Liberalism and the Spirit of Empire* (Princeton, 2005).
4. For women's involvement in the interwar peace movement, see Johanna Alberti, *Beyond Suffrage: Feminists in War and Peace, 1914–1928* (Basingstoke, 1989), and Martin Pugh, *Women and the Women's Movement in Britain, 1914–1999* (Basingstoke, 2000, 2nd edn), pp. 103–7.
5. Priya Satia, *Spies in Arabia: the Great War and the Cultural Foundations of Britain's Covert Empire in the Middle East* (Oxford, 2008), and see also 'Inter-war agnotology: empire, democracy and the production of ignorance' in Laura Beers and Geraint

Thomas, eds, *Brave New World: Imperial and Democratic Nation-Building in Britain Between the Wars* (London, 2012), pp. 209–25.

6. Alison Graham, 'For Women Only', *Headway*, December 1938, p. 34.

7. For a classic account of the tradition of 'dissent' over foreign policy-making, see A.J.P. Taylor, *The Troublemakers: Dissent Over Foreign Policy 1792–1939* (London, 1957).

8. E.D. Morel, *Ten Years of Secret Diplomacy: An Unheeded Warning* (London, 1915), p. xix.

9. M. Swartz, *The Union of Democratic Control in British Politics During the First World War* (Oxford, 1971).

10. UDC, *The Morrow of the War* (London, 1915), p. 4.

11. Arthur Ponsonby was Liberal MP for Stirling Burghs from 1908, having abandoned an earlier career in the Foreign Office. He helped to found the unofficial Parliamentary Liberal Foreign Affairs Group following the Agadir Crisis in 1911.

12. Arthur Ponsonby, *Democracy and Diplomacy: A Plea for Popular Control of Foreign Policy* (London, 1915), p. 114.

13. Helena Swanwick, *Women and War* (London, UDC pamphlet No.11, 1915), pp. 4,12.

14. Cited in Margaret Kamester and Jo Vellacott, eds, *Militarism Versus Feminism: Writings on Women and War* (London: Virago, 1987), p. 40.

15. See p. 130.

16. Final Report of the Committee on the League of Nations, 18 July 1918, MSS Zimmern 82, 7, Bodleian Library, Oxford.

17. Many radicals associated with the UDC were, by contrast, sceptical of the League due to its origins in the Treaty of Versailles, which they viewed as a capitalist-imperialist document designed to shore up the global power of the 'Big Three': Britain, France and the USA. This position was not, however, universally held on the left; the LNU recruited many allies from the Labour and Trade Union movement. See Helen McCarthy, *The British People and the League of Nations: Democracy, Citizenship and Internationalism, c.1918–1945* (Manchester, 2011).

18. Cecil to Baldwin, 31 March 1926, British Library, London (BL): Papers of Viscount Cecil of Chelwood, Add. MSS 51080, fol. 172.

19. McCarthy, *The British People*.

20. 'Heart and Head', *Headway*, May 1929, 91. See also 'Heart and Head', *Headway*, December 1930, 231.

21. S.H.Bailey, *International Studies in Modern Education* (Oxford, 1938), 16.

22. Ibid., and see also S.HBailey, *International Studies in Great Britain* (London, 1933), and John Toye and Richard Toye, 'One World, Two Cultures? Alfred Zimmern, Julian Huxley and the Ideological Origins of UNESCO', *History* (95) 2010, pp. 308–31. For a detailed survey of League-related educational work, see McCarthy, *The British People,* ch. 4.

23. LNU, 'Women of England' (1921) copy in records of the National Council of Women, file marked 'League of Nations, 1921', Acc/3613/03/002/E, London Metropolitan Archives.

24. For full list, see Appendix to Executive Committee minutes, 21 December 1922, LNU/2/5, ff24–5, British Library of Political and Economic Science, London.

25. *Home and Country*, Jan 1934, Vol. XVI, No.1, p. 5.

26. McCarthy, *The British People,* ch. 7.

27. 'Reports of Work' in minutes of Welsh Women's Advisory Committee, 15 June 1935, WNC/B1/127 /3, National Library of Wales, Aberystwyth.

28. 'Women on the Front Line', *The Ballot Worker*, No.8, 23 May 1935, p. 8.

29. 'Frontline reports' *The Ballot Worker*, No.6, 25 April 1935, p. 3.

30. Martin Ceadel, 'The first British referendum: the Peace Ballot, 1934–5' *English Historical Review*, 95 (1980), pp. 810–39.

31. Helen McCarthy, 'Democratizing Foreign Policy: Rethinking the Peace Ballot, 1934–5', *Journal of British Studies* 49 (2010), pp. 358–87.

32. 'Notes of a delegation received by the Prime Minister at the Foreign Office from Societies Co-operating in the National Declaration on the 23rd July, 1935', p. 11. PREM 1/178, The National Archives.

33. For a detailed account of this story, see Helen McCarthy, 'Petticoat Diplomacy: The Admission of Women to the British Foreign Service, c.1919–1946', *Twentieth Century British History*, 20 (2009), pp. 285–321.

34. Evidence of the National Union of Societies for Equal Citizenship to the Tomlin Commission, 26 February 1930, in minutes of evidence, volume 1, p. 460, T169/17, The National Archives.

35. Statement submitted to the Schuster Committee by the London and National Society for Women's Service, March 1934, FO/366/930, p. 238, The National Archives.

36. Dame Edith Lyttelton's evidence to the Schuster Committee, 1 March 1934, TNA, FO/366/928.

37. Cited in Hebe Spaull, *Women Peace-Makers* (London: George G Harrap & Company, 1924), p. 121.

38. Barbara Metzger, 'Towards an International Human Rights Regime during the Inter-War Years: The League of Nations' Combat of Traffic in Women and Children' in Kevin Grant, Philippa Levine and Frank Trentmann (eds), *Beyond Sovereignty: Britain, Empire and Transnationalism, c.1880–1950* (Basingstoke, 2007), 54–79; Daniel Gorman, 'Empire, Internationalism, and the Campaign against the Traffic in Women and Children in the 1920s', *Twentieth Century British History*, 19 (2008), 186–216.

39. Helena Swanwick, *I Have Been Young* (London, 1935), p. 385.

40. Evidence of Council of Women Civil Servants to Schuster Committee, 22nd March 1934, TNA FO/366/928.

41. A tension which has been characterised in terms of 'old and 'new' feminism, although the distinction should not be overplayed. For a useful discussion, see Susan Pedersen, *Eleanor Rathbone and the Politics of Conscience* (London, 2004), chapter 10.

42. Marshall, 'Women and War', p. 40.

43. 'Can the Women of the World Stop War?' from *Modern Woman*, Feb 1934, pp216–220 in Paul Berry and Alan Bishop, eds., *Testament of a Generation: The Journalism of Vera Brittain and Winifred Holtby* (London, Virago, 1985), p. 218.

44. Ibid.

45. *Home and Country*, April 1934, 217.

46. *Labour Woman*, February 1932, DIS/6/11, 25.

47. LNU, *Women, Work for Peace!*, (London, 1934).

48. McCarthy, *The British People*, pp. 196–7.

49. 27 October 1933, handwritten note from Hankey to Cecil, f98, Cecil Papers, Add. MSS 51088.

50. It was subsequently reversed by the incoming Conservative government and then reinstated in 1929.

51. Sir Henry Chilton's evidence to the Schuster Committee, 16 March 1934, FO/366/92.8.

52. Dame Edith Lyttelton's evidence to the Schuster Committee, 1 March 1934, TNA, FO/366/928.
53. Evidence of RCS Stevenson to the Schuster Committee, 21 March 1934, TNA, FO/366/928.
54. See McCarthy, 'Petticoat Diplomacy'.
55. Robert T. Nightingale, *The Personnel of the British Foreign Office and Diplomatic Service, 1851–1929* (London, 1930).
56. A point made by Susan Pedersen in her review of Ross McKibbin's *Parties and People* in *Twentieth Century British History*, 21(4), 2010, pp. 561–4. McKibbin suggests – erroneously – that foreign affairs were electorally marginal in interwar politics. Ross McKibbin, *Parties and People: England, 1914–51* (Oxford: Oxford University Press, 2010).
57. McCarthy, *The British People*.
58. McCarthy, *The British People*, conclusion.
59. 'UNA is launched' *International Outlook*, November 1945, p. 2.
60. Kathleen Courtney, 'The Task Before Us', *United Nations News*, Sept./Oct. 1949, 9.
61. Brittain, *Honourable Estate*, p. 435.

9

'We Were Done the Moment We Gave Women the Vote': The Female Franchise Factor and the Munich By-elections, 1938–1939

Julie V. Gottlieb

From the immediate post-war and post-enfranchisement years to the out-break of the Second World War two issues preoccupied press, politicians and public. The first was how the universal franchise – particularly the women's vote – would redraw the political landscape and alter the nature of politics. Already in 1918 Lord Esher set a fretful tone by foreseeing that 'an avalanche of women has been hurled into the political chaos. Institutions as well as ideas will have to be re-sorted'.[1] The second area of deep uncertainty was the reconstruction of the international order after the rupture and annihilation of the Great War. The mass electorate's imagination was captured by the recasting of international relations, the expectancy placed on the League of Nations, the menace of extremist alternatives at home and abroad, and myriad campaigns promising the path to world peace.[2] The scholarship on each of these themes is vast and varied but, ultimately, quite discrete, tend-ing not to recognise how intimately the two issues were, in fact, overlapping and intrinsic. Indeed, one of the main objections to women's enfranchise-ment was on the grounds that as a sex they were not suited to decide foreign and imperial affairs. This attitude persisted even after the war, and was well illustrated, for instance, by the state's reluctance to remove the bar to women joining the diplomatic service. When the House of Lords debated the Representation of the People Bill, clause 4 of which dealt with franchises for women, Earl Loreburn (L) moved to leave out the sections that would confer the vote on women. He made what was and would continue to be a familiar and familiarly patronising claims about women's moral superiority, and that 'whatever good there was in men was largely due to the affection, the influence, and the teaching of women'. However, that did not mean that women were worthy of full citizenship; on the contrary, they were especially unsuited to take important decisions on imperial affairs:

> He was referring now to questions of Imperial policy, the ultimate end of which was peace or war, and he asked the House to say whether feminine

159

influence ought at once to become very powerful, and most probably in the near future predominant, in matters of that kind. (Cheers.)... He did not doubt that the desire to do right would be as strong in women as in men, but on the whole he held that men were safer than women as judges on grave matters of this kind (hear, hear.) It looked to him a very dangerous 'leap in the dark' to transfer the responsibility on women.[3]

While Earl Loreburn and those who agreed with him would not carry the day in legislative terms, there was much agreement for the next twenty years at least that women's enfranchisement was a leap in the dark, and that where the female electorate's influence was most undue and potentially subversive was regarding these matters of foreign affairs.

This chapter focuses on a few months in the autumn and winter of 1938–39, the Munich Crisis and the subsequent by-elections, when the press and politicians certainly believed that pro-Chamberlain women and anti-appeasement men were on a collision course in deciding the nation's destiny.[4] The Munich Crisis and the history of appeasement have been largely neglected by gender historians. Likewise women, both individual figures and the female half of the polity, have been almost entirely ignored by historians of appeasement. As I will argue here, however, women represented an important if unknown franchise factor in the Munich by-elections, while the representation and the experience of the Munich Crisis was starkly gendered. It would thus be against this backdrop of deep sex antagonism and distrust of women's political judgement on matters of war and peace that women themselves reflected upon their own achievements two decades after they were enfranchised. It was also in this context of the perceived alienation between the sexes that the nation entered the Second World War. The upheaval of the First World War had occasioned a blurring of gender lines, leading 'many in British society to see in a reestablishment of sexual difference as the means to re-create a semblance of order'.[5] If the First World War was followed by the negotiation of a 'gender peace', as Susan Kingsley Kent has persuasively argued, by the eve of the Second World War this symbolic treaty was all but null and void, the breach running parallel to the breakdown in understanding between nations. On the symbolic level, and on the psychological level, Britain stood on the brink of another world war already embroiled in a sex war on the home front. We can see this tense discursive gender peace bending under the strain of international disorder from the Munich Crisis onwards. In the case of the Munich Crisis, many identified a direct causality, namely that the emancipation of women had facilitated the dishonourable policy of appeasement, and, more broadly, sown the seeds of national decline. This was summed up neatly by the former diplomat and now Edenite National Labour MP Harold Nicolson, confessing in his diary less than a fortnight after the Munich Agreement: 'Go up to Leicester. Bertie Jarvis says I have put the women's vote against me by abusing Munich. I expect that the historians of our decline and fall will say that we were done the moment we gave the women the vote.'[6] British women, as a collective, and women voters, as a bloc, were being set up as the fall guys, the fall girls, if you prefer, for the failure of the odious policy of appeasement.

This study takes the path less travelled in the historiography of appeasement by not only turning the gaze to women but to public and popular opinion on foreign affairs.[7] It is a truism that in a democracy the most respected if not always the most reliable indicator of public opinion is the election. By-elections in particular serve a number of functions. They offer opportunities to try out new party tactics, they have been used to test innovations in publicity, and they present opportunities to field new forms of organization, but most crucially they are thought to reveal the state of public opinion in relation to both specific issues and to the likely outcome of subsequent general elections.[8] The anti-appeasement paper the *Daily Mirror* claimed that electoral success hinged upon appealing to women voters, with headlines such as 'Women can Make Premier Change His Policy', on the eve of the by-elections at Fulham and Litchfield.[9] The focus on women voters as a bloc was due, of course, to the addition of 4,750,000 women voters to the electorate with the Equal Franchise Act (July 1928). While empirical evidence shows that women do not vote on gendered lines, it is true to this day that we hear about the women's vote, women's issues, and women's political priorities, conflations not 'paralleled by debates about political men'.[10] The 2010 General Election was dubbed the 'mumsnet election', and the appeasement by-elections of 1938 could well be summed up as the 'Munich Mums' elections. Indeed, the by-elections of 1938 and 1939, especially the immediate post-Munich by-elections, an unusually high number being imminent, were seen as general elections in miniature, and gender played a more significant part in them than has previously been acknowledged. Eatwell has shown how the government did badly in the series of seven by-elections that took place in October and November 1938, even as the Munich Agreement 'was believed to have been received with great rejoicing by the majority of the people of Britain'. However, while Eatwell's analysis is entirely convincing, especially his assertion that 'foreign policy in the two months after Munich attracted greater public attention than at any time since the clash between Gladstone and Disraeli over the Bulgarian massacres', at no point does he stumble upon the oft remarked polarisation of opinion between male and female cohorts of the British population.[11] In regard to the Oxford and Bridgwater by-elections, MacLean does, in contrast, recognize the importance of the perception of women's identification with the appeasers, but emphasizes the lack of social scientific evidence that can prove such a hypothesis.[12]

Allowing for the shortcomings of available data, gender played a part in these by-elections in a number of significant ways, all the while keeping in mind that the integration of women into party politics was slow. In 1922 the three major parties nominated only 33 women for the 615 seats.

The total rose to 69 by 1929, but this was still only 4 per cent of the total number of candidates, and by 1935 it was just 5 per cent.[13] There were many women among the by-election candidates, and, interestingly considering the assumption that women were the strongest supporters and advocates of appeasement, only one of the women candidates was a pro-Chamberlain National Government candidate. The only pro-appeasement woman candidate was Dr Catherine Gavin standing in the South Ayrshire by-election. There was much concern and debate about the impact the female electorate would have on the results – and this could be identified at all points of the political spectrum. Further, the whole appeasement debate and support for Chamberlain had already been gendered by the political parties and the press. The study of the representations of women's engagement in the political process in these post-Munich by-elections speaks for more than the sum of its parts. The relationship between gender and power, and the precarious place of women both in the enlarged electorate and as political actors and agents was part of a dialectical paradigm shift in the discourse that constructed and constricted women's citizenship. This shift was well illustrated by the feminization of the policy of appeasement in the press and in political campaigns.

The West Fulham by-election of March 1938 is part of this story even though it took place before the Munich Agreement was signed. It was at a by-election at East Fulham in late October, 1933 that Labour had snapped up the seat, with a swing of 29.2 per cent, one of the most remarkable ever recorded. The results in East Fulham were among the early motivations for the organization of the LNU's (League of Nations Union) Peace Ballot, as it was perceived that a referendum on international control of armament production and arms reduction by international agreement would demonstrate wide public support.[14]

The West Fulham by-election was similarly newsworthy as it came at a critical time, shortly after Anthony Eden's resignation as Foreign Secretary.[15] Of course Eden himself was very popular with women voters, a matinee idol among politicians. The importance of good looks was seen to be on the rise as 'now that women have the vote, for some reason, a symmetrical set of features is not unhelpful to a candidate'.[16] In Fulham where the by-election was regarded as 'a referendum in miniature on British foreign policy',[17] the candidacy of Labour's Dr Edith Summerskill was significant in itself. Her sex was at once a point of strength and a liability. On the positive side, she had the ear of women voters and played on her distinguished medical career and her specialization in welfare issues.[18] On the down side, it was noted that women voters had little to no interest in the European situation, and it was to this burning issue that Summerskill would really have wished to direct the attention of voters. In the early stages of the campaign she represented herself as standing for the removal of all the disabilities of women whether legal, economic or social, and it was duly noted that she had 'lectured frequently on equal pay and opportunity and the problems of the professional woman and the status of women under democracy and under dictatorship'.[19] In short, she was both a feminist and anti-fascist, as well as a feminist anti-fascist, her European and fascist encounters sharpening her political conviction.[20] Against such a formidable woman politician as Summerskill, it was good practice for the Conservatives to have Nancy Astor in Fulham to campaign for their candidate, Mr Busby, and Astor addressed a meeting of 175–200 women, mainly middle-aged, where she supported the Prime Minister and highlighted the failure of the League.[21]

Even though Summerskill had the support of Lloyd George's Council of Action, the League of Nations Union, and the Liberals (with figures such as Wilfrid Roberts and Megan Lloyd George coming to speak on her behalf), and at the beginning of her campaign at least one-third of her speeches were devoted to foreign policy, she increasingly shifted to social questions. In contrast, Mr Busby, her pro-Government Tory opponent, kept foreign matters and defence policy in the forefront. Sir Archibald Sinclair, an anti-appeaser himself, was leader of the independent Liberals, while Lloyd George had detached himself from the Liberal Party since 1931 and formed his own Council of Action for Peace and Reconstruction. It was a significant player in all Popular Front campaigns. It had the support from across party lines, including Eleanor Rathbone and Labour's Margaret Bondfield.[22] In Fulham it was observed that women voters 'remain, as they have always been in lower middle-class constituencies... concerned chiefly with such things as rent, rates, employment and the price of food'.[23] Once it seemed clear that women voters were not inspired by discussion of foreign affairs – in fact, quite the contrary – Summerskill changed track and downplayed the foreign affairs element of her campaign. She did this to such an extent that another newspaper surmised that she was 'hardly happy when talking of foreign affairs, and her replies, when questioned on Socialist policy in the present tangled skein of international matters obviously failed to carry conviction'.[24] Indeed, Summerskill was bowing to public pressure, and Mass-Observation conducted a straw-poll survey on the eve of the by-election which revealed a number of interesting tendencies. Asked 'Which is more important, home or foreign affairs?', there were some apparent gender differentials, with the predictable penchant of women taking less interest in foreign affairs.

Summerskill was wise to tailor her appeal to the domestic front. Whether it was because she listened to her woman constituent, aged 60, who said 'Don't believe in foreigners' or took M-O's conclusions to heart, Summerskill's strategy could not have contrasted more with that later adopted by the Duchess of Atholl, even when they had in common their passionate opposition to appeasement. As we will see, the Duchess would lose her by-election because she identified herself exclusively with foreign policy and thus, by extension, with war. Hawkishness was seen as unbecoming, especially for a woman politician. In the end Summerskill's strategy was a wise one, winning the seat for Labour with a narrow majority (16,583 votes verses 15,162 for the Conservative Busby).

Eager to congratulate Summerskill on her victory was Ellen Wilkinson. With her win there were now three Labour women sitting as MPs: Summerskill, Agnes Hirdie and Wilkinson. Summerskill was a formidable public figure, and her Fulham win was the beginning of a very successful parliamentary career. Indeed, by-elections were an important route by which women entered parliament. As Pugh has shown, between 1918 and 1939, 31 women contested by-elections for the three main parties, a tactic especially favoured by Labour which provided 18 of them, and of the total of 36 women who became MPs between the wars no fewer than 10 first entered parliament through by-elections:

> The explanation for this is that for the parties rather less was at stake at a by-election than at a general election. The by-election was also a useful test of electors' reactions since it was tempting to focus attention upon the individual candidates, especially if they were women. That women polled very well on these occasions when placed under the limelight makes the parties' reservations about them seem irrational even in this period.[25]

Quick on the heels of the Munich Agreement there was speculation that a general election would be called in order to cash in on Chamberlain's vast popularity with women voters:

> Mr Chamberlain is a bold man, as everybody has come to understand by this time...The election rests with him. He is being pressed by some of his advisers and some of his newspapers to have a snatch election, in which he is to be paraded before the electorate, particularly the women voters, as the man who saved us from war.[26]

But in the absence of a general election, the post-Munich by-elections were the best indicators of the Prime Minister's wavering popularity with the electorate as a whole and with women in particular, and the public anxiety about the power of women as an electoral force. By mid-October seven new by-elections were due to be contested, all of which were understood to provide an instructive reflection of public opinion on the Government's foreign policy. These were Oxford City, Dartford, Walsall, Doncaster, West Lewisham, and Bridgwater and the Fylde Division of Lancashire.

Furthermore, these by-elections were covered at the local, national and international level, the *New York Times* reporting that as a group they represented the 'miniature general election',[27] as well as making frequent remarks in its reporting about the significance of gender differentials. Of the Gallup poll taken in mid-October, it was noted how 'the Prime Minister is much more popular with Britain's women voters – who, incidentally, outnumber the men – than with men voters'.[28] This acute concern with the gender ratios of franchise holders was already typical of the same newspaper's coverage of the lead-up to the Equal Franchise Act a decade before, opining that the significance of women outnumbering men by 2,000,000 electors would be 'that Britannia, not content with ruling the waves, has stepped ashore and intimated John Bull, politely but firmly, that the Englishman's house is no longer his castle, but hers'.[29] This was a fear of men being engulfed by women, and the nation being feminized, and in particular its foreign policy being emasculated.

Oxford City was perhaps the most famous of these by-elections due to the candidacy of Alexander Dunlop Lindsay (Independent Progressive), Master of Balliol College and long-standing member of the Labour Party. Here the conventional opposition parties withdrew in order to give the best chance to the anti-government candidate. Oxford was also a groundbreaking by-election as it saw the first constituency opinion poll ever conducted in Britain. Further, it was in the fight for this seat that the Popular Front was its most united, exemplifying not only the possibilities of collaboration between Labourites and Communists, but more crucially between Labour and Liberals.[30] But while Oxford City has been studied from various angles, it has yet to be subjected to a thorough gender analysis. Here too the ambivalence about the power of the female electorate was very much in evidence. The very motivation for Lindsay's candidature has been attributed to a woman's influence: while he had thus far lacked any parliamentary ambitions, he had an 'enthusiastic' wife.[31] Both Lindsay and his opponent Quintin Hogg (Con.) were reported to be 'wooing the women voters of the constituency by every means at their disposal, by personal canvassing, and by loudspeaker vans which have made electors listen willy-nilly to the claims of either side'. Hogg was even better equipped than his opponent as he was 'admirably supported by Mrs Hogg and a host of women workers'.[32] Lindsay, on the other hand, had cross-party support for his united Progressive Front, including that of some of the most vociferous of the women anti-appeasers Mrs Corbett Ashby, Lady Rhondda, Lady Layton, Megan Lloyd George, Lady Violet Bonham Carter and Miss Ellen Wilkinson. The by-election also caused rifts within families, with Lady Violet Bonham Carter campaigning energetically for Lindsay while her mother the countess of Oxford and Asquith announced she would vote for Hogg.[33] In the end, there was much speculation about what could account for Lindsay's loss, a recurring explanation being women's continuing gratitude to Chamberlain for saving the peace just weeks before. 'The evidence of workers in the recent Oxford by-election showed that even there, almost in the centre of England, a large proportion of women were still obsessed by gratitude to Mr Chamberlain for momentarily averting war.'[34]

M-O's founder Tom Harrisson conducted a snap poll in Oxford on the eve of the by-election and he offered a rather more than usually impressionistic and personalized survey, particularly preoccupied by the gender gap. His report exuded frustration and anger that women were likely to vote against Lindsay.[35]

He remained hopeful that even if women's opinion was pro-Chamberlain, many would ultimately be swayed by their husbands in the end as it remained the case that the 'man of the house is most important'.

Harrisson and his fellow observers found that there was respect for Lindsay and that he was regarded as an outstanding candidate, but that this view prevailed mainly among those within academic circles. When asked

WHAT do you think about Lindsay as a candidate?... Women are undoubtedly far more ProChamberlain than men. I think that the problem of this election is the female vote. Leave the men to vote according to their powerful tradition of that obscure 'fair play.' In this snap sample, with only two hours to do it in, about a hundred people were interviewed. MEN who were favourable to Lindsay equalled in number those against and doubtful. WOMEN for Lindsay were outnumbered by against and doubtful by five to one.

These results, although admittedly not entirely satisfying, led Harrisson to make a number of suggestions that might help Lindsay's campaign along. His suggestion was this: 'Deal all the time with women. In this connection, do NOT forget that women have reacted violently against the crisis, via gas masks, and that the line of approach to them is not likely to work if Anti-Chamberlain, for they feel he saved us from war, and it is impracticable to argue that in this short campaign.' Under these circumstances he averred that 'the line can only be Home Affairs. And the crisis reaction has swung women back onto that with a woosh'. Harrisson allowed his own impressions and partisanship to intrude, much more in keeping with the remit of M-O diarists than with the objective social scientist. He remarked, throwing academic caution to the wind with his free use of expletives: 'The general feeling of men: Fuck Hitler. And we ought to have stood up to him before. The general feeling of women: Anything for peace. Chamberlain did his best. He's a good gent.'[36]

Harrisson's view of the Oxford by-election was a fair prediction of the outcome, but where he and others were mistaken was in the belief that all these closely-timed by-elections would go the same way. The outcome of the Oxford city by-election of 27 October 1938, with a 76.3 per cent turnout, was Hogg (Con.) 15,797, and Lindsay (Independent Progressive) 12,363. Further, M-O's analysis of the Crisis had a wide influence, especially when it was published as part of their Penguin Special. A review in *The Pioneer* summarized M-O's findings as: 'on the whole, women were for peace at any, or Mr Chamberlain's, price; that men were much more bellicose. . . . From the latest figures it would appear that anti-Chamberlain feeling is building up rapidly among men. As enquires from 6,000 women show that 75 per cent vote the same way as the dominant male in their family, whatever they may say when casually questioned, this is a pointer to which the PM should pay attention.'[37] For Conservatives the result was seen to vindicate

Chamberlain. Upon the result Hogg announced that 'It is not my victory. It is Mr Chamberlain's.' In contrast:

> those on the other side have tended to take the view expressed by Lindsay and endorsed by his daughter and biographer: namely that Oxford started the anti-Chamberlain bandwagon, Bridgwater gave it a push and the Norway debate of May 1940 saw it home. This has been contrasted with the view that public opinion stayed with Chamberlain until Hitler occupied Prague in March 1939, and then deserted him.[38]

Nonetheless, this impression of the sway and sensibilities of the female electorate would require some rethinking.

In Dartford the Conservative candidate Mr G.W. Mitchell (Conservative) was running against Mrs J.L Adamson (Labour) in what was considered to be the tightest race of the lot. Adamson had contested this seat in the 1935 General Election, narrowly losing to the Conservative. (In 1935 there was a Conservative majority of 2,646; in 1929 Labour had won the seat with a 10,000 strong majority). Unlike the Fulham contest earlier that year where Summerskill had sought to play down the foreign policy issues, Adamson's race was widely regarded as a referendum on the recent Munich agreement. There was no attempt to deemphasise foreign policy even though the anti-Government candidate was female. She too had cross-party support in the shape of the Council of Action. Further, the centrality of foreign policy was illustrated by the 'unusual incident' of the LNU holding a meeting at the Town Hall in Crayford on the subject of 'Which way to world peace?', where both candidates appeared on the platform to answer questions on a questionnaire.[39] Her opponent was standing or falling by the Munich Agreement, and he asked voters to elect him as a mark of gratitude to and confidence in Mr Chamberlain.

Even as the post-Munich euphoria was fading, there remained serious concern that this by-election would go the way of Oxford City. Women's 'obsession' with gratitude for the PM was reckoned to be even stronger in a largely working-class division that extended along the south bank of the Thames almost from Woolwich to Gravesend, and was thus particularly vulnerable to air attack in the event of war. While there was some evidence 'that a certain number of Conservative male voters will abstain through disgust either at the Government's weak foreign policy or at its rearmament and ARP failures', it was still expected that 'the extra women's vote will more than compensate for those defections'.[40] Of all the by-elections, Dartford was considered the most difficult to forecast because:

> opinion three weeks ago had swung over to predict the return of the Government candidate through the votes for women offered in thankfulness to Mr Chamberlain. Since then shock of the crisis has lifted and

criticism has been poured out by opponents of the Government. It must be largely a matter of guessing how far the pendulum has moved again.[41]

Were women voters still so enamoured with Chamberlain the peace maker?

In the final reckoning, Adamson won with a 4,238 majority (Adamson (Lab.) 46,514; Mitchell (Con.) 42,276). She declared it a victory against the foreign policy of the Government and the betrayal of Czecho-Slovakia and democracy, and she asserted that it showed 'Mr Chamberlain that he had not got the people of this country behind him and he must go.'[42] Further, there was another novelty about Adamson's election – for the fourth time in the history of the House of Commons a husband and wife sat together as MPs, her husband W.M. Adamson representing the Cannock Division of Staffordshire for Labour.[43]

Regardless of the marital accord in Parliament represented by the Adamsons, all was not well in the relationship between the sexes at the national level writ large. The Crisis and the ensuing by-elections created an atmosphere of deep suspicion about women's political influence. Addressing the annual conference of the National Council of Women in early November, Harold Nicolson castigated the women of England for their lack of courage during the recent crisis and for their instinctive pacifism and insularity. He portrayed women as the guilty party, more culpable than any of the men who actually played the real leading roles in bringing about the national dishonour that was the Munich Agreement. He claimed that during the recent crisis:

> English women showed fear, not courage; that women had still to show whether they were brave or not. In no previous time of international difficulty had they felt themselves and their homes to be endangered, it was suggested, and on this first occasion of realising the proximity of danger, while men had been resolute women had only been afraid.[44]

Nor was he heartened by how easily women recovered from their fear and returned to business as usual once the agreement had been struck and war had been, for a time, averted. Nicolson gendered the recent crisis, establishing a very stark bifurcation between the sexes in their emotional and practical reactions to the imminence of war. What was necessary, as implied by Nicolson, was to convert women, to wake them up from their apathetic slumber and to make them keenly aware of the gravity of international affairs.

In some respects the Dartford result provided the necessary counter-evidence to Nicolson's sexist allegations. The Dartford result proved that not only could a woman fight successfully on a foreign policy ticket but also that women voters were not as reliably wedded to Chamberlain's policy as it may at first have appeared. The lesson to be drawn from Dartford, according to

Labour campaigners in the upcoming by-election in Walsall, was the instability of the assumption that women would support the Conservatives out of gratitude for Chamberlain's peace. However, the lesson to be learned from Dartford was not entirely unambiguous as the Conservatives held Walsall. In Walsall it was a National Government win, with the National Liberal candidate, Sir George Schuster, elected with 28,720 votes, and Labour's G. Jeger with 21,562.

The line of thinking and speculation about how women would vote carried through all these by-elections. In the Bridgwater Division of Somerset the Conservative P.G. Heathcote-Amory was running against the broadcaster and *News Chronicle* journalist Vernon Bartlett, who was standing as an Independent Progressive. Bartlett received the endorsement of the Council of Action, as well as letters of support from Eleanor Rathbone and Ellen Wilkinson, among others, support for which he was very worthy considering the vehemence and consistency of his anti-fascism in his journalism. Wilkinson was enlisted to rouse women voters, sending a letter of appeal to the women to vote for Bartlett as a vote 'for a policy of constructive peace'. Wilkinson wrote: 'Peace is not just an interval between wars or a terrified respite bought by giving bullying dictators the lives of other people. True peace can only be secured by removing the causes of war while at the same time insisting on the observance of international law.' She then went on to explain this formulation with specific reference to women: 'The peace-loving nations in Europe were and are strong enough to insist on this if Britain will give the lead. Mr Chamberlain gave way instead, and he has gone on giving way. Can this bring peace? Every sensible woman knows it will only lead to further demands and eventually to war.'[45] Wilkinson's profile, as a woman and a staunch anti-Chamberlainite, with a past as a member of the PPU, rendered her support invaluable in trying to convince women voters. While Bartlett did not receive official support from Labour, he had the strong support of the Liberals, with several major Liberal figures coming down to take part in a big demonstration in his support, including Megan Lloyd George MP, Wickham Steed, Sir Charles Hobhouse, Lady Violet Bonham-Carter and Richard Acland. The Bridgwater result was one of the more unpredictable of these by-elections. The constituency was a Tory stronghold. Further, the new register contained 44,653 electors, and there were about 4,000 more women than men. Yet, in the end, Bartlett won, which was considered a by-election sensation. On 17 November 1938 there was a turnout of 82.3 per cent and the result was Bartlett (Independent Progressive) 19,540, Heathcoat Amory (Con.) 17,208, thus an Independent Progressive majority of 2,332.

There was another woman Labour candidate in the by-election in Fylde. The by-election, occasioned by the death of Lord Stanley, was contested by Captain Claud Granville Lancaster as National Government candidate, and Labour's Dr Mabel Tylecote, a teacher of history to the Workers' Education Association. Tylecote had hitherto been involved in local affairs and social service, but the mounting danger of the international situation drew her to national politics. She was also fighting on an anti-Munich pro-League platform.[46] She described 'Munich as a Mockery of Peace'.[47] She lost to the Government candidate in Fylde.

In Doncaster it was the wife of the National Liberal candidate, Mrs Monteith, who dug the trench that divided male and female over the rectitude of the policy of appeasement. She had taken an active part in her husband's campaign, emphasising that it was the men who wanted war for all the wrong reasons, while women wanted peace. She argued, 'if we had fought in the recent crisis when we were bound by no treaty it would have been a fight to please men who did not like another nation's politics. She asks the women electors to devote themselves to the task of making peace secure'.[48] *The Times* was confident that Alexander Monteith could turn the Labour majority of 8,000 into a government victory due to the large element of Liberal Nonconformists among the railways workers and engineers in the town, as well as 'the support of a large proportion of the vote of the women who support Mr Chamberlain's peace policy'.[49] Doncaster was, in fact, a win for Labour's John Morgan, Labour retaining the seat with a 11,708 majority. So too in West Lewisham, the sixth by-election after Munich, it was predicated that gender would play a decisive role, with an electorate where there were 30,501 men and 37,140 women. Here the Government candidate did win.

Perhaps the by-election that most effectively illustrates the complex and tense interplay between gender and support for appeasement was the one in Kinross and West Pertshire, Scotland, a by-election that was brought on by the sitting member herself, Katherine the Duchess of Atholl (1874–1960). Not only was this one the most revealing in a study of gender and appeasement, but Stuart Ball argues that it is the most significant of all the by-elections as it was the only one to have come about 'as a direct result of the controversies over European affairs and as a deliberately staged test of public attitudes to foreign policy. Furthermore, this was the only contest to involve a prominent parliamentary critic of appeasement'.[50] Possible to view as a feminist in practice – she was the first woman Scottish MP and the first Conservative woman to become a minister as Parliamentary Secretary at the Board of Education from 1924–1929 – but certainly not in ideology – she had been opposed to the women's suffrage movement before the war – the Duchess was hardly the most predictable of committed anti-fascists. A Conservative from the Right of the party on so many other issues, she was not the most likely candidate for anti-Chamberlain scourge either.

The Duchess had gained her nick-name the 'Red' Duchess for her passionate commitment to the Republican cause in Spain, which also provided the route into her acute awareness of and public campaigns to draw attention to the Nazi menace by seeing to it that an unexpurgated translation of *Mein Kampf* was published. For this reason her by-election was given added significance to that of other by-elections of the moment, and 'its results will have much wider personal interest than it would have had before the outbreak of the Spanish rebellion'. Yet she was a personality of contrasts, and puzzled many with her apparent inconsistencies:

> in 1931–2 she was speaking and writing strongly against Russia. About two years later she was eager for Russia's admission to the League. She annoyed her party by opposing the Government of India Bill, though she does not now criticise its administration. She is a strong Imperialist, and her desire for the prosperity of the Empire is combined with an equally ardent desire that it should be faithful to its manifold responsibilities.[51]

For the 1935 General Election her constituency Conservative association had agreed to respect her independence in foreign affairs, but her doggedness to defy her own party strained this relationship to breaking point. While she returned to the party fold for a short time after the Italian invasion of Abyssinia, soon after this she was again in conflict with her own party over Spain. She lost the party whip in April 1938 because of her persistent protests to the Prime Minister, after which she sat as an independent. Indeed, along with a small group of fellow back-bench Conservative dissenters on matters of foreign policy, the Duchess regularly abstained from foreign policy votes throughout 1938. However, she was not part of the inner circle of anti-appeasers and never a recognised member of the Edenites or so-called 'glamour boys'. She resigned from Parliament in November 1938 in order to force a by-election on the issue of foreign policy.

Her Conservative opponent W.M. Snadden benefitted from concerted government support, which included some fifty MPs travelling to the constituency to campaign for him. This included the support of the Duchess's fellow Scottish woman Conservative MP (Dundee), Florence Horsburgh who spoke out against her and argued that the she would not have possibly taken the stand she had if she had been in Britain during the Crisis – the duchess had been in America campaigning on behalf of the Spanish government. Horsburgh remarked: 'I believe it is a tragedy that your Member was not in London or in the House of Commons on September 28 when Mr Chamberlain received the vital summons to Munich or she would not be doing what she is doing now.' Having missed that momentous and emotional event, the Duchess was, it was implied, out of touch with public opinion. 'It was borne in upon us, continued Miss Horsburgh, that we must work for peace, and that we would win through. In the negotiations Mr Chamberlain had shown Herr Hitler that the German people wanted peace. It was no use looking at the past and saying whether the Munich agreement was right or wrong, it could not be undone.'[52]

In the end, the Duchess lost her bid. There was relatively high voter turnout at 67 per cent, but Snadden won 11,809 to her 10,495 votes, with speculation that the proximity of Christmas and adverse weather conditions in the spread-out largely rural constituency may have contributed to her loss. Others have attributed it to her unpopularity locally and her ineptitude as a politician, only compounded by Conservative representations of her as a war-monger.

How did gender issues figure in the Duchess's campaign and its outcome? Stuart Ball's provides a meticulous blow-by-blow account of the progress of the Duchess's political career and the events leading up to and including the by-election itself.[53] However, he only shows a passing interest in interrogating the category of gender in this story. The duchess defied gender stereotypes by caring far less about local issues and more about foreign affairs, travelling a great deal to the world's trouble spots on various missions, and publishing on these topics. While other women candidates in these by-elections either played down international affairs or shrouded their anti-appeasement in the cloak of the opposition's 'peace' discourse, a vote for the duchess was widely regarded as a vote for war. 'One of the duchess's sub-agents later reported how "the slogan, vote for the duchess and you vote for war, often took this form: you are a supporter of the duchess? Yes! Then you want your son to be killed".'[54] Indeed, she came to recognise that her loss could be attributed to that fact that 'the whole force of the party machine...spared no pains to make the women believe that my foreign policy meant war'.[55] It is significant too that she recognised that women, who made up 55 per cent of the electorate, were not her natural supporters, especially in this campaign, further alienating her from any sense she may have had about sex solidarity.

By adopting the role of hawk she allowed herself to appear both unladylike by antiquated Victorian standards, and unfashionable as set against the modish pacifism of many feminists and younger people, which was only compounded by her dour dress and appearance. Furthermore, it did not help that due to a sudden bout of illness her husband, the duke, was unable to take an active part in her campaign, only adding emphasis to her loneliness and her distance from more acceptable models of women's political behaviour. In the Kinross by-election then it is not unreasonable to suggest that the duchess lost because she could not appeal to women voters, either in terms of her policy or in her approach to politics. The duchess's campaign asked voters to take many positions that were counter-intuitive. First, to place country before party and to transcend their allegiances to parties; second, to accept the tantamount importance of foreign affairs in this largely rural and agriculturally based constituency; and third, to accept a woman candidate who took on the role of belligerent against a local male candidate who could appear to be a dove by riding the coat tails of the ashen-faced PM who had very recently declared that he had achieved 'peace in our time' at Munich.

The Duchess of Atholl's spectacular loss would have only added substance to the perception that women remained the best friends of the policy of appeasement. Therefore in East Norfolk, the campaign literature of the National Liberal candidate, Mr F. Medlicott contained messages directed to women voters, with the candidate's wife appealing 'to them to support and encourage Mr Chamberlain and his Government in the task of consolidating the work of negotiation and appeasement'.[56] Indeed, Tories were still trying to capitalise on women's support for appeasement in early 1939. For example, Sir Terence O'Connor, the Solicitor-General and MP for Central Nottingham, told a meeting of his women constituents:

> that it might be that noisy people anxious to test their strength in the House of Commons and the country would suggest taking a more bellicose policy than we did at present. The Government might have to go to the country and ask the people if they really wanted to pursue a policy of peace or to sit down to make ourselves only ready for war. He had no doubt about the result. He would not be a bit surprised if the policy of appeasement had a great deal more support in the dictator countries than many people believed.[57]

It remained the assumption that women constituents would be the more receptive to the underlying message of appeasement, which included trying to convince them that they had allies in their overwhelming desire for peace in the populations living under dictatorship.

What is certain is the high level of support for appeasement and the Prime Minister among women Conservatives. In the absence of systematic holdings in the Conservative Party papers of the Women's Conservative Associations, local newspapers provide some important insight into the mood and content of these self-selecting but still public meetings. During the crisis it was clear that Conservative women worked hard to legitimise, rationalise and promote Chamberlain's foreign policy, running alongside the advocacy of preventative rearmament. Even if one of the most notable women anti-appeasers, Atholl, was from within the party, by 1938 her position was anathema to that of her fellow Tory women. For example, a meeting in Carlisle at which Mr Amery MP was to speak was cancelled in retaliation for his abstaining from voting in the House of Commons recently on the motion of confidence in the Government in the Munich agreement. The Chairman of the Carlisle Women Conservatives said that they had 'no personal objection to Mr Amery, but "we women Unionists are absolutely for Mr Chamberlain and his peace policy, and are nervous about Mr Duff Cooper, Mr Churchill, and Mr Eden, because we fear their policy may lead to war"'.[58] Women Conservatives were on the side of appeasement and any statesmen who spoke in these terms could pretty much be guaranteed their support. This was the case up and down the country. In Cheltenham the meeting of the Unionist and Conservative Association wished 'to convey to Mr Morrison its hearty appreciation of the strenuous efforts of the Prime Minister for peace, and that it approves of any measures that he and the National Government may take to strengthen our Army, Navy and Air Force, and to organise the civil population so that a strong nation will help to ensure the future peace of the world'.[59] At Bridport Simon Wingfield Digby addressed the Women's Conservative Association and explained that 'Most of us dislike Fascism – I certainly do – but I cannot accept that as a reason for hating all Germans and all Italians. That is what the Opposition ask us to do, and many of them would go further and even like to fight Italy and German to overthrow their Fascist Governments. I think that war needs a better excuse than that.'[60] At Cullompton Colonel Troycote, the MP for Tiverton, received an enthusiastic reception when he told the Women's Section of the Conservative Association that the policy of appeasement was 'the only way to preserve peace'.[61] Nor did this approach lose potential and potency in by-elections held nearly a year after Munich. 'The "peace or war" issue of the North Cornwall by-election is one which will probably influence the minds of women electors of the division more than anything else', it was claimed. 'Realizing this, the National Conservatives are pressing home at women's meetings all over the division the debt of gratitude of women of the country owe to Mr Chamberlain for saving their homes and families by his Munich intervention.' Again women MPs were enlisted for the campaign: 'A strong plea to the women of Bude was made by Miss Irene Ward, MP for Wallsend, who appealed to them to show the dictators that Britain was solid behind the Prime Minister by returning Mr Whitehouse.'[62] It was clear that special efforts were being made by local party organisations to target women voters and build on the strong perception that they supported the PM's foreign policy.

Notwithstanding this strong identification of Conservative women with appeasement, we are left with the question of how gender influenced the post-Munich by-elections. Because of the unpredictability of the number, of the frequency, and of the profile of the constituencies that would come up for by-election contest, it is very difficult to identify any definitive patterns or draw any systematic conclusion, at least ones that would satisfy a psephologist. While gender may have played less of a part in the outcome of these by-elections than the media had prophesied, the notion of women's power, and the allegation that they held power without responsibility, left an indelible impression on public opinion. It contributed to a mood of distrust between the sexes, or more one-sidedly, men's irritation that women voters, this still new and untried political force, could influence the course of foreign policy and thus world events. When studied through the lens of gender, the by-elections of 1938 and 1939 taken together reveal an abiding public concern with women as a political force, and, more often than not, as a political problem. Indeed, the inter-war years were obsessed by a series of 'Questions' and 'Problems' – the 'Jewish Question', the 'German Question', the 'Sudeten Problem', etc. – and it is clear that twenty years after enfranchisement the 'Women Question' was not much nearer to a resolution.

But the gender-based interpretation is not all doom and gloom. It is noteworthy that there were a fair number of women candidates, almost all of whom stood on anti-Government platforms, which is ironic when the overlying assumption was that the female voting bloc was predisposed to the Government and its appeasement policy. While it is difficult to meas-ure the popularity or lack thereof of women candidates because of their sex, it is clear that there were many impediments to women's standing for election. For instance, Mrs Elsy Borders, wife of a Kent taxi driver, friend of Ellen Wilkinson, and active speaker, was not yet considering standing for Parliament because caring for her young daughter had to come first. She told the *Daily Mirror* that 'although it was suggested to me a year ago that I should stand in a by-election in the Spelthorne, Middlesex Division, I must always give first consideration to the upbringing of my daughter'.[63] While some of these women candidates in the post-Munich by-elections made an effort to emphasise their traditional gender roles and woman-centred political interests, such as Summerskill, others did not shy away from using the foreign policy card, which would lead to success in the case of Adamson, and disappointing failure in the case of the Duchess of Atholl. In addition, public women played prominent supporting roles in many of the by-election campaigns, and all parties seemed aware of the importance of mobilising their 'star' women politicians alongside women party work-ers and the wives of candidates in bids to influence the presumed decisive women's vote. Furthermore, candidates addressed male and female voters separately, going further to make concrete the rather artificial construction of gender bifurcated voting blocs. Most significantly, and rather ironically, these women candidates were standing on anti-Government and anti-appeasement platforms. The result of all these attempts to woo women voters was ambiguous, as there were constituencies that were identified to have a surplus of women, and majorities of women who were still pos-sessed by feelings of gratitude to Chamberlain, which nonetheless returned the anti-Government candidate, and visa versa. 'Women voters' consist-ently belied expectations, but the bogey of the woman voter, the female franchise factor, continued to play a part in candidates' electoral strategies, the choices of their political technology, and analysis of the result after the fact. Practice had outstripped principle in the evolution of progressive sexual politics.

The study of public opinion is a means of exposing the gender structures that undergirded the policy of and the popular support for appeasement. Why study public opinion to understand the gender dynamics of appease-ment? Any investigation of gender and appeasement must reply heavily on indicators of public opinion as the first step before speculation about the impact of public opinion on eventual foreign policy outcomes. Laura Beers has shown how there was a 'time-lag between the advent of polling and its integration into political life', and she has noted specifically how anti-appeasers were especially keen to use public opinion polling data to substantiate their case, the Liberal *News Chronicle* leading the charge in October 1938 with British Institute of Public Opinion surveys. While 'most of the journalistic establishment lined up behind Chamberlain's foreign policy, the polls were one of the few organs of public opinion that opposition MPs could point to as illustrating a strong anti-Hitler bias within the British public'.[64] Opinion polling was received with scepticism in Britain for a number of reasons, and it did not help that Gallup was an American import. I would argue a further or related impediment to politicians trust in the measurement and the authentic value of 'public opinion' was that it was seen that women represented too high a proportion of 'the public'. The appeasers would have been especially hostile as most of the key figures, such as Chamberlain, were used to defining public opinion as it suited their purposes, relying on the press to create rather than reflect public opinion, and taking as a reliable indicator the contents of their post bags. Reflecting on her life as a Tory grandee hostess, a feminist patriot, and appeaser, Lady Londonderry completed her memoir as it so happened in October 1938, at the height of the Munich Crisis. She wrote:

> The great and increasing share that women are taking in public life, both in politics and municipal life, and on the magisterial bench, is very remarkable when we consider the comparatively short time it is since public opinion recognised the fact that the inclusion of women in responsible positions was of material benefit to the State. I feel convinced that a country in which public opinion represents the views of its citizens of both sexes is less liable to blunder into errors and tumults than those continental nations today where women are allowed no say in the government or national affairs, but are sternly relegated to the home and kitchen.[65]

Lady Londonderry's comment provides a snapshot of some of the major currents of political change in the aftermath of suffrage, including the view that the inclusion of women in national and international affairs has exponentially increased the value of public opinion. In addition, Lady Londonderry confirming other commonly held perceptions, namely that the Conservatives have embraced the fruits of enfranchisement, especially as the party benefits from women voter preference; that fascism and communism are alien to British political culture; that women's growing influence in the affairs of state is intertwined with the national policy and attitude of appeasement; and the gradual acceptance of the value of public opinion within a mass democracy.

Only through a history of appeasement from below can we hope to locate any sizable cohorts of women concerned with foreign affairs – women have very rarely 'been on top' and this is certainly true for both domestic and international politics in this period. Women hardly figure in traditional sources that are relied upon by the IR, diplomatic or foreign policy historian, and this is in part because it would be relatively fruitless to trawl through government and parliamentary papers to learn more about women's influence on Britain's foreign policy. Within those more traditional source bases, the work of the handful of women politicians who were MPs at the time can be gauged and evaluated, and here we do start to see that women MPs were far more invested and engaged in foreign policy than our preconceptions might allow. There are striking examples of women politicians who acted as formidable anti-appeasers, even if their sex remained a disadvantage for earning the respect they would have needed to join in the intrigues of the male-dominated anti-appeasement camp. But aside from the study of these 'women worthies', where we can really find women and identify gender as an important analytical category, and, indeed, as a key source of tension – hitherto almost entirely neglected in the historiography – is at the level of public opinion and media-fuelled perceptions. The by-elections are also an instructive gauge, as they reveal not so much how women voted, but how politicians and the media thought women would vote, as the narratives of women's enfranchisement and Britain's diminishing position on the world stage became intertwined.

Notes

1. Lord Esher, *After the War* (1918).
2. See Helen McCarthy, 'Parties, Voluntary Associations, and Democratic Politics in Interwar Britain', *Historical Journal*, 50,4 (2007), pp. 891–912, and Helen McCarthy, *The British People and the League of Nations: Democracy, Citizenship and Internationalism, c. 1918–1945* (Manchester: Manchester University Press, 2011).
3. 'Electoral Reform: Peers and Franchises for Women', *Manchester Guardian*, 10 Jan. 1918. Lord Loreburn's amendment to delete the women's suffrage clause from the Reform Bill was defeated by an unexpectedly large majority of 134 to 71.
4. Julie V. Gottlieb, 'Guilty Women?', *BBC History Magazine*, 12:13 (December, 2011), pp. 26–9.
5. Susan Kingsley Kent, *Making Peace: The Reconstruction of Gender in Inter-war Britain* (Princeton, 1993), p. 99.
6. 8 Oct. 1938, ed. Nigel Nicolson, *Harold Nicolson: Diaries and Letters 1930–1939* (London, 1966), p. 376.
7. Daniel Hucker, *Public Opinion and the End of Appeasement in Britain and France* (Farnham: Ashgate, 2011) is a step towards closing this gap in the historiography.
8. See eds Chris Cook and John Ramsden, *By-Elections in British Politics* (London: UCL Press, 1997), p. 5.
9. 'Women Can Make Premier Change his Policy', *Daily Mirror*, 21 March 1938.
10. Krista Cowman, *Women in British Politics, c. 1689–1979* (Basingstoke, 2010), p. 170.

11. Roger Eatwell, 'Munich, Public Opinion, and Popular Front', *Journal of Contemporary History*, Vol. 6, No. 4 (1971), pp. 122–39.
12. Iain McLean, 'Oxford and Bridgwater', in Chris Cook and John Ramsden (eds), *By-elections in British Politics* (London: UCL Press, 1997), pp. 130–50.
13. M. Pugh, 'The Impact of Women's Enfranchisement in Britain', in C. Daley and M. Nolan (eds), *Suffrage and Beyond* (New York, 1994), p. 318. Women also were more successful winning their seats at by-elections.
14. Martin Ceadel, 'The First British Referendum: The Peace Ballot, 1934–5', *English Historical Review*, Vol. 95, No. 377 (Oct. 1980), pp. 810–39.
15. Norman Rose, 'The Resignation of Anthony Eden', *Historical Journal*, 25, 4 (1982), pp. 911–31.
16. 'K.R.G. Browne Is All for Youth at the Helm and Putting our House (of Commons) in Order', *Hull Daily Mail*, 5 Feb. 1938.
17. 'Fulham By-election: Bread and Butter Politics', *Manchester Guardian*, 31 March 1938.
18. See Penny Summerfield, '"Our Amazonian Colleague": Edith Summerskill's Problematic Reputation', in R. Toye and J. Gottlieb (eds), *Making Reputations: Power, Persuasion and the Individual in Modern British Politics* (London: I.B. Tauris, 2005), pp.135–50.
19. Mass-Observation Archive, University of Sussex, File 2/B Central Women's Electoral Committee: Woman Candidate in West Fulham by-Election, 26 March 1938.
20. Julie Gottlieb, 'Varieties of Feminist Anti-Fascism', in Nigel Copsey and Andrzej Olechnowicz (eds), *Varieties of Anti-Fascism: Britain in the Inter-war Period* (Basingstoke: Palgrave Macmillan), pp. 101–18.
21. M-O, File 1/B, Conservative Meeting, 30 March 1938, 3 p.m. West Fulham, Box 1 By-Elections – 297.
22. Pugh uses the example of the COA to build his case for the cleansing of Lloyd George's tarnished reputation that was a result of his visit to Hitler in 1936 and his subsequent glowing reports of the meeting. Martin Pugh, 'The Liberal Party and the Popular Front', *English Historical Review*, Vol. CXXI, No. 494, (Dec. 2006), pp. 1328–50.
23. Ibid.
24. 'Keen Fight in West Fulham', *Observer*, 3 Apr. 1938.
25. Martin Pugh, *Women and the Women's Movement in Britain* (Basingstoke, 2000).
26. 'The Election Speculations', *Manchester Guardian*, 5 Oct. 1938.
27. 'Chamberlain Gets Rebuke at Polls', *New York Times*, 8 Nov. 1938.
28. 'Survey Finds British Behind Chamberlain', *New York Times*, 19 Oct. 1938.
29. 'Under the Franchise Soon to be Passed Women Will Outnumber the Men Voters by 2,000,000', *New York Times*, 24 Apr. 1927.
30. As Pugh has shown, Lib. –Lab. collaboration was actually far more effective in giving some coherence to the Popular Front and far more pro-active in the wider fight against fascism than has otherwise been acknowledged, with too much attention having been conferred on Labour-Communist squabbling and resultant anti-fascist strategies. Martin Pugh, 'The Liberal Party and the Popular Front', *English Historical Review*, Vol. CXXI, No. 494 (Dec. 2006), pp. 1327–50. The Popular Front was launched by Richard Acland, John Strachey, G.D.H. Cole and Robert Boothby in December 1936. Megan Lloyd George was one of the parliamentary advocates of the Popular Front, and Lady Violet Bonham-Carter a prominent supporter. Bonham-Carter emerged as one of the most important

Popular Fronters because close connection to both the Liberal leader Sir Archibald Sinclair and Winston Churchill, and together they participated in the launch of Churchill's 'Arms and the Covenant' movement in December 1936, another cross-party anti-appeasement movement.

31. Roger Eatwell, 'Munich, Public Opinion, and Popular Front', *Journal of Contemporary History*, Vol. 6, No. 4 (1971), pp. 122–39.
32. 'By-Election at Oxford', *Manchester Guardian*, 23 Oct. 1938.
33. 'Oxford Poll Today Will Test Opinion', *New York Times*, 27 Oct. 1938.
34. 'Dartford By-Election Campaign', *Manchester Guardian*, 3 Nov. 1938.
35. Noakes notes that Harrisson constructed women 'as a separate and problematic group'. Lucy Noakes, *War and the British: Gender, Memory and National Identity* (London, 1998), p. 87.
36. M-O, Oxford by-Election, First Day of Campaign, Oct. 18, report from Tom Harrisson, File 2/G.
37. 'Mass-Observation', *The Pioneer*, 4 Feb. 1939.
38. Iain McLean, 'Oxford and Bridgwater', in Chris Cook and John Ramsden (eds), *By-elections in British Politics* (London: UCL Press, 1997), pp. 130–50.
39. 'Our London Correspondent', *Manchester Guardian*, 28 Oct. 1938.
40. 'Dartford By-Election Campaign', *Manchester Guardian*, 3 Nov. 1938.
41. 'Voting To-day in Dartford', *The Times*, 7 Nov. 1938.
42. 'Labour Majority of 4,200', *Manchester Guardian*, 8 Nov. 1938.
43. The first three husband and wife teams were the Runcimans, Sir Oswald and Lady Cynthia Mosley, and Hugh and Ruth Dalton.
44. 'Pale Cast of Thought', *Manchester Guardian*, 4 Nov. 1938.
45. 'The By-Elections: Mr Bartlett Making Headway at Bridgwater', *Manchester Guardian*, 11 Nov. 1938.
46. 'The By-Elections', *Manchester Guardian*, 18 Nov. 1938.
47. PUB229/1/8 By-Election Addresses, 1937–39, Conservative Party Archive.
48. 'Two By-Elections To-day', *The Times*, 17 Nov. 1938. Doncaster was, in fact, a win for Labour.
49. 'Nominations at Doncaster', *The Times*, 8 Nov. 1938.
50. Stuart Ball, 'The Politics of Appeasement: the Fall of the Duchess of Atholl and the Kinross and West Perth By-election, December 1938', *Scottish Historical Review*, Vol. LXIX, No. 187 (Apr. 1990), pp. 49–83.
51. 'The Duchess of Atholl: Outspoken Critic of the Premier's Foreign Policy', *Manchester Guardian*, 25 Nov. 1938.
52. 'Candidates Toe the Line at Crieff', *Pertshire Constitutional and Journal*, Fri. 16 Dec. 1938.
53. Stuart Ball, 'The Politics of Appeasement: the Fall of the Duchess of Atholl and the Kinross and West Perth By-election, December 1938', *Scottish Historical Review*, Vol. LXIX, No. 187 (Apr. 1990), pp. 49–83.
54. Ibid.
55. Ibid.
56. 'East Norfolk Contest Appeals to Women Electors', *The Times*, 12 Jan. 1939.
57. '"Solicitor-General and "Noisy People"', *The Times*, 17 Jan. 1939.
58. 'A News Miscellany', *The Essex Chronicle*, Fri. 21 Oct. 1938.
59. 'Twyning Women Conservatives: Crisis Resolution Sent to Mr Morrison', *Cheltenham Chronicle*, Sat. 29 Oct. 1938.
60. 'The Foreign Situation', *Western Gazette*, 18 Nov. 1938.
61. 'Appeasement the Only Way to Peace', *Western Times*, 13 Jan, 1939.

62. 'Issue of "Peace or War": Appeal to Women of N. Cornwall', *The Western Morning News and Daily Gazette*, Sat. 8 July 1939.
63. '"Portia" Puts Child Before Politics', *Daily Mirror*, 23 Feb. 1939.
64. Laura Drummond Beers, 'Whose Opinion?: Changing Attitudes Towards Opinion Polling in British politics, 1937–1964', *Twentieth Century British History*, vol. 17, no. 2, 2006, pp. 177–205. Eleanor Rathbone made reference to polls during her incursions into foreign policy debates in the House. *New Chronicle* headline 'Widespread demand for National Register in Public Opinion Survey: 57 per cent for Chamberlain: 43 per cent Against: More Women than Men are in his Favour',. *News Chronicle*, 19 Oct. 1938.
65. The Marchioness of Londonderry, *Retrospect* (London, 1938), p. 145.

10
'They Have Made Their Mark Entirely Out of Proportion to Their Numbers': Women and Parliamentary Committees, c.1918–1945

Mari Takayanagi

Throughout the suffrage struggle, Parliament was the target of prolonged activism by feminist campaigners. From the first petition presented by a solitary woman asking for the vote back in 1832, through extensive petitioning and lobbying in the 1860s and 1880s, to the militant suffragette 'rushes' on Parliament after 1906, Parliament was the desired destination of women campaigners who wished to have a voice in the election of their representatives.[1] In 1918 this destination was reached, with two Acts passed, one giving the franchise to most women over the age of 30, and the other allowing women to become MPs. A host of further Parliamentary legislation affecting women's lives and gender equality followed over the next ten years, culminating with the Equal Franchise Act in 1928.

However, women in Parliament were few in number in this period. As the introduction to this volume describes, only one woman candidate was elected in the general election of 1918, but she did not take her seat. Whatever difference the vote made elsewhere, it did not lead to a large influx of women MPs. Only 37 women were elected throughout the inter-war period; they remained in a tiny minority, reaching a high of 15 at one time, out of a total of 615 MPs, for a short period during 1931.[2] No women could sit in the House of Lords, a situation which continued until 1958. The few women in the Commons found themselves in a frustrating environment where facilities for women were limited, and the Parliamentary officials there to assist were almost exclusively male.

A leaflet issued after the Second World War by the 'Women for Westminster' campaign, titled *Our Women MPs: What They Have Done for Us*, declared:

> Always too few to counterbalance their 600 odd male colleagues, they have yet by debate and committee service made their mark on the law-making of the last 30 years in a degree entirely out of proportion to their numbers.[3]

181

Of the two types of contribution mentioned, a number of historians have previously evaluated the early women MPs' contribution to debates in the chamber. In *Women at Westminster* Pamela Brookes examined women in Parliament over a long period of time, in a broad approach in which Parliamentary committees were mentioned, but not in detail.[4] Martin Pugh's analysis of what early women MPs made of their time in Parliament focussed on their speeches in Parliament and contribution to legislation; committees were not mentioned.[5] In *Women in the House* Elizabeth Vallance said that, 'Women have always made a contribution, well in proportion to their numbers, in Parliamentary committees', but does not produce evidence to substantiate this.[6]

Brian Harrison's 1986 article on the early women MPs concentrated largely on their contributions to debate, counting the *Hansard* columns and analysing topics on which they spoke.[7] Harrison gives two sentences to their role with committees:

> Much less is known about women MPs' conduct in committees… but in the two sessions of 1929–31 a higher percentage of women MPs than men were summoned to serve on standing committees, and the women attended more assiduously. On select committees over the same period, however, women's attendance surpasses that of the men in only the first of the two sessions.[8]

It is clear, then, that not much is known about this topic. Historians have tended to assume that all significant activity in the House of Commons took place in the debating chamber, and behind the scenes in the club-like culture of smoking rooms and offices. As Richard Toye notes elsewhere in this volume, Parliament has been little studied as an institution in this period.[9] It is perhaps not so surprising then, that the role of Parliamentary committees is poorly understood and largely ignored. Yet Parliamentary committees were an increasingly important part of the working lives of Members of Parliament by 1918. Bills had been routinely referred to standing committees since 1907, to be considered in clause-by-clause detail as part of the legislative process since 1907.[10] The passage of legislation in this period cannot therefore be understood only if debates in the chamber are considered; the picture is incomplete without consideration of the standing committee debates.

Investigatory Parliamentary committee work has been traced back to the earliest time for which records exist; procedures for select committees, which examined subjects, heard evidence and scrutinised public policy and administration, had been established back in the sixteenth century.[11] By the interwar period, eight 'core' select committees on aspects of Parliamentary administration were regularly appointed every session, plus between three and 13 further 'ad hoc' select committees each session on various subjects. The recommendations of such committees might exercise considerable influence on government policy and politics, for example, by advocating legislation on a particular subject, or by advising against such legislation. Even where their reports might not be adopted they still provided a public arena for issues of the day to be discussed and a forum for expert witnesses and members of the public to give evidence and lobby their Parliamentary representatives.

In order to evaluate the impact of women MPs, their committee work therefore needs to be understood. This chapter will consider this hitherto neglected area, the role women played in Parliamentary committee work. In particular it will consider the contribution of women MPs to Parliamentary committees up to 1945. It will consider attendance; the number of committees on which women sat; on what kind of committees they sat; and their contribution. It will do so with particular reference to Parliamentary standing and select committees. This analysis does not include bodies such as Royal Commissions of investigation and government departmental committees, as these are not Parliamentary bodies.

Although only MPs and peers could be members of Parliamentary committees, women were involved in other ways, for example, as witnesses. Women had given evidence in person as witnesses before House of Commons select committees at least as far back as 1852, when Mary Carpenter gave evidence to the House of Commons Select Committee on Criminal and Destitute Juveniles.[12] Women also gave evidence to House of Lords select committees; in 1881 two women gave oral evidence to a House of Lords select committee on the subject of child prostitution.[13] It was nevertheless fairly unusual for female witnesses to be called before select committees in the 19th and early 20th century. When they were summoned this was usually in relation to a subject with a very obvious 'women's angle'.[14]

By contrast, representatives from women's organisations can be found giving evidence to select committees on a number of occasions after 1918, including select committees on Equal Guardianship (1922), Nationality of Married Women (1923) and Equal Compensation (1943).[15] The Select Committee on the General Nursing Council (1925) heard 15 witnesses of whom 12 were women, and the Select Committee on Nursing Homes Registration (1926) had at least 20 women among its 36 witnesses, including owners of nursing homes, nurses and other medical professionals.[16]

Women witnesses could be something of an afterthought. In 1929 it occurred to the chairman of the Shop Assistants Committee in the middle of an evidence session that there might be conditions especially affecting women shop assistants, and he asked the witness present, a trade union official, if it would be desirable to hear women witnesses.[17] The official opined that it would be very valuable, and the committee eventually heard from nine women out of a total of 87 witnesses. This included two female MPs, Marion Phillips and Ethel Bentham. In other cases there was lobbying by female MPs for women witnesses to be heard. Eleanor Rathbone lobbied the Joint Select Committee on Indian Constitutional Reform to hear evidence from the British Committee for Indian Women's Franchise. She herself also submitted a memorandum and gave oral evidence, as did five representatives from Indian women's associations.[18]

Overall it appears that women were heard as witnesses before select committees on subjects without an immediately obvious gender angle more frequently after 1918 than before. This can be attributed at least in part to a greater awareness that women might be affected by issues differently to men, and sometimes stemmed from pressure directly brought by women MPs.

Women could also be involved as special advisors. Although select committees today routinely make use of special advisors to assist their investigations, this was comparatively rare in the first half of the 20th century. Women were involved as special advisors for the first time shortly after the vote was won in 1918, when seven women, including the social reformer Violet Markham were co-opted onto the Select Committee on Luxury Duty. They were put on sub-committees to advise on the possibility of a luxury tax being applied to 'articles used chiefly by women', 'furniture and other household articles', and 'Miscellaneous' items.[19] Excluded from the decision-making as they were not on the full committee, Markham and two other women resigned in June 1918 before the committee reported.[20] Markham wrote privately:

> I have no words to describe how loose end are the proceedings of the sub-committees. Acland, the chairman of the main committee, has never called us together; no instructions have been issued by the parent Committee, and no general principles laid down for us to follow.[21]

Markham was a veteran of public service work outside Parliament, and her insight into the apparently chaotic and amateurish nature of a House of Commons committee is illuminating. Clearly, she had different expectations of how a committee should operate than her male colleagues. Despite the mixed fortunes of this committee, it was held up in the House of Commons as an example of how women could contribute to the work of the House.[22]

From 1919, when Nancy Astor became the first woman MP to take her seat, women could be full members of select committees. Edith Picton-Turbervill, Labour MP 1929–31, wrote of her experiences in Commons committees as follows:

> For almost every committee the chairman nowadays says he would like to have a woman in it. There are many committees and not enough women, they simply won't go round, so whereas many a man can escape Parliamentary committees it is impossible for the women members – even if they wished – to do so.[23]

One might assume from this that every woman MP would sit on at least one committee, but this is not so for select committees, as Figure 10.1 illustrates.[24]

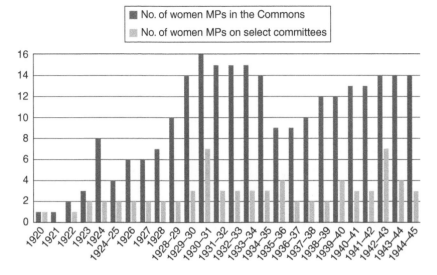

Figure 10.1 Number of women MPs and number of women MPs on select committees

The numbers are, of course, very small given the tiny number of women MPs in this period, but analysis shows that most Select Committees in the inter-war period did not have a woman member; and that most women MPs did not, in fact, sit on a select committee. Picton-Turbervill's observation is more applicable to standing committees, which scrutinise legislation at committee stage in the House of Commons. Figure 10.2 shows that most standing committees in the inter-war period did have a woman member, and most women MPs did sit on a standing committee. Standing committee service was, therefore, a typical part of the work of a woman MP in a way that select committee service was not.[25]

Having considered how many women sat on select committees, it may be considered which committees they sat on. Table 10.1 provides a list of select committees with women members. It shows that through the 1920s, women MPs were consistently placed on select committees dealing with what were defined as women's interests. The first time a woman MP was put on a committee which was not obviously a 'women's subject' was in 1929, Ethel Bentham on the Capital Punishment committee, but there were gender aspects to this issue also; the committee considered, for example, whether the death penalty should apply to women on the same terms as men.[26] Sometimes women were placed on select committees as a result of lobbying by feminist organisations, such as the National Union of Societies for Equal Citizenship who urged the appointment of a woman to the Shop Assistants Committee; Leah Manning was duly appointed, although not until a male

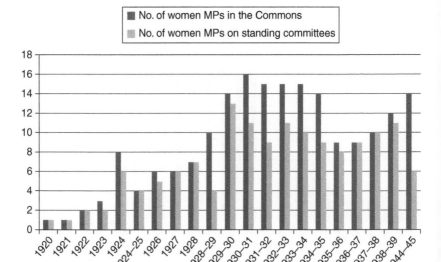

Figure 10.2 Number of women MPs and number of women MPs on standing committees

member died.[27] During the 1930s the 'women's angle' became less and less obvious, with women being placed on the Select Committees on Indian Constitutional Reform, water supply, and Public Petitions.[28]

In the interwar period five standing committees were usually appointed each session, lettered A, B, C, and D as well as the Scottish Standing Committee. Usually, approximately 40 MPs were appointed to each standing committee, although a typical attendance might be half that. Not all members were summoned to every meeting, and MPs were added and removed from a particular standing committee according to interest or expertise.[29] One or two of the standing committees would normally spend the majority of its time on one or two government bills, and another would spend most of its time considering a variety of private members' bills. The Scottish Standing Committee considered legislation affecting Scotland, and the Scottish women MPs tended to be appointed to this; for example, the Duchess of Atholl and Florence Horsbrugh. Both women and men tended to be added as members of a specific standing committee if it was considering something in which they had a special interest or expertise.[30] The subjects women spoke on are considered further below.

Analysis of attendances at select committee meetings show a generally good attendance by women MPs compared to the average attendance figures for their male counterparts.[31] Although there were some poor attendance records, such as Thelma Cazalet failing to attend a single meeting of the

Table 10.1 List of select committees with women members[32]

Session	Select committees with women members	Women members
1920	Criminal Law Amendment & Sexual Offences bill	Nancy Astor (Con.)
1921	[NONE]	[NONE]
1922	British Nationality (Married Women) bill	Margaret Wintringham (Lib.)
	Guardianship of Infants	Margaret Wintringham (Lib.)
1923	British Nationality (Married Women) bill	Margaret Wintringham (Lib.)
	Guardianship of Infants	Wintringham (Lib.), Mabel Philipson (Con.)
1924	Kitchen	Mabel Philipson (Con.), Dorothea Jewson (Lab.)
1924–25	Kitchen	Mabel Philipson (Con.), Ellen Wilkinson (Lab.)
	General Nursing Council	Ellen Wilkinson (Lab.)
1926	Kitchen	Mabel Philipson (Con.), Ellen Wilkinson (Lab.)
	Nursing Homes (Registration)	Mabel Philipson (Con.), Ellen Wilkinson (Lab.)
1927	Kitchen	Mabel Philipson (Con.), Ellen Wilkinson (Lab.)
1928	Kitchen	Mabel Philipson (Con.), Ellen Wilkinson (Lab.)
1928–29	Kitchen	Mabel Philipson (Con.), Ellen Wilkinson (Lab.)
1929–30	Capital Punishment	Ethel Bentham (Lab.)
	Kitchen	Cynthia Mosley (Lab.), Ellen Wilkinson (Lab.)
1930–31	Kitchen	Cynthia Mosley (Lab.), Ellen Wilkinson (Lab.), Countess of Iveagh (Con.)
	Capital Punishment	Ethel Bentham (Lab.)
	Wills & Intestacies (Family Maintenance bill)	Lucy Noel-Buxton (Lab.), Eleanor Rathbone (Ind.)
	Shop Assistants	Leah Manning (Lab.)
1931–32	Kitchen	Thelma Cazalet (Con.), Helen Shaw (Con.)
	Public Petitions	Mary Pickford (Con.)

(*continued*)

Table 10.1 Continued

Session	Select committees with women members	Women members
1932–33	Kitchen	Thelma Cazalet (Con.), Helen Shaw (Con.)
	Public Petitions	Mary Pickford (Con.)
	Indian Constitutional Reform (Joint)	Mary Pickford (Con.)
1933–34	Indian Constitutional Reform (Joint)	Mary Pickford (Con.)
	Kitchen	Thelma Cazalet (Con.), Helen Shaw (Con.)
	Public Petitions	Mary Pickford (Con.)/Norah Runge (Con.)
1934–35	Kitchen	Thelma Cazalet (Con.), Helen Shaw (Con.)
	Public Petitions	Norah Runge (Con.)
1935–36	Kitchen	Thelma Cazalet (Con)/Mavis Tate (Con.), Ellen Wilkinson (Lab.)
	Water Resources & Supplies (Joint)	Irene Ward (Con)
1936–37	Kitchen	Thelma Cazalet (Con.), Ellen Wilkinson (Lab.)
1937–38	Kitchen	Thelma Cazalet (Con.), Ellen Wilkinson (Lab.)
1938–39	Kitchen	Thelma Cazalet (Con.), Ellen Wilkinson (Lab.)
	London Government Bill [HL] (Joint)	Thelma Cazalet (Con.)
1939–40	Kitchen	Thelma Cazalet (Con.), Ellen Wilkinson (Lab.)/Agnes Hardie (Lab.)
	National Expenditure Committee (NEC)	Lady Davidson (Con.), Ellen Wilkinson (Lab.)
	NEC Navy Sub-Committee	*Lady Davidson (Con.)*
	NEC Trade Sub-Committee	*Ellen Wilkinson (Lab.)*
1940–41	Kitchen	Lady Davidson (Con.), Agnes Hardie (Lab.)
	National Expenditure Committee (NEC)	Lady Davidson (Con.), Irene Ward (Con.)
	NEC Navy Sub-Committee	*Lady Davidson (Con.)*
	NEC Supply Sub-Committee	*Irene Ward (Con.)*

1941–42	Kitchen	Lady Davidson (Con.), Agnes Hardie (Lab.)
	National Expenditure Committee (NEC)	Lady Davidson (Con.), Irene Ward (Con.)
	NEC Co-ordinating Sub-Committee	*Lady Davidson (Con.)*
	NEC Production & Supply Sub-Committee	*Irene Ward (Con.)*
	NEC Women's Medical Services Sub-Committee	*Lady Davidson (Con.), Irene Ward (Con.)*
	NEC Fighting Services Sub-Committee	*Irene Ward (Con.)*
1942–43	Kitchen	Lady Davidson (Con.), Agnes Hardie (Lab.)
	National Expenditure Committee (NEC)	*Lady Davidson (Con.), Irene Ward (Con.)*
	NEC Special Inquiries Sub-Committee	*Irene Ward (Con.)*
	NEC Dept Inquiries B Sub-Committee	*Lady Davidson (Con.)*
	Equal Compensation	Megan Lloyd George (Lib.), Thelma Cazalet-Keir (Con.), Mavis Tate (Con.), Agnes Hardie (Lab.), Edith Summerskill (Lab.)
1943–44	House of Commons (Rebuilding)	Eleanor Rathbone (Ind)
	Kitchen	Lady Davidson (Con.), Agnes Hardie (Lab.)
	National Expenditure Committee (NEC)	Lady Davidson (Con.), Irene Ward (Con.)
	NEC Sub-Committee C	*Lady Davidson (Con.)*
	NEC Sub-Committee E	*Irene Ward (Con.)*
1944–45	Kitchen	Lady Davidson (Con.), Agnes Hardie (Lab.)
	National Expenditure Committee (NEC)	Lady Davidson (Con.), Irene Ward (Con.)
	NEC Sub-Committee B	*Irene Ward (Con.)*
	NEC Sub-Committee C	*Lady Davidson (Con.)*

Joint Committee on the London Government Bill in 1938–39, there are a number of impressive examples of conscientious committee service by women.[33] Irene Ward attended all 15 sittings of the Water Resources and Supplies Committee in 1935–36; Joan Davidson attended 60 of 62 meetings of the National Expenditure Committee's Navy sub-committee in 1939–40. The record for most attendances in a session goes to Mary Pickford, who attended 74 of 76 meetings of the Indian Constitutional Reform Committee in 1932–33.

For standing committees, the average female attendance was consistently better than the male between 1928 and 1935, but declined thereafter.[34] Overall on the basis of attendance in this period, however, it appears that women MPs treated their standing committee work more seriously than many of their male colleagues.

Their attendance alone, however, does not mean they necessarily spoke. Select committees produced reports and minutes of evidence, but not records of debate. However, standing committees publish debates, and the extent of the contribution of women MPs to standing committees has been evaluated from Standing Committee *Hansard*, using the same methodology as Brian Harrison's evaluation of women's debate in the chamber.[35] The *Hansard* reports show that women's contribution reached a peak in 1929–30, with 11,162 lines of debate or 4 per cent of the total.[36] No other session comes anywhere close to this number of lines. Comparing contribution to attendances, men's contribution stayed reasonably constant, hovering around 50 lines per attendance, but the women's contribution fluctuated widely – soaring far higher than the men's in 1926 and 1927, but far lower in the period 1931–34 (see Figure 10.3).

Standing committees were a similar environment to the House of Commons chamber, although the number of MPs attending was much smaller with typically 20 people present, and the nature of discussion was much more detailed and often technically complex. The small number of women MPs means that one or two women who spoke a great deal in standing committees skew the statistics, particularly when they held government office such as Susan Lawrence, the Duchess of Atholl and Ellen Wilkinson (see Table 10.2).

Lawrence's figures are partly affected by the period during which she was Parliamentary Secretary to the Minister of Health; in this role she contributed 4844 lines on the Housing Bill in 1929–30 alone. However, she also contributed heavily during the periods she was not in government, contributing 1669 lines on just one bill (Merchandise Marks) in 1926, and 3524 lines on five bills in 1927. Lawrence had a good command of detail and the clause-by-clause nature of standing committee work appears to have been well-suited to this during strength.[37]

Women were noticeably prominent on one of the 'core' select committees appointed every session, the Select Committee on the House of Commons

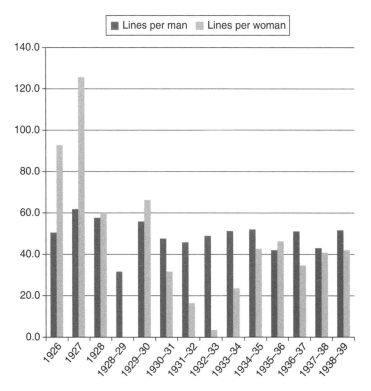

Figure 10.3 Standing committee debates: comparison of women and men

(Kitchen and Refreshment Rooms), usually referred to simply as the Kitchen Committee. This oversaw domestic arrangements in the House of Commons. Although dealing with internal issues rather than matters of public policy and legislation, it shows women MPs influencing at least one part of a very male-centric administration, moving into hitherto all-male spaces, and is therefore worthy of examination. Women formed a high proportion of staff working in the Commons kitchens (14 of 28 in 1924, 16 of 30 in 1936), including barmaids, waitresses and housemaids.[38] It is, therefore, not too surprising that women MPs were put on the Kitchen Committee as early as 1924, as soon as there were more than one or two of them to go round. Ellen Wilkinson was perhaps the most active and engaged female member of the Kitchen Committee. At her first meeting on 17 February 1925, the Kitchen Committee minutes record it was 'Resolved, at the request of Miss Wilkinson, that particulars of the conditions of employment of the staff be supplied to new members.'[39] The committee minutes show gradual improvements to working conditions over time for the staff, male and

Table 10.2   Standing committees: total contribution of individual women MPs

Woman MP	Party	Total lines
Lawrence	Lab.	18,933
Atholl	Con.	8,078
Wilkinson	Lab.	7,387
Rathbone	Ind.	4,479
Astor	Con.	4,295
Horsbrugh	Con.	3,931
Tate	Con.	1,839
Ward I	Con.	1,261
Shaw	Con.	807
Hardie	Lab.	393
Cazalet	Con.	293
Davidson	Con.	282
Copeland	Con.	275
Lloyd George	Lib.	268
Philipson	Con.	235
Bondfield	Lab.	222
Wintringham	Lib.	221
Lee	Lab.	193
Graves	Con.	150
Jewson	Lab.	95
Picton-Turbervill	Lab.	76
Runge	Con.	75
Wright	Con.	64
Ward S	Con.	40
Manning	Lab.	29
Summerskill	Lab.	24

female, including a pension fund set up in 1933 when Thelma Cazalet and Helen Shaw were on the committee.[40]

Away from the Kitchen Committee, the part played by women on select committees varied widely depending on the nature of the committee and the women involved. Sometimes it is possible to see an individual make a real difference. For example, Nancy Astor on the Joint Select Committee on the Criminal Law Amendment Bill and Sexual Offences Bill in 1921, lobbied very hard for the inclusion of a clause which abolished the defence of 'a reasonable cause to believe' that a girl was over the age of consent, and was successful.[41] The same can be seen in standing committees, where sometimes, even though women MPs did not speak much, they played an important role in introducing and amending clauses. Mabel Philipson on the Adoption bill 1926 spoke very little, but made an amendment (that was accepted by the government) on equality of adopted and natural children.[42] Four women were on the Criminal Justice bill standing committee in 1938–39, in which Irene Ward and Mavis Tate both introduced new clauses, and Agnes Hardie an amendment.[43] Seven women were on the Children and Young Persons Bill (1931–32), all speaking and putting forward amendments.[44]

The largest select committee in this period was the Joint Select Committee on Indian Constitutional Reform, set up to consider the Government's white paper on India. It sat over two sessions in 1932–34. As well as sixteen peers and sixteen MPs, there were twenty-seven delegates from the Indian States and from British India.[45] There was one woman MP on the committee, the Conservative Mary Pickford. There was also one woman delegate, Begum Shah Nawaz, who attended the early meetings, but does not appear at all after August 1933. Pickford was an assiduous attendee from the start of the committee until her untimely death in March 1934, and one can only speculate as to how she must have found being the only woman member on a committee with about fifty male members and delegates usually present. The minutes of evidence show Pickford asking questions on many aspects of the situation. She was particularly tenacious in questioning where women's rights were being discussed. Among her questions was one to a witness on a proposal which would enfranchise very few women. She asked: 'The ratio of women to men voters will be 1 woman to 15 men. Do you think that that is likely to give them an effective influence upon candidates and legislatures?' Sir Mohammed Yakub's insistent reply was that: 'Women have never suffered on account of men in the matter of legislation anywhere in India.'[46]

Likewise, in standing committees women MPs were prime movers in bringing forward a female perspective on issues where this otherwise might have been overlooked. For example, on the Universities of Oxford and Cambridge bill (1923) Margaret Wintringham introduced an amendment to include a woman as an Oxford commissioner.[47] The Duchess of Atholl is not known for her sympathy for feminist issues, yet in her contributions to Standing Committee debates she repeatedly brings up women's angles. For example, during debates on the Unemployment Insurance bill (1935–36) Atholl moved an amendment on milking cows, remarking this was, 'a form of part-time employment very common among women'.[48] On the Illegitimate Children (Scottish) Bill (1929–30) she spoke on the need for taking into consideration the means of both parents when setting the aliment (allowance) to be paid for an illegitimate child, and drew attention to the heavy burden that mothers of such children could face in funeral expenses if these were not included.[49]

The select committee with the most women members was the Select Committee on Equal Compensation (1942–43), appointed to examine the inequality in the levels of compensation for personal injury between men and women during the Second World War. Equal compensation was a personal cause of Mavis Tate, one of five women MPs on this committee.[50] For the first time, minutes of evidence of a select committee show an overall high level of questioning from women, especially Tate, Agnes Hardie and Edith Summerskill. They combated arguments from the likes of Sir Alexander Cunnison from the Ministry of Pensions, who argued that a housewife who had lost both her arms and been fitted with artificial limbs could do her duties to 'a considerable extent', at which the committee was understandably incredulous:

> Miss Lloyd George: ...What sort of household duties could she carry out having lost both arms?
> Sir Alexander Cunnison: I am not enough of an expert in household work to say that, but I think there are quite a considerable number of things that the woman normally does in the house that she could do.
> Miss Lloyd George: Could she cook? Could she wash?
> Sir Alexander Cunnison: I should have thought she probably could.
> ...Mr Ridley: I am a thoroughly domesticated animal and I would not like to find myself upstairs trying to make a bed, I being fixed with a potato peeling apparatus. I think rehabilitation to the ordinary housewife is impossible.[51]

The committee reported in favour of equal compensation and the Government accepted their recommendations. This victory for Tate and her colleagues was a great achievement for the women MPs, although it would not have been possible without cross-party support from seven of the ten men on the committee.

However, any idea that women MPs would always agree and band together is repeatedly confounded in standing committee debates. Nancy Astor frequently clashed with fellow Conservatives, women and men.[52] Labour women Susan Lawrence and Edith Picton-Turbervill disagreed on the Town and Country bill (1930–31). And just because a woman MP was on a standing committee dealing with a 'women's issue' did not mean they necessarily contributed to the debate. For example, Wilkinson did not contribute on the Midwives bill (1926), nor did any women MPs speak on the Midwives bill (1927) in the Scottish Standing Committee. Little was said by women on the Widows, Orphans and Old Age Pensions bill (1936–37).

It is not surprising that some women may have hesitated to speak out because there are many examples of male MPs making reference to women counterparts; sometimes to express a courteous attitude to their lady Members, at other times being unashamedly hostile. Leah Manning sat on the Consumer Council bill (1930–31). The impression that she had to prove herself as a woman is given at one point when Conservative MP Captain Harry Crookshank remarked about food rationing: 'I was one of the people who, because they were in uniform, did not have to bother with that sort of thing.'

> Manning: 'I also was in uniform.'
> Crookshank: 'My respect for the hon Lady goes up by leaps and bounds.'

The debate included an exchange over fixing the price of a skirt which veered into some joshing over skirt lengths.[53] There was a discussion on birching during the Children and Young Persons bill (1931–32) where the ILP MP David Kirkwood, father of seven, clashed badly with Florence Horsbrugh. He said, 'Think of the conditions as the Hon. Member must know, in her hell of a town-' Horsbrugh protested at this, but the Chairman had not heard the offending word. Astor asked, 'Is it Parliamentary to call a particular town "a hell of a town"?' to which Kirkwood responded, 'Would it be in order if I said that a woman was a hell of a woman?' The Chairman called for order. 'We must all try to keep a little decency in the Committee.'[54]

Without a record of debate, it is rare to find examples of outright sexism by male MPs to women MPs on select committees. Usually only minutes of evidence were recorded, in which witnesses were present and the MPs are, therefore, likely to have been more careful about what they said. However, the Select Committee on National Expenditure, known as the NEC, has unpublished papers surviving which include transcripts of some discussion meetings along with evidence sessions, and some correspondence enabling a broader view of its operation.

The NEC was appointed each session to examine expenditure on the war and to report on possible economies. Under the chairmanship of Sir John Wardlaw-Milne, the NEC was a very large select committee which published one hundred reports over its six sessions. The NEC had two women MPs among its membership but has been given little weight when evaluating the women who were mainly involved, Joan Davidson and Irene Ward. Joan Davidson's entry in the *Oxford Dictionary of National Biography* by Katharine Elliot simply says, 'She was the only woman MP to be a member of the national expenditure committee throughout the Second World War' and refers in the same way to her membership of the Kitchen Committee, as if managing the finances of the Commons kitchen was of comparable importance and difficulty to auditing the finances of the nation in wartime.[55] Irene Ward's concern with issues of women's employment and equal pay is well known, but her membership of the NEC during the war is little recognised as part of this.

Davidson and Ward produced two reports on aspects of women and the war, 'Medical Services of the Women's Royal Naval Service, Auxiliary Territorial Service and Women's Auxiliary Air Force' in 1942, and 'Health and Welfare of Women in War Factories' in 1943.[56] Davidson and Ward were set up as a two-person sub-committee in order to collect evidence on these issues, in recognition that they could discover facts that their male colleagues could not. The evidence taken by Davidson and Ward shows them questioning top military health experts on detailed and wide-ranging issues including pregnancy and venereal disease, problems resulting from love affairs, lavatory shortages, call-up of prostitutes, shortage of sanitary towels (and the supposed undesirability of 'Tampax' for unmarried girls) and the need for hairdressers. A secret memorandum about illegitimate babies and the return of their mothers to service was (after much discussion) communicated separately by the committee Chairman to the Chancellor of the Exchequer.[57]

Although Davidson and Ward's report on the women's fighting services was well received by their male colleagues, their factories report was very controversial. The report went into a lot of detail which many of the men regarded as trivial, for example, the need to warm up the midday meal for night-shift workers at which Sir Ernest Bennett grumbled, 'I cannot see really why a recommendation of this sort comes in a Report on National Expenditure. It is a thing more fit for Mrs Beeton's cookery book.'[58] Davidson argued that these details were 'perhaps beneath the average man but not too small for us to inquire into', that these apparently small issues were giving women a great deal of trouble and causing absenteeism, but nobody had appreciated them before.[59] One of their male colleagues, Herbert Williams, was supportive, saying:

> The two ladies have gone into these irritants with meticulous detail, and have produced a report which men would not have produced. I think we must be very careful not to be masculinists on this, if I may use a phrase we do not very often hear.[60]

The report was eventually agreed, although Davidson and Ward were not asked to do another such specialist inquiry. They nevertheless played a full part in the general work of the NEC before, during, and after their women's inquiries. Davidson and Ward went on all the many visits arranged for the NEC along with the men, heard evidence, questioned witnesses and contributed to reports on a wide variety of topics.[61] Sometimes they can be found asking questions which might not have been asked by an exclusively male sub-committee. For example, during inquiries into the supply of milk, eggs and other household necessities, Davidson took a particular interest in children's clothes.[62]

Equal pay was a recurring theme of concern to Davidson and Ward who repeatedly found examples of unequal pay for the same work in the Fighting Services, factories and elsewhere. They even discovered it on their own doorstep. Wartime had necessitated the employment of women in the House of Commons Committee Office for the first time. A number were employed as secretarial staff but several female Clerks were also appointed, Clerk being the top rung of staff in Parliament rather than the bottom. Kay Midwinter, the first female House of Commons Clerk, played a full role alongside her male colleagues in administering the work of the NEC.[63] Midwinter clerked Davidson and Ward's women's inquiries, during which they discovered that Midwinter was paid far less than male committee clerks. After much effort by the Clerk of Committees and others, Midwinter's salary was raised to a range of £480–£650, 'being the women's equivalent of £600–£800'.[64]

Returning to the quote with which we began, the campaign leaflet issued after the Second World War declared that the women MPs 'made their mark...in a degree entirely out of proportion to their numbers' in their committee service. It can now be considered to what extent this is true. It is certainly correct that the women MPs were greatly outnumbered by their male colleagues in the interwar period, and despite this, their participation on select and standing committees shows much diligence and useful input in a number of areas. The attendance figures are generally good. Although the contribution of those that did participate is sometimes opaque or clearly negligible, there are good examples of active and solid contributions to the work of individual committees. These include Ellen Wilkinson on the Kitchen Committee, Ethel Bentham on the Capital Punishment Committee and Mary Pickford on the Indian Constitutional Committee. Mavis Tate and her female colleagues on the Equal Compensation Committee played important roles in its investigation and could rightly be proud of their impact. Joan Davidson and Irene Ward were not only very solid members of the National Expenditure Committee generally but made a unique and measurable contribution with their reports into women in the armed forces and in factories.

Some women MPs, such as Susan Lawrence, Ellen Wilkinson and Florence Horsbrugh, excelled in the forum of standing committees. Others did not contribute much at all. Although it must have been a less intimidating atmosphere than the Commons chamber, standing committees were also more demanding in that an interest and knowledge of the subject was assumed, and the smaller numbers meant that there was no place to hide. If you were there, the extent of your contribution, large or small, would be apparent.

Regarding select committees, it is clear that women MPs were initially placed on select committees were mostly deliberately put on committees which were seen to have a 'women's interest', either explicitly (children's guardianship, nationality of married women, nursing) or according to a perception of women's interest being in the domestic sphere (the Kitchen Committee). This marginalisation diminishes during the 1930s, with women being placed on committees dealing with broader topics such as water resources and London local government. However, no women in this period were put on six of the eight 'core' select committees which were regularly appointed each session, or on the regular select committees on public finance, the Public Accounts Committee and the Estimates Committee. It is therefore difficult to say that women MPs made their mark 'entirely out of proportion to their numbers'. Many women MPs never sat on a select committee at all. This includes some long-standing members such as the Duchess of Atholl, and notable Labour MPs such as Susan Lawrence and Margaret Bondfield. It should be noted, however, that many male MPs also never sat on a select committee. In a period with more than 600 MPs in the

House, numbers of men on select committees varied from a high of 212 in 1920 to a low of 113 in 1934–35.[65] Women MPs' participation in select committees is therefore more proportionate than not.

Rather, it is perhaps the case that some of the women MPs who did not participate so much in other areas of Parliamentary activity, such as debate in the chamber or in standing committees, contributed more to select committee work instead. The investigative nature of select committees had similarities to other forums in which women MPs are likely to have participated before they entered Parliament; feminist organisations, charitable institutions, Royal Commissions of inquiry, and government departmental committees. Maybe such similarities helped them feel at ease. Brian Harrison's analysis of the early women MPs' contribution to debates in the chamber mentions a 'top eight' list of contributors who are Astor, Atholl, Bondfield, Horsbrugh, Lawrence, Lloyd George, Rathbone and Wilkinson. This list is similar to the contributors to standing committees, but wholly different to those prominent in select committees; of these eight, only Astor, Rathbone and Wilkinson sat on a select committee, and Astor and Rathbone only on one each. By contrast, Harrison mentions 'reluctant speakers' in Parliament, such as Runge and Shaw; Runge and Shaw did participate in select committees.[66] Mary Philipson's biographer says that she never overcame her dislike of speaking in the House of Commons, but she too participated in select committee work.[67] Perhaps the very nature of committee work, the smaller group of people involved, the concentration on the detail of legislation and gathering evidence, was more suited to some of these women than the avowedly masculine cut and thrust arena of the House of Commons chamber.

This analysis of committee participation fills a gap in the historiography of both Parliamentary history and women's history, and contributes to a more rounded view of participation of women in Parliament. It brings to the fore the contributions of female MPs such as Mary Pickford, Ethel Bentham and Joan Davidson who are often overlooked. It takes our historical understanding of the House of Commons beyond the main debating chamber and into a different, more intimate, sphere of Parliamentary politics. It shows how the extension of the franchise enabled some women to take skills and experience honed by committee work elsewhere, including that of the suffrage struggle, and apply it to the work of Parliament. It highlights a new political role played by women in the aftermath of suffrage.

Notes

1. The presentation of the first petition is recorded in HC Debates, 3 August 1832, vol. 14 c1086.
2. B. Harrison, 'Women in a men's house: the women MPs, 1919–1945', *Historical Journal* 29, 3 (1986).

3. Leaflet issued by the Women's Electoral Campaign, part of the 'Women for Westminster' movement formed in 1943 with the aim of encouraging the adoption of women as Parliamentary candidates. The Women's Library (WL), 7/TBG/1/12.

4. P. Brookes, *Women at Westminster: An Account of Women in the British Parliament, 1918–1966* (London: Peter Davies, 1967).

5. M. Pugh, *Women and the Women's Movement in Britain, 1914–1999*, 2nd edn (Basingstoke: Macmillan, 2000), pp. 194–201.

6. E. Vallance, *Women in the House* (London: Athlone Press, 1979), p. 102.

7. Harrison, 'Women in a men's house'.

8. Harrison, 'Women in a men's house', p. 633.

9. R. Toye, 'The House of Commons in the Aftermath of Suffrage'.

10. W. Ivor Jennings, *Parliament* (Cambridge: Cambridge University Press, 1939), pp. 264–79. Before 1882, legislation was considered in a committee of the whole House of Commons; Gladstone instituted standing committees to help meet the situation caused by Irish obstruction.

11. Jennings, *Parliament*. Despite the long history of select committees, the modern-day select committee system, where each Government department is shadowed by a select committee (for example, the Home Office is scrutinised by the Home Affairs Committee), dates only from 1979.

12. *Report from House of Commons Select Committee on Criminal and Destitute Juveniles*, HC 515 (1852).

13. *Report from the Select Committee on the Law relating to the protection of young girls*, HL 145 (1881) & HL 188 (1882). More famously, the following year Josephine Butler and Mary Webb gave oral evidence to a Commons Select Committee on the Contagious Diseases Act. *Report from the Select Committee on Contagious Diseases Acts; together with the proceedings of the committee, minutes of evidence, and appendix*, HC 340 (1882). Butler had previously given evidence to Royal Commissions on the same subject.

14. For example, *the Report from the Select Committee on Post Office Servants*, HC 380 (1906), included evidence from female employees of the Post Office on behalf of women sorters, telegraphists, supervisors and clerks.

15. *Proceedings of the Joint Committee on the Guardianship of Infants Bill [H.L.], Minutes of Evidence and Appendix*, HL 95 & HL 163 (1924), v, pp. 293–522: *Joint Select Committee on the Nationality of Married Women*. HC 115 (1923): *Select Committee on Equal Compensation: Proceedings of the Committee, Minutes of Evidence, Appendices and Index relating to the Report of the Committee*, HC 53 (1942–43).

16. *Select Committee on the General Nursing Council*, HC 167 (1924–25): *Select Committee on Nursing Homes Registration*, HC 103 (1925). The exact number is unclear as some witnesses are referred to as 'Dr' without a first name and may have been male or female. This can only be discerned if it came out during questioning. For example, it is only apparent that Dr M. A. C. Douglas-Drummond, Assistant Medical Officer of Health, Manchester, was a women from her own reference to herself as a 'medical woman,' p. 179.

17. *Select Committee on Shop Assistants*, HC 176 (1929–30), p. 43.

18. *Joint Select Committee on Indian Constitutional Reform* HC 112(1), HL 79(1), (1932–33). 27 June 1933, 17 October 1933, 2 August 1933.

19. *Report from the Select Committee on Luxury Duty*, HC 101 (1918). The other women were Lady St Helier, Mrs H. B. Irving, Miss M. Craig, Mrs Vaughan Nash, the Hon. Mrs Frederick Guest and Miss Beatrice Chamberlain.

20. Violet Markham and Mrs Vaughan Nash were apparently discharged on 18 June and Margaret Craig resigned on 21 June. Whether Markham and Vaughan Nash actually resigned or were discharged was a moot point; Francis Acland, the Chairman, wrote to both asking them to rejoin the sub-committees on 20 June but they refused. LSE Archives, Markham 2/4. Acland to Markham, 20 June 1918; confidential letter from Markham to A. Spender (Westminster Gazette), 26 June 1918.
21. LSE Archives, Markham 2/4. Markham to J. A. R. Marriott MP, 23 May 1918.
22. HC Deb, 23 October 1918, vol 110, c 816, Herbert Samuel. This was during the debates on the Parliament (Qualification of Women) Bill, which was subsequently passed and allowed women to become MPs.
23. E. Picton-Turbervill, *Life Is Good: An Autobiography* (Frederick Muller Ltd., 1939), p. 172.
24. The statistics on select and standing committee membership, attendances and contributions in this paper were compiled during research for the author's PhD thesis. M. Takayanagi, 'Parliament and Women c.1900–1945' (King's College London, PhD, 2012). Space precludes the inclusion of the complete data here.
25. The statistics on select and standing committee membership, attendances and contributions in this paper were compiled during research for the author's PhD thesis. M. Takayanagi, 'Parliament and Women c.1900–1945' (King's College London, PhD, 2012). Space precludes the inclusion of the complete data here.
26. *Report from the Select Committee on Capital Punishment*, HC 15 (1930–31).
27. WL, 2NSE/A/5/5/1. NUSEC Parliamentary Committee, Minutes of meeting 13 May 1930. Manning was appointed on 24 March 1931, after the death of James Stewart on 17 March. Manning had been elected as an MP only one month earlier.
28. Irene Ward was appointed to the Joint Committee on Water Resources and Supplies (1935–36). Although supply of water to rural households was an issue of concern to some women, this committee did not deal with that angle, concentrating on the technicalities of water supply and the effect on mills, factories and industry.
29. 'Where a standing committee is considering an Agriculture Bill, a member who does not know, and does not care to know, the difference between a turnip and a mangel-wurzel, either ceases to be a member or does not attend.' Jennings, *Parliament*, p. 268.
30. For example Nancy Astor was appointed to standing committees considering temperance reform, and Eleanor Rathbone to standing committees considering family allowances.
31. Compiled from *House of Commons Returns of Standing Committees*. These returns were printed in House of Commons Parliamentary Papers up to 1931. Thereafter they were compiled by clerks and laid before the House but not printed, and can be found in the House of Commons Unprinted Papers in the Parliamentary Archives. Standing committees were not summoned between 1939-1944. Takayanagi, 'Parliament and Women'.
32. Compiled from *House of Commons Returns of Select Committees*. These returns were printed in House of Commons Parliamentary Papers up to 1931. Thereafter they were compiled by clerks and laid before the House but not printed, and can be found in the House of Commons Unprinted Papers in the Parliamentary Archives. The returns for two sessions (1942–43 and 1944–45) are missing from the Unprinted Papers and this data was reconstructed from the reports and minutes of proceedings of the individual committees. Takayanagi, 'Parliament and Women'.

33. Cazalet became Parliamentary Private Secretary at the Board of Education in June 1938, and married in June 1939, so it was a busy time for her in other ways.
34. Takayanagi, 'Parliament and Women'.
35. Methodology as follows: Women MPs debating lines have been directly counted. Equivalent data for men obtained by deducting the women's figures from an estimate for total debating lines each session. The estimate is reached by multiplying the number of columns for the session by 60 (the number of lines per column) and deducting from that figure 929 lines per 100 columns to allow for lines used for purposes other than reporting debate. Harrison, 'Women in a men's house', pp. 630–1.
36. Takayanagi, 'Parliament and Women'.
37. 'Lawrence was a ministerial success; her command of detail secured her authority both in her department and at the dispatch box.' David Howell, 'Lawrence, (Arabella) Susan (1871–1947)', *Oxford Dictionary of National Biography*, Oxford University Press, 2004 [http://www.oxforddnb.com/view/article/34434, accessed 17 May 2011].
38. Parliamentary Archives (PA), HC/CL/CO/EA/2/6. Staff lists among Kitchen Committee minutes, 22 July 1924 and 10 December 1936.
39. PA, HC/CL/CO/EA/2/6. Kitchen Committee minutes, 17 February 1925.
40. PA, HC/CL/CO/EA/2/7. Kitchen Committee minutes, 4 May, 18 May, 16 July 1933.
41. When it seemed that this clause might not be included in the Government's bill, Lady Astor wrote to the Government that, if it were not included, she would move it as an amendment, and, if this amendment was not accepted, she would oppose the whole bill on behalf of all organised bodies of women. The National Archives (TNA), LCO 2/469. Letter from Lady Astor, 15 February 1922.
42. SC Deb (A) 16 Mar 1926 cc.127–8.
43. SC Deb (A) 20 Apr 1939 cc.778–80, 777–8, 787–8.
44. SC Deb (B) 25 February–28 April 1932 cc.1059–1608.
45. *Joint Select Committee on Indian Constitutional Reform*, HC 112(1), HL 79(1), (1932–33).
46. *Joint Select Committee on Indian Constitutional Reform*, HC 112(1), HL 79(1), (1932–33), pp. 1497–8, 1 August 1933.
47. SC Deb (B) 11 July 1923 c. 685.
48. SC Deb (A) 12 March 1936 c. 34.
49. SC Deb (Sc) 10 December 1929 cc. 54, 61–2.
50. Tate chaired a committee of women's organisations dedicated to opposing this aspect of the Personal Injuries (Civilian) Scheme. She also later chaired its successor body, the Equal Pay Campaign Committee.
51. *Select Committee on Equal Compensation: Proceedings of the Committee, Minutes of Evidence, Appendices and Index relating to the Report of the Committee*, HC 53 (1942–43), p. 23.
52. For example on the need for women justices in juvenile courts during the Children and Young Persons bill 1931–32; Astor was opposed by Runge and Graves in the division. SC Deb (B) 25 February 1932 cc. 1087–8.
53. SC Deb (C) 21 July 1931 c 1479, c 1083.
54. SC Deb (B) 3 March 1932 c. 1155. The 'hell of a town' was Horsbrugh's constituency Dundee.
55. Elliot of Harwood (author), 'Davidson, (Frances) Joan, Viscountess Davidson and Baroness Northchurch (1894–1985)', rev. *Oxford Dictionary of National Biography*,

Oxford University Press, 2004 [http://0-www.oxforddnb.com.catalogue.ulrls.lon. ac.uk/view/article/31006, accessed 15 April 2011].

56. *Select Committee on National Expenditure, 6th report*, HC 72 (1941–42) and *Select Committee on National Expenditure, 3rd report*, HC 19 (1942–43).

57. Miss Musson from the National Council for the Unmarried Mother and Her Child wrote to the Clerk, Miss Midwinter, 'it is very cheering to my Committee and other friends in my work, as well as myself, to feel that we have such real and practical sympathisers on your committee.' Letter dated 7 June 1942, with the memo in Parliamentary Archives, HL/PO/CL/CO/AA/AN/1/2. Other correspondence about it in PA, HL/PO/CL/CO/AA/AN/1/6. The discussion in the NEC as to what to do with it is in PA, HC/CL/CO/AA/1/062 – Full 20, 16 July 1942.

58. PA, HC/CL/CO/AA/1/078 – Full 3, 17 December 1942.

59. PA, HC/CL/CO/AA/AA/1/42 – Co-ord 1, 9 December 1942.

60. PA, HC/CL/CO/AA/AA/1/42 – Co-ord 1, 9 December 1942.

61. At one point the Navy sub-committee was at Salisbury Plain watching a demonstration with live ammunition. The Clerk Basil Drennan recorded, 'Lady Davidson was in great form. She said, "I don't want to seem fussy, but was that a bullet that went past my head just now?"' PA, DRE/A/1/17, letter dated 5 June 1942.

62. Davidson said she had received many complaints about this and was concerned as a mother herself. PA, HC/CL/CO/AA/AR/1/10-11 - Departmental Services (B) 21, 5 August 1943.

63. Midwinter was Clerk to the sub-committee on Transport in 1941–42 and Works (A) in 1942–43, as well as clerking the women's inquiries on an informal basis. She was praised for her work by the Chairman of the NEC, Sir John Wardlaw-Milne; by the Clerk of the NEC, Cyril Diver; and the Clerk of the Committees, Sir Gilbert Campion. PA, HC/CL/CH/2/2/107.

64. Salary book, PA, HC/FA/FO/1/171. The Clerk's discussion of Midwinter's salary is in PA, HC/CL/CH/2/2/107, and the Treasury's deliberations are in TNA, T 162/777. Midwinter's Parliamentary career is studied in detail in Takayanagi, 'Parliament and Women'.

65. Takayanagi, 'Parliament and Women'.

66. Harrison, 'Women in a men's house', p. 647.

67. J. Sleight, *Women on the march: the story of the struggle for political power and equality for women in the north-east from 1920 to 1970, told through the lives of seven remarkable women* (Newcastle-upon-Tyne: 1986), p. 53.

11
The Political Autobiographies of Early Women MPs, c.1918–1964[1]

Krista Cowman

Introduction: autobiography, politics and women

In 1948, after having been 'again and again asked for an account of [her] life', the socialist former MP Margaret Bondfield completed the preface to her autobiography. In it she explained how she intended the book to be:

> an account of the life of the first woman who became a member of His Majesty's Privy Council, and a Minister and a member of the Cabinet. How and when and why this came about are matters worthy of some record....for...the younger generation...who will not remember even the more recent of the events here recorded. ...It may be useful for them to read of the kind of path trodden by one who is now in her seventies. ...If, occasionally, it is difficult to separate my personal adventure from the history of the Labour Party, that is perfectly in harmony with the facts. I have been so identified with the Movement that it is not always possible to say where one ends and the other begins.[2]

In writing these words, Bondfield was following a long-established tradition in Western politics. Political autobiographies and memoirs comprise one of the oldest forms of life writing. The urge amongst those at the centre of the events that challenged and shaped their nations during their lifetimes to leave accounts of their part in these for future generations 'has scarcely abated since the rise of literacy in human civilisation'.[3] Rather, it has increased in recent years, augmented by technological developments to include taped diaries, televised interviews and blogs. Familiarity with a politician's personality is deemed as important as knowledge of their policy; the 2008 American presidential election was 'remarkable for the role played by the published life narrative' of its key protagonists (Hillary Rodham Clinton's *Living History*, Barrack Obama's *Dreams from My Father*, John McCain's *Faith of My Fathers* (and his subsequent texts) and, immediately after the campaign, Sarah Palin's *Going Rogue*.[4] In the UK public interest has turned texts such as Blair's *Journey* into bestsellers. The genre of political autobiography appears to be enjoying something of a moment.

This popularity is not reflected in autobiographical criticism. George Egerton, who directed a pioneering international comparative research project on 'Political Memoirs' in the late 1980s, ascribed the lack of critical attention to political life writing to the genre's tendency to blur into other forms including history, political science and journalism. Egerton proposed the term 'polygenre' to capture the breadth and distinctiveness of a body of writing produced by a wide spectrum of writers who could be considered politicians including elected representatives, court ambassadors and military leaders.[5] Three conditions were seen to stimulate its production: 'the occurrence of dramatic events such as war or revolution; the desire of participants...to record their observations...and the provision of necessary leisure time' to do this.[6] Consequently this project considered little writing by women. That which was included came from witnesses rather than participants in key political events; military wives, political hostesses or courtiers, 'well-placed to observe the political elites and their behaviour' from the sidelines, but unable to write as political insiders.[7]

Women are more likely to write of their own direct experience of political participation within the rank and file of political movements. Historians of communism have recently turned their attention to the vast body of autobiographical writings that communist parties encouraged as a means of establishing a distinctive political culture where 'social class, political questions and political action played a central role'.[8] The writing produced by women party members has been said to take a distinctive form, tending more towards introspection and personal detail.[9] Feminist labour historians drew on this approach to interpret the considerable body of life-writing produced by socialist women. Such writing, according to Ursula Masson, countered an emerging male personality cult in socialist historiography through providing an 'alternative...labour history in which the central place was taken by women, and the struggle was the welfare of the women and children of the working class'.[10] Autobiographies produced by liberal or conservative women have attracted less attention.[11]

Analyses of the gendering of communist and socialist life-writing mirror a longstanding school of thought in feminist autobiographical theory that suggests that the form and content of women's autobiographical writing distinguishes it from that of men. Women's written constructions of their lives, it is argued, reflected 'more relational...fragmented selves' hence were less likely to result in the neat linear narratives produced by men.[12] Their content, being dependent on women's social position and concerns, will lean towards addressing 'the personal [and] the intimate' rather than public life or national events.[13] Although this position has been the subject of challenge and review, assumptions of a binary positioning of 'female' and 'male' autobiography have proved remarkably trenchant.[14] Women's autobiographies are still largely seen as the self-presentation of the under-represented, the powerless, the marginalised or the dispossessed.

The political writing of women MPs does not sit comfortably within either of these fields. On the one hand, there is much less than that of men. Only after 1918 could women produce political autobiographies that addressed the authors' own experience as elected representatives. On the other hand, as the few women who did this wrote as leaders rather than rank-and-file activists, their narratives proved difficult to position within an emergent 'feminist autobiographical canon' that was strongly influenced by ideas of 'history from below'.[15] Women MP's life-writing is thus rendered doubly invisible, statistically marginal compared with the output of male politicians but too public in its focus to sit comfortably within studies of women's autobiography.

Suffrage historiography offers a potentially more useful model. As Hilda Kean has noted, many former activists turned to autobiographical writing in the inter-war period to shape the history of their movement and ensure that their pioneering work was not lost to a new generation of younger women.[16] Suffragists and suffragettes used autobiography to justify their position within the movement's pre-war militant/constitutional divide whilst simultaneously attempting to ensure that this position remained to the fore within an emergent suffrage historiography. Thus autobiography became 'a representation of experience....rather than a quasi-objective historical account...through which the suffrage feminists sought to appropriate and develop their own pervious political experience'.[17] Kean's definition may provide a way of approaching the life writing of women MPs. Women elected in the 1920s faced numerous challenges as they sought to carve out a niche for themselves in what largely remained 'a men's house'.[18] External commentators remained fixated on their novelty, placing their every move under scrutiny. Women MPs found that their speeches and campaigns, their dress and conduct, and even the areas of the House of Commons they were able to access became the subject of fierce media debates. As much of this interest was associated with women's scarcity value in parliament, the situation changed little until the 1990s. Yet, within this extensive reportage, little agreement emerged as to what was expected of the new category of 'woman MP' and much of the role had to be shaped and defined by those who acceded to it. In common with ex-suffragettes, some women found that autobiographical writing offered them a means through which they could construct a public identity as well as a way of recoding their contribution to a broader political history.

Egerton believed that political life-writing was most useful to historians.[19] Here, I am using it as a means of exploring one of the most obvious changes to the British polity in the wake of the 1918 Representation of the People Act; the presence of women in Parliament. The Parliament (Qualification of Women Bill) of November 1918 confirmed women's eligibility as candidates as well as voters. As Mari Takayanagi's contribution to this volume reminds us, they were not elected in great numbers. Indeed, between 1918 and 1964 (the end point for this chapter) only eighty women had been returned to Parliament.[20] The year 1964 represented a modest peak – twenty nine – in their numbers. Within women's history the early women MPs have been examined collectively in studies aimed at reclaiming their contribution to politics, and extending knowledge of women's participation in government. The presence of women in Parliament has also raised important questions for historians seeking to uncover exactly what difference the vote made.[21] Whilst there is consensus that most activists in the pre-war women's movement took a pragmatic view of what their presence in Parliament might achieve, the main focus of the pre-war suffrage campaign had been on this arena, making what happened there after women were granted the vote a highly legitimate question. Looking at how women functioned in Parliament, particularly in the inter-war period, may also have implications for broader political history. Despite the brief efforts of Emmeline and Christabel Pankhurst and a handful of their supporters at the end of the war, there was no move to establish a woman's party in Britain. Although a handful of women fought as independent candidates, almost all who entered Westminster came as representatives of political parties to work alongside party men. How these women negotiated the previously masculine Parliamentary world, what areas of work they found assigned to them and what territory they strove to claim tells us much about the gendering of mainstream party politics in the inter-war period.

Thirteen of the women elected by 1964 published book length autobiographies.[22] These texts have informed historical studies by Pamela Brookes, Brian Harrison and Elizabeth Vallance as a means of interjecting personal experience into their analyses.[23] None of these, however, considers the body of writing itself, or attempts to provide a collective analysis of its content, form and purpose. Here, I will discuss what distinguishes women's political life-writing, considering its presentation of a number of common themes to assess what is distinctive about this genre.

Seeking a form: political autobiography, memoir or the autobiography of politicians

Labour women MPs were the most numerous autobiographers. Ten of the thirteen authors discussed here were from the Independent Labour Party or the Labour Party; the remaining three came from the Conservative Party. Socialist culture offered a broader autobiographical tradition to draw on, but Labour also returned greater numbers of women to parliament before 1964. Women MPs' writing differs in form, irrespective of party. Autobiographical theory distinguishes between the memoir, which offers a short and immediate view on a particular event or series of events and the autobiography, which describes an entire life from birth and childhood through to the point of writing, frequently in old age.[24] This division becomes less clear in political life writing where lives can be ostensibly presented in totality, but within a political context such as in the working-class autobiographies discussed by Regina Gagnier which channel 'all experience into one great conflict, the integration of social process and personal development in time'.[25] Neal Blewett distinguishes between a political autobiography which he defines as a work 'focussed overwhelmingly on the political life of the author with little in the way of personal introspection' and a politician's autobiography, 'that kind of autobiography in which the author...grapples with their personal life, their pre-political life...and...other interests'.[26] Applying this criteria to the writing of women MPs shows them producing both political and politician's autobiographies. Although most of the texts record entire lives, some take a shorter focus. Jean Mann's 1962 *Woman in Parliament* may be considered a memoir as it opens not with her birth or family background but with her election in 1945 at the age of forty-six. Yet despite its focus on her twelve years in Parliament, Mann's text is not linear but twists back on itself to describe fragments of her earlier life and political influences. Other autobiographies attempt a less conventional form. Bessie Braddock's *The Braddocks* presents an account of her own life from birth alongside one of the life of her co-author husband, Jack, forming a dual biography which testifies to the importance of their political partnership. In *Working Partnership*, Katharine, Duchess of Atholl switches from autobiographer to biographer between chapters to describe the early life and military and political career of her husband, Tullibardine. Some writers constructed multiple versions of their lives in different formats. Mary Agnes Hamilton supplemented the 'classic' form of her autobiography *Up Hill All the Way* with another book, *Remembering my Good Friends*, which situated aspects of her work as an MP in a series of anecdotes about leading political figures, mixing autobiographical and biographical approaches throughout. Edith Summerskill provided both the traditional *A Woman's World*, and *Letters to my Daughter*, an epistolary record of her career including her time as a Minister, sent to her daughter, Shirley (who later followed her mother into Parliament).

Routes into political life

Most political life writing offers some account of how the author came to be involved in politics in the first place. The political genealogies described by women MPs are strongly gendered. Brian Harrison's analysis of women's work in parliament before 1945 found only a 'relatively muted feminism' at best, which he ascribed to 'the internal divisions among inter-war feminists'.[27] Yet feminism is easily discerned in women MP's autobiographical writings when they place their political genealogy firmly within the context of the pre-war women's movement and the suffrage campaign that made their election possible. Jean Mann's text discussed her links with the suffrage movement. The Suffragette Fellowship had organised a large event at the House of Commons 'to celebrate Emmeline Pankhurst's centenary', on 15 July 1958. Mann, one of the chosen speakers,

> ....recalled how I used to share an open-air platform with Annie Munro... and I told the women that I would like to...get her opinion of our work if she was still living. Just then there was a bustle of interruption and Annie was pushed out of the crowd right up to me on the platform.[28]

Mann may well have spoken for suffrage in her early life although she makes no further mention of this, and it does not feature in biographical accounts of her career.[29] Constructing this anecdote connected her to the pre-war women's movement at a point when its achievements were being publicly celebrated amongst MPs, establishing her credentials as a feminist activist without the need for any further detail. Many women who were too young to have played any active role in the suffrage campaign sought similar connections. Jennie Lee recalled how the suffragette Helen Crawford was a regular visitor to her childhood home, telling the young Jennie tales of 'window-breaking adventures and prison exploits' which made her 'wonder...ruefully if anything at all would be left to do by the time I had finished with school'.[30] Although Bessie Braddock's family politics were more connected to trade union activism than suffrage, her autobiography recalled how she had been dressed up as a suffragette in a Band of Hope pageant before the First World War.[31]

The familial influences that many women MPs credited with shaping their politics were often less woman-centred. In her 2009 work *Climbing the Bookshelves*, Shirley Williams claimed that 'the achievements of women politicians grew out of their father's belief in them'.[32] Williams cited Jennie Lee, Margaret Thatcher and Barbara Castle as 'examples...of daughters living out their fathers' aspirations', and suggested that 'the relationship between fathers and daughters...is...a key to understanding how some women become leaders'.[33] Autobiographies discussed the political beliefs in childhood homes, and the important influence of their fathers' attitudes. In Edith Summerskill's *A Woman's World*, an early chapter, 'the seeds of feminism are watered', explains how it was her father rather than her mother who

> followed with considerable satisfaction...the struggle for women's suffrage and whenever some incident hit the headlines he would comment, "the franchise is all very well, but we must also establish the economic emancipation of women".[34]

For Leah Manning the role was taken by the grandfather who raised her after the rest of her family emigrated to Canada. He took a permissive attitude to her reading and gave her free rein in his bookshelves (an indulgence which Barbara Castle also recalled as critical in forming her own young political consciousness).[35] The young Manning was permitted to sit, 'quiet as a mouse' during the animated political discussions that pervaded her adopted childhood home. Here, she learnt of

> The rights and wrongs of Charles Bradlaugh; the vicious sentence on Oscar Wilde; the queer ideas of Mrs Besant....the white slave traffic; General Booth and Mrs Josephine Butler. ...I would sit...only very occasionally catching the drift of the meaning, yet with the names of the people under discussion indelibly impressed on my memory, and a determination to find out all about them when I could read some of the books on my grandfather's shelves.[36]

In comparison with the autobiographical accounts of suffragists which were often riven with domestic conflict, women MPs rarely recalled any familial disapprobation for their political activities. Many came from political households. The levels of engagement varied. As a civil servant, Barbara Castle's father was debarred from political affiliation, yet he still managed to take up the editorship of the ILP paper *The Bradford Pioneer* under a thinly disguised pseudonym.[37] Jennie Lee recalled a childhood in which the Socialist Sunday School and outdoor ILP meetings defined her week.[38] Not all formative political experiences were shaped by party. Although both were Conservative, the politics Margaret Thatcher learned from her Alderman father were a matter of civic duty' where 'party was of secondary importance'.[39] In Thelma Cazalet Keir's family it was a politician's social potential rather than their party affiliation that mattered. Her mother was an active hostess, and her dinner guests who included Kipling, H. G. Wells, the Webbs, Lloyd George and Stanley Baldwin were presented by Thelma as decisive 'among the factors which helped to strengthen my instinctive taste for politics and surmount my natural inadequacies'.[40]

Gagnier's analysis of working-class political life writing highlights the importance of the conversion moment to this form, which distinguishes it from other less climatic forms of non-bourgeois autobiography.[41] Conversion moments remain a key marker of suffrage autobiography where the discovery of a political movement forms an important point in the subject's self-discovery.[42] In women MPs writings, they are less common. Although a third of Edith Picton-Turbervill's *Life Is Good* deals with her time in parliament, there is little explanation as to how she got there. The text simply noted that '[t]he following entry appears in my diary for January 15 1919. "Joined the Labour Party! After months of consideration"'.[43] Any interior discussions she engaged in during these months of consideration are not revealed. Mary Agnes Hamilton is the only author to describe something approaching a conversion moment when, in explaining what predisposed her towards socialism, she isolated one single event:

> on a very cold, wet day in 1913, I was held up, as I sought to cross the road, by a coal cart. I had on thick shoes, a warm overcoat; over my head was a stout umbrella; on the cart, with only a ragged sack over his thin shoulders, a man sat perched on the bags of coal; not a young man; a man with a fine intelligent head, although his face was grimy. ...Here was something surely needlessly wrong.[44]

Whilst Hamilton cited this as '[t]he incident that, finally, settled' her politics, it could just as easily be read as a confirmation of the 'democratic faith' she learned in her childhood home.[45] Most writers presented their politics as emerging gradually from a secure home, even in cases where there was a moment at which they became conscious of having an individual political consciousness. Jennie Lee, who was ten when the First World War broke out, derived much secret shame from her parents' socialist pacifism as it cut across a childish sense of convention.[46] This changed when she encountered the Covenanters in a school history lesson. At an ILP meeting the following Sunday, she realised a strong parallel with her family's socialism:

> Were we not a persecuted minority? Were not some of our members in prison? Were we not forced to meet in the open country miles outside the town? ...That decided it. We were the modern Covenanters. ...Nothing could now make me feel ashamed'.[47]

Although the moment left Lee 'happy and proud, spiritually at one with my family', this was less a moment of conversion, and more one of an acceptance of the ideologies surrounding her since birth. For most women MPs, the process of becoming political involved the gradual development of familial principles throughout an unfolding life rather than a dramatic rejection of these which signalled a new era.

Relationships between women MPs

A key issue for historians exploring immediate political changes that might be ascribed to women's suffrage has been the ways in which the earliest women MPs negotiated the competing demands of party and gender politics at Westminster.[48] The autobiographical writing of women MPs acknowledges that their sex placed them under very particular pressure, intensified by their small numbers. The Duchess of Atholl summarised the dilemma that faced any woman who was

> sent to the House of Commons by the votes of the men as well as the women of her constituency....But when you get there.... The women of

the country have a charming habit of thinking that it is they who have sent you there and that you are only responsible to them![49]

Many women MPs described resisting the limitations they felt that this placed on them. Athol feared pressure from the external woman's movement for a woman's party, believing that this would 'inevitably have antagonised men, and in doing so would have created a gulf far more difficult to bridge than the cleavage of party or of "class"'.[50] In common with many inter-war feminists outside parliament, she was anxious to promote a new, inclusive form of citizenship that would unite men and women rather than perpetuate pre-war sexual friction. Other women MPs were sensitive to the needs of the parties which had sent them to Westminster. Mary Agnes Hamilton refuted Nancy Astor's hope that the fifteen women elected in 1929 'should function as a woman's party', as she felt no need 'to be other than the Labour M.P. as which I had been returned'.[51] Parties could be less clear about what they expected from their women representatives, however, wishing them to prioritise party loyalty over gender solidarity, but presuming, at the same time, that they were best equipped to represent the needs of British women at Westminster. This presumption did not diminish when the novelty of women's enfranchisement wore off. Margaret Thatcher cited the resignation of Pat Hornsby-Smith from the cabinet in 1961 as instrumental to her own promotion because 'it was thought politically desirable to keep up the number of women in the Government'.[52] Many male politicians had difficulty moving beyond the situation Ray Strachey noted in 1918 when the Representation of the People Act led MPs to discover 'that every Bill...had a 'women's side' and the Party Whips began eagerly to ask 'what the women thought?'[53] When Thatcher was appointed to Edward Heath's shadow cabinet in the 1970s she still felt that she was 'principally there as the statutory woman whose main task was to explain what "women" – Kiri Te Kanawa, Barbara Cartland....and all the rest of our uniform, undifferentiated sex – were likely to think and want on troublesome issues'.[54]

Certain autobiographical theorists have emphasised the importance of collective identity in shaping women's accounts of their own lives. Women MPs writings often demonstrate 'their awareness of group identity' although the competing demands of their identity as party loyalists render this complicated.[55] In most of the texts the authors position themselves within a cross-party group of women M.P.s at some point even when they were not consistently comfortable with this. Mary Agnes Hamilton was dismissive of both 'the silly business' of the group photograph on the terrace and of newspapers' tendency to 'talk...of the women MPs as though they were some kind of peculiar animal', but her discussion of her female parliamentary colleagues presented them as a unit, albeit 'a mixed' one, 'resistant to feminist grouping'.[56] Women acknowledged the value of support of other women which could transcend party boundaries. Shirley Williams felt this stemmed from a common understanding that all of them, regardless of party, 'were up against the unstated but pervasive view that women weren't up to the hard choices of politics'. She recalled one particular instance of female solidarity when, after facing an hour of hostile questioning during her tenure as Secretary of State for Prices and Consumer Protection, she turned to

> just see a figure behind the Speakers' Chair intently watching my performance. It was Margaret Thatcher....When my ordeal was finished, I retreated to the Lady Members' Room where she was ironing a dress. 'You did well', she said. 'After all, we can't let them get the better of us'.[57]

Other women described the importance of deeper female friendships across party lines. Leah Manning recalled her admiration and liking for Patricia Tweedsmuir and Megan Lloyd George, her companion for 'noon-day visits to the cinema', whilst Edith Picton-Tubervill gave three pages of her autobiography to a glowing description of Lady Astor.[58]

Common circumstances framed many autobiographical descriptions of sexual unity. Brian Harrison's group study explained how Westminster's gendered spatial arrangements which excluded women from certain bars and smoking rooms promoted 'a certain solidarity' amongst those who shared the small women member's room.[59] Autobiographical writings reveal a more complex, contradictory set of attitudes to this space. Jean Mann gave a romantic description of its atmosphere where 'the political women mixed together well, avoided controversy and even praised each others' speeches'. When the number of Conservative women increased in the 1950s, Labour women sought to preserve the neutrality of the women member's room and 'began to look over their shoulders to see if any of the "enemy" were present before indulging in an angry blast against their opponents'.[60] Yet not all autobiographers presented this room as a haven. Edith Picton-Tubervill complained of one (unnamed) inhabitant who persisted in 'keep[ing] up lengthy conversations in a loud voice to "dears" and "darlings" on its one telephone whilst others struggled to deal with constituency correspondence'.[61]

As the extract from Picton-Turbervill suggests, women did not automatically praise their women contemporaries. Manning claimed to have liked all women MPs except for Jean Mann who she disliked on account of her fondness for making 'malicious' and 'catt[y]' comments towards other women in the House.[62] Mann's vituperative attacks on her fellow Labour MPs Barbara Castle and Judith Hart show how internal political divisions as well as cross-party conflict could assert themselves over gendered commonalities. Writing from the right wing of a divided Labour Party, Mann implicitly emphasised her own working-class origins and lack of higher education when she placed Castle and Hart at the centre of a group of

> educated women Members...who go out in a big way to influence the whole of their party in its policy. ...The trouble with Barbara is deep

within herself – feverish hypertension – constantly driving (always left). She never even notices the signals at the road junctions. She knows. She knows. The 'come on' Green should be altered to Red. She feels confident she can change the signs...

Hart, who had children, gained slightly more sympathy 'as mothers are so scarce in the House of Commons', but her criticisms of the 'rampant individualism' of many post-war housing developments were not welcomed by Mann, who was a keen supporter of cottage-style council housing. 'We needed talented, presentable-looking women like Judith,' she admitted, '[b]ut some of her left-wing views were not such an asset'.[63] Eight years later, Leah Manning (who did not feature in Mann's book) used her own autobiography to repudiate the attack on Castle and described some of its affects:

Barbara, brilliant indeed, was not nearly as tough as she liked to make out...in the early days of the 1945 Parliament she did not have an easy time. Her very success as a young member aroused jealousy, and I had often to put up a fight for her against the malice of Jean Mann whose book *Women at Westminster* was positively splenetic about Barbara...more than once I found [her]...in tears in the Lady Members' room.[64]

Castle's own autobiography, written in 1993, made no mention of Mann, who by this point had been dead for almost thirty years. By this time, a long political career that had taken her through the European Parliament to the House of Lords, gave Castle a broader context for her political life in which smaller personal battles could be glossed over or omitted entirely.

* * *

Such contradictions in their autobiographical selves reflect the dual expectations which weighed on early women MPs. On the one hand they were all party women, more interested in vindicating their personal political positions in the partisan world of party politics than in offering exemplars for a wider feminist movement. On the other hand, external observers and the internal arrangements of the House combined to present them as a reasonably homogeneous group, an identity which permeated their writing even when they strove to deny it.

Women's interests?

Analysis of women MP's careers has noted how the expectation that they should represent their sex was in part borne out in the areas of policy they were encouraged to colonise. Questions that suffragists had argued would be better served by women in parliament – temperance, child welfare, and issues that impacted disproportionately on women – quickly became identified with women MPs after 1918. Harrison has argued that this equated to a separate 'metaphysical space' for women, a segregation which could be both confining and empowering.[65] Certain areas allowed women greater opportunity to participate. As Vallance observed, 'it was very much easier for [women] to catch the Speaker's eye when the debate was one on social questions or education, than when it was on, for example, the economy'.[66] Other areas, by implication, remained more difficult to penetrate.

Autobiographical reconstructions of policy areas confirm this sense of dichotomy. Women's descriptions of their work in Parliament located it across common areas such as welfare, education, health (especially of women and children), woman-focussed questions, moral issues and international affairs. Whilst these replicate Harrison's summary of women's interest areas drawn from analysis of their contributions to parliamentary debates up to 1945, their more reflective tone reveals the complex set of motivations that channelled women into these fields.[67] Gender played a role in encouraging women to concentrate on a number of issues in parliament, but it was not the sole force. Autobiographies suggest that experience, class and party political loyalties were of equal importance, although disentangling these from gendered motivations is not always straightforward.

Life writing that outlines a subject's life from birth shows how the political priorities of many women MPs priorities originated with their pre-parliamentary experience. Some writers drew direct links. Edith Summerskill trained as a doctor during the First World War when women medics were still a rarity. Like many other women doctors of her era she developed a special interest in 'questions concerning mothers, children and the inferior position of women' through her work as a practitioner and her time as a co-opted member of her local Maternity and Child Welfare Committee.[68] Although she went on to hold ministerial positions for Food and National Insurance, Summerskill's autobiography also dwelt on her intervention in parliamentary discussions on issues such as anaesthesia in childbirth, abortion and birth control, showing how such things continued to preoccupy her. Margaret Bondfield wrote of her work as the first woman cabinet minister, but believed her 'greatest contribution...to the Labour Movement in Great Britain' was 'connected with women's work' which she knew first hand as well as through her organising work for a variety of women's trade unions.[69] Shirley Williams' autobiography did not reflect on her own schooling when explaining her priorities when working at the Department of Education and Science. Nevertheless, a previous section described how, by attending school in an era when 'education mirrored class and class mirrored education', she 'learned early on how unjust the education system was' by watching it fail her classmate, Amy, whose family were 'unable to afford the school uniform required for grammar school'.[70] The echoes of this earlier passage are clear when Williams defended her support for the controversial policy of comprehensive education. This, she hoped, would deliver

'An inclusive, cohesive society of which the schools would be the building block...not...a narrowing ladder, with pupils falling off.'[71] Connecting their pre and post-parliamentary political interests, women MPs offered versions of their lives which rooted them firmly in campaigns for equality and social justice, especially around issues which impacted disproportionately on the lives of women and children.

There was some blurring around the edges of those areas of parliamentary work that were seen as better suited to women MPs, especially in issues of foreign affairs. In Harrison's analysis of women's participation in parliamentary debates up to 1945 this emerged as the second most popular area (after broadly-defined welfare issues) with 14 per cent of their contributions located there. Heightened political tensions in the inter-war years loaned a feminine dimension to this; although issues of defence and national security were generally numbered amongst the 'hard' areas of politics, an identification between political women and international pacifism going back to the First World War made the preservation of international peace an obvious arena for their voices to be heard. The development of the League of Nations was also important in allowing women to access the arena of foreign affairs. Many feminist organisations established bases in Geneva between the wars; women MPs found congenial hosts amongst these when visiting the city on political business.[72]

Most of the autobiographers had no experience of foreign travel before their political involvement. The Duchess of Atholl was an exception, having 'follow[ed] the drum' as an upper-class army wife, tending the wounded of her husband's Scottish Horse regiment in Johannesburg during the Boer War, and again in Egypt in 1916.[73] Most of her contemporaries in the House travelled abroad through politics. Socialist parties were keen to internationalise their politics in the inter-war period, and many socialist women visited the Soviet Union before and after election. Political perspectives coloured women's writing on Russia. Barbara Castle, who was sent to write a series of articles for *Tribune*, was impressed. In particular she remembered the enthusiastic egalitarianism of the steerage quarters of her ship, 'warm and alive with chatter...officers...sharing the same simple but ample food. After the meal we all...gathered round the piano to sing international songs', although with hindsight she admitted that 'this period of classlessness did not last long'.[74] The Duchess of Atholl reached a different conclusion. She recognised that many viewed the country as 'a genuine and inspiring attempt to raise the conditions of the world's workers', but found in Russia 'a system utterly repugnant to British traditions', where '[w]omen....and even children were being conscripted for various forms of heavy industry'.[75]

In most cases, women's descriptions emphasised the humanitarian dimensions of international work. Common female experiences such as maternity were important. When the Fellowship of Reconciliation sent Leah Manning to Germany in 1918, she realised that '[t]he blockade as a weapon of war was more terrible than any of us could have guessed, especially for the children'. Femininity could also impact on women's reception when travelling in parliamentary delegations. Edith Summerskill learned 'with some amusement' that 'the fact that I was a woman Minister, married, travelling with two male Civil servants, without my husband' loaned 'special significance' to an official visit to Egypt in 1950.[76] This novelty could mean that expectations were laid on them. When Jean Mann was 'the only woman in a British parliamentary delegation of men' to Switzerland, she found that her 'presence was seized upon by the Swiss women' still fighting for the right to vote.[77] Gender was sometimes a powerful tool for opening subjects that could be overlooked on the political agenda. When the Duchess of Atholl began a campaign against female circumcision in Kenya in the late 1920s her membership of a Select Committee to enquire into the question enabled her to address the issue on a world stage.[78]

Despite the suggestion of pragmatism underpinning analyses of their adherence to particular causes, the autobiographical writing of women MPs shows many of them retaining an active interest in foreign affairs on leaving parliament. Some had simple motivations for this. Jennie Lee, who was voted out of office at a time of high female unemployment, found the North American lecture circuit offered a lucrative proposition for 'the youngest woman ever to have been elected to the British House of Commons' when she lost her seat.[79] Others found that their political work had opened up new directions. On losing her seat, Edith Picton-Turbervill was invited to join a commission investigating the question of Mui-Tsai or child slavery in Hong Kong and Malaya in 1936. After a harrowing visit she authored a separate Minority Report, convinced that only legislation would succeed in putting an end to the practice.[80] For a number of those who wrote retrospectively of their experiences, losing their seats coincided with the rise of international fascism which provided a clear focus for their energies. Leah Manning (now out of Parliament but joint secretary of the Co-ordinating Committee Against War and Fascism) and the Duchess of Atholl played prominent roless in arranging the evacuation of Spanish children to Britain during the Spanish civil war and wrote emotive accounts of this work.[81] Its maternal dimension united women across party lines. Atholl had been scathing in her depiction of the Soviet Union, but offered a weak defence of the alliances she was forging through her Spanish work, explaining to irritated Conservatives that they were wrong to accuse her of having joined in singing *The Red Flag* at a Glasgow meeting appealing for funds for Spanish children 'as I knew neither the words nor the tune'.[82]

The area of foreign affairs reveals how women MPs' experiences could differ between political generations. There is a noticeable shift in their presentation in the autobiographical writings of Margaret Thatcher and Shirley Williams, the most recently-elected of this group of autobiographers who entered Parliament in 1959 and 1964 respectively. By this point women MPs drew less attention for their novelty value, and both Thatcher and Williams held Ministerial posts and offered more assured accounts of foreign travel.

In *The Downing Street Years,* Thatcher described numerous overseas visits where military and economic matters rather than the social conditions of local women or children held centre stage. Her descriptions of earlier visits in *The Path to Power,* prior to her leadership of the Conservative Party, showed the same priorities; she recalled 'the hardness of life for ordinary people', especially 'working mothers' she saw on her first visit to Russia in 1969, but gave more space to reproducing her repeated defences of NATO made to the Russians accompanying her delegation.[83] Williams' writing on overseas trips from the 1960s onwards is similarly less concerned with what might be considered feminine priorities, describing issues such as political and religious freedom in pre-Revolutionary Iran, or increasing educational and scientific links between the UK and China.[84]

The political and the personal

Re-presenting their lives through the intensely personal genre of autobiographical writing enabled early women MPs to consider particular gendered difficulties that surrounded their careers at a point when they were still too few in number to be considered anything other than exceptional. The most common of these was maternity. In an early study of the autobiographies of five internationally prominent public women, Patricia Meyer Spacks argued that their writing shared a tendency to emphasise the personal costs of public life, as a form of self-deprecation.[85] Women MPs autobiographies counter this observation. Many authors downplayed personal sacrifices, situating the conflicting demands of career and motherhood within the context of a broader political landscape to assert their public commitment over private concerns. One extreme example of an author's attempt to lessen the impact of deeply personal events is Leah Manning's description of the death of her three week old daughter in the last months of the First World War. Manning spared just half a paragraph for her experience of pregnancy and neo-natal death, within a longer section that addressed the end of the war and its implications for the Labour Party:

I was pregnant and I suppose I had a *crise de nerfs.* ...In the summer my baby daughter was born. She only survived three weeks. I couldn't grieve. All my tears were shed. Lloyd George brought us some cheer, but what we needed was a morale booster...[t]hen suddenly it was all over...[t]he crowds in Trafalgar Square that night were delirious...all that mattered was that we were at peace. What were we to make of such a peace?[86]

Manning's writing does not avoid personal problems entirely, but they are not foregrounded in an autobiographical discourse which is focussed on her public life and its events. Other, more introspective accounts of maternity did not entirely jettison a political focus. Shirley Williams observed that the series of miscarriages she experienced whilst her husband was working in African universities 'taught me quite a lot about the differences in the treatment of women among obstetricians', but was less detached in describing her own feelings after giving birth, writing that her daughter 'was to me a miracle, a tiny human being with every finger and toe perfect'.[87] Margaret Thatcher's brief account of giving birth to twins by emergency caesarean conceded that 'the pull of a mother towards her children is perhaps the strongest and most instinctive emotion we have', a confession she immediately qualified by adding that she also 'needed a career because, quite simply, that was the sort of person I was'.[88]

In writing about maternity, women MPs admitted its pressures, but countered these with depictions of a variety of elaborate domestic arrangements they evolved to ease them. Class and party had some input over the shape of such arrangements. Jean Mann recalled James Maxton telling her how she 'was known as "haud the wean" Jean' throughout Scotland, and that her public meetings prompted discussions in local socialist branches as to 'who would take the chair; who would lift the collection and who would "hold her bairn"'.[89] Mann's justification that 'The children enjoyed accompanying me...they insisted on coming with me, after they had well outgrown the need for it', was replicated in similar accounts by other writers. Shirley Williams described life in her communal household where three couples shared the care of five children, explaining that 'the stress and guilt that afflict so many families were minimised' in this way.[90] And Margaret Thatcher wrote frankly of the complexity of balancing demands, sharing the school run with other mothers, keeping in touch with her young twins when parliamentary duties detained her beyond bedtime, which were helped through her being 'able to rely on Denis's income to hire a nanny to look after the children in my absences'.[91] Through such detailed explanations, women MPs justified their choices and asserted that they were capable of balancing the demands of public life and motherhood without reducing their effectiveness on either side.

Detailing their experiences of maternity offered women MPs a means of countering the accusation of being 'unsexed females' which beset them, particularly in the first decades after suffrage. This accusation could also be challenged through dress, which autobiographies reveal as an equally fraught area. Although the young Jennie Lee fumed that she 'simply could not understand why what I looked like, what I wore...had anything to do with the serious political purposes that engaged my working hours', her irritation reflects her recognition that this was an issue for outside observers. Dignified and appropriate dressing was more difficult for women than for men. A small number followed the example of Susan Lawrence who Leah Manning recalled as 'mannish-suited'; others attempted to find an appropriate style of their own.[92] Jean Mann described how this could be complicated when combining engagements: 'I was to be at a reception...and had rigged out in brown velvet...unobtrusive or so I thought...when I rose...cheering broke out..."Dressed like a bride" someone said. I never wore that brown velvet again'.[93]

Margaret Thatcher admitted that she 'took a close interest in clothes, as most women do; but it was also extremely important that the impression I gave was right for the political occasion'.[94] Early in her career she approached a man – Donald Kaberry at Conservative Party Central Office – for advice, presumably as he embodied the views of most party selection committees, and attended her selection meeting in a 'black coat dress with brown trim'.[95] Later, she relied heavily on her personal assistant, Cynthia Crawford, who would 'discuss style, colour and cloth' after Thatcher became Prime Minister and kept a note of each outfit to ensure that none was repeated on successive occasions after sessions became televised.[96] Dress was not an issue that women MPs could afford to take lightly.

Conclusion

In recent decades studies from within women's history have overturned perceptions of 1918 as a cut-off point for the pre-war women's movement. Whilst there is broad agreement that inter-war feminism lacked the unifying focus of the single demand of the vote, it is now accepted that organised activities continued across diverse locations ranging from the political education provided by local Women's Citizens' Associations to work on a global scale at the League of Nations. Looking across such a range demonstrates the results of the 1918 Representation of the People Act in some unexpected quarters. One unintended consequence of women's admission to Parliament was the opportunity it brought them to join the ranks of male political autobiographers, and alter the gendering of this genre of life writing.

In a discussion of attempts to theorise the growing use of life writing in twenty-first century political campaigns, Sidonie Smith has noted the importance of approaches from literary and cultural theory which have expanded understanding of 'the political' in ways historians of women's politics will find familiar. Within this expansion, the study of autobiographical material has been seen to 'provide the evidentiary ground for understanding the everyday life of political discourses, institutions, actors, events and ideologies...that is, the lived experience of politics'.[97] The writing of women MPs suggests that some of this experience – concern over dress; the balancing of maternal and political responsibilities; personal, first-hand understanding of the problems of women's health, childcare, managing family budgets or domestic arrangements that underpinned twentieth-century welfare policies – was uniquely feminine. Through their exploration of such themes, women MPs produced autobiographies which were attentive to the interior dimensions of their lives, suggesting that their presence in Parliament was beginning to affect a change in its gendering, albeit at the level of personal awareness rather than institutional or structural alteration.

Nevertheless, the experiences of women MPs cannot be separated from the broader political history of the time. Much of the writing they produced, especially when addressing the inter-war period, shares features with contemporary masculine accounts.. Internal political issues such as the direction of party policy or the balance of power within party structures all feature prominently in accounts of lives which are simultaneously public and private. There is little space within this writing for discussions of a broader feminist movement (aside from occasional nods towards its legacy) as most authors are keen to present themselves as party women rather than as feminist pioneers. The public nature of much of this writing makes it difficult to position within a distinctly female autobiographical tradition as the demands of party are emphasised over those of sex in authors' accounts. Also, although not all of the texts considered here describe lengthy parliamentary careers, they are all to some extent success stories where selection, then election are navigated with relative ease by the writers.

The autobiographies of women MPs formed a small but significant group of life writings through which the first elected women sought to order their public lives and reflect on how these intersected with their private selves. Personal concerns are not muted in this writing, but neither do they hold centre stage as women seek to represent themselves as active political agents, equal to if different from their male colleagues. The women who produced this writing can be seen as duel pioneers, as the first group of women MPs but also the first female political autobiographers able to write of their experience on the same terms as men. For the post-suffrage generation, the political memoir could no longer remain the preserve of the male politician.

Notes

1. I would like to thank Amy Culley for her suggestions on an early draft of this chapter.
2. Margaret Bondfield, *A Life* (London, 1948), p. 9.
3. George Egerton, 'Politics and Autobiography: Political Memoir as Polygenre'. *Biography*, 15, 3, Summer 1992, pp. 221–42, p. 242.
4. Sidonie Smith, 'Autobiographical Discourse in the Theaters of Politics'. *Biography*, 33, 1 (Winter 2010) pp. v–xxvi, p. v. Hillary Rodham Clinton, *Living History* (New York, 2003); Barrack Obama, *Dreams from my Father: A Story of Race and Inheritance* (New York, 1995, repr. 2004); John McCain and Mark Salter, *Faith of My Fathers: A Family Memoir* (New York, 1999); Sarah Palin, *Going Rogue: An American Life* (New York, 2009).
5. George Egerton, 'The Politics of Memory: Form and Function in the History of the Political Memoir from Antiquity to Modernity' in Egerton (ed.), *Political Memoir: Essays on the Politics of Memory* (London, 1994), pp. 1–27, p. 16.
6. Egerton, 'Introduction', p. xv.
7. Egerton, 'The Politics of Memory', p. 16.
8. P. Kaihovaara 'A Good Comrade, A Good Cadre: Autobiographies and Evaluation Reports as Part of Cadre Policy in the Finnish Communist Party during the 1940s and 1950s' in K. Morgan, G. Cohen and A. Flinn (eds), *Agents of the Revolution: New Biographical Approaches to the History of International Communism in the Age*

of Lenin and Stalin (Oxford, 2005), pp. 245–64, p. 250. See also Claude Pennetier and Bernard Pudal 'Communist Prosopography in France: Research in Progress based on French Institutional Communist Autobiographies' in Morgan, Cohen and Flinn (eds.) pp. 21–36; D. P. Koenker, 'Scripting the Revolutionary Worker Autobiography: Archetypes, Models, Inventions and Markets'. *International Review of Social History*, 49 3 (2010), pp. 371–400.

9. J. Barrett, '*Was* the Personal Political? Reading the Autobiography of American Communism'. *International Review of Social History*, 53 (2008), pp. 394–423, pp. 403–4.

10. UrsulaMasson, 'Introduction' to E. Andrews, *A Woman's Work Is Never Done* (South Glamorgan, 2006), p. xxiv.

11. This mirrors the comparative position of women in the historiographies of socialist, liberal and conservative parties.

12. T. Coslett, C. Lury and P. Summerfield (eds), *Feminism and Autobiography: Texts, Theories, Methods* (Routledge, 2000), p. 2.

13. D. Stanton, *The Female Autograph: Theory and Practice of Autobiography* summarised by L. Stanley, *The Autobiographical 'I'*, p. 92.

14. For an overview see Siodnie Smith and Julia Watson, 'Introduction' in Smith and Watson (eds.), *Women, Autobiography, Theory: A Reader* (London, 1998), pp. 3–56.

15. Stanley, *Autobiographical I*, p. 90.

16. Hilda Kean, 'Searching for the Past in Present Defeat: The Construction of Historical and Political Identity in British Feminism in the 1920s and 1930s'. *Women's History Review*, 3, 1 (1994), pp. 57–80, here pp. 60–1.

17. Kean, 'Searching for the Past', p. 61.

18. Brian Harrison, 'Women in a Men's House: The Women MPs, 1919–1945'. *Historical Journal*, 29, 3, 1986, pp. 623–54.

19. Egerton, 'The Anatomy of Political Memoir: Findings and Conclusions', in Egerton (ed.), *Political Memoir* pp. 342–51.

20. Eighty-one were elected, but the first, Constance Markievicz, did not take her seat.

21. For example by Cheryl Law, *Suffrage and Power* (London, 1997).

22. The works considered here, in order of the author's election, are: Katherine, Duchess of Athol, *Working Partnership* (London, 1958); Margaret Bondfield, *A Life's Work* (London, 1948); Jennie Lee, *This Great Journey: A Volume of Autobiography, 1904–45* (London, 1963); Edith Picton-Turbervill, *Life Is Good* (London, 1939); Mary Agnes Hamilton *Remembering My Good Friends* (London, 1944); *Up-hill All The Way* (London, 1953); Thelma Cazalet-Keir, *From the Wings* (London, 1967); Leah Manning, *A Life for Education: An Autobiography* (London, 1970); Edith Summerskill, *Letters to my Daughter* (London, 1957); *A Woman's World* (London, 1967); Bessie Braddock and Jack Braddock, *The Braddocks* (London, 1963); Barbara Castle, *Fighting All The Way* (London, 1993); Jean Mann, *Woman in Parliament* (London, 1962); Margaret Thatcher, *The Downing Street Years* (London, 1993); *The Path to Power* (London, 1995); Shirley Williams, *Climbing the Bookshelves* (London: 2009). The autobiography of Margaret Mackay, *Generation in Revolt* (written as Margaret McCarthy, London, 1953) was written and published before her election, so is not included.

23. Pamela Brookes, *Women at Westminster* (London, 1967); Harrison,' Women in a Men's House'; 'Elizabeth Vallance, *Women in the House* (London, 1979).

24. See, for example, Sidonie Smith and Julia Watson (eds.), *Reading Autobiography: A Guide for Interpreting Life Narratives* pp. 3–4; Laura Marcus, *Autobiographical Discourses: Criticism, Theory and Practice* (Manchester, 1994) p. 3.

25. Regina Gagnier, *Subjectivities* (Oxford, 1991), p. 160.

26. Neal Blewett 'The Personal Writings of Politicians' in Tracy Arklay, John Raymond Nethercote and John Wanna, (eds.), *Australian Political Lives: Chronicling Political Careers and Administrative Histories* (Canberra, 2006), pp. 91–7, p. 91.
27. Harrison, 'Women in a Men's House', p. 643.
28. Jean Mann, *Woman in Parliament*, p. 53.
29. For example, her entry in the *New Dictionary of National Biography*.
30. Jennie Lee, *This Great Journey*, p. 52.
31. *The Braddocks*, p. 12.
32. Williams, *Climbing the Bookshelves*, p. 152.
33. Ibid., p. 152.
34. Summerskill, *A Woman's World*, p. 19.
35. Manning, *A Life for Education*, p. 20; Castle, *Fighting*, p. 32.
36. Manning, *A Life for Education*, p. 20.
37. Castle, *Fighting*, p. 29.
38. Lee, *This Great Journey*, especially ch. 3, pp. 39–52.
39. Thatcher, *Path to Power*, p. 21.
40. Cazalett Keir, *From the Wings*, p. 27.
41. Gagnier, *Subjectivities*, p. 43.
42. Kean, 'Searching for the Past', p. 70.
43. Picton-Turbervill, *Life Is Good*, p. 154.
44. Hamilton, *Remembering My Good Friends*, p. 163.
45. Hamilton, *Up Hill All the Way*, p. 23.
46. Lee, *This Great Journey*, p. 41.
47. Ibid., p. 41.
48. Harrison, 'Women in a Men's House', p. 634. Valance and Brookes also touch on this theme throughout their work. See Elizabeth Vallance, *Women in the House: A Study of Women MPs* (London, 1979); Pamela Brookes, *Women at Westminster* (London, 1967).
49. Atholl, *Working Partnership*, p. 139.
50. Ibid., p. 138.
51. Hamilton, *Remembering my Good Friends*, p. 180.
52. *Path to Power*, p. 117.
53. Ray Strachey, *The Cause: A Short History of the Women's Movement in Great Britain* (London, 1988 [1928]), p. 367.
54. Thatcher, *Path to Power*, p. 144.
55. Susan Stanford Friedman, 'Women's Autobiographical Selves: Theory and Practice' in Shari Benstock (ed.), *The Private Self: Theory and Practice of Women's Autobiographical Writing*' (London, 1988), p. 44.
56. Hamilton, *Remembering My Good Friends*, p. 181.
57. Williams, *Climbing the Bookshelves*, p. 148.
58. Manning, *Life for Education*, pp. 204–5, Picton-Tubervill, *Life is Good*, pp. 230–3.
59. Harrison,'Women in a Men's House', p. 634.
60. Mann, *Woman in Parliament*, p. 25.
61. Picton-Turbevill, *Life is Good*, p. 185.
62. Manning, *Life for Education*, pp. 203, p. 205.
63. Mann, *Woman in Parliament*, pp. 33, 34.
64. Manning, *Life for Education*, p. 203.
65. Harrison, 'Women in a Men's House', p. 636.
66. Vallance, *Women in the House*, p. 110.
67. Harrison, 'Women in a Men's House', p. 637.

68. Summerskill, *A Woman's World*, p. 36.
69. Bondfield, *A Life's Work*, p. 329.
70. Williams, *Climbing the Bookshelves*, p. 21.
71. Williams, *Climbing the Bookshelves*, p. 175.
72. Carol Millar, '"Geneva – The Key to Equality": Inter-war Feminists and the League of Nations', *Women's History Review*, Vol. 3, No. 2, 1994, pp. 219–45 See also Bondfield, *Life's Work*, pp. 347–8; Hamilton, *Remembering*, pp. 184–92.
73. Atholl, *Working Partnership*, pp. 42, 92.
74. Castle, *Fighting*, p. 84.
75. Atholl, *Working Partnership*, pp. 185, 182.
76. Sumerskill, *Woman's World*, p. 161.
77. Mann, *Woman in Parliament*, pp. 58–9.
78. Atholl, *Working Partnership*, p. 178.
79. Lee, *This Great Journey*, p. 118.
80. Picton-Turbervill, *Life Is Good*, pp. 294–304.
81. Manning, *Life for Education*, pp. 112–40; Atholl, *Working Partnership*, pp. 208–17.
82. Atholl, *Working Partnership*, p. 221.
83. Thatcher, *The Path to Power*, p. 155.
84. Williams, *Climbing the Bookshelves*, pp. 198–9; pp. 230–3.
85. Patricia Meyer Spacks, 'Selves in Hiding', cited by Marysa Navarro, 'Of Sparrows and Condors: The Autobiography of Eva Perón', in Donna C. Stanton (ed.), *The Female Autograph* (London, 1987), p. 185.
86. Manning, *Life for Education*, p. 54.
87. Williams, *Climbing the Bookshelves*, pp. 132–3, 140.
88. Thatcher, *The Path to Power*, pp. 80, 81.
89. Mann, *Woman in Parliament*, p. 120.
90. Williams, *Climbing the Bookshelves*, p. 141.
91. Thatcher, *The Path to Power*, pp. 102–3, 82.
92. Manning, *Life for Education*, p. 89.
93. Mann, *Woman in Parliament*, p. 36.
94. Thatcher, *The Downing Street Years*, p. 575.
95. Thatcher, *Path to Power*, p. 95.
96. Thatcher, *Downing Street Years*, p. 576
97. Smith, 'Autobiographical Discourse', pp. v–xxvi.

12

'Women for Westminster,' Feminism, and the Limits of Non-Partisan Associational Culture

Laura Beers

The year 1918 witnessed not only the partial enfranchisement of British women but also the removal of the bar to women serving as members of parliament. Yet, while women were quick to exercise their voting rights, the entrance of women into Westminster was a much slower process.[1] One woman was elected to parliament in December 1918, the Countess Markievicz; however, the Sinn Fein candidate refused to take her seat in the Commons. The first woman MP did not enter parliament until a year later, when Nancy Astor replaced her husband as member for Plymouth Sutton – more a triumph for dynasty than for feminism. Until the 1945 general election, only 38 women served as MPs, leading Brian Harrison to refer to them as 'Women in a Men's House.'[2] As Adrian Bingham's chapter in this volume underscores, initial assumptions about the momentum towards greater equality in the 1920s often failed to live up to expectations. Several arguments have been put forward to explain the failure of women to make greater inroads at Westminster, both in the more immediate aftermath of suffrage, and in more recent years. These have included resistance to the nomination of female candidates by male-dominated selection committees, or an unwillingness to allocate women winnable seats; the reluctance of voters (male *and* female) to vote for women candidates; and women's comparative lack of interest in running for office.[3] Feminists have long decried allegations that women are biased against female candidates, and there is no definitive evidence to suggest this.[4] Yet, the absence of such bias does not imply that women voters put gender before party and supported women candidates out of feminist solidarity.

The literature on women's organizations in the aftermath of suffrage has tended to focus, not on party politics, but on civic associations and international activism.[5] From such studies, female associational culture would appear to have been exemplary of what Arthur Marwick has characterized as the 'climate of agreement' in 1940s politics.[6] The case of the Women for Westminster society paints a different picture. Women for Westminster, which even at its height remained a marginal group of less than 10,000 paid-up members, has tended to be either overlooked or mischaracterized by political historians.[7] Yet, despite its comparatively small size, an examination of the society's aims and its ultimate failure offers new insight into the impediments to women's entrance into parliamentary politics in the aftermath of suffrage, while underscoring the centrality of party politics both to British political culture more broadly, and (a less widely appreciated fact) to many female political activists.

Women for Westminster was founded in 1942 and hobbled on until 1949 when it was subsumed into the National Women Citizens Association, an organization that explicitly abjured involvement in party politics. The society's goal was to train women for political life, and to assist female candidates at general elections. Women for Westminster was a self-professed 'non-party (or all-party) body,'[8] but given the centrality of party to British political life, it proved impossible to avoid conflict with party organizations and partisan women. At the national level, the organization's leaders tended to view its mission in terms of supporting women across the board. However, the national leadership's apparent willingness to support partisan female candidates, regardless of party, sat poorly with many local members who perceived this as a breach of the organization's commitment to nonpartisanship. In addition, both the national and local branches of Women for Westminster suffered from accusations of partisan bias as a result of the center–left predominance amongst the organization's membership. Those branches that did survive worked hard to neutralize threats posed by political partisanship, either through a strict adherence to an 'agreement to disagree' at election times, or by virtually boycotting partisan engagement. But the seemingly inherent contradictions between Women for Westminster's civic and feminist mission and its intervention in partisan politics ultimately proved unsustainable; and, by 1949, only eight branches of the organization remained active.

A significant amount of misinformation exists about Women for Westminster. Andrew Thorpe, in his recent study of wartime politics, claims that the organization 'fizzled out' in late 1943, when in fact it continued to run an active program of national and local activities through 1947, and was not formally wound up until 1949.[9] Others have claimed that the organization, which was formed *sui generis* in 1942, was a direct successor of pre-existing societies. *The women's suffrage movement: a reference guide, 1866–1928* wrongly states that 'the Women's Electoral Committee ... after the Second World War became Women for Westminster'; and Deborah Thom, in her DNB entry for Teresa Billington-Grieg, incorrectly identifies the organization as the successor to the Women's Freedom League, and dates its genesis to 1945.[10] The confusion is heightened by the organization of the Billington-Grieg archive at the Women's Library in London, which includes her Women for Westminster papers, as well as documents detailing her involvement with various other women's organizations. These include a file on the shortlived Central Women's Electoral Committee (CWEC), founded in 1938 and wound up in 1939, erroneously labeled 'Formation of Women for Westminster papers 1937–38.'[11] The following section provides an overview of the formation and progress of Women for Westminster, comparing its difficulties to those faced by the CWEC before the war.

While Billington-Grieg took over as chairwoman in 1945, Women for Westminster was the brainchild of the Labour MP Dr Edith Summerskill, and was established by her, the Liberal women's organizer and internationalist Margery Corbett Ashby, the Zionist feminist philanthropist Rebecca Sieff (wife of the Marks and Spencer mogul Israel Sieff), and the radical equal rights feminist Dorothy Evans. Unlike the organization's other founding members, Summerskill did not have a background in the feminist movement. Born in 1901, she was seventeen when women were first included in the electorate, and was studying for a medical degree in London. Despite her exceptionalism as a female medical practitioner, she faced comparatively little sex discrimination in pursuing her chosen career. In 1925, she married a fellow medical student Edward Samuel, and the two went on to establish a joint medical practice. The history of Summerskill and Samuel's marriage shows a remarkable commitment to equal rights feminism by both partners. Summerskill not only kept her maiden name after marriage, but both their son Michael and their daughter Shirley took Summerskill's name. When Shirley Summerskill followed her mother into parliamentary politics, a journalist asked Samuel how he felt about his children's surname. 'It's quite unfair for the children always to take on the name of the father,' he responded. 'I was glad to make my small contribution to redress the balance.'[12]

Although Summerskill advocated gender equality in her own marriage, and was active in founding the Married Women's Association which sought to redefine marriage as an equal partnership (she sponsored the bill that led to the 1964 Married Women's Property Act), what brought her into politics was not feminism but socialism. Her interest in public health and urban poverty spurred her successful run for the Middlesex County Council in 1934. Her professional expertise and force of personality (not to mention her independent financial resources) helped her rise through the male-dominated Labour hierarchy. While Labour's National Executive Committee did not go so far as to offer her one of its (admittedly few) safe seats, she famously won a by-election victory in West Fulham in April 1938 with the aid of Mass-Observation, in the organization's first foray into political polling and consultancy.[13] (Summerskill's West Fulham campaign was one of the few to receive help from the Women's Electoral Committee before it folded in 1939.[14])

Summerskill felt marginalized within parliament to a greater extent than she had been in her medical career, and she attributed her marginalization to the 'unmistakable evidence that men are prejudiced against women.'[15]

Her sense of isolation, and of the costs to women of their lack of representation in the House, led her to make contact with the Women's Publicity Planning Association, a coordinating body of women's organizations founded at the outset of the Second World War by Sieff and Corbett Ashby. Summerskill met with the WPPA in January 1942 and proposed the establishment of a new national committee that would be tasked with furthering what she saw as the seven principal prerequisites to women's greater inclusion in the political sphere:

1. compiling a list of women who are doing work in the constituencies;
2. drawing up a large map of constituencies to find out where there are likely to be vacancies;
3. arousing the interest of women by lecturing in every area throughout the country, particularly in places where good seats are likely to be gained;
4. teaching the women public speaking, and encouraging the timid ones by telling them that their apparent disabilities and inexperience are shared by men;
5. encouraging and directing women who want a political career;
6. circularizing women about meetings and lectures; and
7. instructing likely people in the methods and procedure of local and central government.[16]

Summerskill's agenda for action focused as much, if not more, attention on civic education as on political organization. As such, it had much in common with the work of existing women's organizations. As James Hinton and more recently Helen McCarthy and Pat Thane have emphasized, societies such as the Townswomen's Guilds, the Women's Institutes, the Women Citizens Associations, and the mixed-sex League of Nations Union trained women for active citizenship, both by educating women in issues of local government and international relations, and by training women in committee and propaganda work.[17] Yet, these other organizations, McCarthy argues, 'wished to keep party politics compartmentalized, and to preserve a place within associational life for creating responsible and publicly engaged citizens free from the demands and discipline of a party machine.'[18] In contrast Women for Westminster, in order to achieve its ends, would have to work with the existing party apparatus.

The organization sought to diffuse the tensions inherent in such a dual mission by encouraging women of all political affiliations to work together to forward the political education of women citizens outside of election times, and to allow its members to divide into political camps during campaigns. Women who indicated that they were politically undecided or 'independent' would be encouraged to consider seriously the positions of all women candidates, but Conservative women would not be asked to support Labour women's candidacies, or vice versa.[19]

In so doing, the new organization sought to sidestep the controversy that had undermined Billington-Grieg's initial effort to promote female political candidacies: the CWEC, established in 1938. The CWEC was the brainchild of several members of the Women's Freedom League, an equalitarian women's organization founded in 1907 as a non-violent offshoot of the Pankhurst-led Women's Social and Political Union, whose membership included both Billington-Grieg and Corbett Ashby. Since the early 1920s, the WFL had given financial support to female parliamentary candidates through its 'Women-in-Parliament fund' (WFL).[20] This, however, was not seen to be enough. The leadership of the WFL believed that women's parliamentary representation would only increase if the full strength of the women's movement were marshaled behind the cause. In 1937, the WFL submitted a resolution on election policy for discussion at the annual conference of the National Council of Women (NCW), the coordinating body of British women's organizations; but the resolution did not make it onto the conference agenda.[21] Failing to raise the issue through the NCW, in October 1937 the WFL leadership convened a conference at the Caxton Hall in London on 'More Women in Parliament,' under the chairmanship of Corbett Ashby and with Billington-Grieg as convener, to which representatives of 50 national women's organizations were invited.

Even before the conference was held, the WFL's initiatives encountered suspicion from women who feared an attempt to sidestep the existing party structure. The Conservative MP Mavis Tate wrote to Florence Underwood, the secretary of the WFL, that in her view the best way to increase female political representation would be for women to 'get themselves elected to the selection committee of which party they belong to, in which constituency they reside, or contribute to the local party funds on the definite condition that, when choosing a candidate, women applicants shall have an equal chance with men of being selected.' Alternatively, women could contribute to their party headquarters to support 'women candidates who might be chosen for good seats but who cannot compete with men who might be able to provide large sums of money.' The key point was that women candidates should be supported on the basis of party credentials. Tate ended her letter with a warning: 'Any suggestion on the part of any women's organization of putting forward women candidates on the grounds of sex only, would instantly cause me to sever (if necessary publicly) any connection I have had with such a body.'[22] At the Caxton Hall conference a resolution that the new committee should 'run their own independent candidates pledged to feminism and not to party' failed. Ultimately, the women present endorsed an alternate resolution put forth by the Edinburgh branch of the WFL: 'This Conference considers that a Women's Party is at present impracticable but that women should endeavor, both individually and through the various societies to which they belong, to secure a larger proportion of women as candidates for parliament.'[23]

Even given this innocuous remit, several women's groups – including the National Council of Women, the London and National Society for Women's Service, the Standing Committee of Women's Industrial Organizations, the Open Door Council, the Six Point Group, the Saint Joan's Social and Political Alliance, and the Manchester and Salford Women's Citizens Association – declined to cooperate with the newly established CWEC.[24] The women's organizations of the principal political parties proved similarly unenthusiastic. At the CWEC's first meeting in February 1938, Billington-Grieg reported that an organizational meeting in her own constituency of Hampstead had been a success, but that similar efforts in Manchester had shown 'less happy' results. Ms I.H. McLelland of the Glasgow Women's Electoral Committee admitted that in Scotland they had had 'to recognize that the affiliation of the Party Women's organizations would not come quickly – and to set out to create the right atmosphere by friendly discussions and explanations, and an examination of the possibilities of mutual usefulness.'[25]

Three months later, at a meeting of the executive of the CWEC, the women recorded their frustration at the continued lack of party enthusiasm for their plans.[26] That June, the executive committee reported to the CWEC membership that, 'Our original suggestion was that party women of all political views should sit on the Central Women's Electoral Committee, but this has not been favorably received. The party women themselves felt that it might run counter to party loyalties and create difficulties beyond solution for the Central Committee itself.' The executive reported their proposal that the CWEC restructure itself as a non-party body with three affiliated committees, one for each political party, and that each of the party committees should work as an 'independent unit, doing its own work in its own political field.'[27] There is no evidence, however, that these new partisan committees ever took shape; and after the death of one of the CWEC's founders, Dame Maria Ogilvie Gordon, in June 1939, the remaining members of the executive formally wound up the committee.[28]

Three years later, Women for Westminster encountered similar hostility from the three national parties, and, despite its best efforts, ultimately lost support at the local level over the issue of party politics. In its first year, the national committee ran organizing conferences in Manchester, Ipswich, Southend, Blackpool, Bournemouth, Bristol, Leads, Harrogate, Hull, Southampton, Swansea, Cardiff, Bangor and Epsom. They invited the leading members of local government (male and female) to speak at the conferences, as well as national politicians committed to increasing female participation in government.[29] While the organization's files do not include records of local branches before 1946, its first annual report records the establishment of branches in Birmingham, Blackpool, Bournemouth, Harrogate, Hull, Leeds, Manchester and Southampton.[30] The Manchester branch, which was run by the Conservative party activist and former

Lord Mayor of Manchester, Dame Mary Kingsmill Jones, sponsored a robust program of events throughout the war. These were often advertised in the *Manchester Guardian*, which in turn reported regularly on the activities of that branch.[31] The national organization's statement of income and expenditure for its first year notes income from subscriptions of £274 10s 5d, indicating a paid up membership of over 1000 – a comparatively small, but not insubstantial achievement.[32] The subscription income amounted to less than a quarter of the organization's operating costs in its first year, the balance being made up by individual donations, including £500 from Rebecca Sieff.[33]

In seeking to gain recognition and cooperation from the national political parties, however, Women for Westminster proved less successful. The three principal parties were all suspicious of the organization. Before approaching the WPPA, Summerskill had already made contact with Nancy Adam, the secretary of the TUC Women's Advisory Committee, asking for her support in furthering female parliamentary candidacies, only to find that, as she put it, 'the TUC is very prejudiced against women.'[34] After the establishment of Women for Westminster, Summerskill and Freda Corbet of the London County Council wrote to the Women's Advisory Committee of the Labour Party to suggest consultation between the party and the new organization on the selection of female candidates. The party's chief woman officer, Mary Sutherland, reported the letter to the NEC's elections sub-committee, which, after discussion, 'resolved that members of the Labour Party be asked to disassociate themselves from the Women for Westminster Committee.' The Labour leadership objected both that a 'self-appointed' committee should presume to advise it on its own administration, and that Labour women should be engaged in joint activities with women of other party affiliations.[35] Under pressure from her party's national executive, Summerskill gave over the presidency of the organization to Corbett Ashby. However, she refused to dissociate herself from the organization, and many Labour women remained involved in local branches.

When, that summer, a representative to the Labour party's national women's conference put forth a resolution urging the party selection committee 'to give favorable consideration to women candidates when submitted by the constituency parties,' the leadership encouraged abstention given the origins of the resolution in the Women for Westminster movement. Jennie Adamson, MP, argued from the stage that, while 'they accepted the principle of the resolution,' 'they had received many protests at Head Office from women's sections against members of the Party associating with Liberals and Tories in demands for more women MPs.' The resolution failed 211 to 192, largely due to a high number of abstentions.[36]

A heated correspondence between Summerskill and the party secretary J.S. Middleton that winter got at the nub of the distinction between Women for Westminster and other cross-party associations. In response to a further instruction to desist with her Women for Westminster activities, Summerskill noted that:

> I understand that our Party associates with all Parties on the League of Nations Union, the Society for the Overseas Settlement of British Women, the National Council for the Unmarried Mother, Women's Group of Public Welfare – not to mention organizations like 'Fight for Freedom.'
>
> It would be interesting to learn why my efforts on behalf of women should be criticized in view of the precedent which has already been established by these Associations. ...
>
> I would like to make a strong protest against this potty heresy hunting which is a reflection on our Movement.[37]

The distinction, of course, was that while the aforementioned organizations were ginger groups devoted to furthering policies already in line with the aims of the Labour movement, Women for Westminster pitted two potentially contradictory goals against each other: getting more women into parliament, and getting more Labour MPs into parliament. If women were encouraged to privilege female representation too highly, they might be persuaded to support Conservative, Liberal or Independent women against Labour men.

For the Liberal and Conservative women's associations, the fear appears to have been more the seeming left-wing tilt of the organization. Corbett Ashby, who briefly replaced Summerskill as the organization's president before Billington-Grieg took the helm, had a long involvement with the Liberal Party. She served as president of the Women's Liberal Federation in 1928–29, and ran unsuccessfully for parliament as a Liberal candidate seven times. Yet Ashby's association was not enough to reassure the WLF about the organization. In October 1942, the honorary secretary of the WLF, Marguerite Dixey, sent a curt note to Dorothy Evans: 'I am not filling up any form or sending any subscription until I am more convinced than I feel at present that Women for Westminster is a genuine all-party organization – Your autumn programme does not suggest this.'[38] Evans attempted to reassure Dixey that

> the Women for Westminster Movement is progressing steadily on inter-party lines. There are active groups of women working within each party and these are in close touch with us at Headquarters.
>
> It is true that the speakers at headquarters in October are members of the Labour party, but the subjects which they are talking are academic and in no sense do they make it an occasion for party propaganda. We have had speakers from the Liberal and Conservative organizations and the audience is composed of women of various parties and a number of non-party women.[39]

Ultimately, Dixey acceded to a meeting of interested Liberal women with Evans on October 28 to discuss the organization and promotion of Liberal women activists and would-be candidates across the country.[40] The WLF's annual report for 1942–43 states that Corbett Ashby was appointed as the Executive Committee's official representative to Women for Westminster. However, by 1945 the organization was no longer included amongst the list of women's societies to which the WLF sent an official liaison, suggesting that the organization had fallen out of favor with the Liberal women.[41]

The WLF's suspicions of the organization's supposed Labour leanings was echoed by the Central Women's Advisory Committee of the Conservative Party. Rebecca Sieff wrote to the CWAC in March 1942, asking its chairman Lady Davidson to meet with her about forming a national Conservative Committee of Women for Westminster. Davidson circulated the letter for discussion at the CWAC, where 'the view was strongly expressed that association with Mrs. Sieff and the WPPA was not advisable, though several members felt that an observer should be appointed.' Ultimately, Miss Bowker, a relatively obscure Conservative local councilor from Lymington was elected Chairman of the Conservative Committee of the Women for Westminster Movement and Lady Davidson reported that 'this provided a most satisfactory solution as, although the Party was in no way committed, we were kept informed of the activities of the Movement.' In the discussion which followed the Committee agreed that 'watch should be kept on this movement which appeared to be spreading to all areas.'[42]

Discussion of Women for Westminster at subsequent meetings of the CWAC reflects a growing paranoia about the organization. In April 1943, Mary Hornyold-Strickland, who took over from Davidson as CWAC chairman, reported the party view that 'Women for Westminster was far from being a democratic organization, and that, while under the control of the its present officers, its tendency would always be left wing and there could be little hope of a fair deal for those holding Conservative views.' Committee member Miss Dowling reported her resignation from the movement in the wake of their support of Jennie Lee's candidature as Common Wealth candidate in the Bristol West by-election. After discussion, the committee agreed that the organization was 'making an appeal to many women who would not wish to have any connection with it if they were aware of its tactics and political background.' On the basis of that discussion, they decided to decline a request from Women for Westminster to come speak to the organization, and to sever their connection with the group.[43]

The increased activity of Women for Westminster in the run up to the 1945 general election did, however, prompt the Conservative women to re-establish contact with the organization in order to 'keep a watchful eye to see that at no point is political influence brought to bear.'[44] During the election campaign Women for Westminster rented a shop at No. 7 Whitehall where they distributed party pamphlets to women voters, as well as their own leaflets, including one to 'The Woman Voter' that began: 'Women – No call in War'

Time found you wanting. This is again your Hour of Duty. The New World we are promised – The Good Days for which we have fought – Your Own Future and the Happiness of your children – All this will depend upon the Member YOU elect for Parliament. USE YOUR VOTE.'[45] They increased the number of local and national events. The national organization held discussion meetings or 'Brains Trusts' (modeled on the successful BBC talks programme) at the Caxton Hall in Westminster and the Conway Hall in Red Lion Square, and organized public demonstrations in Hyde Park.[46] The activities of the local organizations, which now numbered around 40, varied. The Muswell Hill and Highgate Branch limited itself to working on behalf of the Liberal candidate for Hackney North, Mrs. Doreen Gorsky. In Bournemouth, in contrast, the local branch 'organized meetings of the women electors to be addressed jointly by all three candidates, getting great Press publicity, both national and local. Clerical and other help was given by members to help their parties and to gain practice in Election routine.'[47]

The general election, however, was both a high point for the organization and the beginning of its demise. In the years that followed, the number of members plummeted, and several branches folded. Less than a year before the election, there had been 32 active branches of Women for Westminster.[48] By 1949 there were only eight and the total branch membership of the organization had dwindled to 382 women, and the organization's total membership (branches and national members) was less than 700.[49]

* * *

The following section considers the histories of the two largest surviving branches at the time of the organization's absorption by the Women Citizens Association in 1949 – Glasgow and Chorley, and of one branch – Bournemouth – that did not survive. Glasgow, by 1949 the largest remaining branch organization, was (alongside Bradford) exceptional, in that it retained a commitment to training women for party politics and was able to contain members of all political stripes without undue controversy.[50] In contrast, Chorley, the second largest branch by 1949, appears to have survived largely on the strength of its social appeal. In practice, little differentiated the Chorley branch from other women's civic organizations; but, in contrast to many branches, this did not detract from its popularity.

While more detailed records exist for Bournemouth than for other branches, the reasons for that branch's dissolution appear to be similar to those that undermined others around the country. Specifically, they found it impossible to convince potential supporters that they neither privileged one party over another nor sought to forward a feminist agenda at the expense of party politics. Instead, most groups focused on political education, as opposed to activism, but once partisan activity had been removed from the branches' remit, they found it difficult to distinguish themselves from other women's civic organizations, and hence, as the Bournemouth branch secretary reported, 'suffered in difficult times from members having little leisure for Service.'[51]

Of the 382 paid-up branch members on Women for Westminster books in 1949, 119 were members of the Glasgow organization. Glasgow feminists had long shown a willingness to cooperate across party lines to further women's political representation. Even before the creation of the Central Women's Electoral Committee in 1938, organized Glasgow women had been involved in campaigning on behalf of female candidates. In 1937, a group of Glasgow women formed a Women's Representation Committee for the Election of Women to Parliament, Local Councils, and other Public Bodies. Its secretary, Miss I.H. McLelland, was also the honorable secretary of the Glasgow branch of the Women's Freedom League, and the committee was active in the formation of the CWEC.[52] In a letter to Billington-Grieg sent a few months after the committee's establishment, McLelland reported that '[t]he party difficulty [was] still to the fore to a certain extent' within her organization, but that the members dealt with this by "agree[ing] that no member shall be expected to support a candidate against her conscience."'[53]

In fact, while candidates supported by the group may have run for local government under party colours, it is not clear that any of the parliamentary candidates who received help from the Glasgow organization held party affiliations. Billington-Grieg's files include a circular from the Glasgow group supporting Dr Frances Melville, the mistress of Queen Margaret College, Glasgow University, and a prominent feminist activist in Scotland, who ran as an independent candidate in the February 1938 by-election to fill the Scottish Universities seat after the death of Ramsay MacDonald.[54] On top of the file box in which the circular is held is a handwritten note by Billington-Grieg identifying four female candidates helped by women's committees between 1937 and 1938, including Melville and Violet Robertson, a local government bailie who ran unsuccessfully in the June 1937 Glasgow Hillhead by-election, also as an independent candidate. Yet, agreeing to disagree also meant not forcing the organization's partisan members to support feminist candidates merely on account of their sex.

The tradition of political activism on behalf of parliamentary women in Glasgow likely encouraged the early success of Women for Westminster in setting up a branch in that city. The Glasgow branch retained its strength after the 1945 general election, even as the branch in Dundee folded due to declining membership.[55] A draft manuscript for a 'Book of the Branches', compiled by Billington-Grieg in 1946, but never published, notes that:

> Glasgow is one of our largest and liveliest branches having a membership of 120 and the most active local group of outside speakers organized to address the West of Scotland. Meetings of all kinds including Guilds, Business and Professional Women's Clubs, Trade Unions, Institutes and Girls Training Corps.

The Branch has several suburban study groups chiefly on Local Government and economics.

Among the resolutions carried by the branch and sent to Prime Minister, Scottish MPs, and local government councils were those on Clean Food and U.N.O.

Social events run by the Branch are largely attended. They raise money and generously distribute it, as is shown by the cheques for £25 and £50 which reached headquarters during the year.

Election work was done by members as individuals chiefly for the women candidates within reach of Glasgow.[56]

Again, the emphasis on group members working as individuals to support those candidates with whom they personally agreed politically appears to have been a key element of the group's continued success. This was particularly crucial as the Glasgow branch, unlike some of the other branch organizations, does not appear to have been dominated by members of a single political party. A letter from the branch secretary to Billington-Grieg, written in 1946, indicates the extent of the membership's political engagement. The Glasgow group membership included 10 women serving on ward committees, and three women who had fought (unsuccessfully) in municipal and county elections. In June 1946, Glasgow women of different political stripes participated in a mock parliament organized by the Edinburgh branch of the organization.[57] The Glasgow women – like their sisters in Bradford, whose Women for Westminster branch membership at one point included the Labour Lord Mayor, the chairman of the Women Liberals, the secretary of the Women's Conservative Association, and two women communists who were candidates in the recent municipal election – successfully managed to square their commitment to encouraging women's political representation and their party political allegiances.[58]

Such high-mindedness was, however, exceptional. The six other branches which remained in existence in 1949 – Bristol/Bath (24 members), Chorley (86), Finchley (25), Hampstead (27), Harrogate (33), and Muswell Hill (30) – appeared to have maintained their membership by shifting their focus from political action to civic education, and by emphasizing socializing as much as, if not more than, activism.[59] The Chorley branch provides a particular example of this trend.

Chorley's Women for Westminster branch was so popular that, even after the absorption of the organization by the Women Citizens Association, the group continued to meet separately under the leadership of Miss L. Mercer, honorable secretary, and continued to run its own separate program of activities. Its printed programs identified the Women for Westminster branch as an independent organization until the 1951–52 Autumn and Winter Session when the program cover was changed to read 'Women for Westminster (Chorley Branch) (Amalgamated to NWCA).' Clearly the local branch maintained an independent identity well after the national organization had ceased to function.

This was not, however, because the Chorley branch maintained a commitment to encouraging women in party politics which set it apart from the aims and objectives of the local WCA. Rather, a survey of the events sponsored by the group between 1945 and 1954 is notable for the absence of partisan discussion.[60] In the aftermath of the 1945 general election, the Chorley branch of Women for Westminster did hold a series of five talks by representatives of the Liberal, Conservative, Labour, Commonwealth and Communist parties. However, they did not hold any party-political events before either the 1950 or 1951 elections. Other than the talks series, their only two events with a party-political focus were a talk by Clifford Kenyon, the local MP, in March 1946 titled 'Why I became a Socialist,' and a roundtable in October 1951 on 'The present finance bill and the housewife.' In January 1947, the branch did hold a mock parliament, but the event was not repeated.

In place of politics, the group specialized in more general talks and discussions on current events, such as 'Discussion – newspapers & their influence on the nation's thoughts' (26 Nov. 1947), 'The YWCA in Greece' (26 Mar. 1947) and 'My Work as a Hospital Radiographer,' by Mrs. F.B. Wood (14 Jan. 1947). While educational, these events were not particularly geared towards training women for a career in politics. Much less so was the debate that the group sponsored over the merits and demerits of the New Look in women's fashion. Yet, the group's continued success suggests that these events held a popular appeal. The fact that the group hosted a variety of social events, including not only usual Christmas and summer garden parties, but more unusual events like the June 1946 'Mystery Charabanc drive' and the April 1948 'Peddlers' Fair' likely did not hurt its popularity. The survival of the Chorley branch of Women for Westminster is illuminating as an insight into post-WWII associational culture in the northwest, but it does not provide a model for how to reconcile feminism and party politics.

The experience of the Bournemouth branch underscores the difficulties of reconciling the two. The General Purposes Committee, the executive of the Bournemouth branch, was a left-leaning, but genuinely all-party organization. A poll of those present at the 14 April 1943, GPC revealed eight professed independents (apparently including a few with Communist leanings), four Labour women (including a municipal councilor, Mrs. B.A. Middleton, representative for Moordam North), three Liberals and one Conservative.[61] One of the branch's first endeavors was to organize a series of talks by representatives of each of the political parties. However, the fact that most of the women on the GPC leaned to the left politically meant that they had an easier time securing speakers from the progressive parties. Consequently, the first two talks were by representatives of the Labour and Communist parties. This seeming bias led to 'questions ... being asked about the movement's political flavor,' with the result that the GPC had to scramble to find a Conservative speaker to address its September meeting.[62]

Over the next several years, the group strove to reconcile the integrity of its members' party-political identities and its commitment to Women for Westminster's goal of encouraging women's political participation. In June 1944, the group invited a Miss Court, who taught elocution through the WEA, to give a talk on 'Public Speaking and Voice Production.' After her presentation, '19 members expressed their willingness to join the series of classes to be conducted by Miss Court.'[63] In 1944–45, the group organized a series of Brains Trusts where local politicians and experts addressed questions of particular interest to women. The first of these, held on November 18, 1944, was a town-wide affair, with the mayor acting as question master, and several local councilors on the stand. The event sparked considerable local interest and the local branches of the Townswomen's Guild and the Women's Voluntary Service cooperated in the organization of the event. However, these two women's organizations stipulated that they 'could not be named officially' as working with Women for Westminster, a reticence that likely reflected residual suspicions surrounding the organization's political agenda.[64] In the months that followed, the group organized several local brains trusts, including one in Southbourne and one in Northbourne in 1945. In June 1945, they hosted a meeting for the women electors addressed by all three candidates, a successful venture that netted the group £8.8.3. A similar meeting was held during the by-election campaign that November. During the elections, '[c]lerical and other help was given by members to help their parties and to gain practice in Election routine.'[65] Here, as in Glasgow, the emphasis was on members acting individually to support their own parties, and not on the organization acting collectively on behalf of female or feminist candidates.

While the Bournemouth women cooperated successfully on the local level, despite early suspicions of partisanship, the members were increasingly uneasy with the perceived attitude of the national organization towards the question of gender solidarity versus respect for party political identities. When a member of the Bournemouth branch reported back on her attendance at the organization's National Advisory Council Meeting in London in March 1945 that 'the general feeling at the meeting was vote for women [in the upcoming general election],' the branch members recorded their own view 'that it was not right to vote for a women just because she is a woman.' While it was one thing to vote for '[a] woman with the right policy,' it was another to 'vote indiscriminately' for a woman candidate out of 'favoritism.'[66] Prior to the Annual General Meeting of the national organization that September, the Bournemouth GPC resolved that its representative should press for 'some reference to be made that the Women for Westminster Movement is all Party' in the movement's official statements.[67]

The records of the Bournemouth branch peter out after 1945, with a few loose-leaf notes from 1946 and 1947 tucked into the back of the GPC minute book. By 1949, national headquarters had no record of the group's existence. While the reason for the organization's dissolution is not explicitly stated, the discomfort of the members, several of whom were committed party supporters, with the perceived feminist agenda of the national leadership, which put supporting women *qua* women before maintaining the right of women to disagree over party politics, was a repeated source of tension within the branch.

While some branches, such as that in Glasgow, managed to square their dual goals of training women for active citizenship and supporting women as political candidates by 'agreeing to disagree' over the party-political beliefs of their members, the conflict between feminist and party allegiances was ultimately Women for Westminster's undoing. In 1946, at the organization's annual national meeting, the Scottish region tabled a resolution that 'no monies of Women for Westminster or any Branch or Committee thereof be used to support candidates,' and the Bedford branch recorded 'that in the opinion of this branch, no political bias should be shown by any speaker sponsored by headquarters.'[68]

As of 1947, Women for Westminster still had 4,000 members,[69] but during 1947–48 they 'lost several branches – [including] three large ones, two of which were very generous' with the consequence that the national organization saw its financial situation crumble, and was reduced to laying off its paid organizer and cancelling its summer meetings.[70] Bradford's membership decreased from 90 in December 1945 to 39 in March 1948.[71] By 1949, Leeds branch, which had had over 100 members in 1946, had folded.[72] In a letter to branch officers sent 30 March 1948, Billington-Grieg attempted to explain what she saw as the reasons for the movement's decline:

> We wanted to do our particular work in the right feminist background – a background which would only be provided by a women's federation for consultation and common action. Because there was no such federation we tried to create one within our own movement. Let us admit that our experiment has failed, and that our work needs to be sectionalized under some three heads [Conservative, Labour and Liberal].[73]

The leadership ultimately decided not simply to disband the rump organization, but to seek its amalgamation with another feminist body. The equalitarian Six Point Group put themselves forward, but Billington-Grieg instead pursued a merger with the National Women Citizens Association, a group founded by Eleanor Rathbone in 1917 to train women for active citizenship.[74] The decision reflected a recognition that the organization had been most successful in its attempts to educate women about current affairs, and least successful in its furtherance of gender equality in local and national government.

The NWCA members ultimately endorsed the merger, but it is notable that several of members expressed a profound uneasiness with Women for Westminster's links to the party-political system. As one member from the Dulwich WCA said at the extraordinary general meeting to discuss the merger in March 1949:

> our feeling in Dulwich is that we hope to be political without party, that we are extremely anxious not to have party introduced. ... [I fear that if we go ahead with the merger] instead of going on with the general subjects that are so dear to our hearts, the welfare of Children and so on, all the things that appeal to us as National Women Citizens, we should sometimes, especially when feeling got heated in the country, be swamped by ideas put to us by one point of view and the other.

Both Billington-Grieg and Corbett Ashby devoted the majority of their time at the meeting to reassuring the NWCA that Women for Westminster, being 'all party,' really was in effect 'completely non-party.'[75]

An examination of the genesis and collapse of Women for Westminster can shed light both on the failure of women to make further inroads into party politics, and, more broadly, on the movement for non-partisan (or at least cross-party) association in interwar and 1940s Britain. In the decades after the vote was won, women, even committed feminists, showed a greater commitment to the existing party system than to a feminist political agenda. Women for Westminster's branches thrived only as long as partisan identities were not contested, and members 'agreed to disagree' at election time. Investigating the limits of cross-party cooperation can broaden our understanding of why Britain's parliamentary system remained so firmly entrenched at a time when countries throughout Europe saw their own multi-party systems come under threat and collapse. While civic associations (and especially feminist organizations) supported goals that often transcended party boundaries, they were also wedded to a political system characterized by partisanship.

Notes

1. For anecdotal reports on British turnout, see, e.g. 'Keen Women: 80 percent expected to vote,' *Daily Mail*, 2 Nov. 1922; *Daily Express*, 30 Oct. 1924. Harold Gosnell, *Why Europe Votes* (Chicago, 1930) cites an analysis of voter turnout in constituencies pre- and post-1928 to conclude that young women's participation more or less equaled that of men. However, he also cites tickers' sheets from 3 'typical' polling districts in the 1924 election as evidence that '10 percent less of the women electors than of the men electors voted in 1924.'
2. Brian Harrison, 'Women in a Men's House the Women M.P.s, 1919–1945,' *Historical Journal*, Vol. 29, No. 3 (Sept. 1986), pp. 623–54.
3. For an overview of these arguments see Joni Lovenduski and Vicky Randall, *Contemporary Feminist Politics: Women and Power in Britain* (Oxford, 1993).
4. For an early dismissal of such arguments, see Eleanor Rathbone, 'Changes in Political Life,' in *Our Freedom: and Its Results*, ed. Ray Strachey (London, 1936),

15–76, 29, 31. As noted in the introduction to this volume, Rathbone tended to attribute women's poor performance in election campaigns to the biases of selection committees, which rarely allotted them winnable seats.

5. E.g. James Hinton, *Women, Social Leadership and the Second World War: Continuities of Class* (Oxford University Press, 2002); Leila Rupp, *Worlds of Women: The Making of an International Women's Movement* (Princeton, 1997). See also, Pat Thane's chapter in this volume.

6. Arthur Marwick, 'Middle Opinion in the Thirties: Planning, Progress and Political "Agreement",' *English Historical Review*, Vol. 79 (Apr. 1964), 285–98, at 286. Most studies of women's activism between the wars have focused on either civic organization or women's internationalism, Andrew Thorpe's recent *Parties at War: Political Organization in Second World War Britain* (Oxford University Press, 2009) is notable in focusing on women's party political identities in this period.

7. The organization's membership peaked during the 1945 election campaign. While no membership figures can be found for that year, by 1947 the organization still retained a membership of around 4,000. (See 'Our London Correspondence,' *Manchester Guardian*, 23 May 1947.)

8. 5WPP/D2: Report of National Organizers, Mar. 1942 to Mar. 1943. Women's Publicity Planning Association papers, Women's Library, London.

9. Thorpe, *Parties at war*, 89.

10. Elizabeth Crawford, ed., *The Women's Suffrage Movement: A Reference Guide, 1866–1928* (London: Routledge, 2001), p. 56. Deborah Thom, 'Greig, Teresa Mary Billington-Grieg (1876–1964),' *Oxford Dictionary of National Biography* (Oxford University Press, 2004).

11. 7TBG1/2c: Formation of Women for Westminster papers 1937–38. Teresa Billington-Grieg papers, Women's Library, London Metropolitan University.

12. Edith Summerskill, *A Woman's World: Her Memoirs* (London: Heineman, 1967), 65. On Summerskill's feminism, see Penny Summerfield, '"Our Amazonian Colleague": Edith Summerskill's problematic reputation,' in R. Toye and J. Gottlieb, eds, *Making Reputations: Power, Persuasion and the Individual in Modern British Politics* (London: I.B. Tauris, 2005), pp. 135–50.

13. Tom Harrisson Mass-Observation Archive, Sussex University (hereafter M-O) File Report A7.

14. 7TBG1/1-3: On the top of the cardboard box containing these files is written: 'Getting women elected: Candidates Helped: Dr. Summerskill – West Fulham, April 6th 1938, Ms. Hannah Miller, East Finchley, May 3rd 1938; Scotland: Miss Violet Robertson, Hill Head, Glasgow, Miss Helen Melville, Scottish Universities candidate.'

15. 5WPP/D1: Minutes of the Special Meeting of the Women's Publicity Planning Association to meet Dr. Summerskill, MP, 7 Jan. 1942.

16. Ibid.

17. Hinton, Helen McCarthy, 'Parties, Voluntary Associations, and Democratic Politics in Interwar Britain,' *Historical Journal*, Vol. 50, No. 4(2007), 891–912. Pat Thane, 'The Impact of Mass Democracy, 1918–1939,' Chapter 3 in this volume.

18. McCarthy, 899.

19. 7TBG/1/10: circulars of January and April 1943, appealing for and reporting on election work in Bristol Central and Ashford by-elections.

20. The Women's Library, *Appendix 2-7 (2WFL)*. Available at: http://www.londonmet. ac.uk/library/e72435_3.pdf (First published online 22 Aug. 2007.)

21. 7TBG/1/2b: Women's Freedom League to Tereas Billington-Grieg, 17 Sept. 1937.

22. 7/TGB/1/2a: Tate to Underwood, 13 July 1937.

23. 7/TGB/1/2a: Billington-Grieg's annotated copy of Caxton Hall conference agenda.
24. 7TBG/1/2c: Report of the formation meeting of the CWEC, 24 Feb. 1938.
25. Ibid.
26. 7TBG/1/2c: Minutes of Executive Committee meeting, 9 May 1938.
27. 7TBG/1/2c: Second Report of Executive Committee of the CWEC, 22 June 1938.
28. The Women's Library, *5BWW Appendix 5.1* Available at: www.londonmet.ac.uk/library/n33630_3.pdf. (First published online 22 August 2007.)
29. 5WPP/D2: Report of National Organizers, Mar. 1942 to Mar. 1943.
30. Ibid.
31. See, e.g. classified advertisements in 10 Dec., 11 Dec. 1942 issues of the *Manchester Guardian* for conference held at the Onward Hall 12 Dec.; and announcement and report of the conference in the 12 and 14 Dec. issues.
32. 5WPP/D3: Income and Expenditure Acct 7 Jan. 1942 to 30 June 1943. 5s. of local subscriptions were meant to be forwarded on to the national fund.
33. Ibid. SUFF8/006: Audiotape of Brian Harrison interview with Margery Corbett Ashby, Women's Library, London Metropolitan Univeristy. Ashby suggests that the organization relied on Sieff's financial support throughout its existence.
34. 5WPP/D1: Minutes of the Special Meeting, 7 Jan. 1942.
35. NEC elections subcommittee minutes, 15 Apr., 13 May 1942. Filed in NEC minutes, Labour Party Archive, Manchester.
36. *Report of National Women's Conference,* London, 24–25 June 1942, p. 44; minutes of Standing Joint Committee of Working Women's Organizations, 9 July 1942, filed in NEC minutes.
37. Summerskill to Middleton, 4 Jan. 1943, filed in minutes of the NEC elections subcommittee.
38. 7TBG1/16: Marguerite Dixey to Dorothy Evans, 8 Oct. 1942.
39. 7TBG1/16: Evans to Dixey, 12 Oct. 1942.
40. 7TBG1/16: Draft circular on the inaugural meeting of the Liberal Committee of the Women for Westminster Movement, 28 Oct. 1942 (written by Evans, amended by Dixey).
41. DM 1193/4/6: Women's Liberal Federation Reports, 1943 and 1945, held at Liberal Party Archive, Bristol University Library.
42. CCO 170/1/1/2: Minutes of 25 Mar., 8 July 1942 meetings of the CWAC, Conservative Party Archives, Bodleian Library, Oxford.
43. CCO 170/1/1/2: Minutes of 13 Apr., 8 July 1943 meetings of the CWAC.
44. CCO 3/1/24: Majorie Maxse to Mrs Allen, 17 May 1945.
45. CCO 3/1/24: Women for Westminster leaflet, 1945.
46. CCO 3/1/24: Women for Westminster, 1945–49.
47. 7TBG/1/4: Papers related to proposed 'Book of the Branches,' 1946.
48. 5BWW/2: Mrs Hillman's report of the annual general meeting held in Leeds on 9 Sept. 1944, made to the Bournemouth branch meeting, 6 Dec. 1944.
49. 7TBG/1/10: 'Members of Women for Westminster.' Handwritten scrap of paper, dated Apr. 1949 [date written in later in different pen].
50. On Bradford, see 7TBG/1/4: Manuscript draft 'Book of the Branches,' by Billington-Grieg, n.d. [1946].
51. 'Book of the Branches'.
52. 7TBG/2(c): Letter, dated 13 Oct. 1937, from I. H. McLelland to Billington-Grieg.
53. Ibid.
54. 7/TBG1/2a: Circular supporting Dr. Frances Melville's candidacy, 1937.
55. 7TBG/1/4: Handwritten report on the Scottish Regional Council, 24 May 1946, by I. McClelland.

56. 'Book of the Branches.'
57. 7TBG/1/4: Report of Edinburgh Branch, 5 July 1946, sent to Billington-Grieg by Elizabeth Scally, Hon. Sec.
58. 'Book of the Branches.'
59. The importance of socializing to the success of political organizations was highlighted by Martin Pugh in *The Tories and the People: 1880–1935* (Oxford: Basil Blackwell, 1985). More recently, Lawrence Black re-emphasized the link, again in the context of Conservative politics, in his 'The lost world of young conservatism,' *The Historical Journal,* Vol. 51, No. 4 (2008): 991–1024.
60. For a complete list of events hosted by the organization see 5NWC/2/I/2/1: Programmes of the Women for Westminster Chorley Branch, 1945–54, The Women's Library, London.
61. 5BWW/1 Papers of the Bournemouth branch of Women for Westminster, Women's Library, London Metropolitan University: Bournemouth Women for Westminster branch general purposes committee minute book, April 14, 1943. The inference that some of these women had CP leanings is drawn from the ease with which the group secured a Communist speaker for its talks series and the fact that, in the summer of 1944, the group became actively involved with fundraising for Aid to Russia (see minutes, 15 Aug. 1944 GPC).
62. Ibid., 9 June 1943.
63. 5BWW/2: Minutes of Bournemouth Women for Westminster branch meetings.
64. Ibid., 24 Oct. 1944.
65. 'Book of the branches'.
66. 5BWW/2: Minutes of Bournemouth branch meeting, 21 Mar. 1945.
67. 5BWW/1: 11 Sept. 1945 GPC meeting.
68. 7TBG/1/6: Minutes of the forth national annual meeting, 15–16 June 1946.
69. 'Our London Correspondence,' *Manchester Guardian,* 23 May 1947.
70. 7TBG/1/10: Circular to branches from the National Chairman, 20 Apr. 1948.
71. 7TBG/1/21: Summary of the work of some of the branches for the year ending 31 Mar. 1948.
72. 7TBG/1/10: handwritten notation by Billington-Grieg, dated Apr. 1949.
73. 7TBG/1/6: Billington-Grieg to Branch Officers, 30 Mar. 1948.
74. Teresa Billington-Grieg, Carol McPhee and Ann Fitzgerald, *The non-violent militant: selected writings of Teresa Billington-Greig* (London, 2001), 22; Martin Pugh, *Women and the Women's Movement in Britain, 1914–1999,* 2nd edn (London: Macmillan, 2000), 51. Rathbone had started the first women's citizenship association in Liverpool in 1913. See Susan Pedersen, *Eleanor Rathbone and the politics of conscience* (Yale, 2004) pp. 128.
75. 7TBG/1/21: National Women Citizens' Association, Extraordinary general meeting, 22 Mar. 1949.

Selected Bibliography

Alberti, Joanna, *Beyond Suffrage: Feminists in War and Peace, 1914–1928* (London, 1989).

Beddoe, Deidre, *Back to Home and Duty: Women Between the Wars, 1918–1939* (London, 1989).

Breitenbach, Esther and Thane, Pat (eds), *Women and Citizenship in Britain and Ireland in the Twentieth Century: What Difference Did the Vote Make?* (Continuum, 2010).

Brooks, Pamela, *Women at Westminster* (London, 1967).

Canning, Kathleen and Rose, Sonya O. (eds), *Gender, Citizenships & Subjectivities* (Oxford, 2001).

Cook, Chris, *The Age of Alignment: Electoral Politics in Britain 1922–1929* (London and Basingstoke, 1975).

Cowling, Maurice, *The Impact of Labour 1920–1924: The Beginnings of Modern British Politics* (Cambridge, 1971).

Cowman, Krista, *Women in British Politics, c. 1689–1979* (Basingstoke, 2010).

Gullace, Nicolette, *The Blood of Our Sons: Men, Women, and the Renegotiation of British Citizenship during the Great War* (Basingstoke, 2002).

Harrison, Brian, *Prudent Revolutionaries: Portraits of British Feminists Between the Wars* (1991).

Hunt, Karen, *Feminists: The Social Democratic Federation and the Woman Question, 1884–1911* (London, 1996).

Kingsley Kent, Susan, *Aftershocks: Politics and Trauma in Britain, 1918–1931* (Basingstoke, 2009).

Kingsley Kent, Susan, *Making Peace: The Reconstruction of Gender in Inter-war Britain* (Princeton, 1993).

Law, Cheryl, *Suffrage and Power: The Women's Movement, 1918–1928* (London, 1999).

Ross McKibbin, *Classes and Cultures: England 1918–1951* (Oxford, 1998).

McCormack (ed.), Matthew, *Public Men: Masculinity Politics in Modern Britain* (Basingstoke, 2007).

Overy, Richard, *The Morbid Age: Britain Between the Wars* (London, 2009).

Pugh, Martin, *Women and the Women's Movement in Britain, 1914–1959* (Basingstoke, 1992).

Rose, Sonya, *Which People's War? National Identity and Citizenship in Britain, 1939–1945* (Oxford, 2003).

Spender, Dale, *There Has Always Been a Women's Movement This Century* (London, 1983).

Smith, H. (ed.), *British Feminism in the Twentieth Century* (London, 1990).

Daley, C. and Nolan, M. (eds), *Suffrage and Beyond: International Feminist Perspectives* (New York, 1994).

Seldon, Anthony and Ball, Stuart (eds), *Conservative Century: The Conservative Party since 1900* (Oxford, 1994).

Tanner, Duncan, *Political Change and the Labour Party 1900–1918* (Cambridge, 1990).

Williamson, Philip, *Stanley Baldwin: Conservative Leadership and National Values* (Cambridge, 1999).

Index

Printed and bound in Great Britain by
CPI Antony Rowe, Chippenham and Eastbourne